LEAVES OF CHESTNUT RIDGE

By

Ann Littlefield Coleman

Ann Littlefield Coleman

ISBN: 1-4107-5178-3 (e-book)
ISBN: 1-4107-5177-5 (Paperback)
ISBN: 1-4107-5176-7 (Dust jacket)

Library of Congress Control Number: 2003093025

This book is printed on acid free paper.

Printed in the United States of America
Bloomington, IN

1stBooks – rev. 06/24/03

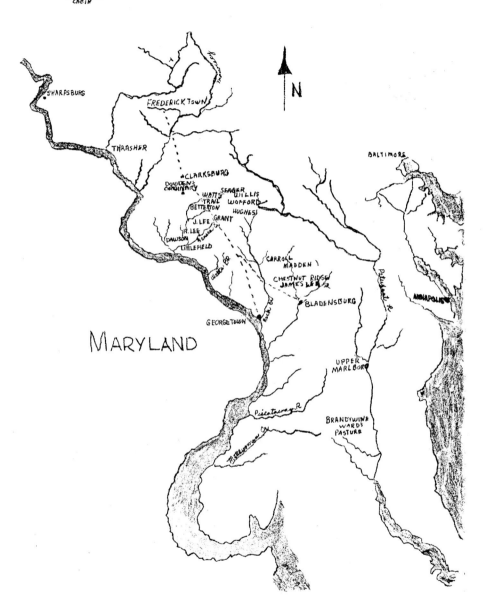

FREDERICKTOWN

Acknowledgements

When I first began gathering material for this novel, little did I know the willingness of total strangers. Without it I could never have put the words together to make a story. In the beginning it was Beverly Littlefield who never stopped sharing her mammoth collection of files and her many books on the history of Maryland. To Jean Lee McCrackin for her early research on the Lee family and those who responded to my queries for information, your help was essential. When it was time to move into the Maryland countryside and meet the people of the 1700's it was my good fortune to have Patricia Andersen, now editor of Western Maryland Genealogy, serve as guide. And when the research was complete it was my wonderfully patient and insightful editor, Jolie Lamping Roth, who took the story to heart and watched over my every page. Without these people there would not be a novel today. To 1st Books Library and Dan Heise, I say thank you for guiding me through the world of publishing. And what would a book be without its cover? A special thank you to James, the professional artist and fifth generation Lee-Littlefield descendant, whose artwork lets you walk among the graves on the lonely hillside of Chestnut Ridge.

Equally important was my sister Athie Strickland, who kept pushing me to finish, even though she was not that interested in family history. In the end, the story won her over. To her granddaughter, Hillary, and my grandson, Erik, who begged to be told the stories of Rebeckah and William on our trip from Canada to Oklahoma—what fun! You made me want to find the facts. I say thank you to my sister Lurland Raibourn who first handed me the handwritten will of James Lee, and when I hit a dead end it was her daughter, Gail, who would pick up the search. To my neighbor, Vernadene, who took page after page of the story and showed an eagerness to read on, you have no idea how much that helped. But most of all, I say to my husband and the love of my life, you were my constant inspiration beyond the call of duty. You fast learned the telephone number of the carry-out food service.

From the past to the future—Craig, Rob, Katie, Taylor, Erik, Drew, Savannah, Danny, Austin and Parker. This book is for you.

Author's Note

In April of 1978 I traveled with my father to his boyhood home in Adamsville, Tennessee. I watched as he stopped, old and feeble, leaning on his cane at the porch of the old run-down house. He had been away for seventy-two years, and I wondered about the emotions and memories this trip evoked. Could it be he was hearing his grandmother Artemesia scolding him for staying away so long? It was at this moment I knew I would someday write the story of my father's heritage. Little did I know it would take me back to the 1700s for this first book. Sadly, he could not wait long enough to read it.

Leaves of Chestnut Ridge is historical fiction, in part taken from the printed pages of American history when life was hard for the colonists. The documents, wills and land deeds, on which many of the events are based, are true. James Lee and his children were real people, as well as their neighbors and many of the people they met in the shops and taverns and along the roads.

Many of the businesses and structures detailed in this novel existed and some still exist today, though not in their original locations. Dowden's Ordinary is no longer in existence, but a stone marks its location. The All Saints Church still opens its doors for worship, although in a new location. Likewise the courthouse in Fredericktown, with its cracking window glazing, is still in operation, but it is also in a new location. The Bailey's Dictionary, dated in the early 1700s, is still in the possession of one of the Littlefield descendants, as well as an old cane, possibly the cane James Lee entrusted to his grandson.

However, the day-to-day comings and goings of those within the story have been fictionalized. Try as I might, I could hear only what was left behind of their whispering voices. So in many ways this book could be entitled, "The Way It Might Have Been."

I wrote with an overzealous imagination, based on the research compiled over thirteen years, sometimes going several generations into the future to find residual characteristics needed to make the earlier family prove real.

This novel has been a labor of love for family, past and future. May we always appreciate those who went before us to set our path for what we are today.

Chapter 1

January 1764
Chestnut Ridge

The frozen rain made a clinking sound as it hit the rough wooden box that held the body of James Lee.

A strong wind whipped the frozen tree branches at the top of the hill and carried the mournful dirge down to the creek bottom. The cold gnawed at the very bones of the solemn gathering huddled together with their heavy cloaks pulled tightly around them. Late January was always cold in Maryland.

Rachel Lee's eyes were fixed on the reader sent out from her church to give the burial lesson for her father. Somewhere between the words, "dust to dust, ashes to ashes," her thoughts of the past few days crowded in around her. It had been one week ago today that she had come in from milking the cows and announced to her father that it was beginning to snow. Her father always liked the first snow of the season. He called it a passage to a new year. Then, after his illness, he had added, "And maybe this year I'll be well again."

One week ago, he still had hope. He had started to talk about the snow coming late, but before he could finish his sentence, he began gasping for breath. His hand made a feeble attempt to clutch at his chest, and then his limp body slid from the old chair before Rachel could get to him. Those were his last words, although he lingered until yesterday late.

Her brother John sent the Madden neighbor men to advise the family to come, as the end was near. Now, on this cold day everyone but her sister Eleanor stood by the graveside.

Rachel, her thoughts interrupted by the movement of feet near the grave, raised her head in time to see her oldest brother, James, standing at the head, and Robert at the foot of their father's grave. They looked like two sentinels in a well-rehearsed ceremony, guarding the coffin.

She felt proud of the honorable gathering. It was a tribute to such strong and loving parents. Her brother John was the youngest of the eleven children, and she was two years older. She could still hear her father telling friends, "Those two have always been so close. Where Rachel is, John will not be far behind." And now, he stood beside her for support. Her parents had reasoned she would need John to look after her in later years if she

1

never married. They had even gone so far as to divide the home place between the two. Of course, that could be because the other children already had purchased land on the Seneca Creek, a good day's journey away.

Rachel looked around at her sisters with their husbands and children, scattered around the coffin on the steep hillside, holding onto each other for support against the wind. Thomas Thrasher had brought Martha from their land some miles on the lower side of Fredericktown. Their wagon had pulled up the road only hours before her father took his last breath. William Littlefield had started with Rebeckah almost as soon as the rider bearing the bad news had left. Rachel wondered if that was wise since Rebeckah seemed to tire so easily with this baby. But, thank the Lord, she came. Rebeckah had always helped Rachel defend the decisions she was forced to make, and they relied on each other to speak the same opinion to the family. Sarah and Alexander Grant stood next to Rebeckah, as if to help William support her. Maybe they should have insisted she stay back at the cabin. What if she began to drop the baby right here in this cold?

Mary and John Wofford had picked up Elizabeth and Richard Willis. Poor Richard could never have made it without their help. Elizabeth fought hard to keep up appearances. One glance at Richard now gave them all reason for concern. But as usual, no one in the family dared approach Elizabeth about his illness, and they waited for her to volunteer an answer. Ever since William Norris, Elizabeth's now departed second husband, had caused so much disgrace to the family, Elizabeth had chosen to keep to herself any problem she might have.

John Seager had come. It was hard to accept him as family after Margaret's sudden death when he rushed her burial. In fact, the family might have admitted to being pleased to have John stay away on this emotional day. But he and his new wife had come, so everyone tried to be cordial enough, even if their heart felt otherwise.

Rachel's sister Anne and her husband, John Hughes, stood apart from the rest of the family on the hillside. She could only imagine why, but so be it. That was just their disposition. Anne tilted her chin a little more upward as if to profess, "I am different than any of you and will not stoop to show my emotions in public."

Anne did look different than the rest of them. She wore finer clothes. Rachel looked down at her own faded gray linsey-woolsey dress with no lines of distinction of bodice. Her old cloak showed the wear of many seasons. She let her fingers blindly find the patch on the left sleeve and began to push at the frayed seam. In her rush to get everything tidied up this morning, she did not have time to change into something finer. The thought almost made her laugh. She did not own anything finer. But if she had known this day was coming so soon, she would have made sure the old file dress she had been repairing was stitched back together.

Rachel looked at her sister's clothes. They were dressed in much the same attire as she, but without the tattered condition. Sarah wore a gray cloak. Martha had a black one, the same as Rebeckah.

She looked again at Anne wearing a fine new black cloak with a shiny lining. Rachel could only surmise it was left open to let everyone admire her new dark green silk dress, delicately sewn with lace insertion across the bodice. Sadly, all this fine dressing did nothing to help her sister's once pretty face. It had turned to stone, leaving no room for a smile. Even today before they'd started down the hill to the burial, when grief was close to their hearts, Anne had dictated, "Genteel families do not show emotion in public."

The cold wind brought Rachel's thoughts back to the burial as the reader started on yet another page of the service. She pulled her cloak tighter around her and tried to listen more intently to the words meant to comfort.

On the other side of the circle, William Littlefield also felt the cold and pulled his scarf higher around his neck. He shifted from one foot to the other, turning his ear toward the speaker to hear the words spoken from *The Common Book of Prayers*. But only a scattering of the words could be heard over the howling wind, and they did little to comfort.

Rebeckah began to sob, and William awkwardly slipped his hand into his wife's cold hand. Guilt nagged at his conscience for speaking so harshly to her for staying so long at her father's bedside. By his reasoning she had been sickly carrying this child. He turned to their oldest son and said, "Your mother is grieving hard at the thought of putting your grandfather in the ground on such a cold day."

William turned to his brother-in-law Alexander Grant who was standing behind him. "I'm just thankful we were able to dig the grave before he died. Think what it would have done to their grief if we had been forced to freeze his body in the icehouse while we waited for the ground to thaw."

"Sarah still blames us for his final breath," Alexander said.

"Why? Pray tell."

"She thinks he heard us talking about digging his grave."

William did not bother to answer the accusation.

The men stood in silence for a time before William nodded his head toward Rachel. "What is going to happen to the farm with Rachel having the control?"

Both men knew that when James Lee was alive and sickly, the entire family had been willing to help bring in the crops. Now it would be different.

"She knows less to nothing about farming," Alexander complained.

"Now be fair, Alexander. The last eight years she tended the sick beds of her parents," William said, coming to Rachel's defense.

"Well, it is her inheritance and her responsibility," Alexander said, with a hint of sarcasm. "I have burdens of my own to handle now."

William sensed Alexander was putting voice to rumors he had heard from the others. The family land, at least the part that had gone to Rachel, should have gone to the sons who could keep it up.

"I'd hate to see her marry someone we do not like and he ruins the Lee family land."

"Maybe Robert or James Jr. will see fit to buy it before some ne'er-do-weller comes courting," William said.

"John would be the logical one. He already owns the other half of the home place," Alexander suggested.

"Too strapped for monies right now. He spoke of that out of his own mouth," William confided.

"James or Robert have the monies, but they live so far away."

"That is probably true," William agreed.

The men were left to plan in silence when Sarah turned to show her displeasure at their talking. But that did not keep an occasional thought from surfacing.

Alexander groaned when a more urgent thought came to him. "If she sells the land she would have to come live with one of us."

William turned to face his brother-in-law with a frown on his face but said nothing.

"Maybe she could become a nanny or housekeeper for someone like the Daniel Carroll household. His wife just died," Alexander suggested.

"Or maybe his mother could employ her full-time. She has a large house and social status," William said.

"Doesn't Rachel work for her at times?" Alexander asked.

"You know John Hughes will be the first to try to get it," William said bluntly.

"What better feather in his cap than to tout the purchase of the family land."

"Even in this time of grief, old John Hughes is probably making a tally of the tools he plans to take on the sly," William suggested.

"He has declared the mare as his payment for the half-rotten seeds he gave them last year," Alexander said. Then he added, "You know John Seager will want to buy the land. He always tries to be the one to buy up new land before anyone can make an offer."

Both men shook their head in agreement. "It would give a sour taste if he came to the land after the way he handled Margaret's death." Margaret was the sister who helped with her mother's illness, and burial, during the terrible outbreak of smallpox, only to go home to her own death. John had put her in the ground on his place before he even sent word that she was ill. That disturbed her family, even to this day.

"Too bad John Wofford could not buy the land," William said, knowing John had been forced to help pay off the debts his family left behind. "He just has the old cabin on fifty acres, and the Wofford family cemetery."

Both men turned to see their brother-in-law Richard Willis feebly grasp at his wife's body as he began falling to the ground. His stepson, Will Sierra, reached out to help Elizabeth half carry Richard to the same wagon they used to bring her father's body to the grave. It was all she could do to keep the blanket over Richard's head to shield against the cold wind.

William was so involved in the ordeal with Richard he failed to notice four-year-old Solomon yanking at his arm. "Look, Papaw, there's a big mean bird over there," he said, pointing to a large hawk diving up and down from the frozen creek bottom in search of food. Solomon began tracing its flight with his finger, and when the hawk suddenly let out a screech, he clung to his father's leg and demanded loudly, "I'm cold, take me home."

William wondered about the sanity of standing in the cold for such a long ritual with the children. But he knew they needed to be here to say good-bye to their beloved grandfather. On every visit to *Chestnut Ridge*, they had sat on the floor around their grandfather's feet, listening to him recite the old stories of his youth. They loved it when he would send them out to the ridge to cut a small limb so he could carve a whistle for them. William thought about those times when the children bragged, "This whistle is so good, it makes the sound go all the way over the ridge to our Uncle John Lee's house!"

William bent down to talk to his son. When he heard the shuffling of feet on the frozen leaves, he knew the mourners had begun to move from the grave, signaling the end of the service.

Mary Wofford walked over to the wagon where her older sister Elizabeth stood with her husband and reached out to embrace her. It was not what was said but what the embrace implied that was shared between them. Elizabeth had seen more than her share of grief. First, it was the death of William Sierra, just after her second child was born. Then the death of the schoolmaster husband, although not everyone was sorry to see William Norris go. And now, if Richard did not regain his strength, she might indeed be widowed again.

The mourners began to move through the small cemetery, stopping to look at other tombstones, smiling the usual, sad smiles. The grave next to James Lee's had not been there that many years, but too long for some of the younger ones to remember how their grandmother, Mary Lee, had looked. Rachel went to stand by her mother's grave and bent down to dust the leaves from the tombstone. Rebeckah came to stand with her and ran her fingers over the marking. "Oh, Rach, I so wish we had thought to have a painter put Mother's face on a canvas. I am afraid her looks are only faintly before me as I grow older."

She turned to look for her children, wanting to show them again their grandmother's grave, but she saw William taking them to say a last good-bye to their grandfather and did not wish to disturb them.

William should have known Solomon would be scared of this unfamiliar gesture. Nonetheless, he was unprepared for the reaction. The child began to cling to his father's neck, screaming loudly, "No, no, no." William quickly moved him back from the grave, leaving the others to decide on their own how they wanted to say good-bye. John, at fifteen and coming into manhood, felt awkward with the emotion. To hide his feelings he busied himself with brushing off a leaf that had fallen onto the box, then stood up and pushed Absolom to the edge. At twelve, Absolom chose to follow in his brother's example and only paused to look at the grave before stepping back. Nancy, a year older than Absolom, was not afraid to show emotion as tears streamed down her face. She reached into her cloak pocket for the yellow ribbon she had brought with her. She bent down to put it on the box, before moving to stand beside her mother at Mary Lee's grave.

When it was young William's turn, he stepped shyly to the edge of the grave, looking away as if trying to decide how he should react to this moment. In all of his eight years he never remembered touching a dead person's box and was not sure it was something he wanted to do now. But this was his grandfather, and there was no one else he loved more. He would not walk away like John and Absolom had done.

He had a lot of words to say for an eight-year-old but did not know how to start. This time of emotion issued a rite of passage from young childhood into something far more demanding, and when the words finally began to spill out, he spoke with unabashed eagerness. "Grandfather, I didn't want you to die like old Chester did." The boy was referring to the family dog that sat at his grandfather's feet, and no better friend to all the children. When the dog died their grandfather had explained it was for the best because his work as a hunting dog was finished. "This is different, Grandfather. You weren't finished telling us the stories about that little Indian boy you called Yellow Bird."

As other mourners came close to the coffin, young William would stop talking, only to talk again when they left. "Remember that rock you found at the bottom of the creek? It had gold specks and colors in it, and when you held it up to the sun, all those colors just jumped out at you. You took it to the fair, and the judge stood up on the high steps and told everyone that your marble was the prettiest he had ever seen. Every time you told that part we always cheered, didn't we, Grandfather?"

The afternoon sun began to cast shadows on the hillside. Young William looked up at the cabin with the lighted candle in the window and thought about his grandfather's old chair sitting there. Would Aunt Rachel let anyone sit in it tonight? For as long as young William remembered no one else had ever sat in that chair.

Two neighbor men came with shovels to cover the grave. The thud of the dirt hitting the coffin made the child cover his ears as tears streamed down his face. His words raced on as if time was running out to speak.

Young William turned and ran from the sound until he was almost to the top of the hill. Suddenly, he darted back down the hill. By the time he reached the grave, the box was almost covered. Unashamed of his emotions, he called out over the sound of the dirt hitting the ground, "I promise you, Grandfather, I will always take care of your cane. I won't ever forget."

The warmth of the cabin would be a welcome relief to the cold, Rachel thought, as she fumbled with the old door latch, making a mental note to get it fixed. She needed to put another log on the fire before Rebeckah, who was right behind her, reached the cabin. William had insisted his wife leave the graveyard. As Rachel pushed the door open to the small room, the smell of food brought back the work of the night before when she and her sisters had cooked all night to make sure the time-honored burial meal was up to the reputation of their mother's recipes.

She picked up a long spoon and stirred the heavy pots of stew that hung from ropes hooked to the top of the fireplace, then she twisted each rope to keep it spinning. It was something she had learned from her mother to keep the pot from scorching. As she tasted the turnips warming at the back of the fireplace, she made a face. "These need more seasoning," she said, as she bent down to remove the lid from the lard crock and scooped a ladle full into the turnips. "It takes a lot of lard to season these turnips to Father's liking." The words came without thinking. It hurt so much to think he would never again sit in his chair. She turned to Rebeckah who was standing at the fireplace still wearing her cloak and trying to rub some feeling into her frozen hands. "Father always loved the way Mother cooked. I think he would be proud of all we did to honor his name." The burial meal among relatives and friends was an important happening, and if the survivors did not put forth a good effort, the whole reputation of the deceased could be damaged.

"Poor Eleanor, she must be suffering a broken heart right now, all set apart from the family. What do you suppose made them all so full of sickness?" Rebeckah wondered.

"Sarah and Alexander went to their place just yesterday. Everyone had taken to their beds, bad off with heavy chills and sour stomachs." Rachel was about to say something more about the family's illness when she heard a wagon creaking near the door. They were bringing Richard Willis to the cabin.

Rachel cupped her hand close to Rebeckah's ear. "Do not mention Robert's wife, Elizabeth, to our sister Elizabeth. They have had a tiff over something and our sister called Robert's wife into court calling it assault."

Rebeckah was puzzled. But that could wait. What She was interested in, now that their father was dead, was to talk to her sister about her long held secret. Richard getting sick was making it hard to find a place to question her in private.

It did not take long for the rest of the family, as well as all of the friends, to find their way back up the hill to the small cabin. Martha went from person to person, handing out mugs of hot cider. The other sisters hurried to find places at the center of the long table to set a big skillet of bear meat and roasted turkey leaving little room left on the table. "It is a truly good thing all our sons know how to aim a gun rightly, lest this meal would not have made it to the table," Anne Hughes commented proudly as she watched her sisters continue to cook. "You can never have enough food for an occasion like this—unlike some burial meals I have attended."

Sarah confided to her sisters in a soft voice, so not to be heard by the guests, "I cannot imagine anyone saying we did not furnish enough food to give Father honor." Just as she was about to reach for the plate of ham Rebeckah had been slicing up, she noticed her sister leaning against the fireplace for support. "Becka, you sit yourself down, and let us take care of this meal. We have no room on the floor to step over you," she jested with the tone of an older sister, while pushing Rebeckah toward the bench.

"Anne will take your place," Martha spoke up, motioning to Anne who was sitting at the end of the table in her fine green dress, giving orders as to what each should be doing.

"Did someone add Mother's herbs to that fish?" Anne asked, as she pursed her lips around her words. They always knew when Anne was feeling superior because she screwed up her mouth in a funny weird way. "Rachel, I cannot believe you did not remember this recipe. Go on now. Find Mother's bag of herbs and give it a pinch. For Father's meal we need to follow her recipes to her exact ingredients. It just seems you never put a full effort to a job."

The sisters hated it when Anne put on her airs. Sarah tried to soften the attack aimed at Rachel by saying, "Mother would have had a meal like this put together with no effort at all, and it has taken all of us working the entire night to get it ready."

8

"Something is burning!" Anne shrieked, sniffing the air but making no move to find the cause. Rachel pushed her out of the way, and bent down to lift the biscuits from the baking oven sitting on the fireplace floor. She tried to find a place on the crowed table to set the pan, but there was no room. She finally resorted to setting it on the mantel. "This kitchen is as hot as the hillside was cold this afternoon," she said, as she wiped her flushed face with her apron.

Anne turned to face the men who were standing around talking at the other end of the one-room cabin. As usual, she wasted no gentleness on them. "Robert, we need more table makings. There is no place to put the rest of the food." The men paid their sister little mind, giving Anne an added need to fire another arrow. She sharply spoke again, "James, now you an Robert go on to the barn and find the boards Father always brought in for Mother to make more table—now go." Then she turned around and continued her tirade, "And where is Rachel? As usual, she never finishes a job. Is it any wonder she is not married? Thirty-four years old and still not married. Mr. Hughes says it heaps shame on this family."

The sarcasm brought Rebeckah to her feet. Her back stiffened, and with anger in her eyes, she confronted Anne. "Rachel is without a husband because she stayed with Mother and Father in their old years." She took a deep breath and continued. "It has not a tittle to do with staying or not staying in one place. It has been years since Mother and Father gave Rachel and John the home place, and you and John Hughes have been hard to get along with ever since. The room is full of guests, and you have had the gall to embarrass everyone here." Rebeckah looked around the room at the faces of her family. She had dared to speak a truth they all had known.

Anne's jaw dropped in shock at the thought of someone in the family daring to accuse her of something so mean. When no one came to her defense, she added just the right quiver to her voice to gain sympathy and said, "I've loved this family all my life, and I have sacrificed for Mother's and Father's well being."

Everyone seemed to draw in a breath, leaving the room silent, just at the same time Rachel climbed up through the cellar door. Her face red from the cold, she sensed something happened in her absence. She looked questioningly from one face to the next but no one ventured an explanation. "I can't believe I had forgotten the apples. I've saved them for a family meal, and here I was about to forget to put them on the table." Sensing the strain in the room, she nervously continued to talk. "Father's apple trees give the tastiest fruit of any orchard around. They are so delicious, everyone is always asking for a seedling from his trees."

Awkwardly, John's wife, Betsy, plunged her hands into the big wooden tub being used to wash the dishes and began rattling the pots loudly from side to side. Annie, James Jr.'s wife, rushed over to grab the drying towel. "Betsy, you need help with these dishes, yes?" she asked, saying it much too loudly. Sarah picked up a whisk and began stirring the corn fritter batter with such vigor she slung a portion onto the seat next to the table. The other women followed her thought and found equally unimportant jobs to break the tension.

The barn door was open when Robert and James begrudgingly went in search of a board. They could see John Hughes on his knees before their father's old toolbox. "Looks like you had a mind to help yourself to Father's tools before the will is read, eh, John?" James bent down and picked up the small silver-handled knife, rusted from neglect, that John had set on the dirt floor. Beside it set a broad axe, a nail header, and a bow drill. John still held a pair of wool shears in his hands.

Robert walked over to look at the contents still in the box. There were a few wooden hammers and small saws along with a long rod used to make the nails. He pulled out a worn out strap with two rusty sleigh bells still attached. "Look at these, James. Father loved to put these on the sleigh and take us all for a ride on the first night of the snow season." He turned to his brother with a grin and confessed, "We saw you give Annie your first kiss on one of those trips." He laughed, then suddenly changed his mood and slammed the lid down on the old box and turned to John. "Taking the inventory before the will reading gives the look of stealing from the dead."

John Hughes stood up, breathing a word of sarcasm.

The men climbed the ladder to look for a board for the table and heard the barn door slam.

"I was wondering how long it would take him to get his hands on Father's tools," Robert said, with disgust.

The neighbors continued to come, offering kind words of the recently departed, but maybe more importantly, to partake of a good meal among friends. The questions became tirelessly the same as William listened to the Sopers, the Ryleys, and to the man who lived over the ridge whose name he could not remember. His mind wandered from the talk to thinking about the trip back home. Rebeckah came to stand with him. Rev. William Williams was there to give his blessings, and Mrs. Carroll, from the plantation next to them, sent a servant with a basket of food and words of condolences. The room was overflowing by the time Richard and Susannah Watts began to say good-bye. They had come from the Clarksburg settlement just this morning to sit awhile with the ailing James Lee, only to find he had already slipped from life. Considering they were the parents of Robert Lee's wife, they felt the need to stand by the family at the burial. Leaving at this late hour meant they would not reach home by nightfall. Elizabeth motioned for Robert to convince her parents to sleep over with them at the Madden household.

"Libby, we will be fine," Richard told his daughter. "And besides, we came along with James and Rachel Trail, and it would not be fitting to impose our stay over on them."

"Don't fret, Elizabeth, we have spoken to Lucy Brooke when she came to pay her respects at the burial. She has a house at the edge of *Dann* and has so benevolently promised a blanket for us to roll up in and hay for the horses in the barnyard," Susannah told her daughter.

James Trail had come back to the door. "The sun is going down fast, Richard. Say your good-byes, lest we find not the road."

No sooner had the wagon pulled away from the gate, than another one pulled up. This time it was Thomas Thrasher's brother, William, coming with his family. William helped his wife, Margaret, out of the wagon, gripping her arm tightly against the stiff wind on the path.

Rebeckah called to her sister, "Martha, Margaret has come back with William. Do you think this is wise?"

Martha came to greet her sister-in-law with a knowing nod. "The way your back was hurting last night as you peeled our potatoes, I thought you would be birthing this baby before morning."

Margaret smiled at her sister-in-law. "Babies come when they so choose. A basket of potatoes will make no difference."

Next, Henry Willson and his wife and son, Zadock, struggled to the door. It was the understanding of those in the room that this Mr. Henry Willson had recently bought the old John Madden's home place close by.

Mrs.Willson wasted no time in introducing herself to the family. "I'm Folsome Willson. I just wanted to tell you how much we so liked your Mr. Lee. He always gave such a friendful smile when we sat with him." She turned to Rebeckah, "Pray tell, dear, how far did you come to be with your father?"

Rebeckah explained they lived on the Great Seneca between the Potomac River and Dowden's Ordinary near Clarksburg.

Folsome pursed her lips, shaking her head in sympathy. "How did you ever put all your belongings in the wagon and come so quickly?"

Rebeckah repeated again the same account, as they had done all day. "When we saw Dennis Madden coming down our road, followed by a cloud of dust, we knew something was very wrong."

On and on the recite continued. Rebeckah explained how helpful the Madden boys had been to her parents. "My brother James once owned the land Dennis and Anastasia live on. That was before they moved down to the Seneca Creek."

Ninian Beall, another long time friend of the Lee family, came over to speak to Rebeckah. Still making the most of a hefty piece of pork rib, his voice softened. "Miss Rebeckah, I just wanted to tell you, I was talking to the Magruders today, and they agreed, we will walk a long road to find someone as fine as your father."

Sometime during the conversation with Ninian, an old man staggered in the door unseen. With him came an equally unkempt woman. The stench that accompanied their entrance gave one to picture the pigpen in the heat of the day. His slurred speech was loud. "I just heard 'bout the poor old man's going down, and I thoughts to meself, and to me Mrs. here, oh, I for sure need to pay my re-spects to his me-me-me-mem-or-ee."

Folsome Willson, still standing next to Rebeckah, whispered, "If my mind tells me rightly, the man has never heard of James Lee until his name was spoken outside the door. The smell of good food will bring in the strangest of fellows." Rebeckah could not help but laugh at Folsome's choice of words.

The conversations had gone from the death just before nightfall yesterday, to the hardships of the recently ended French and Indian War, to the weather and the price of tobacco. William finally had all he could take of this babbling verse he had recited since the meal started and reached for his cloak from the hook by the door and headed outside. Just as he reached the gate, he noticed the Madden brothers, along with their wives, coming up the path. He called out a greeting and walked back to the house with the group.

"If I remember correctly, Dennis, your name along with Joseph's appear as witness to Father Lee's will. The courts will need to have your voucher. I pray to ask as to the next time you will be inclined to go into Fredericktown?"

Dennis turned to his brother. "Joseph, when was it that we witnessed Mr. Lee's will?"

Pulling up one of the points on his hat, Joseph scratched his head. "Well, now, it seems like it was in the spring of the year because we were planting our early garden when one of the boys, I think it was John, came to get us. As we stood around Mr. Lee's bed that day, he was breathing so hard we all thought he was going to die before the night ended."

Anastasia Madden broke into the conversation. "Dennis, I remember it was on a Wednesday because that is the day I always quilt. Remember that, Mary?" She turned to her sister-in-law. "You were there quilting with me, and I was just about to take a stitch when John Lee knocked on the door so hard it near scared me to my death. I stuck my finger with the needle. That quilt still bears the stain. That's how I know it was a Wednesday, because that is the day I always quilt."

Frowning at his wife's recitation at a time like this, Dennis hastened to speak, "I remember we rushed on over. Poor old man, he would rather have been dead than in his useless body all these years."

Dennis started to move away but came back. "If my mind serves me right, Mother Lee was to handle the work of the will. Mind my asking who will be taking her place on handling the business?"

Rebeckah was quick to volunteer the answer. "Oh, it will be Rachel. After Mother died, Father made certain of that. He always told us he thought Rachel had the best head for figuring."

Chapter 2

I Bequeath

The cabin was cleared of all outsiders and the floor swept clean. What was left of the foodstuff was taken to the cellar. The younger children had been bedded down on pallets on the attic floor overhead, while the older ones had been sent over the hill to their Uncle John Lee's house to listen to some of the cousins tell pirate stories.

Rachel hung the last pot back on the wall and looked around at the old cabin that now seemed more drafty, more dark, more empty than she ever remembered it to be, even with the house full of siblings standing around. The table in front of the fireplace where the family had sat through the years, listening to the stories seasoned with laughter or tears, now looked too small and scratched to have held the satisfying foods of their mother's makings. The rug their mother had hooked, that once offered up joy just to find your own worn out dress or shirt woven somewhere within, now looked dirty and worn.

The old rocker, carefully carved by their father, now sat empty. Not one person, even the children, made an attempt to sit in it, at least not tonight. Next to the chair stood the table with their father's whittling tools. No longer would the sound of his knife be heard trimming a small limb in preparation for a grandchild's whistle.

Rachel's hand reached for the wall to steady her balance. The day—the week—had left her tired to the bone and drained of life. But life must go on, she reasoned from somewhere in her soul. Their father had trusted her to do the right thing, and now her heart cried out as to what that might be.

As the afternoon light gave way to darkness, Rachel busied herself lighting more candles. She paused at the window that looked down over the hillside. The frosty panes concealed most of the view, but she knew just below the ridge road the graves were hidden among the trees.

As much as it broke Rachel's heart to do so, the hour had come when she must read her father's final message to the family. She went to the back of the room and reached for an oblong bark-covered box sitting on the shelf above her father's bed. Sometime after he had moved to this place, he had painstakingly stripped the bark from the old chestnut tree that stood at the edge of the ridge near the cabin and covered this business box where he kept his important papers.

The room fell silent. Every eye watched Rachel pull the lid from the old box and unfold the long yellowed paper. This was the time in each descendant's life whereupon the deceased spoke for the last time by giving, or withholding. Each of James Lee's children began to position themselves against the walls or on the cold floor of the old cabin.

Rachel looked up to face the crowded room and made a mental roll call of the family.

It seemed only natural that James, the oldest, had taken his place at the front, next to the fireplace. His wife, Annie, came to sit on the trunk next to him and pulled the blanket up over her small son, Amos, who had finally gone to sleep in her arms.

Robert leaned up against the front wall next to his wife, Elizabeth. Rachel watched as Libby pulled her shawl tighter around her shoulders to guard against the cold.

Sarah and her husband, Alexander, found a place next to her sister Mary Wofford. John Wofford had spotted a three-legged stool and placed it in the center of the room so Elizabeth could bring Richard to sit close enough to hear. But as they began lowering him into a sitting position, he cried out in pain so loudly they were forced to help carry him back to the bed.

John Hughes began to work his way to the front of the room for better hearing of the will. Impatience took hold of him, and he kicked the unused stool to the side of the room, hitting Anne on the leg as she came to stand next to her husband. She grimaced, but said nothing as she reached down to rub the pain. Her submissiveness looked unnatural. Were they seeing a secret side of Anne Hughes? John paid her no mind, and took a step forward. He was stiff backed, and his demeanor gave the impression he would not hesitate to pick a fight if someone was given more than he and Anne. He had always been an angry man about any and all things, but this was probably the most intense he had been while at a family gathering.

Thomas and Martha Thrasher were standing against the back wall, as far away from the reading as possible so Martha could nurse baby Keziah into sleep. But the effort was not working, and she resorted to swaying back and forth with the baby. Even Thomas, in an unaccustomed attempt, could not quiet the baby as her tiny legs pulled to her chest in obvious pain.

John Seager and his new wife, Judith—at least that is how everyone still thought of her, although Margaret had been dead several years—had come to stand next to the Thrashers at the back of the room, and watched the struggle with the crying baby. It did not matter to them if they were close enough to hear. No one had made much conversation with them all day. Margaret's memory was too fresh on her family's minds on this day, and Judith could not help but feel like the outsider that she was perceived to be.

Martha's back ached as she walked the baby. Finally she turned to Thomas saying, "There is nothing to do but go outside with her until the reading is over. I so wanted to hear Father's will, but no one can hear over this crying. I should never have insisted Mary and Ruth go to John's house. They could have taken the baby out for me." As Martha started for the door, Judith Seager stepped forward, almost apologetically. "Could I bounce the baby for you while you listen?" Everyone in the room seemed to take note of the gesture. For the first time their faces showed some small degree of acceptance as Judith pulled her cloak from the hook and covered the baby in a large quilt and went out into the cold night.

William Littlefield had brought an empty cider barrel from the yard and placed it against the wall for Rebeckah to sit on during the reading. The exhausted look on her face made him wonder if they should have made this trip.

Rachel turned to John and Betsy, who had come to stand by her near the table. "They are all here except Eleanor and Thomas," she said, moving closer to the fireplace to allow the light from the new log to shine on the paper.

Her voice trembled as she began to speak, unsure of her new role. She unconsciously reached down the side of her skirt and twisted the edge of her apron with one hand. Her siblings had always unfairly considered her the unmarried sister, the one who knew nothing about how to manage the family business. And now she was being forced to prove them wrong.

The next few words took all the courage she could call up as she meekly brought the family to order. "This is Father's will and he wanted me to read it after the burial."

The flickering firelight played tricks with the words on the paper, as she began to read slowly, faltering at first, from the old document. "*In the name of God, Amen—*"

"If you have to be the one to speak for this family than be bold about it," John Hughes interrupted. Under his breath he uttered an unkind comment about a woman not being smart enough to do this job.

Hughes's retort sent a disapproving gasp among the family and embarrassed her, but at the same time, the act had given her a resolve. She cleared her throat and began again in a much stronger voice, "*I, James Lee, of Frederick County, in the Province of Maryland, Planter, being now weak in body but of sound memory (blessed! blessed!), do this seventeenth day of March, one thousand seven hundred fifty-six, make and publish this my last will and testament in the manner following—*"

Rachel paused, asking John to bring the candle closer. Looking out into their faces, she continued, "*I give to my loving wife, Mary Lee—*"

At this mention of their mother, Martha Thrasher let out a sob. Their mother was to have been the one to remain after James Lee was gone but had been taken from them first.

"*I give to Mary Lee the tract of land I now live on called* Chestnut Ridge, *containing by estimation one hundred acres, to hold to her, the said Mary Lee, during her natural life, she making no willful waste or destruction there upon and from after her decease, I give and devise to my daughter Rachel Lee, her heirs, and assignees forever the one half part of the said tract of land called* Chestnut Ridge, *including my dwelling house, outhouses, orchard, and plantation. The same moiety to, or one-half part, to be laid out in the south part of the said tract of land.*"

Rachel struggled to read the faded letters in the dim light and was forced to press the paper with her hand when the creases hid the words. "*Also, I give and devise the other half part of the said tract of land called* Chestnut Ridge *after the decease of my said wife, Mary Lee, unto my loving son John Lee, his heirs, and assignees forever, his half part to include his dwelling house and plantation with the land adjoining. Also, I give to my loving wife, Mary Lee, during—*"

John Hughes once again interrupted. "For the King's crown, woman, if you can't speak up, have someone else read it."

Rachel stared straight at John Hughes. Then in a calm, stern manner, with a strong voice of determination, she started the sentence over. "*I give to my loving wife, Mary Lee, during her life, the use of my household stuff and all my furniture of what kind or nature so ever. Also, I give to my wife, Mary Lee, the use of my stock of horses, cattle, hogs, sheep, plantation tools and utensils to use during her natural life, and after her death, the said household stuff, furniture, horses, cattle, hogs, sheep, plantation tools and utensils are to remain to my said daughter Rachel Lee and assignees.*"

This last mention of Rachel's name was too much for John Hughes. He turned and kicked at the door. When he disappeared out into the freezing night with no concern to return the door to its proper place, William Littlefield quietly moved from his spot and pushed the door shut. He had the urge to lock the heavy lever in place, leaving his brother-in-law out in the cold but decided not to cause any more of a commotion than had already taken place.

Rachel gave her brother a questioning glance. "Should I go on?"

John nodded to continue.

"*Also I give unto my loving children: James Lee, Robert Lee, Mary Wafford, Anne Hughes, Sarah Grant, Margaret Seager, Elizabeth Willis, Martha Thrasher, Eleanor Betterton, John Lee, and Rebeckah Littlefield—*"

No one seemed to breath as they strained to hear what their father had deemed to share from his lifetime.

"—*eleven shillings current money of the Province of Maryland, and no more except what I have before given and devised to my son John Lee, to be equally divided amongst them the said children. Share and share alike.*"

Only a few whispers could be heard among the family, as Rachel paused to take a sip of cider from the mug left on the table. She felt a sense of relief that the reading was almost finished and continued, "*Also, all of the rest of the residue of my personal estate whatsoever I give to my wife, Mary Lee, and I make and ordain my said wife, Mary Lee, my sole executrix of this my last will and testament. In witness where of I, the said James Lee, have to this my last will and testament set my hand and seal the day and year above written.*"

Rachel set the paper on the table and looked up into the eyes of each family member. "You can all read it for yourself and witness Father's mark on it," she said, then remembered, "William has today talked to the Madden brothers, who witnessed this when Father wrote it and arranged they should come swear an oath declaring they heard Father giving it."

Robert Lee was the first to walk over to the table to look at the yellowed paper. He turned to Rachel. "You will need to take this into the courthouse as soon as you can. I was just over to Fredericktown in November for jury duty. I recommend you stay with a Miss Phoebe Graves. You will find her place on Second Street about a block from the courthouse. I've been told it is a fine boarding place, and she keeps only women. You will be safe from any riffraff that might wander into town."

Robert's wife, Elizabeth, had come to stand with her husband. "You should take the time to have her cut a dress for you," Libby said, as she eyed the worn out dress her sister-in-law was wearing. "Heaven knows after all you have been through, you deserve one. Besides it will occupy your spare time while you are waiting for the court to file Father Lee's will."

Satisfied that the will had been properly read, the men left the women to tend to the children and went out into the night air, already heavy with dampness. Someone had built a large bonfire in the barnyard, and some of the men went to stand around it before going on to finish their chores.

The conversation settled in on what they had not received in the will and on past to talk about new renegade Indian sightings along the lower Potomac.

The rumors were not new to William. They all knew about the new more bloodthirsty breed of renegades. "White Horse has always been able to scout out and handle any situation that has come up with other Indians," William said. The old Indian that had resided on the banks of the creek since before William bought the land.

"Sure would like to hear some good news for a change," Alexander said, as he was about to walk away.

18

William Littlefield was quick to respond to his comment. "It so happens Ninian Beall did tell me some good news today."

Any time Ninian Beall passed on news, men could be sure it was worth hearing. Beall owned a tavern near the Great Seneca, and through his door, there was an endless trail of travelers bringing news from all parts of the colonies.

Thomas Thrasher and John Wofford set their feed buckets down and turned back to listen.

"What, what?" John Wofford asked, impatient to be told.

"It has to do with the border war."

"I hope you are telling me they have decided on where to set the border," Alexander queried.

For years there had been a heated dispute between the Pennsylvanians and the Marylanders over where the line should be drawn. If a settler did business in what he thought was Maryland, there was always the threat he was really standing in Pennsylvania, and if that were true he could be arrested. Especially if it was for a deed of land. Neither state wanted to give up an inch of ground. And that is exactly what had happened to several well-known settlers.

"Does it have anything to do with Cresap?" someone called out from the barn door. The Maryland side loved to hear stories about their hero, Col. Thomas Cresap.

Each man loved to recite how Cresap dared to build his fort just over the Pennsylvania side, and when the people of Pennsylvania heard about it, they marched over and arrested him. Then the Pennsylvanians paraded the defiant Cresap through the streets of Philadelphia. The spectators lined the streets to see this Monster Marylander, as they liked to call him. The story was told that Colonel Cresap had stood up, swinging his arms triumphantly through the air and proclaimed in a loud voice, "Why this is the prettiest city in the Province of Maryland."

Colonel Cresap still kept the anger hot even after Lord Baltimore had come to the borders some thirty years before and tried to settle the differences. Just recently a new treaty had been set, and the men had watched with interest to see if it would work.

"William, if you have news, then out with it," one of the men called out.

"Hold thy tongues, I will set it out for ye," William said, still using part of his English-born words when he spoke. "According to Ninian, a man coming from the upper part of the state stopped for a meal and they engaged in conversation."

"Get on with the news, William," John Wofford complained, knowing William often enjoyed the details as much as the main news.

"Well, according to Ninian, the traveler said he was at the river Delaware and witnessed two men and a group of assistants pulling a chain along the countryside. They put stakes down to set the border of Maryland and Pennsylvania. A boy keeping the donkeys said that someone from both sides had ordered up special carved stones to be brought from England, so when the chains are finished, they will go down the line putting the stones in place."

"We have plenty of stones over here. Why do we need to get stones from England?" one of the men yelled out, and they all laughed. If there was one thing a farmer knew about, it was the excess of stones in every field.

William ignored the comment. "It will be called the Mason-Dixon Line, seeing that the surveyors leading the marking are named Mason and Dixon."

"Seems to me it will take a long time to carry that chain with all the mules and supplies up and down those mountains. Did this man allow when it would be safe to do business near the line?"

"Well whatever it takes, it is about time the province secures our land from those Pennsylvania raiders," John said, picking up his feed bucket again.

As the men turned to leave, Alexander needled his brother-in-law with jest. "How did you like all that mourners' duty today?" The men laughed, knowing how William hated being the one to speak to all those who came through the door. "Guess you noticed we kind of left you alone to it." The men laughed again. Enjoying a good ribbing in William Littlefield's direction felt good, as he rarely was lighthearted about anything.

William, in a rare mood for a change, let them laugh and then said, "Guess I thought I'd make more monies when the will was read if I tended to the duties, but as it was, didn't see anymore increase than the rest of you ragged travelers." Again the men all laughed. They had not expected much. James Lee did not have much to give away.

With chores still to do, the men started to the barn to feed their horses. Before they could make it to the barn, Aquilla Compton came out of the house and called to them. "Wait up. Did any of you hear Ninian talking about the new Parliament ruling?"

"Where have you been? We have handled all the news and I'm just about ready to roll up in my blanket," Thomas Thrasher said rather shortly.

"I had to help prepare Richard for the night," Aquilla said as he came closer to the fire. "Ninian was speaking of a new ruling set to come out of the Parliament."

"What—what about Parliament?" William asked, his jaw set. William, and his beloved England, always brought out the stiffness to the jaw any time he set out to defend the Parliaments rulings, no matter what the topic was.

Thomas groaned. "I heard it." He, as well as the other men always avoided talk like this with William. You never knew how he was going to react.

"Stop being so jumpy, William. When you push your feelings upon us we stiffen our backs as well. I, for one, did not hear much more than Aquilla. Ninian said Parliament is in conflict among themselves about the colonists not paying for the recent war, since it was on our lands. It was the belief of Ninian that it was worthy news, and he was quite upset upon hearing it," Alexander explained.

"If you are talking about the war with the French, I would have to ask who voiced the news and how do we know it is true?" William defended.

"Take it or leave it," Alexander said, as he touched his small torch into the fire and held it up to be seen. "All we heard was that a traveler had, just two days before, come off the ship from England. Ninian said this person spent a big part of the day retelling the news to each new traveler, and his facts never varied."

"If that be so, how are they planning on detailing it for us?" Aquilla asked.

"According to Ninian, the man said King George's cabinet is set on passing a document to insure we pay for the war," Alexander said.

The rumors that the British were setting up a new trade commission to keep the colonists in line concerned everyone. William and John Wofford, were about the only ones standing around the fire who still held a strong allegiance to King George.

James Jr. began to protest. He did not agree with William Littlefield on most subjects of Parliament or the King, for that matter. Usually, when the two became embroiled in debate, one had no doubt as to who was taking what side. "Now wait up. It was not our idea to get into that war in the first place. King George did that when he sent General Braddock and all those fine-dressed soldiers over here," James argued. "Not a one of you believed he did it to protect us. All he wanted was to seize more land."

The debate became more heated when William questioned, "It was at our request that King George get the Frenchmen off our backs. And he did that—agreed?"

"But we did not ask for a war," Aquilla said.

"They want us to pay for the war and for the continuing protection." James said, heavily angered by William's comments.

Alexander held his torch up higher to be seen. "I have not seen the King's officials traveling our country roads to do business. Oh, but they are at the ports, all right."

"Yes, with a little payment slipped into their pockets, say ye." The men all laughed, each knowing bribery was alive and well in the colonies.

By now James let his voice grow louder. "I've heard the King gives full power to Grenville to do what ever he wants."

The men went on to discuss the woes placed on them by the new minister Grenville, and how he had opened the books and discovered the colonists did not make a practice of paying for the services, whatever they might be. And that included patrolling the new land from Canada to Mississippi.

John Seager, who had been quiet throughout the talk, piped up to give one last spark to the anger-fed men. "I was at the docks helping a man unload some of his cargo. He said he had been outside the Parliament doors speaking to the vendors when someone came out, and knowing he was about to depart for the colonies, told him, 'Tell those people over in the colony they better sit up and take notice. Grenville is out to get them.' He made a point that we should meet every ship coming in to port from the docks of London. The tax list just might be disguised as a 'fine how do you do' when unbeknownst it is a right smelly piece of rotten fish."

The men broke into laugher at the vendor's description as Seager finished his story.

"All this just when the church has levied us for seven pounds of tobacco a year to take care of the parish. I wonder sometimes why we try so hard. Our good fortune will just be called in to fill someone else's coffers," Robert said.

The men finally broke up the gathering, satisfied they had done and said all they could, and one by one went to handle the chores left from before the burial.

Inside the cabin, Rachel carefully placed the will back in the old wooden box and set it on the mantel. She stood with her hands close to the fire, looking deep into the flames as if to wish for their answers.

Rebeckah had gone to the cellar to return some of the larger cooking utensils, and she scared them all with her yelling when she came running up the steps. "I found *Robinson Crusoe* and *Gulliver's Travels*," she said, blowing the dust from the basket of old books. "Do you remember these, Martha?" Martha and Sarah both came over to see what Rebeckah was holding.

"Father made us walk with these on our heads," Martha laughed. "I always dreaded the days Mother set these out on the table. That meant it was practice day."

Rachel turned around to see what her sisters were laughing about and walked over to look at the books. "You think you had it bad having to practice with those. My life was nothing if I wasn't under the control of *Poor Richard's Almanac*."

Elizabeth Willis left her husband's bed to come see what all the commotion was about. "Mother and Father didn't think you were strong enough to go into the fields, Rachel."

"It always seemed to us that you were the fortunate daughter being allowed to stay home," Rebeckah remembered.

Sarah began to laugh, "Maybe we were the lucky ones getting to escape to the fields."

Rachel performed her straight-back act by walking across the room with one of the old books on her head.

"You may have walked like a lady, but it sure didn't help you get a husband," Anne Hughes said, turning around from the trunk she had been looking through. "Father always said I had the best walk in the family."

To change the subject after Anne's cruel remark, Martha picked up the small bell she had found on the steps in the cellar and began to ring it. "Look, it is Mother's bell. Remember how each time we went out into the fields with the high grass, she made us carry it. If we got lost we could ring the bell, and she would know where to find us." Several of the sisters chimed in at the same time, "It was always you, Martha, who got lost, and we had to come follow the bell to find you." They all laughed remembering how Martha looked.

"There you were standing in the field, ringing the bell, bawling at the top of your lungs," Sarah teased.

Anne Hughes made no pretenses to have fun with her sisters. "Seems to me it is shameful to have such fun on this night, just after we buried our dear father." She turned back to her mother's trunk and continued to search for anything she might want to claim for herself.

The hour was late by the time all the families settled into their assigned sleeping corners and pulled the quilts over their heads as protection from the drafty floor.

As William pulled the quilt over his head, he announced to Rebeckah, "I didn't like the feel of the damp air tonight. A storm might be brewing on the other side of the Blue Ridges. Start thinking of your good-byes now. We'll be leaving in the morning.

Chapter 3

Late January 1764
Lower Seneca Creek

It was still dark outside the following morning when William hitched the horses to his wagon. He sent his son John to make sure he had remembered to place the grease bucket back onto the hook at the rear of the wagon after greasing the wheels yesterday. Rebeckah hurriedly carried Solomon out from the house, wrapped in several quilts. Nancy and young William followed slowly behind their mother, not at all wishing to leave the warmth of the cabin for the cold morning air.

"John, you will find a bundle of clothing on the table. Get it, but be careful not to unroll them. I do not desire to see my clothes flapping all the way home." Rebeckah then searched out Absolom standing on the other side of the wagon. "Go bring the foodstuff your Aunt Rachel packed for us."

Picking up the lantern William had left on the wagon seat, she held it high above the wagon bed to make a detailed accounting of the quilts John had brought out earlier. She called out to Absolom before he got to the door, "And I've left the new squared quilt where we were sleeping. Bring it when you come." If there was one thing you made sure of when you took a trip, it was that you returned home with as many quilts as you had arrived with.

William was impatient with the slowness of his wife's inventory and came back to take Solomon from her and placed him in the wagon next to Nancy. His voice was gruff. "Young William, there will be no fighting between you and Solomon, mind you, lest you want me to stop and whip your behinds."

A sound behind William brought him around to face James Lee's wagon as well as Robert's wagon just turning into the road behind him.

"William, get Rebeckah and the family loaded up. We are tired of waiting," James fussed.

William did not like to be instructed on how to manage his departure but knew James was right. He went over to pull the lighted torch from the stand next to the gate and handed it to his son. "John will lead the way on foot with the torch light until it gets light of day," he said, as he motioned for Rebeckah to climb into the wagon with the children. But after making two attempts at lifting herself up over the side, William became exasperated and went to help her get a foothold.

As the wagon creaked slowly down the familiar path in the darkness, Rebeckah turned for a final look at the home place. She could see the shadowy forms of the remaining sisters standing just inside the door of the old cabin. Life on this ridge would never again be the same without her father.

John Lee stood by the gate with a lighted lantern in his hand and waved the wagons on their way, yelling a final, "Godspeed."

Rebeckah sat with her back braced against the front seat. She could faintly see the lanterns on her brothers' wagons as they rocked along on the rough path. Their plans were to reach James and Annie's cabin in time to take a late noon meal.

The roads were never easy between *Chestnut Ridge* and the *William and John.* But today Rebeckah had been lulled to sleep by the sway of the wagon. Suddenly she was awakened by the screams of the children and felt the wagon sliding off the road. It all happened so quickly. The horses had gotten up too much speed, and the curve at the top of the hill had come on without warning. The wagon leaned sharply on its side, in danger of turning over. The children were holding onto the sides of the wagon, terrified. When the sliding finally stopped, William pulled the horses to the side of the path and climbed down to check the wagon. Rebeckah could see beads of sweat on his face.

"Now sit down and don't make a sound. The horses are spooked," William said as he climbed up to take the reins. Solomon reached out for his mother and tightened his grip around her neck when the wagon began to rock from side to side as it started down the steep incline. Rebeckah pulled the children closer to her to keep them from seeing the deep crevices on either side of the path.

As the small wagon train picked its way over the rough paths, intended more for a single horse than wagon loads of family, the midday passed without notice. When they approached the main Fredericktown and Bladensburg road, the mountain ridge loomed in the distance, and rising behind was the dark and threatening enemy. William had been right about the damp feel of a storm brewing.

At James's plantation they stopped only long enough to eat hot broth and water the horses before heading down the road.

Annie begged them to stay the night. "It is not wise or kind, William, to make Rebeckah travel any longer. What if you get caught in the storm?" But the more Annie tried to persuade her brother-in-law to wait out the storm, the more the idea met with the curt English pride that had caused him to come to the colonies in the first place. "I've tested the likes of this storm, mind you, and I'll take to my own bed tonight, thank ye kindly just the same."

25

Rebeckah knew William's moods, and when he was being pushed too far or he was overly worried, he always fell back on his old countries speech patterns. There was nothing to do but gather the brood back into the wagon without anymore discussion. Her husband had spoken, and it was of no use to question him.

William's decision prompted Robert to continue on as well. And by the time the two families reached the cutoff to Robert's land, *Rich Valley,* the first fingers of lightning slithered across the dark unknown sky. Fear griped the small group. Both families would reach their cabins about the same time, if luck were on their side. William had known all too well that the only way to beat the storm was to take the shortest road from this point on. But that meant he had to forge the small creek that leaked off of the Great Seneca. If a rain had preceded the last cold front, then the creek would be treacherous. His mind had calculated any signs of logs or debris washing up over the banks along the path that might predict high water. But nothing looked out of the ordinary, and he decided to cross the creek next to his land.

His thoughts again gave way to worry, as the icy wind blew straight from the north and bit at their faces. He yelled back to Rebeckah, "I should have been here to help White Horse round the cows up before the storm arrives. Cattle can freeze to death." He spoke with an edge to his voice. "I could lose everything I came to the colonies to gain just so you could wait for death to come."

Rebeckah knew this was William's way of reminding her how she had begged to go to her father's bedside to wait. She also knew that sometime during William's upbringing in the old country, he had been forced to forget about how it felt to be sensitive to one's heart. She reckoned he did not mean to be ill spirited about her father's death. He could only balance his life with what made sense. And when James Lee could not speak or hear death coming, it made more sense to William's livelihood to just wait for the burial time before going. Rebeckah shuttered at the thought of not being there to wait with the others.

The wind had turned into frozen shards by the time they reached the corner of the *William and John*, somehow giving a fitting end to their ordeal, leaving Rebeckah cold all over, inside and out.

The next morning, Rebeckah sat transfixed, unable to pry herself from the chair as she stared at the snow that had fallen in the night. This was the first big snow of the season and the day she would have gone into the hills to say her prayers. But today there was no will or strength. God would forgive her, after all that had happened. She felt empty of spirit as she thought back over what had transpired over the last week. She shifted in her chair and pulled her shawl tighter around her shoulders, as if shielding herself from the family around her.

William had put this window in her kitchen so she could put her chair close and look out on her garden and past the apple orchard, up into the hillside. Most cabins in these backwoods didn't have windows, but she had asked him for one and he had obliged. Now her garden was all but covered in one white blur that mimicked her feelings.

Rebeckah's thoughts were abruptly challenged. Solomon was tugging at her sleeve with dirty hands. Annoyed by this intrusion, she scolded her young son, "You are four years old and you can well speak your mind. There is no need to constantly be tugging at my sleeve." He was finished with his porridge and was ready to be cleaned up.

"I want to go out in the barn to see young William and Absolom," he protested as Rebeckah cleaned his face.

"Solomon, we have been through this before. I told you no." This was going to be one of those days when she would lose her patience all too often, and Solomon was the first to test her.

"I always get to go out and slide down the rope and jump into the hay every morning. Absolom lets me do it. And I get to count how many eggs the hens have laid."

"You what? So that is why I'm not finding as many eggs from my hens now," Rebeckah fussed. "It is far too cold to let you go. Besides Absolom and young William's chores should be almost finished," she said, as she looked again out her window for any sign of them coming.

William had taken John with him over the hill to search for the cattle that had scattered while they were away. It was so unlike White Horse to leave the place while they were gone, and William had been concerned that something had lured him away. She secretly wondered if he had felt the place was being visited by the death angel, and he ran away after hearing of her father's pending death. You never could tell what the old Indian was thinking or what spirits he subscribed to.

Rebeckah worried about William insisting John go along to help him round up any difficult strays. It seemed to her he was more frail than most boys his age. At fifteen, he should be stronger and taller. Her sister Anne had once again reminded her of this fact at the funeral. When she told William about their conversation, he had dismissed her fears as just women talk and refused to listen.

The sound of Absolom and young William racing for the door jarred Rebeckah from her thoughts. They would be hungry, and she had not started their midday meal. The fire also needed another log. Why was she so unwilling to leave her thoughts behind. So many feelings had been put away with her father, and then William's harsh words last night cut at her heart.

She slowly pulled herself up from her chair and unlatched the heavy door so the boys could come in. Their faces were beet red. "Have you seen anything of your father and John?" Not waiting for an answer she asked, "Did White Horse ever come back?"

White Horse would have known his way in this storm. When William and Rebeckah had first settled the *William and John* they soon realized they were not the first to call it home. The old Indian lived in a dugout cave, in the side of the hill at the edge of the creek. He had never told them where he came from, but the word among the other planters suggested he was left behind by the Nanticokes after his mother died and the tribe moved all the ancestral bones to New York. One of his eyes had been gouged out and a portion of his left ear was missing. The rumors spoke of a fight between White Horse and the chief's son. Afterwards, White Horse had been cast out of the tribe. Whatever the trouble, the old Indian now lived peacefully among the colonists, and this latest disappearance puzzled the Littlefields.

Rebeckah pulled another log to the fireplace and laid aside her worries. Her younger children had to be fed. Being gone for a week had left the food supply at risk. And with the storm, she had resisted going out to the food shed in the cold to dig under the hay to find any potatoes worth cooking. Oh, for the breath of spring to make her table live again. She loved what her garden could do. The first herbs should be peeking out from under the house in a few weeks. A deep sigh gave way to a moan. She felt tired all over. This afternoon she must gather her strength to make foodstuff, but for now, she pulled the large brown bowl from the shelf and threw in a handful of meal she had ground before they had left. Journey cakes would have to fill their empty stomachs. Maybe she still had some fatback in the kettle outside the door.

Young William had his nose pressed against his mother's window looking at the snow coming down. They always referred to the window as "Mummy's window." That is what their father had deemed it after making such a fuss over having to cut it out of a "perfectly good log wall." Just as he turned to move closer to the fireplace, he had glanced up at the path his father and John had taken that morning. "Mummy, come look. Someone is crawling down the hill. He must be hurt."

Rebeckah dropped the scooping spoon and ran to the window. "Oh, my soul. Is it William or John?" Rebeckah yelled for Nancy, who was rolling yarn into large balls. "Come get Solomon." She stooped over and ran her hand into the trunk at the end of the table. "Where are my gloves?"

Young William sensed the fear in his mother's voice and begged her not to go out in the snow. Absolom rushed to pull her cloak from the hook by the door, all the while protesting that his father would be upset for her to go out in this storm. Solomon began to cry.

"I can go—and Absolom can go with me," Nancy begged.

Young William went back to the window. The struggling figure was still trying to crawl down the hillside. "Mother, it's John!" he shouted.

Rebeckah bolted toward the door. The wind took her breath away as the hood blew from her head. The snow was coming down so fast it made it almost impossible to see where she was going. All she could think about was getting to her son. "Where is your father?" she yelled against the wind in vain. "What has happened?"

By the time she reached him, he had fallen facedown in the snow. She pulled at him, trying to turn him over, but it was no use. "Oh, please, God, help me." Her fingers were numb as she covered his head with the front of her cloak and rubbed his face. Absolom had come up beside them. Following his mother's lead, he began to try to rub life back into John's near frozen body.

"Where is White Horse?" Rebeckah asked accusingly.

She looked around in the blowing snow and saw something move at the top of the hill. "John, John, where is your father? Is he hurt?" John was muttering, but Rebeckah could not make out what he was trying to tell her. Looking back toward the hilltop she saw someone moving in the blowing snow. "William—William?" She thought she saw a flailing signal, but the voice she heard was not that of her husband but that of White Horse. She let out a gasp. He was half carrying, half dragging William behind him.

Somehow, by the grace of the Almighty, White Horse, with the help of Rebeckah and Absolom, had managed to pull William back to the cabin and help John, staggering beside them.

When they reached the door of the cabin, young William and Nancy were ready with quilts, and more logs had been pulled onto the fire.

In the corner of the room, Nancy stood with Solomon and young William in shocked silence. They had never seen their father like this. He had not uttered a word since they had brought him in and laid him on a pallet next to the fireplace.

White Horse had never entered their cabin on any occasion no matter how many times they had offered, but today there had been no hesitation. He knew Rebeckah did not now have the strength to work on both William and her son. White Horse was always around William when he worked. It was an unspoken allegiance, and they both respected the other's code of living.

Rebeckah and White Horse worked together pulling at the frozen clothes contoured to the bodies of William and John and rubbing the flesh to bring back some warmth. Maybe it was John's youth or maybe he had been in the water for a shorter period but before long he had asked to be helped over to lean against the wall next to the fireplace.

William's lifeless body did not respond to White Horse as he softly chanted something over him. Rebeckah continued to talk to her husband but to no avail. Tears flooded her eyes as she watched William try to get a breath. He had started to tremor uncontrollably. The water had been too cold and he had been in it too long. His frozen clothing had only added to the danger. After awhile she stood up, staggering to the bench by the table. "He needs more than words."

Rebeckah stood in front of the fireplace stirring the broth, adding from her supply of bottles on the shelf above. Again she doubled over, moaning softly as she held her stomach. White Horse noticed but said nothing as he continued to rub down William's feet with some salve he had brought in his blanket.

Rebeckah knew she would not be able to stand much longer. The pains were coming closer together and lasting longer. Possibly her travail started yesterday on the rough ride home, or today when she did not know if William was alive when they got him in the cabin. She began to realize her helplessness. Panic surrounded her and she sat down to think more clearly before calling for her children.

Nancy, at thirteen, would be ushered into the education of childbearing before the night ended, unless someone dropped by the farm to pay a visit after seeing their wagon had returned. Oh, how she prayed that would happen. They needed all the help good neighbors could bring. If it had been in the summer, there would be no problem. Help was everywhere on the farm. But this was the dead of winter when families stayed close to the fire and waited for the blizzard to pass.

She bit her lip to mask the pain as she explained to the children, "Sometime during this night our new baby will be born. Absolom, you must keep the fires going and help John tend to your father. I need you to bring in several buckets of clean snow to put in the kettle over the fireplace. We will need water. Nancy, you will be with me in the loft room." Rebeckah turned to the boys and issued a stern warning, "And if she calls to you for help, do not neglect her bidding. Young William, you will be in charge of little Solomon." There was a deep sigh as this assignment was made. Solomon did not listen to anyone but his parents, and young William knew it all too well.

Rebeckah continued the instructions, pausing every few words to take in a deep breath. "Listen carefully to White Horse when he talks and do what he asks. Your father's life depends on it."

Rebeckah turned her attention to making a large kettle of broth using the last of the fatback and a handful of corn and beans she had in her jugs. Then she cut two onions from the long string of onions tied together, hanging on the wall next to the fireplace. There was no time to go to the cellar to get supplies. The weak broth would keep them through the night, doing little to fill out their ribs, but they would not starve.

She went to stand by William, watching to see if he had made any movement. There was nothing else she could do for him now until the birth of their child. He would have to pull through on his own.

She fell to her knees in the shadowy dimness of the room and took his feverish hand in hers. Holding it for strength, she closed her eyes and offered up a prayer. She stood up, still clutching to his hand, and said, "William, I need you to be here when I come down." Her voice broke as she squeezed his limp hand. "Oh, please be here when I come down."

Chapter 4

Late January 1764
Lower Seneca Creek

The blinding snow made it almost impossible to see the road as Thomas Dawson headed for home. Elizabeth would have spent last night and the better part of today watching the road for a glimpse of his horses. It should have been only a day trip, but the storm had changed that. Hopefully, she had reasoned he would find refuge at a farmhouse or tavern along the way. It was never a good time to have to be away from home, but when your plantation needed supplies, there was no other way.

He turned his horse onto the icy bridge and tugged at the packhorses carrying the supplies. But it was no use. They refused to take to the bridge.

Thomas dismounted and cautiously led them across. He looked down at the road to see if any wagon had come by recently. The Littlefields had been gone for over a week. The gnawing feeling he had felt since crossing the main road told him he should go past their cabin before going home. Their cattle might need extra feed dumped into the troughs by now. But then surely White Horse would have tended to them. He wondered what might have taken them away so quickly without passing the word as to why they were leaving. Even before Thomas left for the warehouse, White Horse had not been seen around the place. He paused for a moment, contemplating. What would it hurt to just take the road past their cabin. He would most certain sleep better knowing he had checked. But the thought of not reaching home before nightfall made him reconsider the plan. He got back on his horse and headed straight across the path toward home. Tomorrow he would try to come back. It wasn't like William Littlefield to leave without letting them know they would be gone so long. And to leave the cattle out in the field during this time of year led him to believe they had been called away rather suddenly.

The feeling he should go check on Littlefield's place still pestered him. If he took the turn to their place, it would cause him to miss another meal at home. He had supplies in his saddlebag to keep him going, so he dismissed that excuse. If the Littlefields were there, he would take the meal with them and be on his way. And if they were not there, he could pull some hay from the loft and leave the barn door open for the cattle to get in out of the storm. Then maybe he could go in peace.

He wiped the snow from his face and gave a hard tug to the reins of the packhorses to get them moving. "We'll just take a quick look and be home tonight," Thomas said to his horses, as he picked his way along, careful not to veer off the snow-covered path next to the creek. The wind was picking up. Maybe this wasn't a good idea, but he did not turn back.

An ice-ladened tree cracked and split from its trunk causing the horses to bolt. The storm had hit harder in this part of the territory. He was nearing what seemed to be the edge of Littlefield's land when his eyes caught sight of someone running toward him with their arms waving frantically. Thomas realized it was a child and knew there must be trouble at the house. "Son, is there trouble?" he called out.

At first Absolom could not tell who it was coming down the path when he yelled out, "My father is hurt and my mother is birthin' a baby!"

"Are you Littlefield's son?" Thomas Dawson yelled.

Absolom's words spilled out, "Yes sir. I was looking out our mother's window and saw you coming down the road. White Horse sent me to fetch you. He is trying to keep Father from dying, and Nancy is with our mother, but she doesn't know what to do. We need help bad."

Thomas Dawson looked toward the house, trying to decide if he should go first to check on William or seek help for Rebeckah. If White Horse was taking care of William, then he better get help for Rebeckah. If he remembered correctly, the Littlefield girl was too young to know how to birth a baby. He turned to Absolom. "Tell them I've gone for help, but first take the packhorses to your barn," he said, as he dropped the rope.

Absolom watched as Thomas put the spur deep into his horse's flank and turned up the north road in a race for life. Once the packhorses were in the barn, the boy ran into the house to deliver the news that Mr. Dawson had gone for help.

White Horse said nothing, but his eyes spoke. William Littlefield was no better. Solomon started crying. "Young William won't let me go see Mummy."

As the hours passed, the snow continued to fall. Solomon had fallen asleep sitting next to John, who was still leaning against the fireplace. The numbness in his feet and legs was not as debilitating as before, but his strength had yet to return.

White Horse stood vigil, forcing hot broth into William's mouth, while Absolom kept the fireplace fed. Young William sat at his mother's window watching the snow pile up around the barn door. An occasional moan from the loft room would chill the quietness of the room. A hard pounding on the door caused them to jump. Absolom ran to unlatch the lock.

A rush of cold air accompanied two women and Mr. Dawson through the door. The short plump Mrs. Sittler, whose family worked on the

Littlefield crops, and Mrs. Posey, who worked for the Birdwhistles on land across the creek and who on many occasions was called on to deliver the babies, rushed up the steps to the bedchamber.

They said nothing to the children. Their minds were only on getting to Rebeckah. Thomas Dawson stood looking at William on the pallet. Then he turned to John. "Son, what happened?"

John tried to get up but slid back down the wall. Before he could speak, Mrs. Sittler rushed down the stairs. "I need ye to gather up some rags to be put in that pot hanging over the fire." Speaking to young William, she said, "Young man, your kettle needs to be refilled. Go out and bring in more snow, and be careful not to get any barnyard mess in it." She abruptly swung around and was back up the stairs.

The moaning sounds, shrouded with long muffled cries, were closer together now since the women had arrived. Nancy came down the stairs looking pale. She said nothing as she walked over to the fireplace and stood staring into the flames. Every crackle of the log, every breath their father took and every moan up above marked a signal point for life or death. No one in the room dared utter a word for fear it would tilt the point in death's direction. Even Mr. Dawson stood staring into the fireplace.

Again, Mrs. Sittler came back down the steps and walked over, standing on her tiptoes to whisper something to Thomas Dawson.

All eyes in the room watched, trying to decide what all this meant. Had their mother died? They had heard of this happening many times before in other neighbors' houses. Mrs. Posey had taken in her sister's baby boy when his mother had died during childbirth. The children had overheard stories about that sad day. Could it be happening to them? If their mother died and then their father didn't wake up, what would happen to them? This thought was going through each wide-eyed child watching the secret conversation going on in the corner.

Mr. Dawson shook his head and said nothing as he pulled on his coat and went out the door. Mrs. Sittler looked at the children but said nothing. Then she turned and went back up the steps. Young William was the first to go to Nancy. "What is wrong with Mama?" he asked, calling her what the older children called her. Mummy was a term for someone that took care of the babies and little children, and now instead she needed their care. He did not want to cry, but the tears were making streaks down his face. "I don't want to go live with another man and woman," he pleaded. "Who will take care of us?"

The door opened and Thomas Dawson called to Absolom and young William. "You boys come help carry these feed bags up to the top of the stairs. Mind you, hold them tight. It will do Rebeckah no use if you spill the corn on the way up." Absolom backed up the steps with the large sack firmly gripped in his hands, while young William's small hands clung to his end with an urgent need to help his mother. Solomon tried to make a run for the steps but Nancy caught him by the shirttail. Solomon protested loudly, flinging his arms in an attempt to break free. John took control of the situation by firmly issuing a command in a voice none of them had ever heard before. Solomon stopped his bawling and turned to look at John. It had taken all the inner strength John could muster up to issue that voice, but now that it had been done, he felt stronger for it. "Solomon, you will stay down here until our mother calls for us. Do you hear me?" Before John could say anything else, Mr. Dawson and the two boys had come back down the stairs.

Absolom went over to Nancy. "Why did Mrs. Sittler need those big bags of corn?" Nancy looked puzzled, not knowing anymore than the others.

Mr. Dawson finally spoke to them. "Children, your mother is having trouble getting this baby to be borned, and the women needed the heavy bags to help her. That is all I can say. That is all you need to know." Thomas Dawson went over to tell White Horse he was going home, and then he made an attempt to wake William from his deep stupor. It was obvious to everyone in the room that the rattle that spilled forth from William was now louder and more frequent.

Thomas turned abruptly and went out the door. Young William watched from the window as Mr. Dawson's horse disappeared down the road. Fear griped the thoughts of all those in the dark cabin.

From the loft, screams of pain slit through the darkness, forming an uneasy balance between William's labored breaths and White Horse's whispered chants. Mrs. Sittler came down from time to time to request more hot water and some broth. Nancy had been sent in search of more quilts. A warming iron was prepared to put to Rebeckah's back to make her more comfortable in the cold night air. Never had the night seemed so long. After a time, all but Nancy and White Horse slept. Hour after hour passed as more logs were laid on the fire.

The rattling sound of death from William's chest surrounded the room. Nancy had heard that same sound just a few days ago while waiting for her grandfather to die. She moved closer to her father's pallet and watched his chest go up and down, and wondered which breath might be his last.

Finally, Nancy went to her mother's window to stare out into the darkness. As the first streak of light wove itself to the edge of the sky, a new sound broke through the night. A tiny whimper, at first so weak Nancy could not be sure she really heard it, was followed by a stronger cry that filled every corner of the cabin. Mrs. Sittler and Mrs. Posey both were uttering loud words of praise. The commotion brought everyone to their feet. Everyone except William, who did not respond. "It's a baby girl you have up here," Mrs. Sittler called down in a tired voice. And in a weaker voice, above the tiny muffled cry, their mother said, "Tell the children they can come up to see her just as soon as you have her wrapped." Solomon didn't wait and ran past them, crawling up the steps before he could be caught, crying, "Mummy, Mummy!"

The creaking of the rocker lulled Rebeckah as she sat in the candlelit room next to William's pallet. Her work was done for the day, and the younger children had been put to bed in the loft. The older boys were in the barn with White Horse, finishing up the late evening chores. Her husband had fallen asleep early this night. His strength had been slow to come. Everyone said it was a miracle that he had recovered, and they all had rejoiced when he first opened his eyes. Robert Lee and his wife, Elizabeth, had come to help. They thought it was the cry of the newborn baby that had brought him forth from his deep sleep. Other visitors felt it was the Indian chants of White Horse, and possibly the secret herbs he had slipped into the broth they had forced down him that challenged him to awaken. But Rebeckah had known differently. William was a Littlefield, and he had told her more than once that the Littlefields of the mother country possessed a strong inner will. A Littlefield didn't give up. She had seen that same self-will fight back adversity over and over again. He would recover, and he would go on to make the plantation produce.

Rebeckah leaned back in her rocker and closed her eyes, savoring the things she held dear in her heart. Her cabin was far different than the first log room with a dirt floor. When she and William had first come together to make a home, life had been very hard in this part of the backcountry. Each landowner was left on his own to clear the land. Even her brothers had been too busy with their own land to offer much help.

Opening her eyes again, she smiled at the sleeping baby in her arms. She traced the contour of her tiny face. Mary was such a perfect baby. She had chosen the name Mary to give to this little one as a memory of her own mother, and William had agreed. It had been a hard birth, the hardest of all her babies, and she wondered if it was to be her last. After Solomon's birth, it seemed there would be no more babies. Her body was aging sooner than natural. She was only thirty-seven and by now should have had at least two more children.

She looked over at the mat where he lay. At forty-six, his graying hair gave him a distinguished look. She spoke aloud without thinking, "You still take my breath away, William Littlefield. What would I do without you?" To her surprise the voice from the mat, uncomfortable over the shower of sentiment, responded impatiently, "Oh, for the King's crown, Rebeckah, I'm not dead yet!"

Chapter 5

10 February 1764
Fredericktown, Maryland

It had been the understanding of John Lee, if he brought Rachel to the Littlefield's cabin they would take her to the court appointment. But upon arriving at the *William and John,* they were shocked to find William had almost drowned in the creek while trying to rescue a calf, and was still not strong enough to make the trip into town. And even more surprising to Rachel was finding Rebeckah nursing a new baby sooner than expected. Rachel had promised to come for the birthing but as it often happened, Mother Nature had intervened with a different plan. Maybe it was just as well that it turned out this way. There was not enough time to take care of the division of her father's will and see to Rebeckah and a new baby.

Because of illness back home, John had been forced to return the very day he had brought Rachel, leaving her to wait for another ride. William was able to send for the Sittler's who lived at the edge of the *William and John* and who tended to the Littlefield crops in the spring and summer. As luck would have it, they had plans to make the trip into Fredericktown for supplies that very Friday.

As the Sittler's wagon lumbered through the streets of Fredericktown Rachel grew more apprehensive. The late afternoon shadows cast a foreboding feeling over the town. Only once had she been here and remembered how most of the shopkeepers only spoke their native words of German. How would she ever communicate with them?

"Miss Rachel, I s'pect you will do just fine here at Miss Phoebe's. She will see to it that nothing unseemly comes your way," Mr. Sittler called back to her from the seat up front as he pulled the horses to a halt.

Zadock Sittler and his son Seth deposited Rachel's satchel and food basket at the bottom of the steps just as the door opened. The house looked to be mostly a boarding house.

"You must be Miss Lee," the lady said. I received your letter from one of the riders who picks up my mail from Dowden's Ordinary."

Rachel looked up into the friendly face of Phoebe Graves, and the welcome seemed sincere. "You have a nice place, Miss Graves," she said, as her eyes searched the front of the narrow house with lace curtains at the windows.

Miss Graves was a tall thin woman with a cheerful voice. And Rachel thought to herself that Robert was right in suggesting that she would be comfortable here.

As Rachel followed Miss Graves up the tiny stairs to the guest rooms, she could see the dress shop just off the hallway below. This must be the shop Robert's wife had spoken of. Maybe she would think about having a dress made. Her room was at the front of the house past another closed door. "You'll be able to see out to the street from this one," Miss Graves pointed out. "Most ladies like this room during court days, as it lets them see the festive goings-on from a safe distance. It is too bad you are a week too early for that. Everyone loves the street dances and jolly making around the illumination at night." Miss Phoebe opened the door and stepped back to let Rachel enter the room. "I'll send Cottie for you when it is time for the meal."

Rachel set her satchel on the bed and turned to look around at the pleasant surroundings. A fire in the small fireplace shed a soft glow to the darkening shadows. There was a table holding a water jug and bowl for easy washing, and on the floor a colorful rug had been placed to keep her feet warm. It held more colors and designs than she had ever seen in a rug. She could imagine every time Miss Phoebe cut a dress for someone in her dressmaking shop, she had gathered the scraps to put in a rug. Miss Phoebe had hooked the look of different colored flowers in the center and outlined it in a dark blue color. A small chair with rockers was placed next to the fireplace. Rachel was not accustomed to so many pretty things. It was such a contrast to her bare cabin. Maybe she could remember how nice this room was and try some of the ideas at home. But then she thought if she tried to bring a color to her place someone in the family would accuse her of wasting all her monies.

After a time warming by the fire, she went to the satchel and pulled out her old green faille dress. She had spent months taking it apart and cutting out the faded material. It happened when someone visiting from her family had let the curtain fall down in the upstairs bedchambers last summer, leaving her dress exposed to the hot afternoon sun. She had been sewing on it when her father fell to his death. There were still places showing a lighter color on the front, but it would have to do. She hung it on the hook on the wall, taking pains to carefully press the cotton petticoat out with her hands. It would have been nice if she had finished the repairs in time for her father's burial, but now, at least, she could look her best when she went before the court.

It had been two years since she had been off *Chestnut Ridge*. Would she know how to conduct herself mannerly? Everyone in the family had come to her after the will reading and told her how to act on this trip. And her sister Anne had spent a good portion of the morning after the burial instructing her on what to say. Now if only she could remember their instructions as they were needed.

She went to the window and peeked out through the lace curtain. The street below was deserted. A stray dog darted from behind the house and stopped only long enough to bark at something in the yard before disappearing around the corner.

A knock on her door startled Rachel. She started to reach for the doorknob, then stopped. William Littlefield had warned her not to open a door without knowing who was standing in the hallway. "Who is there?" she called shyly, her voice faint.

"It is Cottie, Miss Lee. I've been sent to fetch ye to the food table."

Rachel was hungry, and the smell of the meal gave her a strange sense of being cared for.

Her knees proved weak as she followed Cottie down the steps. She would put on her good face and meet the other lady boarders and hope she said the right words in her conversation. Immediately she chided herself for thinking that way. After all, her father had trusted her enough to put the affairs of his will into her hands. And now she must prove to herself that she was capable.

As she entered the dining room, she was surprised to see there was only one other woman sitting at the long table, her back to Rachel. The woman spoke to her in a biting tone, but she did not turn around. "No need to tiptoe in, I don't bite."

Rachel was stunned at her curtness. Thankfully, at that moment, Miss Phoebe came into the dining room carrying a bowl of thick broth with chunks of beef and vegetables sitting on top of the thick liquid. Cottie followed with a plate of yellow meal bread. Most ordinaries did not have food like this, so Rachel again felt privileged to be staying in such a nice place.

Miss Phoebe turned to the older boarder. "Miss Lucy, have you met our newest guest, Miss Rachel Lee? Her father just passed over, and she is in town with the sad task of seeing to his will papers."

Miss Lucy looked up at Rachel for a brief moment, her eyes burned, and her jawbone set in defiance but she said nothing, then shrugged her shoulder and went back to eating. Even when their host tried to engage the two in conversation, the old woman said nothing. Just as Rachel wondered if the woman could not hear, she was shocked by Miss Lucy pointing a crooked finger in her face and saying in a sour voice, "You must have talked a sweet talk to get your father to turn over his will to someone like you."

No one had ever accused Rachel of sweet-talking her father into anything. Before she could defend herself, Miss Phoebe quickly picked up her large Bible and began to read the daily scripture, as was her custom, both morning and night.

The light from the candle shrouded the old woman in eerie shadows against the wall, sending a shiver through Rachel. Suddenly she was reminded of a woman in a dream she once had as a small child. In the dream, an old woman with long gray hair blowing in the wind had come to their cabin door demanding to be let in. Rachel remembered running to her parent's bed, crying uncontrollably. Her mother had convinced her it was just a dream and had held her tight until she fell asleep. Seeing Miss Lucy in the shadowy light brought back the fear encased in that dream. What was it that made this woman sitting across from her so mean spirited?

No sooner had Miss Phoebe finished the readings than she began a conversation with Miss Lucy, probably to divert a confrontation.

Rachel excused herself and climbed the dark stairs back to her room. The night was cold, and she felt so alone. For the first time in her life, there was no one there to calm her fears. Oh, how she wished for a good long afternoon with her most-loved sister Rebeckah. But sadly, that could not happen now. Rebeckah was too busy for her silly chatter.

Once in her room, she latched the door and went to the window, slowly pulling the curtain back to look at the town by night. To her surprise she could see someone had lit several firepots on the courthouse square. She watched as some of the people stuck small sticks into the pots to create their own little light. With each movement the lighted sticks danced in the night darkness. Somehow it made her think of the years when her mother would put the tiny candles on the Christmas branches. That was when all the family was home and life was good.

At the edge of the group a few people began to step out a fast dance as others clapped the lively rhythms.

Rachel let the curtain fall from her hand and turned back to her room, forcing away the thought of that happy life. "Life goes on," she said out loud, vowing to forget the notions of the street below. At thirty-four she knew her future had been decided, and she would always be alone.

She reached for the small scrap of paper sitting on the bedside table and began to set a shopping list. Once she was at the mercy of the Sittler's schedule, she was forced to be in town longer than planned. It made sense to make the most of it by doing some much needed shopping for the coming year. Ever since her father's illness these last years, she had to rely on family to make her choices for the farm. Even her personal items were at the liking of whoever might be going to town.

She looked down at her stockings. They were so patched they hardly remained a true stocking, so she wrote "*stockins*" at the top of her list.

Only once before in her life had she had the luxury of time to shop for items, and the thought made Rachel smile. It was when her mother and father had decided to divide the home place between her brother John and herself. She felt sure her parents had worried about what would happen to their two youngest children if they should die before their lives were set. This was before John had married Elizabeth, and Rachel had no marriage date set. The rest of the brothers and sisters all had spouses and enough land of their own to raise their children. James and Mary Lee wanted the home place safely registered in the courthouse books as belonging to the unmarried children.

Rachel stood for a moment wrapped in the memory. Both she and her brother John had been so full of dreams. She was twenty-three and there was a special man in her life. Tobias wanted to marry her just as soon as he made enough monies to buy some land. John was twenty-two and had spoken for Elizabeth's hand. But this mature age did not stop them from acting out the silliness of a couple of kids seeing the town. She and John had gone from shop to shop to see the wares and even tasted some of the bakery sweets for the first time. John had bought a red bandana and blue and white striped stockings that were the latest fashion back then. Oh, he looked so jovial adorned with the trappings. They had laughed until their sides hurt when their father and mother first looked at him. Rachel had spent her monies on yards of ribbon of different colors. She had worn them until they were nothing but shredded pieces of string and had taken them to the hillside to release into the wind. Once on a walk down by the creek, she thought she saw one hanging from the weavings in a bird's nest in a big oak tree. That all seemed so long ago.

She counted on her fingers the years since all this had happened. Eleven years was a long time and so much had happened in those years. Rachel let out a deep sigh. It was what had not happened that was the most revealing. Shortly, she went back to writing her list.

Her list was simple. Only the most needed items, but even then she wondered if there was enough monies to make the deals. She went over it one last time before she blew out the candle and crawled into the high bed, pulling the cover up over her head. It was a good bed, and again, Rachel was glad to be staying in the safety of Miss Phoebe's rooming house.

Sometime in the middle of the night, a noise outside caused Rachel to sit up with a start. Someone was banging at the front door of the boarding house. She could hear Miss Phoebe coming down the hall calling for Cottie to get the gun. The banging continued. Rachel could feel her heart bumping in her chest. She had heard horror stories of rowdy men snatching women travelers from the ordinaries never to be seen again. And here she was staying in a house without a single man to guard over them.

The rapping became more urgent, and she heard Miss Phoebe demand, "What do you want? It is the middle of the night, and I don't open up until morning." Rachel slipped out of bed and went to the window to see if she could make out who was there. From the small sliver of the moon, she could see children spilling over the sides of an old wagon. Some were not even wearing cloaks. In weather like this they could freeze to death. Who would be so unkind, she wondered? A cry of fear erupted from the smaller ones, as a big man swung a whip in the air to rush the unloading. Rachel gasped in horror. What would all these children be doing here in the middle of the night? She had heard from Mrs. Carroll how some families sold all their children out to slavery in order to pay a debt and had explained it was called indenturing. Whatever it was called, if this was why these children were being brought here in the middle of the night, without as much as a blanket to keep them warm, it was cruel. Was Miss Phoebe working indentured children?

Rachel went to the door to listen.

"Miss Lucy isn't expecting you until day after tomorrow," Miss Phoebe said.

The man's voice was insultingly stern. "You take them as you get them, that were the deal. I can't help how fast the horse trots."

By now Miss Lucy had joined the others at the door. "I'll take charge of this old coot, Miss Graves." Miss Lucy ushered the children into the cold hallway and told them to go to sleep until morning. Rachel just hoped someone had provided some warm bedding to shield against the drafts.

When Cottie came to fetch her for breakfast, Rachel had inquired as to whose authority it was to bring these poor children to this place. For fear of being scolded for passing information, Cottie cupped her hand to Rachel's ear and whispered, "It is Miss Lucy; she always gathers the little ones, and some big ones as well, and takes them to the courthouse. The courthouse man puts their name on a piece of paper, then she takes them to the men who pays to keep them until they are all grown up. Miss Lucy gets a pocket full of monies to do this."

Rachel had never before witnessed this much terror in a child as she had the night before.

Her heart broke as she passed the children with their sad eyes peering out from under matted hair. And when she heard their heartrending cries coming from the dark corners of the hallway where they were being kept, she wanted to go snatch them away. If she had a husband with means, she would take them back to their parents and pay the debts in full. But there was nothing she could do about the heartbreaking cries of, "I want to go back to my mamma!"

The breakfast and noon meals at the boarding house were informative. Several more boarders had registered that morning, and the new ladies talked freely about where to shop, what the townspeople liked best, what you should be wearing, and who was expected in town the next week. But strangely, no one mentioned the children in the upstairs hallway. Every time Rachel started to ask questions about it, the subject was changed. One woman did stop long enough to tell Rachel she should not be a troublemaker and to just go about her own business as that was the way things were in this day.

Reluctantly, Rachel gathered up her list, tucked her monies safely into her underskirt pocket, and went down to the street. She wanted to get the shopping done before the men started drinking. It was not her desire to be the object of their drunken stares and calls.

As she crossed the road she noticed a mother leading her children across the street, and it reminded her of the decision to pick up candy for the children. If she couldn't take the children back to their parents, then she could at least give them one thing to be happy about.

Gradually she was able to forget the pain that occupied the boarding house. Everywhere she walked there were exciting things in the windows. Each shop beckoned her to come in and buy. And to her delight from what she could hear, it sounded like most of the merchants had now learned to speak English. She walked past the shoemaker's shop. The sign said the owner was Valentine Adams. From the looks of the window display, Mr. Adams could make shoes with pointed toes and little black heels for women. She had never been graceful, and that was an invitation to fall flat on her behind if she tried to walk in those. The more serviceable style, even in the simple cut, was more attractive than the ones made by her neighbor Dennis Madden. Dennis had kept her shoes wearable for as long as he had kept the shoe frames at his house. She saw no need to change now. But she did wish he would pattern the fixings after some of these. His words were, "If the shoe fits, do not twitter about how it looks."

The next shop was a neat little whitewashed shop called Combs by Mary. Mrs. Carroll's daughter Elizabeth had spoken how every best-dressed lady at the socials was wearing combs to secure the long locks of hair. She counted at least five different kinds of combs in the window. One comb had little stones fixed in the top, and another was made from gold. The one that caught Rachel's eye was even more exquisite. It was made from a beautiful rich looking wood, and the artist had carved small roses across the top of the comb. Rachel could see her reflection in the window and wondered what she would look like wearing one. Timidly, she looked around to make sure no one was watching and released her hair from the tightly twisted knot at the back of her head. It fell to her shoulders and engulfed her face. She let out a gasp at what had she done? What if someone saw her fixing herself up right here in public? She tried to recapture her wayward hair but it was no use. Before she could twist the knot again, two women with beautifully controlled hair came out of the shop. Rachel quickly pulled it to the back of her neck and secured it with the string. She would fix it back in the knot when she was out of sight. When would she learn that trying to be something she was not always made her look foolish?

The next shop was a dress shop, and when she walked in, several women inside were being fitted with new dresses. Miss Phoebe Graves had expressed regret this morning at not having enough time to cut one at this time. Rachel knew the feeling of not having enough time. She had crops to put in the ground and a barn to clean when she got home—not to mention putting a new roof on the cabin after the last rain had soaked the coverlets in the attic. There would be no time for frivolities like making a dress.

While waiting for the dressmaker to finish attending the other customers, Rachel walked among the rows of brightly colored calico fabrics all stacked neatly on top of the other. There were more selections than she had ever seen in one place. She picked up a brown with yellow colors on it and thought it would be really serviceable and not show soil. But it did nothing for her spirit. She put it back on top of the stack and moved to a black material with different colors. Even a bolt of yellow material looked unappealing. As she looked past the aisle she noticed a woman pick up a bright blue piece. Instantly she knew it was the piece she wanted. But someone else had found it first. Rachel took a deep breath of relief when the woman set it back on the stack and went to another row. Quickly, she went over and picked up the bolt. It was possibly the prettiest piece of calico she had ever seen. It had tiny yellow and red threads woven into it. When she held it up to her face in front of the looking glass, the seamstress turned around and said, "Oh, that piece will surely look good on you. It brings your blue eyes right out." Rachel felt warm all over and almost laughed. No one had ever said something looked good on her.

After the woman took her measurements, Rachel asked for a scrap of the material to take home to show her sister-in-law. Betsy would want to hear all about her shopping trip. That was the way Betsy was, always excited over something good happening to someone.

Once she was out on the street again, Rachel wondered why she was acting so foolishly. It had taken all her willpower to keep from ordering two

Sunday dresses. When did she think she would ever engage her life enough to use two new dresses at one time?

She quickly walked to the end of the street, passing mostly legal shops there for the purpose of running the courts. Several signs announced that the attorney-at-law offices occupied the lower floors of the houses. As she passed she could not help but overhear the conversation between two men standing in a doorway of one office. They were obviously speaking of the powers of the Parliament over the colonies.

Not really intending to eavesdrop, but being forced to stop while someone loaded a wagon in that very spot, she heard a man almost shouting the words, "I thought we made our own laws. Are we not in control of our own lives?"

"Yes, we are. But remember," the lawyer reasoned, "the King's governors have little monies to enforce any of the new laws they pass. They are too busy dealing with their own problems. I guarantee they will not waste time on us."

"True," the man said, then stood shaking his head, contemplating what the lawyer had said. "I guess you are right. The port official can't get to us if he doesn't have monies to hire the people to work the ports."

"And Lord Baltimore does not have the monies to give to the port official."

"I see what you are saying."

The man in the fine satin coat, who Rachel assumed was the lawyer, gave her only a glancing look as she stood waiting for the wagon to move. He continued to lecture the man on the street. "You have land don't you?"

The other man nodded.

"So why are you so distressed? You have land and landowners elect the assembly. We just have to make sure we elect the men who will make the laws we want."

Rachel wondered what fears had fostered the men's exchange. It made her think about the land she owned and maybe she should be paying more attention to who was elected. A smile came across her face. What would John Hughes say if she helped elect someone he didn't like just because she was a landowner and had the freedom to do so? She felt like laughing out loud at that thought.

Finally, the wagon moved out and she could continue down the street to Jacob Cline's Tailor Shop. This must be the shop where the lawyers went to be fitted for their garments that made them look so fine.

Her attention was diverted to another very successful business. The shop was small but its large sign, William Banks Watts Barbershop and Wig Settings, could not be missed. She could see several men sitting in chairs enveloped in a mist of white powder as the wig maker readied the selected piece for wear.

Rachel stood for a moment looking down both streets. The sign for the next building, in the shape of a large tankard, claimed the distinction of being the Tavern Across the Street. This must be the spot her brother had told her about, where the long-winded orators quenched their thirst. The tavern appeared to be full even on this off court day. She had been warned not to expect the clerk to stay on schedule. They were at the mercy of the lawyers who liked to hear themselves make long speeches. And even if her case did not need a lawyer, the clerk would be tied up with their cases. As she stood on the corner waiting to pass across, a patron could be heard making a long speech of some sorts. And to her surprise, he was ousted from the door before she could move. The obvious drinker looked up at her from the ground below. "Well now, my pretty thing, how about a drink?" In disgust, she rushed between two wagons on the street to get away.

Rachel decided to cut through the courtyard where she could see the sign Weaving by Andrew Fogle. And directly under his name were the words Stockings by SueAnna Catherine.

Rachel desperately needed new stockings and opened the shop door. To her surprise there were stockings of just about every color hanging from the racks overhead. She had never worn anything but the serviceable black ones. Her hand ran down the extent of the wonderfully woven thick wool stockings in vivid colors. There were green ones, brown ones, gray ones, a few dark red ones, and even bright blue ones. And hanging near the window were a line of beautiful white linen stockings made for only the rich to wear at very special times. She knew about these from Mrs. Carroll's daughters, Mary and Elizabeth, who wore them to socials.

Rachel stepped up to the table to address the weaver's wife. "I'll take a pair of the black ones," she said, then laughingly lifted her skirt slightly to show SueAnna Catherine her old worn out stockings. "I don't expect any amount of thread will hold these old ones together for another wearing." As SueAnna Catherine reached up to remove the stockings from the hangers, Rachel stopped her. "I've changed my mind. I'm inclinable to try a colored pair," she said.

By the time she left the shop, she carried under her arm, wrapped in paper, a pair of green ones, a pair of dark red ones and even a pair of light gray ones. But more astonishing to her was that she had not bought a single pair of black ones. She vowed to herself that some day she would come back to buy a fancy pair of the white linen stockings.

Once out on the street, she felt light-headed. Was it the shock from spending so many monies for stockings? She had been so careful all of her life to not place a value on unnecessary clutter. Had she lost the sense God had given her? All these years tied to the home place because of her father's illness must have numbed her sense of reason. Now there was no one to tell her what she should or should not do. She was free to make her own decisions. If this was true, then why did she feel shaky all over? She scolded herself over her unwise buying. How dare she chance losing the land or going hungry over some colored stockings.

She stood in the street trying to decide if she should go back to the shop and return them for a single pair of black ones. That is what she would be expected to do if her family had been with her. Common sense prevailed and she turned to return the hose. Suddenly a commotion next to the courthouse caught her attention. A wagon had pulled up to the log building behind the courthouse. Rachel could see a struggle between a young man and several older men who were trying to pull him into the building. The group of shoppers crossing the street pushed her along with them to go see what was happening.

Rachel could hear the German words of a couple greeting each other but could not remember what *ach himmel* meant or the response of *nicht*. Thankfully, another woman came up beside her and spoke in English.

"I think that is where the jail is," the woman offered.

A man standing nearby added further to the intrigue, saying, "It appears to be the same boy I encountered at the edge of town, running between some houses." The crowd was shouting all at once, each person trying to find out more about what was going on. Rachel had never been in the midst of such a commotion and started backing out of the crowd, having been warned to watch out for purse-snatchers in these situations. When she turned around she was almost knocked down in the excitement.

A storeowner came out of her shop to watch and turned to Rachel. "Looks to be the likes of us are none too safe. I says to meself often, they ought to hang em all, those rally risers."

Rachel walked over to the street corner and stood for a time trying to decide if she should just go back to the boarding house for safety. In the excitement she forgot about returning her stockings.

A heavy bank of dark blue clouds appeared to the north, and she suspected cold weather was on the way. If she did not get her shopping done now she might never get it finished in time. She pulled the crumpled list from the inside pocket of her heavy cloak and began looking for the millinery shop. As much as she wanted a new hat, she knew there were not enough monies for such foolery. That did not take away the desire to see what was being offered. Just maybe, she could get an idea on how to remake her old one using the scraps from the new dress being cut.

Street vendors cried their wares on each of the corners. The smell of roasted pork and corn spilled into the air. She stopped to ask the vendor selling hot chestnuts where she could find the Millinery shop. He pointed to the group of small shops at the end of Counsel Street.

Rachel picked up her pace. It was getting colder and a few snowflakes were beginning to collect on the storefront window frames. When she stepped up on the step that connected two shops, she could see a posting on the door: Closed To Bury Husband.

Rachel stood looking at the sign feeling sympathy for this woman's grief, then turned her attention to the hats sitting on the window shelf. She took a step back to leave. That was when the sign in the next shop window caught her attention: Portrait's By Daniel Wolstein. She paused at the door. She had never had her face painted, and she wondered what it would look like. It was a silly thought. No one had ever said, "Rachel, you are so pretty you should have your face painted." She could only imagine the ridicule she would receive at the hands of her family. As she turned from the door she saw, for the second time that day, a faint image of her face. And for the second time today, her hands pulled at her hair. This time she pulled only a few stands from the front, like those she had seen on the young woman at the dress shop. Before she could pull it tight again, the door opened and a man hurried out without considering someone might be standing on the porch. They had been saying something about a man whose name she could not make out. Before she could move, she felt herself being hurled to the ground. A man with curly red hair looked down at her without as much as an offer to help pick her up.

"What were you doing listening to our business?" The man grabbed her by the shoulder but not as an attempt to pull her to her feet. "You stupid wench. I'll teach you not to spy."

Rachel was afraid he was going to hit her. What had been so serious that he did not want her to hear? Would he kill her for thinking she was listening. Something happened which she had no control over and unless she acted to defend herself she would be at his dealings. She kicked the aggressor and scratched at his face causing him to release her. Unlike the shy Rachel the family knew, she retorted, "How dare you call me a wench. I'm Rachel Lee. And I've a right to be here."

The man stood up in pain. He wiped the blood from his face and swore a word she did not know. He limped to the street and disappeared between the houses. Rachel stood up, forcing her body to move.

Shaken, but not terribly hurt, she quickly picked up the rolled up parcel of stockings that had fallen out of her arms and decided there had been enough close calls for one afternoon. Wrestling with the old mother sow in the hog pen at home had never been this challenging to stay afoot. These people were rude and fast moving. But she prided herself in the fact she had not cried in the face of her adversary. Not only had she not cried in the face of adversity, she had, in fact, fought.

As she retraced her way back to the corner, the limp was not because of her confrontation but from walking in her tight-fitting shoes all day. By now the cold wind whipped at her cloak leaving her hands numb. It was time to forget her list and go back to the boarding house.

She made her way to the square where some children were playing with the snowflakes that had begun to fall. Seeing them, she realized she had forgotten to buy the candy for the children and began looking around for the candy store. She would not let her fear take away their surprise.

She worked her way around the shoppers, and spotted the small sign reading Sweet Bites tucked in between the printing shop and another store. The shop window had ruffled lace curtains hung behind the glass shelves and each shelf held pretty china plates with candies. She walked inside and the sweet smells of sugar and molasses gave her a wonderfully pleasing feeling. Along the wall the narrow shelves were lined with ruffled paper. There were pink and white round swirls—clear red sugar drops, probably made from chokecherry jelly, she reasoned. There were dark maple sugar squares, little nuts dusted with sugar, horehound drops, and always the favorite, taffy. Rachel put her hand in her pocket to count the monies she could afford to spend on the children. "Let's see, there are four, no five— and the big boy." In her mind she saw each sad face. "I'll take the pink and white swirled sugars." Rachel looked around the room again and decided on another. "Oh, I'll take a scoop of those clear red drops also, please," Rachel added. She couldn't help but share the reason with the clerk. "The children will enjoy holding them to the light."

The lady behind the counter smiled as she carefully lifted the candies from the plates and began to make conversation. "You are a loving mother to take home candy as a treat. If I may ask, how many little ones have you been blessed with?

Rachel felt a stab to her heart. That same feeling like all those times she realized she would never hold a baby of her own. It would take too long to give the explanation. A deep sigh accompanied the painful words, hovering over the counter like the dust from the sugar candy and stuck in her throat. All she could say was, "I have no children of my own to love."

She took her package from the lady behind the counter, and walked out onto the street. The thought bore into her heart that this surprise was likely to be the last good thing the children would have until they were grown. The daylight sky was disappearing fast and the snow had begun covering the street. She had no desire to be alone on these side streets in the darkness and rushed to find her way back to the boarding house. She could hear music coming from the center of the square. A group of young people were dancing around an illuminary to the rhythm of clapping hands and a high-pitched flute. When the big clock on the courthouse began to chime, a rather large man came to stand on the steps. He was dressed in a black coat with gold bands around the wide cuffs. The bright gold buttons, closely set, lined the front of the coat and along the top of the cuffs. Every time he moved, the buttons caught the light of the nearby fire and sparked the darkness. He held a big bell in his right hand, and in his left hand, he clutched a large paper piece. It must be the town crier she thought. She had never witnessed hearing one, but her brother John had told her how the crier bellowed out the news of the day and how everyone in the larger towns relied on the criers to keep them informed. In fact, she knew her family often mentioned some news they had heard while at Dowden's Ordinary, news that had been brought by someone hearing the town crier the night before. Rachel looked again at the darkening sky and wondered if she would be safe standing here alone. The boarding house was just a little over a block away, and if she stayed only while he called the news, she would not be out that much longer.

The music had stopped and a crowd began gathering around the man. He lifted his arm and swung the bell several times to silence the crowd. Then with a distinctly clear command of his deep voice, the words began to echo off the courthouse wall, out into the cold night air.

"*Hear ye, hear ye, today Saturday, the eleventh day of February in the year of 1764, in the Province of Maryland, the place of Fredericktown. Long live King George III.*

"*Two days ago hence, the British ship Friendly Traveler made dock outside the fair city of Annapolis with news that King George III has assigned his new minister, George Grenville, to form a new financial affairs sheet in order to assure our protection.*

"*Be it known this day our honorable sheriff has brought to our jail Winchell Thurman, a thief, reported to have stolen Widow Sealy's horse with harness and saddle on its back. He is to be housed in Fredericktown in the county of Frederick, Maryland, until sentencing to hang, if indeed be the wishes of the said judge.*

"*Hear ye, hear ye, this day the news of our venerable neighbor Thomas Cresap is scheduled to make his way from his fort at Oldtown to Fredericktown to attend to court matters.*

"*Hear ye, hear ye, today the news of an Indian raid in newly founded town of Sharpsburg, on border of the*

Province of Virginia. A settler's wife and young boy child found slaughtered at site.

"Hear ye, hear ye, so say the constable of said Frederick County, Maryland, on this day, the eleventh of February in the year of 1764."

The report of the Indian raid caused those standing around to frantically question what might have been heard before the crier called it out this night. It had happened just over the ridges, surely only half-a-day's travel from this corner. Panic registered on the faces of the women standing nearby. Rachel had no one to turn to for safety. Fear gripped at her chest. Why had fate handed her the task of coming alone to this rowdy city. She wondered if her family had heard the news about the slaughters.

Hurriedly, Rachel started towards the boarding house, running as fast as the snow allowed. As she reached the front of Miss Phoebe's, she could see a wagon being unloaded at the front step. Miss Phoebe had come to the front door and was ushering in two women.

Rachel slowly followed the women up the steps, eager to see the surprised look on the children's faces when she handed out the candies. But she found the upper hall empty of the small urchins. She could see Miss Lucy standing in her doorway watching as Miss Phoebe settled the new guests into their room.

"Where are the children?" Rachel demanded, daring to address Miss Lucy in such a voice.

"I had them put in the shed. I got tired of hearing their whimperin' and beggin' to go home," she said in a flat uncaring voice.

The thought of the helpless children being stored away in a building without heat, where the wind came in between the boards like they were not even there, was more than she could stand. And with this snow they could freeze to death. She turned to Miss Lucy. "How can you be so cruel?"

Rachel ran back down the steps to Miss Phoebe's door. "Miss Phoebe, I can no longer abide by this mean-spirited demeanor. You either put the children in my room, or I will be forced to take my bed to them and tell others of your practices." Her voice was strained, and she could feel the veins tighten in her neck.

Miss Phoebe stiffened her back, eyeing her for a moment. Then in a somewhat sharp tone she said, "Very well, Miss Lee. I will see they are brought to you. But mind you, you will be responsible for their behavior until Miss Lucy registers them on Monday."

"Miss Lee!" A curt challenge was being laid down at the top of the stairs. It was Miss Lucy who had overheard the conversation. "How dare you try to interfere with my authority. These are nothing but ignorant

51

leftovers of debts unpaid. Their families should have thought of this before they chose to come to our new province."

Rachel's temper was rising as she came back up the stairs. "And how dare you tell me what I should or should not feel about a small innocent child?" Rachel wondered what her brothers would have thought of her now. Would they have said she lacked courage? It was obvious from the look on the old woman's face that no one lately had dared to refute her authority.

Rachel threw her purchases on the bed, trying to control her tears. She was being forced to take a stand on something important, and in some strange way, it felt good to speak her mind to Miss Lucy. What she would liked to have said was, "Close up your mouth you haggard old woman." But again, the teachings of her mother had prevailed and thanks be for that. What would the courts think of her if she appeared before them with a black eye?

When she heard Miss Phoebe bringing the children up the stairs, she rushed to open the door, anxious to see their excited faces. But the children who stood before her were not what she thought she would see. Instead, the look she saw was like a caged animal after being tortured. And when she reached out to them they drew back. The little girl in the front began to scream in terror. She did not dare ask Miss Phoebe's help to calm their fears. Finally, the oldest boy addressed her as the self-appointed spokesman of this fear stricken group of indentured debt payers.

"My name is Samuel. We want to know why you want us up here now, when you just threw us out in the cold."

Rachel spoke directly to the boy who appeared to be about thirteen years of age. "Samuel, it was not I who had you and the others sent to the shed. I was doing my shopping, and when I found you gone, I insisted Miss Phoebe bring you here."

"Are you taking us back to our places?" Samuel again spoke for the group.

Oh, how Rachel's heart ached with that question. She so wished she could answer yes, but all she could give them was a night's security in a warm room.

"Oh, how I wish I could, but that is not my decision to make. But I do have a surprise for you—something I bought for you today."

The children shyly entered the room looking as if they had never seen a room like this. And that was probably true. After all, she herself had been impressed with the room. Rachel pushed the log around in the small fireplace to make more heat and motioned for the shivering children to sit on the floor to warm. She pulled the blankets from her bed and wrapped them around the little ones. Then she produced the sugar treats and watched their eyes grow wide. The look on their faces would rest on her heart for the remainder of her life.

One by one the shy children came to hug Rachel's neck. Her heart was breaking as their tears melted away any loneliness she felt.

As the evening shadows fell around the sad-faced children sitting on the floor in front of the warm fire, Rachel felt their helpless feelings, only in a grown up sort of way. She too was forced into something she did not want to do.

Finally, as the evening wore on she heard the names of each child and found out something about where they lived, if they even knew. Frantically, her mind raced to think of a way to get them to forget their plight. "Would you like to hear a story that my father used to tell me?"

The little ones shook their heads eagerly. The older ones knew it was just a way to keep them quiet. But as she began the story, they became as transfixed as the others. She started from the beginning of her father's young years and worked her way through the friendship with the little Indian boy, sometimes making up something to keep their attention, like when the boy James was lost from his parents and the Indian child helped him find them. The children sat quietly, transported from their bleak future, to hope in finding their own way back home.

It was Samuel, again, who spoke. "Is that a true story?"

Before she could finish the story, Rachel heard the bells peeling from the All Saints Church on a distant street below. She remembered Miss Phoebe telling her to listen for them. It was a custom that the German people had brought from their homeland, and each Saturday night, the ringing of the bells reminded them of their heritage. The children softly tiptoed down the steps as Rachel led the way out onto the street below.

The snow fell softly on their dirty faces huddled silently together. The sound of the bells echoing through the crisp night air offered up a sense of peace to those who listened. Rachel's thoughts turned to a sad realization that there was no peace for these little ones.

In the quietness of her own heart she asked, "Please, dear God, find a place of hope for these children."

The sun broke through the mist in the early morning sky. It was Tuesday, and the day Rachel had told the Madden boys to meet her at the courthouse to vouch on their witness marks. By midmorning tomorrow she could be on her way home. That is if her brother John and her sister Martha's husband remembered to come in time to vouch for the sureties.

Last night her dreams had been crowded with the thoughts of the last few days. Probably it had to do with the emotions she had felt yesterday while waiting outside the courthouse door as the children came out one by one. Some were too young to fully realize their names had just been matched to a person indenturing them for twenty years.

Her heart still ached remembering the sound of their cries as they climbed onto the wagon and Miss Lucy's scornful voice yelling at them to stop crying.

But that was yesterday, and today there was a different reason to go to the courthouse. Rachel put her feet to the floor and pulled on the old worn out black stocking held together with a mesh of new mending threads. She would never forget the smiles on the children's faces yesterday as she slipped their new snug green, gray and dark red wool stockings over their cold feet just before the wagon pulled away. It had taken her most of the night before to cut up and sew the pretty stocking she had purchased for herself on Saturday. She smiled as she wiggled her toes. "Someday I will again buy colored stockings."

A knock on the door caused her to jump. She was not expecting anyone to come for her. When she inquired as to who might be at the door, she was pleasantly surprised with the reply.

"It is Betsy. Let me in."

It was her brother John's wife and not a better face to see. Rachel pulled open the door in excitement. "Oh, you are a sight for sore eyes, to be sure. Where's John? Where are the children? Are you feeling better? Where did you stay last night on the road?" The questions spilled out. Until now she had not realized how alone she had been.

"Since Dennis Madden was having to come, Anastasia insisted she keep the children and told John he needed to bring me with him. Wasn't that sweet of her? She is like that. So John went over to the Bealls and asked if he could hire their servant, Magdalina, to help Anastasia with the children at the Maddens. Remember her?" Betsy asked.

"I know the one; she has such a pretty face and name but such blank eyes. I hope baby Elizabeth will not be afraid of her," Rachel fretted.

"I wanted to come so badly. John was not so sure at first, but then I told him you needed help with your shopping," Betsy giggled. "Well, did you shop, Rachel? And what about the new dress? Are you having one cut for you?"

Rachel pulled the scrap of material she had brought from the dress shop out of her pocket. The women both agreed that it was the prettiest calico they had ever seen.

"Oh, Rachel, they are going to be so surprised when you go to church wearing the first new dress you have had in years," Betsy teased.

As the two went down to breakfast, the conversation continued without pause. You would have thought Rachel had been away for a year or more by their chatter.

After the breakfast at Miss Phoebe's table, the two started for the courthouse. Most likely by now, John Lee and the Madden brothers were already pacing the front, wondering what had kept Rachel and Betsy so long.

When the women stepped out onto the street, they found the ground had thawed just enough to allow the mud to slip with each step, leaving their shoes caked with the heavy red clay. Both women grabbed at their skirts, gathering the fullness up to their knees in an effort to keep the clay from soiling them. But this did not keep Rachel from pointing out some of the goods in the store windows as they walked to the courthouse. In her excitement, she failed to move out of the way of a man coming around the corner. Betsy had to reach out and grab her sister-in-law to keep her from falling but not before they both had been roughed up.

"Get out of my way, you simpleton wench."

Rachel turned when she heard the voice, a familiar voice from a man who had addressed her in the same manner at an earlier time. She realized it was the same red-headed man who had been in front of the portrait painter's shop on Saturday.

Rachel and Betsy watched the man break into a run and dart between two houses. Then Rachel turned to her sister-in-law and told her about the event that led to the happenings on the second night she was in town and how this man had so rudely knocked her to the ground.

Rachel pointed toward the street with the candy store in the middle. "That is where I bought the candies for the children. Did I tell you they each hugged my neck that night?"

Betsy looked at her sister-in-law. "You would make a good mother, Rachel."

Rachel put her hand on Betsy's arm but said nothing. Wanting to change the subject, she began describing the people in the town. "Many still speak no English, and I cannot remember much German now, since mother has gone. She was the one that taught us the words, you know."

When they reached the street in front of the courthouse, Rachel pointed out where she had seen the men struggling with a man before taking him into the jail. "That was when two boys grabbed the purses of two women. Oh, you have to be so careful when you come to town," Rachel counseled.

The dull thud of the bell in the tower of the courthouse sounded the hour as the two women crossed the street. Realizing they had spent too much time talking, they picked up the pace. "We should have already been in line. John and the Madden boys are going to be upset with us," Rachel feared.

The two-story brick courthouse with its long white-pained windows stood in the middle of the courtyard square. As they approached the building, Rachel pointed out to Betsy, "There is the pillory. I saw a man and woman with their heads and hands put through the holes yesterday when I came to see the children off. I never heard what their crime was, but they were protesting loudly about the harsh punishment. I'd like to see that rude name-calling man sentenced to the pillory." They both laughed at the thought, then Rachel went on to explain how the court worked with wayward women. "Do you know what they do to women who quarrel and lie to their husbands? I've been told, they tie them on a long pole and dunk them right down there in Carroll Creek."

Betsy stood with her mouth open in disbelief. "I shall remember that when I speak again to my John Lee." The women both laughed, and Rachel said, "Tis it any wonder that I wish not to engage with a husband."

The women were halfway around the courthouse when they spotted John and the Madden boys waiting by the side of the building. "There is John now," Betsy said and waved but he did not see her.

John was busy inspecting the window structure while Dennis Madden looked on. "This glazing has begun to crack already. Robert told me when he was here for jury duty in November last year that there was talk with the courts that the repair had not gone well."

After sizing up the frame, Dennis stood back and looked at the full length of the tall window. "I admire the idea but seems to me it does not work the way intended. They say the inside is as cold as it is out here."

"John, look who I found standing on the street corner begging for a coin," Betsy called out to her husband.

The men had not seen the women approaching and turned to acknowledge them but wasted no talk in their direction. Utmost on the men's mind was the structure and what should be done to fix the problem.

By the time Rachel could pull the men away and they moved around to the front of the courthouse, a long line had moved ahead of them. She whispered to Betsy, "That woman and man over there were at the tailor's shop on Saturday. I talked to them after they had bought a new suit of clothes for their son who is leaving for London next month to study the law." Then she pointed to another person. "And see that woman in the gray cloak? She was at the dressmaker the same day I was."

"What color did she buy? I'll wage it wasn't as pretty a color as yours," Betsy giggled.

Dennis and Joseph Madden had gone over to speak to a man they knew from the road into town, leaving John to talk with his wife and sister.

The subject of Anne and John Hughes came up as it always did when there was the talk of money. "I expected to see them sitting on the top step just to make sure you are doing everything to their liking."

"I'm sure there is still fussing enough to come," Rachel agreed.

The sound of pigeons squawking on the ledge around the bell tower created such a commotion that they all looked up. In a rare moment of gaiety in her role as administrator, Rachel pointed to the foul, "Well, as I live and breathe, I do believe they are arguing about who inherited the family farm." They all, even those standing next to them, could appreciate the humor and laughed at the thought.

It seemed everyone was settling family affairs, and court day was not even until next week. A man standing with some men next to the line were upset over the way the currency was losing value with the British bank. Rachel wondered if that would affect her dividing the will assets. She would need to remember to ask. As the long line moved toward the door, they were told that only the one doing business could go into the crowded courtroom and anyone needing to sign as witness would be called in after the words were set in the book.

When Rachel reached the door, John turned to his sister and patted her on the shoulder, "I am so proud of you, Rach."

As she took hold of the door handle, tears were stinging at the edges of her eyes. If this had been for any other reason but her father's death, it would have been an exciting time for a poor country girl. She turned around and gave John a hug and waved to the others as she took a step inside the small room that served as the entry room.

A deep voice broke into her thoughts, "Next. Next." His gruffness embarrassed Rachel. She should have been paying closer attention but how could she when the man standing at the door barking the orders had no knowledge that his breakfast had been slopped down his red vest, still wet from the hour. This in some way made her feel less frightened. He was not as much in control of his arrogant self as he wished her to believe.

A desk by the door had a sign plate on it that read John Darnall, Clerk. As she moved up the line, Rachel felt very insignificant standing in front of this man in his well-tailored green velvet suit. He wore a white wig and had heavy black eyebrows. His eyes stared right through her. His sharp voice relayed an unfriendly manner toward women doing business before the court. "Sir, I am Rachel Lee, and I am here to register my father's will."

In a cold, disinterested voice he said, "Your father's name?"

"James Lee Sr," She said with a slight quiver to her voice.

Mr. Darnall took his pen from the inkwell and wrote the name in big scrawling letters. Then he looked up at her. "James Lee was your father?"

"Yes, sir, we buried him late January."

With his pen still in midair, the clerk paused to look up at Rachel. A kinder tone replaced the sharpness in his voice. "He was a fine man, a very fine man. I once lived near his place." He motioned to a young boy on a long bench behind him. "Take Miss Lee to Thomas Bowles's table to write her father's will into the book."

Rachel followed the boy into the main part of the courthouse. The large room was lined with long benches on both sides, and at the far end there was a high platform with a pulpit stand like the kind ministers delivered their sermons from. Just below the platform on the floor part were three long tables. Three men, dressed somewhat alike with white powdered wigs, were seated, one at each table.

As she was led to the far right table, she noticed another woman sitting at one of the tables. She felt more confident to see she was not the only woman doing business on this day.

The man taking her in told her to sit down and wait for Mr. Bowles.

While waiting she could not help but observe that Mr. Bowles did not seem to be doing official business, but rather it appeared town gossip was on trial by a group of men standing next to the table. She could hear King George III mentioned. It seemed they thought he was a fair and impartial King, and they were all satisfied with the dealing of the officials at the ports. After they stopped talking about the King's business, the men began to talk of the recent ending of the French and Indian War and how grateful they were that it was finally over. Now they could begin to buy wagons again and even find a few good horses for sale.

The men talking of buying new wagons made Rachel think about her conversation with the wagon builder just last week. Just a few weeks after the war was over last year, her father had sent word to Mr. Jacobs that he would be needing a new wagon shortly. Then just after her father died, Rachel had gone by to see how soon her name would come to the top of the list. To her shock she was told since it had been reserved in her father's name and he had died, the name had been removed. And now her name was at the bottom, giving her reason to wonder if she could ever stop borrowing her brother's wagon.

Rachel's thoughts were interrupted when a man whom the others called by the name of Peter Mallot, walked over to Mr. Bowles's table. After shaking hands, they began talking about the latest news of the Indian uprising. "Joseph Chapline and I just came from Sharpsburg to tend to some deeds, and all along the way, the farmers were jumpy every time their dogs growled. We saw evidence of some of the burned out barns and houses. We had to put our wives up at Miss Graves's boarding house this morning because they were so terrified. My wife, Rachel, was so upset she could not even think of shopping. That alone should tell you something." The men laughed a hearty laugh at the thought.

These words caught the attention of Rachel because of the wife's name and also that she was staying at Miss Phoebe's. They must have come in before Elizabeth had come because she did not see any new people at the door.

One of the men agreed to the concern and said he had followed fresh Indian tracks all along the lower Potomac near the point of rocks when coming to the courthouse yesterday.

"I heard they had gotten as far as the lower Monocacy," the clerk volunteered.

Rachel gasp out loud. One of the men turned around to look at her. "They are headed toward my brother-in-law's place," she explained as to why the concern.

Rachel knew Thomas Thrasher would never bring the family out or leave them alone if he had heard of this danger. If Thomas did not come, she knew this was a wasted trip. Her brother John could not prove he had the monies to stand for the surety alone. And without the promise of sureties, the courts would not file the will.

Her thoughts were again interrupted by a commotion at the next table. A man in a ragged cloak had presented a paper that was not signed, and the clerk said it could not be proven to be real. The man had grabbed the recorder by the throat, and Rachel was sure he intended to strangle him right then and there by the way he held his neck. The man's voice was shrill and desperate. "What am I to do with the man's old lady. It means there is no inheritance?" Several bystanders had come to the aid of the recorder and restrained the angry man.

Rachel wondered if this was how most people reacted in court when things didn't go their way.

Finally, Thomas Bowles called for her paper. His voice seemed kind as he took the fragile yellowed paper from Rachel. Then he reached under a pile of books and found a large brown leather-bound book with big gold writing on the spine. He opened it to somewhere near the middle, looking for the last page he had written on.

He looked at the names on the bottom of the yellowed will, then asked Rachel, "You do know, Miss Lee, it is necessary that the witnesses listed here," he pointed to the names, "must come in to make oath of their testimony?"

"Yes, sir," Rachel started to explain, "Mr. Butler has passed on. I'm uncertain to the exact date, but I've been told sometime before 1762. But his wife, Elizabeth, says she would be willing to speak of his signing if you need her to come at a later date. The Madden brothers are waiting in the outer room to make oath."

"Very well." He looked up at her as if surprised at her ability to take care of the details. "I'm aware that Mr. Butler is deceased, he did business for us, you know."

Mr. Bowles took time to read most of the writing and again stopped about halfway down the page. "And why is it, Miss Lee, that Mary Lee did not come to file the will?"

"That is my mother and she died before my father. You will see down here he underlined my name when he selected me to answer for him."

This explanation seemed to satisfy Mr. Bowles as he continued to read. Finally he looked up. "I am satisfied everything is in order if you say Mr. Dennis Madden and Mr. Joseph Madden are both here to vouch." He looked up at Rachel, at which time she nodded yes. He dipped his pen in and out of the inkwell several times, then pulled the point over the lip of the glass edge to make sure it would not drip on the paper. Having forgotten to number the page, he turned back to the previous page number before going on. He carefully lined up the numbers 1.9.4 at the upper left corner of the blank page.

Rachel could tell this was a job he had done many times by the careful way he let the words glide onto the faint blue-lined paper in an effortless motion. And he did not waste the paper by making the words too large, like some scripters did.

"What is this name?" he asked, pointing to the word.

"It is Betterton, my sister Eleanor Betterton."

Mr. Bowles pointed to several other names and Rachel repeated the names of Mary Wofford, which he said was spelled as Wafford on the will paper. He continued, "Martha Thrasher and Elizabeth Willis? Oh, and down here, what is this?"

"I'm not too good with the reading so I don't know what Mr. Butler was writing but the name is Margaret Seager. It sure looks like he was starting it with an *L* but it is Seager. John Seager was her husband." Rachel's voice took on a tenderness as she explained, "My sister is dead now."

Mr. Bowles looked up at Rachel, then said, "Oh, I see now that is an *S* and not an *L*. Some of these writers don't make their words plain enough to read. It is a wonder the possessions get to the right people."

Mr. Bowles pointed to a line where she should make her mark. "Miss Lee, you can go home and tell your people your father's will is safely written into my book, and you can expect the appraisers at your house within the month. It is very important that you not give away one single item until I so instruct. No matter who wants it."

When Rachel stood up to go, Mr. Bowles took the liberty to speak a word of caution. "It is best if you are not traveling alone, Miss Lee. I guess you have heard about the renegades who have terrorized the river dwellers the last few days."

A cold chill swept over Rachel at the warning, but at the same time, she felt shy that this man had been concerned for her safety.

Once outside, Rachel looked around for her brother and sister-in-law, but they were nowhere in sight. Had news of the murdering savages scared those outside as well as inside the courtroom?

A man running by her yelled, "Cresap is down at the creek with news of the savages."

She watched as several more people from the houses close by came out of their doors to join in on the search for news. Had John, Betsy, and the Maddens gone down to the creek as well? Most likely so, she thought, and decided it seemed a safe enough thing to do, and followed two women who had come from the courthouse. By the time Rachel had reached Church Street, she could see John standing on the corner.

"What is going on to cause such a gathering?" Rachel called.

"Colonel Cresap and his party of fighters just came into town. The news in the courtyard was that Cresap exchanged gunfire with some men coming over the ridge." John pointed to the Blue Ridges west of Fredericktown that lay between the outer limits of the county. I sent Betsy back to the boarding house for safety. You should have gone there as well.

The crowd was clamoring around them to get closer to Cresap's boat. John and Rachel followed, all the time looking around at the outer areas. In their minds they knew no one would come this close to a crowd in full daylight, but cautious habit prevailed.

When they reached the creek, they could see Cresap, a tall muscular-bodied figure, dressed in shirt and leggings made of leather. Long fringes dangled from the bottom and sleeves of his shirt. It made him look more Indian than his old Indian friend, Nemocolin. They pulled their weight up the steep embankment, and the gathering let out a gasp when they first noticed their muddy clothes streaked with blood. Rachel turned to John, nervously asking, "Where did the blood come from?"

"Did you get the murderers?" A man in the crowd shouted, hungry for gory details, while others wanted to know how many Indian scalps had been taken lately. But Cresap and his men were not there to entertain.

The crowd knew if anyone could protect them, it would be Cresap. He was loved by all as the defender of the public and had a history of fights to prove the point. Cresap wasted no time with the crowd, yelling back to them, "No, we didn't kill savages. The blood is from a mad bear." With the crowd following, he hurriedly walked toward the courthouse leaving the questions unanswered.

Rachel relayed all the happenings of the morning to her brother as they walked back to the boarding house. "Mr. Bowles said he would appoint two men."

"Ah, the appraisers," John said.

Rachel continued, "Yes, that's what he called them. They will come to the farm in a few weeks to make a listing of everything Father owned. I suppose they will want me to gather it up before hand."

"We'll leave for home tomorrow after the signing for the surety money. When you go back to the boarding house, gather up all your belongings and pack your satchel. I sent word to Thomas by a rider that he would be needed at the courthouse tomorrow. And he returned word that he would come."

"But he won't come if he has heard the news."

"Rachel, he said he would come and he will come."

The boarding house had a cold and forlorn feeling when Rachel walked in the door. Just as she started up the steps, a new lady came from the dining room and met up with her on the steps. She introduced herself to Rachel as being Rachel Mallot, the wife of Peter.

"You are truly a brave woman to be out on the streets by yourself," Rachel Mallot said. We just came from Sharpsburg this very morning, and I do not wish to be out there," she said, pointing to the street.

Rachel realized she had probably missed the noon meal and suddenly felt hungry. "Has Miss Graves finished serving the meal?" she asked the new boarder.

"Oh, no, because of the troubled news we are much later than usual today, she told us. Her helper refused to go out to the farm to secure the food. Miss Graves had to make the trip herself."

"My husband just heard Thomas Cresap report to the courthouse that the Indians have taken some families outside of Sharpsburg, and we are anxious to return home." The woman excused herself and rushed on up the steps.

As Rachel opened the door to the dining room, she could see the other boarders standing over a very distraught woman.

When Betsy saw Rachel, she called out, "Oh, Rachel, have you heard about the simply terrible thing that has happened? This is Ruhammah Chapline; you may have met her. She is the Reverend William William's daughter. He lives over by the Ryley's place, near us I think. She and her husband have started selling the lots for that new town named for Governor Sharp. They're calling it Sharpsburg. Cresap just brought word about the renegades striking close to their town shortly after they left yesterday. Ruhammah and her friend Rachel are worried sick about their small children they left back home with some neighbors."

Rachel realized she had seen the tall woman at the courthouse, just this morning. Ruhammah Chapline had been standing at the next table when she first came in, and Rachel had overheard the other clerk say something about having to sign her name to all the dower releases for the lots they had sold.

Miss Phoebe quickly spoke up, as if to assure the women that all was well. "Sharpsburg is a real fine town, I hear." The room seemed to stand frozen in place as the women boarders stood looking at Ruhammah who continued to sob. A banging on the front door caused them all to jump.

It was the man they called Peter Mallot at the courthouse with another man Rachel guessed to be Ruhammah's husband. She had heard his named called Joseph Chapline by someone at the court house this morning. Both men impatiently asked to have their wives sent out. Each woman in the boarding house helped to carry Ruhammah Chapline's and Rachel Mallot's belongings down to the waiting wagon.

The news had scared every woman in the boarding house, and Betsy and Rachel wasted no time that afternoon browsing through the shops. They went straight for the item that would be needed to keep their houses running in the months ahead. After rushing back to the boarding house for the evening meal, they bedded down early. It would be a long trip home the next two days.

John had bedded down at the small tavern within sight of the courtyard and was waiting at the courthouse door when Thomas Thrasher rode up early the next morning. Thomas had come alone after securing Martha and the children's safety with a group of settlers who had taken refuge from the Indian threat.

The signing for the surety took only a few minutes, and as soon as the clerk stamped the paper *15 February 1764*, the two men walked out onto the street and said their good-byes.

It was official. James Lee's will was now a matter of record.

Chapter 6

February 16, 1764
Chestnut Ridge

John Lee turned his wagon up the south road of *Chestnut Ridge*, thankful to be home. It had been a long ordeal for all of them, and now maybe life could get back to order for a time. He pulled the horses to a halt and helped Rachel climb over the side. He wondered why his father's dogs had not come out to greet them. Usually you could not keep them from barking. He turned around to see if they were coming. "Here Blacky— General," he called. Strangely, they were nowhere around. Had Rachel been gone so long the dogs had moved on to another barnyard?

He pulled Rachel's satchel from the back of the wagon and began lifting out the baskets of supplies she had purchased while in Fredericktown.

"Is this your jug, Rach? Why did you think you needed another one?" he fussed as he set it on the ground.

"I need it to put the milk in when I set it in the creek. Sour milk is not to my liking." Rachel was somewhat annoyed that her brother thought he needed to scold her for something she felt necessary.

Rachel picked up her satchel, exhausted after the trip. The stay over at the Grant's cabin last evening had been nice, but she and Betsy had stayed up too long telling Sarah about the events since their father's death. They had left their place before sun-up and today's ride had been long and tiring. And even after they arrived home, she had to go with her brother and Betsy to pick up their children at the Maddens and return the servant girl to the Bealls.

As John crawled up onto his wagon he noticed Rachel still had not opened the cabin door.

"What's wrong, Rach? It's cold out here. It would be wise to go on inside."

Rachel tried the door again. Finally she resorted to giving it a swift kick to get it to yield entrance after being untampered for a time. At least no one had broken in while she was gone, she thought. She didn't want the court to reprimand her for losing her father's possessions before they were counted. Once the door was open she heard John's wagon wheels begin to turn. She turned to watch as it rumbled over the hill.

Slowly, she unfastened her cloak and removed the hood from her head. Her eyes surveyed the neatness of the cold damp cabin. Suddenly she felt like an intruder. This was not her cabin, although she had lived here most of her life. Only the small corner of the attic belonged to her. The rest belonged to her mother and father. It was their choice as to what went on in this house.

She picked up two logs from the woodpile next to the large fireplace and set them on the ashes left from the smolderings of last week. Tomorrow she would clean out the fireplace, but today she just wanted to sit by the warm fire and let the soft flames talk to her. Was this lonely feeling going to follow her the rest of her life? Was it because she had experienced the lively big city that now she felt so unsatisfied with a room full of shadows?

The sun had begun to set over the ridge by the time the chores were finished, and she ate a bowl of mush. An eerie feeling settled in the corners of the cabin. She got up from the table and lit more candles than she really needed. For the first time since her father's death she was afraid. "No, no, no, I can't do this alone," she cried outloud as she looked out at the sliver of pink at earth's edge. "Oh, Jehovah, Father Almighty, send someone that needs me," she prayed.

From a distance she could hear old General and Blacky barking as they came up the path. Maybe God had answered her prayers. At least, something seemed normal again.

She turned away from the window and noticed the books sitting on the table. Rebeckah had brought the books from the root cellar when she was here, and Rachel had not had time to take them back down. Besides, they would need to be shown to the appraiser. She dusted off the top book and set it in a basket. When she picked up the next one something fell out. It looked like a petal from a flower. She ran her hand down the spine and opened the book to the page where the flower was pressed. It was a faded red rose—one that her mother had planted when they first moved to *Chestnut Ridge.* Rachel bent down and smelled the faded flower, and remembered how her mother had watched it bud and bloom with such delight each spring. After the buds were fully opened, she would let the children gather them in the small basket she kept on the shelf by the door. Rachel could still see her mother on her hands and knees scrubbing the rough wooden floor with the brush made from straw, all the time fussing at the family not to step on the floor until it was dry. Then she would let the girls scatter the sweet smelling rose petals over it. They would laugh at seeing who could step on the most flowers. Oh, it made the room smell so sweet.

Rachel looked again at the old book in her hand and tried to read the note written in the margin. She moved closer to the firelight to inspect the scripting. "I came so lately to your—" she turned the book sideways to read the next word, "heart" then repeating it, "I came so lately to your heart, amidst the autumn colors. The red to brown, no longer found, the colors of our love." Rachel looked at it for a long moment then set the book back on the table. It was a note of love from someone—but from whom—when?

She sat down in the old rocker by the fire and began easing back and forth into a comforting motion. Her father had made this rocker from one of the first chairs he had carved for her mother when they first married. It was just after the first rocker was introduced to the colonies that he had gone to the barn and sawed the rounded pieces to fit the chair. Since that day she had heard her father say many times, how every baby in his family need not lack for a lullaby and a rocking chair.

Her thoughts wandered, going in search for any words of the past that would settle the longing she felt tonight. Her mother used to calm her tears by telling her to have happy thoughts and she would feel better. If only life could be that simple then maybe those happy thoughts would do some good. If her mother had not died—if her father had not gotten sick—there were so many ifs. She let out a sigh. Oh, it would not have made any difference. She was not pretty. That was the problem. Her thoughts dared to go back to a boy she once knew. They were in love for a time until a pretty girl caught his eye. That was the way he had called it out when he broke the engagement.

Rachel had reasoned after that no one wanted such a plain wife—at least not the boys that she would partner with. She had chosen to stay in the safety of her parent's home. She closed her eyes, lulled by the sweet smell of the dried rose pedal that had fallen under the old rocker and slowly drifted off to sleep among the memory of her mother's words. "Someday Rachel, someday you'll love."

The clerk at the courthouse had not been specific as to when the appraisers would visit the cabin to make an accounting of all that James Lee had owned, or more likely what he did not own. Rachel spent the next few days setting the household items in clear view and sweeping the dust from the surroundings.

It was cold away from the fireplace when she went to the attic to pull out the plunder from under the beds and along the roofline. Rachel reached for a shawl stored in one of the old baskets. It was one her mother always wore, now half moth-eaten, but it would keep her warm. She put her hand in the pocket and discovered a small stone. The sunlight caused the brilliant colors to dance before her eyes. Her father had found it as a young boy so many years ago. She could still hear him telling the story to the grandchildren, and time after time, they begged to hear it again.

James Lee had given that special stone to his best girl before they married, and she had kept it all these years. Her mother had carried the rock as a good luck piece. And when she was deliriously ill with smallpox, she had asked for it over and over again, but no one could find it. Rachel caressed the edges, worn smooth by her mother's fingers. She pressed it to her cheek as tears watered her eyes. She could not help wondering if they had found it, would it have given her Mother the will to overcome the disease.

At midmorning, Rachel climbed down the ladder from the attic. It was time to make an accounting for what she had set out.

The shelf at the far end of the cabin held her father's stack of paper. Her mother had called it her father's "registering paper." He had learned how to make out the words but not set them to paper. Rebeckah's William had tried to teach him, but her father had been too impatient. She could still hear him argue, "My mark has served me well enough all these years; I don't see reason to switch now." And he would take the pen and form his usual *J* and defiantly show the others his mark.

Rachel had learned to set down enough words to get by and even set some of her father's business words, but it embarrassed her, as she put it, when someone else visualized them. She had thought of having William teach her the rules. Ever since her sister Elizabeth had lost the husband, William Norris, to death they had turned to William Littlefield as the family teacher. The family always felt a sense of pride when they could say to others, "He is of educated means, you know."

Dipping the pen in the inkwell, Rachel thought about how little she knew about words—words that would be needed to do this task. She felt self-conscious at the thought. After a few tries at sounding out the words she vowed to spend some time with Rebeckah after the crops were laid in, and have William teach her how to make her words right. She spun the pen around like she had seen the scripters do. The ink dropped in a puddle on the paper but she kept writing: *2 Chessts, 2 Tabelles, Box irrons and heeters, Cyder cask, Parsel of old books.*

She wondered if she should write down the name of each book? Finally, she put the pen back in the well and got up to look at the books.

When she picked up the first book, the mystery of the love words again caught her interest. In the daylight she could see the writing much more clearly. The smooth flowing words were set by someone who had practiced many times before. She fingered through the book. Nothing was familiar to her. It was an old book, but not one that her mother had placed on her head to teach her how to walk straightly. Besides it was much too small. Her mother only put big heavy books on her head for that. She turned it over several times. The faded cover yielded the imprint of a young woman in a blue dress. As she leafed through it, she noticed the last few pages were water-soiled and wrinkled.

Rachel's thoughts were interrupted by the sound General and Blacky barking at someone coming up her path. She set the book down quickly and went to the window. Two men on horses were coming up the road. She recognized one as Andrew Heugh, but did not know the man riding with him.

She pulled at her hair to tighten the knot in the back and smoothed the front of her shift, feeling flustered at not being presentable for company. She rushed over to put on her white cap.

When she opened the door, the two men greeted her with respect. "Miss Rachel, this is Mr. Adamson who will help me take the inventory," Andrew Heugh explained.

Rachel had known Andrew as living on the land called the *Forrest* on the far side of *Joseph's Park* some miles away, and also through her brothers-in-law's family, although she was told that he spelled his name with a more sophisticated sounding spell than did John Hughes. She could trust him being in her cabin. Besides, the courts trusted them so that was all that mattered.

Her embarrassment of being surprised by the visit must have been apparent, because the men apologized for not sending word of their intentions. "We found ourselves finishing up on another business sooner than we allowed and thought, beings the weather is passable through these parts, we'd better come take the accounting of your father's belongings." Rachel acknowledged them and ushered the men into the cabin.

"I just started setting down the plunder. You can take that over now. I'm not very practiced with the scripting," she said, as she handed Andrew Heugh the paper.

"Just tell me what you need and I'll bring it to you, or you can go see for yourself. There's a root cellar door under the rug there. And the attic has belongings, as well. The ceiling is hung low to the floor and seeing now that you are so tall, might be that your heads could get bumped off." The men laughed at her reasoning as they began writing down the inventory.

Rachel stood by the window looking at the bare treeline, watching the dogs sniffing out an animal scent. She almost laughed out loud when the thought came to her and she wondered if Mr. Heugh and Mr. Adamson would have to list old General and Blacky on the inventory.

The men went from belonging to belonging, writing down the description of each item of plunder, sometimes making conversation about the item. Finally, after what seemed like part of the day, they told her to sit down and they would recite the list.

Mr. Heugh straightened out the paper on the table and began to read. He remembered there was something he needed to ask, "Miss Rachel, we didn't see a wagon on the premise. Do you not have one?"

"No sir, Mr. Benjamin Franklin came through this way, and he took every wagon around here for General Braddock's army. My brother John Lee just happened to be into the blacksmith shop that day getting his wagon wheel repaired or they would have taken his also. That put a real strain on everyone in these parts. Mr. Franklin saw to that. He was responsible for taking the horses to pull them as well. If my father's old horse had not been almost lame, they would have taken him. I have to admit I still feel anger each time I consider what they did. I could have taken Father to visit my brothers and sisters if he would have had the wagon. But as it was, he had to stay here and wait to die." Rachel's voice trailed off.

The two men did not say anything when she finished. There was nothing to say. Everyone in the county had given up something for the war. And a wagon was just one of the things lost.

Andrew Heugh picked up his list again and began to read, "Starting where you left off on your paper, in the barn I found tools—not many—but enough to make a mention of. Your father didn't do much work these last few years and most of the things rusted out. But the three wedges, the plows and plow irons, and a harness were in fair condition. You had better check the rings on the harness before you try to use it again. There was a leak in the roof and it dripped down on part of that harness. It's badly cracked and could break in two if used. He looked back down the list then said, "Oh yes, there are several sifters."

"Miss Rachel, could I bother you for some of that hot cider you have over the fire? My throat is rather coarse," Andrew Heugh asked.

Rachel quickly took two tankards from the hook above the fireplace and dipped the steaming drink into the mugs and set them on the table. The reading continued. "Did I mention the hackle? One hackle. There are some good pieces of lumber sawed just recently from the looks of them."

Rachel spoke up, "My sister's son came up from the Middle Seneca to do some sawing for us after we lost some trees during the bad storm last year. We thought about building a covering for my father to sit under during the hot weather. Oh, he did like to sit outside and look up the ridge and down into the valley. Everyone of those Chestnut trees were special to him, I suppose."

Mr. Heugh cleared his throat and Rachel stopped, realizing she was conversing too much. She felt her face flush with embarrassment and fixed her eyes on the floor.

"Well yes, it would have made a good shelter," he said before he picked up where he had left off, "a long wheel, old lumber—" Mr. Heugh went on

69

reading the list which included spoons, a box of knives and forks, a butter pot, box irons and heaters, cyder cast, parcel old books, one drawing knife, old tubs, palls, piggons, old pot skillet, 30 pounds pewter, old canisters, 2 jugs, basket, soap, and 2 chamber pots. The men stopped reciting to take a break.

Rachel realized the dinner hour had come and gone and wondered if she was expected to feed them. Finally she asked, "I would have been proud to offer you a meal but you came unannounced this day. I can put some journey cakes on the spade if you like."

John Adamson stood up to stretch his stiff body. "Lucy, that's my wife, didn't fix enough this morning to hold my stomach satisfied. That would be a fine thing, if it proves no bother to you. You—I mean your father had more to him than we thought. It's taking more of the day than we first laid out for."

Rachel listened to the talk between the two men as she gathered the makings for the meal. It was news she had heard little bits and pieces of when she was in Fredericktown and it gave her a sense of being a part of the talk.

Mr. Heugh was saying he had occasion to shop on the lower end of Fredericktown last week and noticed strange happenings between the fellow who claims to be a painter. "I think he goes by the name Daniel Wolstein. He appeared to be an acquaintance of a red headed, no gooder, shifty-looking fellow. And I'd wager he was not there to have a picture of himself painted either." The men laughed at the unlikely thought. "When I walked passed their standing, they were conversing with an intense tone. The talking halted when I came close. I could tell from their eyes they were questioning what I might have heard. I've never trusted his purpose of the late night hours he spends on the creek bank either. I've been told the sheriff had inquired as to why he was there and he said the waterfront reminded him of the times he used to sit on the waters of his own homeland. Seems to me that is a lame excuse considering the looks of our Carroll Creek."

Rachel's interest in the conversation heightened after the mention of the portrait painter, and she ventured into the talk, "That man was at his shop when I passed it last week. He came out so fast he knocked me to the ground and I thought he was going to hit me."

Both men looked at her, but said nothing. Andrew Heugh continued, "Someone at the ports where the painter landed said they had heard he was accused of being involved in some smuggling in Germany. He may have even been one of those convicts brought in by King Billy." He turned to Rachel, and asked, "What did you see Miss Rachel? Was anyone else there with them? Did you go in to talk to him?"

Rachel started to answer but before she could explain, the smell of burning journey cakes caused her to rush over to yank the food from the fire. Nothing they had been talking about seemed as important as the food at hand, and the subject never came up again.

Once the last edible journey cake was eaten and the cider downed, the men thanked her for the meal and explained what to expect next. "You'll hear from the courts about coming back in to attest the inventory. Probably sometime during summer court."

After they had ridden down the road, she went back to the fireplace and dumped the scorched journey cakes into the wooden scrap bucket to feed to the hogs. As she went back to the table, she noticed Mr. Heugh had forgotten to take the rolled up papers with him.

She unrolled it and read, "*Parcel of linen, wool and basket, 15 3/4 pounds of yarn, 1 box of old cards, 1 old linen wheel, leather and 2 hides.*" Where had they found the hides? They must have been on the rafters of the old barn. She had not known of anyone in the family having skinned anything for years. "*Two yearlings, 1 cow, 1 calf, another cow, 1 indifferent cow,*" she laughed, wondering what old Boggs would say about being called indifferent. "*One heifer, 1 steer, 14 hogs, 1 horse, 1 mare.*" She rubbed her finger across the words, "*1 horse, 1 mare*" and thought how the old horse was not long for the world and the mare had been promised to Anne Hughes for her payment of the seeds for last year's crop. Just as soon as the will was settled she would be losing her.

Rachel put the paper down on the table. From the looks of the list she should have been okay for life if it had been all hers. But more of it was promised out for favors done while her father was alive than was left.

"No, Mr. Heughs I do not have a wagon," she said outloud. "And if my name comes up it looks like I won't have the monies to pay for it anyway."

She looked around the room at all the plunder sitting out for the counting and tiredly shook her head and thought to herself—no I have no wagon, but sure a lot of plunder.

She was again reminded of her father's old adage, "Not as much as some, but better than many."

Chapter 7

March 26, 1764
Seneca Creek

The sounds coming from the upstairs made Rebeckah stop her spinning wheel and consider the problem. "William, what are you doing up there?"

"I am trying to find my contrary wig," William bellowed from the bedchambers up above.

Rebeckah quickly took to the steps to stop what would be a disastrous mess if she knew her husband correctly.

"William, stop fretting. You act as if I've set a plan to make your life hard." Out of breath from climbing the final step, she took one look at the room and let out a moan. Clothes and keeping items were thrown around the room from his search through the trunk.

"William, you know how Solomon loves to tease the dogs with your wig when you leave it in plain sight," Rebeckah said, as she went to reach under the mattress for the hairpiece. The flattened out wig looked at the moment like it had seen its last wear, and she hastily began to pull at the curls. "There, as good as new it is," she said, not at all convinced it was even wearable but refusing to admit her unwise decision to hide it in such a place.

William was feeling more than frustration over the wig. "If I do not get on the road soon I will not get to the meeting in time tomorrow morning. If only I could have left early this morning," William complained. "I'm taking the wagon and that will slow me down."

Even without the wagon it was a slow, tedious trip, up and down the rut filled road leading to the inn. Dowden's Ordinary sat at the intersection of the roads leading from Fredericktown to Blandensburg and coming from the Potomac going to Baltimoretown. It had been a favorite spot for men interested in hearing all the news since before the French and Indian War and had seen its share of the gossip between the British and the colonists. The talk from the travelers was always good and full of news of the old world as well as the happenings in the Province of Maryland.

"When can I expect you home?" Rebeckah asked.

William was impatient with his answer. "You have been married to me long enough to know you can never predict these things, Rebeckah. I will go on past the ordinary to see about some supplies, and most likely stay at

Wofford's tonight. Tomorrow I'll go back down for the meeting. I will stay the night at Dowden's and be ready to go to the *Zebulon's Blacksmith* the next morning. Today is Monday, so that puts me home on Wednesday. At least that is my plan."

Rebeckah always liked for him to go to these gatherings because it meant he would bring back news from her family, but she hated the long hours at home with him away.

"Did you hear me say I will be taking the wagon? The new plow is supposed to be ready," William reiterated. He was anxious to finally get it in his barn, as all iron products had been hard to come by since the war. "Zebulon will be taking a sweeter price for it if I don't get there to claim it."

Zebulon was a well-known blacksmith in their area and had on other occasions cheated men out of bringing home a promised item. His pockets swelled from the monies slipped under the table for an already promised piece of machinery. The men still used him because of the closeness to Dowden's Ordinary, but they knew that they had better be there to pick up an order when it was ready.

Rebeckah listened as she went about picking up the mess he had caused. "I do tell, William, you make my work two times as hard when you pull a mess out like this."

William did not seem to hear her or chose not to make a comment. Instead he began to talk about sharing the plow with Thomas Dawson.

"My plow has almost rusted out, and Thomas broke his last fall. He has put his name on the list at that blacksmith's over by Thomas Thrasher's place. I can't recall just now the fellow's name. He runs a ferry over the Monocacy when the river is up."

Rebeckah ventured a guess, "Do you mean Daniel James?"

William again showed impatience. "Yes, yes—that is the one. I agreed with Dawson that one between us is better than none. We will just have to do some scheduling." William pulled on his gray wool stockings and dusted off his black square-toed shoes. He bent down and straightened the silver buckle on the right foot. Then he picked up the wig to put it on. "Can't get this thing to set right," he fussed.

Rebeckah dropped what she was doing and went to help him adjust it to his head. Then she took the big comb and tried to smooth out the loose hair. Always before she had liked the way he looked in this wig, now she was not so sure. She stood back to look at him.

"William, are you loosing more hair? This doesn't fit like I remember. It rather slides off to one side." He waved her off as he put on his coat.

She liked the way this green velvet waistcoat and knee breeches fit and began to run her hand over the wide silver-threaded braid on both sides of the front and along the sleeves. Then she counted the long row of silver buttons that lined the front to make sure they were all there. "Oh, William, you do look fine today," she bragged.

"With John away on the road work it leaves you without protection. Absolom is not that good with the gun yet so you and the children stay close to home. Send White Horse for help if anything suspicious comes this way."

"Now, how am I going to do that, William, seeing that White Horse never comes around when you are away," Rebeckah responded.

"This time he will. You scared him when the baby was coming and I took to the bed," William reasoned.

"You are a fortunate man to be alive and don't you forget that. My thinking tells me the Almighty hasn't forgotten what he had to do to bring you back to us."

William reached down, and kissed her hand. "You are a good wife, Becka." Then he added, "Maybe not the best but a good one." His smile teased her as he led the way down the steps.

Rebeckah could feel the hot afternoon sun on her head as she watched William's wagon disappear over the hill. She went back to the job of keeping her family cared for, husband or no husband.

"Absolom, we need wood for the woodpile. The sun may be good now, but once it falls, a fire will be needed. Nancy, you and the young ones can help grind down the wheat after the evening meal. I will make a skillet of fresh wheat cakes for you to eat with some of the fresh berries I'm going down to the road to pick." Tonight she desired their company and called back as she went to the road with the basket, "I might even read some words to you from the big book." Solomon and young William let out a squeal of excitement.

As the afternoon wore on, Rebeckah had come out the door to see if young William and Solomon were still playing in the dirt down by the old tree stump near the road. They had been creating barriers for some ants in the warm earth. Such good-looking children she thought. Her heart swelled at the blessings. As she turned to go inside she noticed black puffs of smoke rising from somewhere down at the edge of the hill near the Great Seneca. It was more smoke than the fireplace would usually give out. As she watched, the sky blackened. It could be a very large grass fire.

"Someone must be burning the dead crops," she said to Absolom who had come to watch with her.

The sun was just slipping over the hill at the back of the house when she called the children in from their play. Rebeckah could hear the soft call of the cows out in the field. It was a good day. Spring had arrived.

That night the children ate their turtle soup made with thick cream and torn from the loaf of bread left over from yesterday's meals. They talked of pleasant memories of the summers before. "Will we go to Aunt Martha's this summer when the crops are finished?" Absolom asked.

The children liked going to the Thrashers and the good things their Aunt Martha fixed for them.

"Aunt Martha laughs good, doesn't she mother?" young William said, eager to join in on the conversation. "Was she funny like that when you were a little girl?"

"I like her," Solomon said, too intent on eating the last of the honey-covered wheat cakes to look up when he spoke.

"Uncle Thomas took us into that big town and let us buy a feather painted with pretty colors. Remember that Nancy? A young Indian girl was selling them on the street corner," Absolom said.

"You lost yours and told Uncle Thomas someone had stolen it, and he believed you," young William claimed.

Rebeckah felt this talk was turning into name calling, and it was time for something pleasant to hold their attention. She went to her old trunk that she kept under the window and took out the big book. The book had been given to her as a small child on her birthday. It was one of the few things in her life that had been truly just her own. She opened the book where the marker held the waiting page.

Rebeckah sat with her back to the fireplace letting the firelight shine on the page as she began to read *Jacob picked up the hot poke and turned around just as the big bear was about to pounce on the boy. The bear's teeth glistened like daggers poised to strike.*

The children's eyes were wide with fear as they listened to their mother slowly pick at the words of the story of great suspense. Never had they heard anything so scary, and real, even scarier than the stories their grandfather Lee had told them.

A log in the fireplace rolled over and fell from the grate, and they all jumped. Even Rebeckah was so taken up in the story that she gasped.

It was then they heard their dogs barking down near the road, and Solomon came to stand closer to his mother. Rebeckah questioned who could be coming at this hour. It was too late at night for someone to be paying a social visit. Rebeckah looked toward the door to make sure she had fastened the door latch to the wall hook.

The threatening growl of the dogs told Rebeckah someone was coming very close to the cabin. Should she let them in or just act like no one was home? Rebeckah handed the baby to Nancy and told her to take young William and Solomon with her to the corner of the room. She motioned for Absolom to get the gun down from the hooks over the fireplace.

The knock on the door was made by a man with intentions of being let in. His deep voice demanded, "Littlefield, let me in." When Rebeckah answered, it was with all the courage she could muster, "Who is it? What do you want?" One of the dog's began to growl a deep threatened response, then it yelped as if it had been kicked.

"I've been sent by the sheriff to get Mr. Littlefield to come help in a search. Someone burnt down a cabin on the creek." Rebeckah drew in her breath. That was what had caused the black smoke today.

"My husband will not be home until later," she said, all the while knowing William was not to return home for at least two days. "Go down about a mile and you will find the cabin of our worker, Mr. Sittler. He will help you." Rebeckah could hear the man's footsteps leaving and let her grip on the gun relax, feeling a flush of weakness in her knees. But before she could sit down, the man was back at the door with a warning, "You better be prepared to defend yourself while your man is away. Whoever did this thing is real mean. They killed the men and a woman there and dragged the little ones away. We found one of 'um dead by the side of the road. It's an awful thing someone did, probably an Indian raid."

She couldn't let the children see how afraid she was. With as much courage as she could muster, she said, "You children have had your story reading, and now it is time to be abed. Absolom stay here for a time. I need help banking the fire while I tend to the baby." What she really wanted was to form a plan with her son for their survival. Oh, why did William allow John to work with the road crew just when he was going to be away?

Absolom listened to his mother with wide eyes. He would have to see to the children if something were to happen to his mother while dealing with an intruder. Finally, their plans set, she sent him on up the steps to his bed with the other children and went to sit in her rocker, pulling a quilt up around her. The baby would stay with her for the time but if the dogs started barking, Absolom was to come for her.

Rebeckah again checked the heavy latch on the door and counted the shots for the rifle before leaning it against the doorframe.

All through the night fear bounced around in Rebeckah's head and she imagined every wild animal rustling for food and every birdcall outside the cabin as a threat against their lives. She even admitted William was right about her window. He had tried to convince her that the new cut out window was an uninvited entry into the cabin.

Oh, where was White Horse? Although she would feel safer with him close by, it probably was a good thing he was nowhere in sight of the men searching. They did not trust any Indian and White Horse was just another Indian to them.

The sun was just creeping out of the night when she pulled the covers from around her and took in a deep breath, thankful for light that allowed her to see outside the cabin. There were chores to do, and White Horse was probably already in the barn feeding the milk cows. She called to young William and Absolom that it was time to go to the barn.

Rebeckah cautiously released the heavy latch from the door as her sons waited. At the first glance, they could see the tracks left by the man the night before. The dogs had been sleeping by the big tree near the road and came to greet her, wagging their tails, giving Rebeckah a sense that no one was lurking nearby. "Go on boys, I will be watching." She stood inside the doorway as the boys started toward the barnyard. White Horse always opened it first light of day but today it was still closed. Maybe it was because William was gone. He was under no obligation to them to come since he didn't really work for them; he just came to help because he wanted to. "Boys, tell White Horse I need to talk with him," she yelled as they opened the barn door. Oh, how they had depended on this old red man through the years.

Rebeckah was well into her own chores for the day when she stopped to question what could possibly be taking the boys so long tending the stock. By now they should have been back to eat their morning meal.

She stacked the wood on the back of the fire hole, gathered the washing tub from the back wall, then picked up the water bucket to go to the creek for water. She called for Gabby to follow her, knowing that going to the creek alone could be dangerous. If Gabby bristled she would know someone was around. The old dog got up slowly from his spot next to the tree and came to her. As she passed the barn she again called to the boys, but there was no answer. By now, the sun was over the edge of the earth and full of promise. Normally a bright spring day like today would be a moment for rejoicing, but today her mind was only on the safety of her children.

As she lugged the third bucket full of cold creek water up the bank, she stopped to listen. All was quiet on the creek. Apprehension gave way to losing patience with her sons for not coming back home. It was so unlike the boys to disobey, if that was what they had done. Was it because their father was away and they thought they could abandon the work and go to practice with their bow and arrows in the woods?

She poured the cold water into the tub sitting on the fire, and felt the steam rise up to her face. Then she picked up the strong smelling bar of lye soap and was reminded of how this last batch seemed stronger than the others she had made. During the last wash it had brought blisters to her fingers almost tearing the skin away. Rebeckah went to find the old smooth scrub rock her father had found for her mother. It had been passed on to her when she and William first set up housekeeping. She always kept it under the dead tree stump and gave orders to the children that no one was to move it. While the clothes soaked, she would go look for the boys, then come back and use the rock to scrub any leftover stains.

Her back ached from bending over the wash tub. It would take her most of the day to do the wash, hang it out on the tree branches to dry, then as she always did, she would scrub the floors with the leftover wash water. That would leave very little time to see to the ironing before the evening meal.

By now, Solomon had come out to watch his mother and ask questions about why Absolom and young William had not returned from the barn. "Let me go see where they are? I promise I will come right back, please?"

"Solomon, you know your father never lets you go alone to the barn. What if your brothers have gone to take the cows to the pasture? The barn is not a safe place for a young child alone." His mother's reasoning did nothing to quiet the child's whining, but after a time, he gave up and went to dig in the dirt by the road.

She was halfway through the wash when Nancy brought baby Mary out to nurse. Rebeckah sat down on the ground enjoying the moment to rest her back. Washing was hard work, and she was anxious to finish before the sun was too hot. Nancy came out again to ask her mother what she should do about the meat that had scorched on the fire. Rebeckah let out a moan and went inside the cabin. She pulled the stew from the flame, threw some salt over the burned meat, added more water, and set it back in the fireplace. It was wash day and they would just have to fill up on burnt stew, like it or not.

When she returned to the yard to finish the wash she glanced to where Solomon had been playing but he was not there. And neither was Shadow. They had named the dog that because he was so black and he never left Solomon's side when he was outside. Even when the child was just beginning to walk, the dog just a puppy then, had followed Solomon everywhere, and if anyone scolded the child the dog protested loudly.

Rebeckah called several times but there was no answer. In a frantic run, she circled the cabin to look for the young child. "Solomon, Solomon, where are you?" Her calls fell on silent places. She remembered how he had wanted to go to the barn to slide down the shoot. She ran back to the cabin door and yelled for Nancy. "Solomon has disappeared. Put the baby in the cradle and come with me to look for him."

She thought of the manhunt the night before and felt a shudder go through her body. Horror stories raced through Rebeckah's mind as she ran for the barn. Solomon was such a curious child and had no fear. She remembered stories of other children having fallen to their deaths from the lofts in the barn when left unattended. And the child of the family down the road that had hanged himself while getting ready to swing from a rope, and another falling from the door used to throw hay from the loft. "Solomon, Solomon, answer me." Rebeckah could hear baby Mary screaming in a mad high-pitched cry. She did not like being left in the cradle when awake, but that did not matter now.

Rebeckah and Nancy raced from one side of the big barn to the other. The cows had been let out to pasture so that meant Absolom and young William had been there earlier. Panic welled up around her. What if the boys had been taken by the same men that killed the family yesterday? She raced up the ladder, all the while yelling for first Solomon, then Absolom and young William. She stood still, listening for an answer, but there was no sound, just that of bees swarming around their nest near the hot roof. She went to the door of the loft and pulled the heavy stack of hay away from the opening to look out over the fields below. She saw nothing. A sick, dizzy feeling came over her.

"Nancy, go back to the baby. Lock the door and do not open it until I get there." She turned to go to the other side of the barn to look out the cracks in the wood. From this point, she could see a great distance all the way to the creek. She pulled a board from the siding, and stood watching for any sign of movement. But all was quiet. The cattle were slowly eating their way from the barnyard with no sign of someone disturbing them. No one was there, but neither were the boys.

She wearily slid down the ladder and as she did caught a splinter in the palm of her hand. She sat down and began to cry, not so much out of pain, but from the terror she felt. By now, the children could be lying dead at the hands of the raiders. She dared to look up into the sky for any sign of vultures circling something dead.

Her heart stopped. On the other side of the forest, she saw a movement way up in the sky, too far to tell what they were circling. But there was something.

"Mother come here," Nancy yelled to her mother. She jumped up and ran frantically until she could see the door of her cabin. Standing in the door with Nancy was Solomon looking surprised at all the attention. "Where have you been?" she asked as she grabbed him in her arms, smothering him for safe keeping. Shadow as usual, wasted no time protesting.

Nancy spoke for him, "He had been playing near the road and followed a baby rabbit that had been beside the road." As the rabbit went farther into the thicket so did the curious child. Rebeckah put her son at arm's length, "Solomon, you have caused us a heart full of fear this morning. I thought someone had—" She realized she was about to scare him and changed her scolding, "I thought you had gone to the barn. I could not find you. She gathered her dirty little boy in her arms again. When he wiggled loose she took his hand and led him inside the cabin. "How would you like some of my maple syrup for a treat?" she asked, sitting him on the bench by the fire. When Solomon looked up at his mother, he traced with his small dirty finger the tears that had fallen down her face. "Why are you crying?" He didn't wait for an answer, "Can I have another spoon of syrup?"

"Solomon, did you see your brothers while you were following the rabbit?" Rebeckah softly asked so not to scare him. Solomon shook his head from side to side as he licked the last of the brown syrup from the spoon.

Rebeckah went to the side of the room and motioned for Nancy to come to her. There was a nervous quiver to her voice as she whispered, "Nancy, what I am about to say will scare you but it is most urgent you understand. We do not know the seriousness of what happened yesterday but I do know we could all be in danger. Absolom and young William do not respond to my calls. It is not like them to slip out of sight, especially when your father is away. It is up to you to keep the little ones safe while I go to look for them. If only there was someone to help me."

Nancy sensed the gravity of the situation. "I'm not much afraid, I will go real fast to the Sittler's cabin."

Rebeckah protested with fear. "No, no, never would I have you go unless someone was attacking us.

Rebeckah called for Gabby to follow her as she again went in search for the boys. She picked up the rifle and made sure more shots were tucked into her pocket than before.

But the search proved useless as she went to the fields, the orchard, the barn, and even walked along the road. By the time she returned home, the tub of wash water with the strong lye soap had boiled dry. She would have to go back to the creek to fetch more water. If left with that much lye soap on them she feared it would eat through the threads of what was most of their year's supply of clothing. There was nothing she could do but return to the creek for more water. With each slip of the dirt along the creek she jumped in fear, imagining the men were lying in wait for her very soul.

After finishing the wash and hanging it on the trees to dry, she wore a path between the cabin and field and back to the road, each time stopping to call Absolom's and young William's names.

Finally she went back into the cabin and sat by the table to think about what she should do next. The afternoon sun slid down the kitchen wall and left her sitting in the shadows. Only the light from the fire lit the darkening room. Rebeckah slipped out the door one more time while there was still some light. Maybe, just maybe, she could see someone coming along the road. If only John would come home from the road work early. Or if someone came by their place she could send word to the Dawson's or her brother, Robert, to come help. If it had been just a week later there would be help. The field hands would be swarming in the fields getting the ground ready to plant the tobacco. She stood looking in every direction listening for the slightest sound of something unusual. From the road she could see the vultures more clearly. It had not been her imagination. There was something past the forest that they were attending to. The sound of thunder in a distance could be heard. Normally, an early spring shower was a welcome thing but not tonight, not with her sons out there in danger. She turned and walked back to the cabin.

That night after Mary's last feeding Rebeckah handed her to Nancy to take her upstairs to sleep with her. It was unsafe to have her downstairs if she found it necessary to fire the rifle.

Afterwards, Rebeckah went to her window to watch the angry streaks of lightening come closer. If only she had been able to go into the forest to look for the boys. But to be gone that long or that far away from the cabin, leaving only Nancy to protect the defenseless little ones was cruel. Nancy had failed to learn how to aim the gun enough to hit her mark.

She tried to console herself by knowing the boys were old enough to try to devise a plan for their safety. But in the same breath she began to relive the story where they had found an earlier neighbor's son's, all five of them, slaughtered one at a time along the side of the road. They had not been found until the wolves had cleaned their bones. Rebeckah shivered and pulled the shawl closer to her body as panic began to clutch at her throat, leaving her weak.

She reached for the rocker and wearily leaned back to take solace from the rocking motion. She was waiting for a sound. A sound of the dogs barking a welcome home or of her boys calling out to be let in. She began to sob openly as her life seemed to come apart. It was all her fault. If she had not sent them to get White Horse. No—no, it was not her fault. White Horse should have been there to take care of them. He had always been there when William was away. Then the thought came to her that terrified her very being. What if White Horse and the boys were all killed by these vicious murderers. She frantically began to recite the minister's words as best she remembered, finally calling out her own personal appeal to her God.

A plan began to form in her mind. She could not leave her sons out there, dead or dying from their wounds. She must tend to them. Once the sun was up, she would take the children and they would go for help. It would be dangerous walking out in the open with the children, leaving them all vulnerable to an Indian attack, but there was no other way.

The rain and hail began pelting the cabin violently. Then just as it had come, it moved on and the silence seemed louder, more menacing.

She did not move from the chair. Not even to look out the window into the dark night. The clock chain began to pull the gong into place, One—Two—the deep hollow sound echoed in the cold damp room. Silence again. Only the sound of fear waited, keeping her from sleep.

Chapter 8

Dowden's Ordinary
March 27, 1764

It was midday when William rode into the back lot of the Dowden's Ordinary. He was thankful to have found time to come before the grueling work in the fields started. A quick look at the threatening sky made him hope the boys got the chores done before the rains started. What he did not want was to come home with the new plow and find they had been slackers. Rebeckah tended to be soft with the children when he was away.

Unhitching the wagon, he gave a swat to the flank of his horse and watched it trot into the back pen. A young stable boy was already busy emptying a bucket of feed into a trough at the back. If a big ordinary were to receive a license from the courts to open, they had to agree to provide provisions for the horses as well. And this was a big ordinary. The Dowden family had build it with heavy log walls and a wood shingled roof to hold the warmth and many dormer windows jutting out to let the sunshine in. It was known far and wide for the comforts.

William lifted his satchel from the back of his wagon and painfully picked his way between the dung to the front door of the tavern. He could see his brother-in-law Thomas Thrasher waiting for him at the door.

"What's causing the pain in the foot?" he called out after noticing William's limp.

"Oh, Rebeckah left my shoes to dry in the sun after the last rain and they shriveled up smaller than my foot intended."

A sharp streak across the sky, accompanied by the loud clap of thunder made the two men rush for the door as the rain began to fall.

The smell of tobacco filled the familiar dark room where the walls were a topic of interest as much as the conversations. There was a feeling of familiarity to the men that walked into this room.

On one wall, now chipped with age, someone during the French and Indian war had painted Benjamin Franklin's creation of a cut up serpent, each section depicting one of the thirteen colonies, and the words *Join, or Die* at the bottom. It had become the symbol for the rallying call all over the colonies. On the other side of the room someone else had drawn the map of the colonies and the seaports that fed them, as well as those ports across the vast ocean.

The men walked over to the fireplace to dry. A smoldering log rolled from the grate, sending out sparks in its wake, leaving it to sizzle against the wet stocking. Each man selected a pipe from the rack and ceremonially dipped it into the decanter of strong smelling tobacco before dropping a coin into the jug on the mantel. Everyone rented a pipe, whether they made a practice of tobacco or not. This time honored tradition between travelers created a brotherhood of sorts, giving refuge for a time to the demanding work just outside the heavy tavern door.

William's eyes were becoming accustomed to the darkness, and acknowledged a few men with a nod of the head. One was the older Flayl Pain who lived down in Thomas Thrasher's part of the county. "What purpose do you suppose brings old Flayl this far?" William asked his brother-in-law.

"Someone told me Flayl has been ailing of late," Thomas said.

"You wonder if he knew his name Pain would be so foretelling?" William suggested. "I've heard some refer to him as Frail Pain. Sadly, it seems to have caught on, and now he does look sickly."

William nodded to Thomas. "Is that Edward Northcraft sitting with the Trail boys?" William asked.

"Has he been sick?"

"I hardly recognized him." William said, as they went over to exchange a greeting with the men.

When they went back to stand by the fireplace, Thomas told William, "Poor Elizabeth, she will find herself a widow if he continues to change."

Thomas continued to pull the smoke from his long pipe as the men stood in silence for a time, watching the travelers mingle with stories of their own making.

Several men were talking about how long it was taking the Maryland boundary line to be set on the Mason Dixon line. Another group was voicing concern about what would happen if the British banks could not support the value of the local currency. Would they all go broke if more paper monies were not made good. Across the Potomac in Virginia they were already feeling a severe hardship and no one seemed to have an answer.

Two men sitting at the corner of the large room seemed to have something all together different on their minds. William nodded toward the men to his brother-in-law, "Do you know these men?"

"Cannot say I recognize them," Thomas admitted. The man sitting next to the wall, dressed in a handsome blue satin suit with lace ruffles on his shirt, gave the look of a man of worth and probably of educated ways. It was obvious that something had disturbed them. The older man sitting across from him, angrily slapped the tip of his cane on the floor. The more upset they got the louder their voices became and everyone stopped to listen. At this point the man in the blue suit obligingly stood up.

"We have come this day from Annapolis to collect a large number of crates shipped from London," the man said using his strong Irish accent to pronounce his words. "The port officials were swarming around like bees on sugar cane. Then they hiked the prices on us again. Someone told us it was the King's new minister, Grenville, that is setting the prices. Seems to be he is set on making a name for himself before the King. The British officials threatened to throw our crates overboard if we did not pay the extra duties.

This accusation caught the interest of William Littlefield who was never shy in confronting some colonist about how they judged parliament and the King. "You speak serious words. What name do you answer to and by what authority do you come with this news?" The men standing around looked at William and wondered why he was getting a little more than heated over this talk.

The man in the blue suit directed his answer to William, equally unafraid to speak his mind. "My name is Graves McIlvain and I am a plantation owner near Taneytown, as well as doing business in western regions of the province. My authority is the same as yours, making a living for our families in the colonies."

A traveler standing at the fireplace next to William and Thomas, nodded understandingly in agreement. "I dare say, Graves McIlvain, we are all in your shoes."

"Since our last King George put this man Grenville in charge, the officials are more aggressive with each ship," another man chimed in.

Mr. McIlvain waved his hand, letting those in the room know he had something more to say. "I've been shipping goods for twenty odd years without so much as a nod from the officials. But I shan't try to claim I did not slip a wee bit extra over the crate to make them look the other way."

The rest of the men in the room knew it was true. The officials up to now had paid very little attention to what was brought in or where it was to be shipped as long as something was slipped into their hand. It all started when the King sent the British officers over here to keep peace on this side of the ocean. Those officers found it to their liking to live in this supposedly self-ruled land where no one watched their every step. This allowed for bribes to fill their money pouches. Now, someone was calling for more money, and no one could tell if it was the King himself or the officers filling larger pockets.

The older man sitting at the table with McIlvain pulled himself up with his cane, struggling to breathe as he began to talk, breaking up his words until another breath could give him voice. "Yesterday a British pulled his pistol on someone he accused of receiving lace without duty."

Did they arrest the man?" a man called out.

"Didn't see," the man's words trailing off to a whisper for the lack of breath.

Mr. McIlvain, sensing his friend's difficulty, took the floor. "Like I said, it is getting hard to do business with Grenville in charge."

"So you are ready to set blame on the King and Grenville for the new changes?" William again demanded an answer.

"Indeed, that is what is taking place." A man standing close to the fireplace angrily stood up to William. "Grenville knows what it takes to be favored by the King."

A group of men had just come in the door and stood listening for a time while waiting for a table to empty. One of the men began polling the audience. "Do you not know the ships are being searched, some even stopped on the high sea to check for a complete listing of contents, then if they suspect someone is trying to cheat the King they crack it open?"

"What do you mean—a complete listing of contents? It is none of their business what I buy or sell." The man in the corner stood up to take issue.

Mr. McIlvain was all but irate over the subject as he talked. "They are suspicious you might try to ship something forbidden, like your wife's homemade laces for selling abroad. Or you have ordered something you and the merchant agreed not to declare, enabling you to save paying the tax or duty. On occasions they have thrown your already paid for crate overboard and when you go to pick it up, they arrest you for not declaring it. It happened to me two days ago." Mr. McIlvain had again shown his knowledge of the shipping trade in the colonies.

A man sitting on the far side of the smoke filled room yelled out. "Each of you have heard how the tax on sugar all but ruined the rum making business in New England, haven't you? Plain and simple, if they can control our livelihood, they can set the rules as to who makes the monies."

William turned to Thomas and began complaining, "This man is going to cause trouble for the colonists. He is trying for a revolt."

One man thought he had a solution to the problem, and stood up to offer it. "Well, why don't we just send our goods to the West Indies and forget about England?"

All but a few men in the tavern put their tankards in the air and shouted their agreement.

"We have always been able to deal with them. They like us and we like their monies," someone yelled over the cheer.

Mr. McIlvain took a step forward. "I'm glad you brought that up, sir," he said as he took the older man's cane from him and walked over to the map on the wall. "Here is the problem with that theory."

By now every man in the room watched what Mr. McIlvain was about to do, as he pointed to the Annapolis shipping port. "From where our ships load up at Annapolis or Baltimoretown it is true you could just drop straight down the coast here and you are at the West Indies." He dramatically pulled the cane down the painted outline of the map and tapped it on the island of West Indies. "That would be smart. Save money on shipping and get good deals. Right?" He turned to the men in the room to look for approval. He again tapped the cane on the wall for attention. Pronouncing the words loudly for effect, he continued, "But before we can sell our goods at a much better price to West Indies here is what is happening. The King tells the port officials to be on the watch for any ship planning to go anywhere but to the English ports. And if they try they are to be told no. That is forbidden. And if they try they are to be intercepted and turned back to the right waterway."

"And why is that?" Thomas Thrasher called out.

Graves McIlvain again tried to explain. "The peoples of England are rioting in the streets because of their increased taxes. They say we should share in the cost of the recent war. Grenville agrees with them. And the only way to make enough monies is to collect a duty on everything shipped out or coming in."

Mr. McIlvain walked over to his table to take a swig from his cup, wiping his mouth with the back of his hand, being sure to keep his fancy blue suit protected. He then went back to the map while everyone watched in anticipation of his next words. "So the ship carrying our crates are forced to go to the London port first. See—here we are now."

He again tapped the cane on the Maryland coastline and pulled the cane with a scraping noise across the painted-in ocean, and tapped it at the spot marked London.

"Okay, the captain did as he was told. He went to the ports of London. He paid the duty. Now he is ready to continue his journey to West Indies. But wait!" Mr. McIlvain speaks up with a loud shocked voice to gather any wavering attention. "He hears someone call out his ships name just as his sailors are lifting the anchor. He sees the port official is coming toward him, waving a paper."

William Littlefield had enough of this ranting and went to find a table in the corner for the family meeting, hoping he could not hear Graves McIlvain. But no matter how much he tried to ignore what was going on he could still hear his overpowering voice.

Mr. McIlvain pointed into the crowd. "Still more rules passed by the parliament! The Captain of the ship reads from the paper." Mr. McIlvain picks up a scrap of paper left on the table, acting out reading, *"Given by the authority of King George III and Parliament and Grenville."*

Mr. McIlvain puts it down and speaks to each man, enjoying the attention he has caused. "The man bringing the paper tells our captain he must pay a duty before he will be allowed to leave his port."

There was grumbling throughout the tavern. One man waiting to leave turned back to ask, "Who pays the captain for all these extra duty charges?"

Another man yelled out, "Our captain does and then he charges us for it."

McIlvain waved the cane in the air as if applauding the man's understanding of the matter. "The gentleman is correct. What started out as getting a decent price for our goods is now only enough to pay the shipping fee. Do you see what is happening? The English need our monies to pay their bills, and they are not concerned as to how we will have monies for our own family."

A man in the back of the room yelled out, "They say the war cost them more because we refused to co-operate in fighting the French."

This last comment filled William Littlefield with anger. If he spoke out much more they would start booing him. No matter how much he tried to defend his ideals they would not listen. But he could not let this pass. He stood up from the back of the room. "Tell me, gentlemen. Who benefited from getting the Frenchmen off our backs? We did. What is so wrong about paying what we received. We still govern ourselves through the assemblies. Just watch. It will turn out to our advantage."

James Jr. came through the door just as William finished giving his opinion about the King, and promptly disagreed in a loud voice. "That is hog wallow. We did our part. I marched up those hills just as fast as any of those British fighters. Not once did I stop fighting so why should I pay for them fighting the war?"

By now, there was not a man in the room that was not worked up over what was happening. It if wasn't because of the King and Grenville, it was because of what William had said, and James Lee's challenge.

The man in the blue suit looked at William and shook his head. "Sir, feel free to pay more any time you please." The crowd applauded Mr. McIlvain for standing up to William, then they began to pat James Lee on the back for giving fight.

If William had not felt it important that he stay for the family meeting he would have walked out the door right then. The only way he could tolerate this crowd was to not listen. Besides, he was used to these ups and downs with the men. One day they would be for what the King was doing, especially if it meant more trade for them, and the next meeting they would be doing what had happened today.

They all recognized what was once believed to be a strong allegiance for the way the British saw the trade system, was now being whittled away. And the way you felt about it was based on which side you stood or who could speak out the loudest.

John Wofford and Thomas Betterton arrived at the tavern in time to hear the last few comments.

"What is going on?" John Wofford asked of his brother-in-law as he went to the rack for his pipe.

Thomas Thrasher began to explain, "John, it does not sound good for anyone trying to ship tobacco—or anything for that matter, to ports other than the English held port."

"Each hogshead of tobacco we roll to the ports for shipping, is now worth less than last week?" John questioned.

By the time most of the family men arrived at the tavern William's point had been forgotten by the crowd, and he was able to get on with the business they had come for. They all moved over to sit at their usual meeting table at the back of the room. It was quieter there and out of the other travelers' earshot. The men all felt the same way. When you were doing family business it was wise to keep some items to yourself.

The last man to arrive for the family meeting was Alexander Grant. "I'm drenched to the bone," he said and went to stand in front of the fireplace to dry out.

The men liked to be informed, and the purpose of these meetings was to hear what was happening among the other farmers. It was their belief if they stood together on issues they would be able to protect their holdings against the foes, be it Indian raids or the British official sent by the King to make life hard. Their time together allowed them to exchange family news, as well. This alone was a worthy reason to gather together. A contented spouse was like monies in the pocket, and nothing like news of family could make a wife happier.

William walked over to a table by the door to get a pen and ink well. The tavern kept them for the writing of legal documents, which was often the occasion for a visit to the tavern. It was a natural place to meet and discuss a will, or set a land deed. You could always be assured of finding a witness at the table next to you or standing by the fire.

An almost dried out Alexander Grant walked over from the fireplace and called the meeting to order. He had been elected several months back by the brothers-in-law to speak for them if the need arose and to keep peace within the family meetings. The men believed in orderly records of what was spoken so they had also voted William Littlefield, who was blessed with the educated use of the pen, to be the scripter for the group.

The men married to the Lee women, all but poor ailing Richard Willis, and John Lee were accounted for. At the roll call it was noted that John Lee had sent word by way of a rider coming to the ordinary, that he would not be able to attend.

William sat down and began to swirl the quill around the paper in a few practice runs then said, "Give me the first order of business."

This list was somewhat of a legal document or at least the brothers-by-law felt it to be so. They might be forced to prove who said what if future issues were in dispute.

John Wofford brought up the condition of the roads. John Seager agreed with him. James Lee wanted to find a way to get the captain of the ship to post at dockside the latest news when a ship came in.

Aquilla Compton had joined the group to give his father-in-law, Richard Willis a voice and agreed with James. "We don't hear much from the town crier out here."

Alexander Grant brought up a controversial topic when he said, "Gentlemen, I am disturbed at having to bring this issue up before all of you here, especially because of you, James and Robert. I was back at the home place and what I saw grieves me. Rachel is not able to keep up the Father Lee's place and the first thing you know some man will be coming 'round sweet talking her into letting him move in, and then he will take the land for himself."

When John Hughes jumped up the others were not surprised. They just wondered why he was not the one to bring the subject up first. "I think I should take the land off your hands, seeing my wife gave her father the seeds for his crops the last two years." He turned to Robert and bluntly told him, "Robert, what was your father thinking, giving a woman that land?"

Robert shook his head at John Hughes and his determination to always assume he had a right to everything. "I'm sure father had a plan in giving Rachel the land and by law we cannot change that without going to the judge and showing she is irresponsible. I, for one, will not go against her."

James Lee, rather awkwardly spoke up, "Father always hoped by the time he died, Rachel would already be married. It sure would have solved things if that were true."

With that suggestion, it opened the door for a long discussion among the men.

"That won't be easy. She may already be too old to bear a husband children, and without the possibility of children she wouldn't be worth the price of calling a minister to marry them."

"Can anyone think of a widower with a ready borned family? That would work."

"It has to be someone that we can trust with the land. But who?"

William, his pen in hand, interrupted the speeches, trying to make some sort of progress on the issue. "Gentlemen, give me names—give me prospects."

The men started one by one to offer suggestions or denounce it. They suggested names of those living close by the family land, someone they already knew.

All the men agreed the land was important and they had to be careful as to who would take it over once the marriage was signed. Someone suggested it would be nice if he had money.

"Gentlemen, give me names, give me names," William repeated again, this time rather impatiently.

Finally, someone listed a name they all could agree on. "I suggest we look to Daniel Carroll. He has money, more than any of us put together, and a fine house."

James suggested something for the first time. "They could put us all up in that big house." The men found that amusing, but true.

"We would sure be able to sit a spell." Aquilla Compton volunteered the information he knew as fact. "They have near as I could count twenty seven chairs."

The men shook their heads in disbelief. "Oh, go on with you. Where did you hear that?" This fact stretched all of the men's imagination since most of them had no more than two chairs in their cabins.

"I know the caretaker that unloaded the cargo as it had been shipped in from foreign ports just last summer," Aquilla bragged. "He said Mr. Carroll's mother asked him to put all twenty seven chairs in her son's room."

"Were they having some kind of a meeting in there?" John Seager asked.

Wanting to get back home, Thomas Betterton finally called his vote. "Daniel Carroll it is. He has everything we could hope for, including enough chairs." The seriousness of his recent widowhood the year before and three small children to care for gave them a good feeling about his need.

"I suspect his grieving time has surely reached its full term," William suggested.

"And he already has borned children," John Seager suggested.

The men turned on John and one spoke out. "John, you can come to our meetings. But since your remarriage you no longer have a voice to vote for matters that deal directly to our family. You are free to vote for the tobacco or the wheat or how we feel about the parliament, but not Rachel's husband."

John Wofford continued with the suggestions. "Rachel has worked for Mrs. Carroll in the past at odd times, so she would know the house."

"The Carroll's have status and that is important," someone reminded the others. "And they wouldn't even have to pay her."

The men laughed a coarse sort of manly laugh at the suggestion.

"The horses would not have to be rested during the move over, it is so close," Thomas Betterton said. Again they all laughed. .

"Well, she doesn't have much to take." The men continued to jest. At first, even Robert and James Jr. laughed but it was beginning to sour.

When William looked up from the paper he realized they needed to move on. "And who will go talk to Daniel Carroll?" He asked again to the silence. "I said, who will go to Mr. Carroll?"

No one volunteered. "Under the circumstance, I have no other solution but to strike his name."

Finally, John Wofford asked for a reading.

William squinted his eyes to read his writing, pushing the paper to arms length. "Let's see now, I have the Duvall name. Anyone desire a comment on this choice? John you put up his name. What say ye of him?"

"He just lives up by Rachel. I thought they might know of someone wanting to marry."

After a few more tries William realized the suggestions were going nowhere. William continued to read the list, and with each name someone found a reason to scratch through it.

"How about the Beall family? Thomas, your family lived close to them for years when your father was alive. Any thought on them?"

Thomas admitted, "The Beall family would be a fine family for her to marry into."

William dipped his pen in the inkwell and wrote Thrasher in the margin after the Beall name. "Thomas, next time you are up to your father's land, go talk to them about any one of them needing a wife."

"How about a Spriggs man. You all remember that Osborn Spriggss mother was a Lee, don't you? Maybe someone there would find a kinship." William continued to recite the names on the list.

"And the Northcrafts would be good. Junior, the Trails live up by you. Can you talk to them about someone willing to marry Rachel?"

"William, I can't do that to Rachel," James said. "It is one thing that she find a husband, but I won't force her to marry."

"Allen Bowie's name is next on the list," then William reminded them who the man was. "His mother married Thomas Cramphlin Sr. He is the one that ran a mill close to *Chestnut Ridge.* Also, father Lee owed money to them at the writing of the will."

"Oh, it wouldn't do much good. Allen Bowie has an eye to marrying his stepsister I hear," Thomas Thrasher told the men.

William took his pen and scratched through the Bowie name. "Looks like that one got away. It's a shame too, because his father had willed him some good land when he died."

"George Washington occasionally comes through on this road on his way to the mountains," John Wofford jested in desperation of names.

"Ah, yes, the young George. He married some widow woman once married to a Custis fellow in the last year or so. I heard it when I was at the tavern of late. But then you never know, she may have died by now."

By now laughter was too easy, William realized. Before it was over, he had recited names like reading a tax list of the wealthy and the poor as equals. If they had a man in the family that would take Rachel off their hands, they now had position. The Cramphlins, the Edmonstons, the Dawsons, the Allisons, the Birdwhistles, and after those even the lower class had been added.

William put his pen down, and viewed the list. He wondered what Rebeckah would say. They had all but raffled off her sister to the highest bidder. Even a low bidder would suffice at this point. It had all been done under the rationalization that what they were doing was for Rachel's own good. But somehow it was sounding more like they just wished to shuffle the problem of the run-down farm and the aging spinster sister-in-law off to someone else's back, as soon as possible.

The sun began to slide past the barn at the back of the horse pen when the men finished the meeting. "Betterton, if you are intending to ride along side of me, we better be taking our leave. I'd like to be in my own bed tonight," Alexander suggested. "Sarah gets worried if she has to do the chores without me there. This Indian problem has her awful jumpy."

Thomas Betterton stretched and got up. "I like knowing Eleanor will be my bed partner. Can't say the same for the likes of the beds in this establishment or how many will be close to me."

The other men knew all too well what he meant. There were only so many beds available, and if a large crowd came in for shelter, you shared your bed with strangers.

"Are you making your way back tonight, William?" Robert asked.

"No, the blacksmith has sent word my plow will be ready tomorrow, so I am spending the night whether I like the sleeping accommodations or not," William said.

Thomas Thrasher nodded his agreement with the bedding down problems. "Every time I come to one of these family meetings I get caught not making it back home before night fall. I figure it is better to take my chances with a bad bed partner than meet up with a not-so-friendly bear on some dark riverbank."

After going outside with the others to stretch, the two came back to the corner table to wait for the leg of lamb turning on the fireplace spit to be pulled off and served up. It was the custom that the innkeeper always furnished the meal if you were planning on staying the night. The conversation settled in on the business that had just transpired. "Seems to me there could be some mighty strong arguments coming our way by the women if we don't handle Rachel's husband finding real orderly like," Thomas confided to William.

Before William could make a suggestion, their conversation was interrupted by a group of burly looking men that had flung open the door and were shouting, "Any one of you coming this way catch sight of some Indians traveling from the Great Seneca?" The anger in the voice of the man talking caught the attention of every man in the tavern.

Life was hard in this part of the province, and when someone tried to do something to make it more difficult, it enraged the planters. Surviving the Indian raids brought down the guns from the hooks above every fireplace like nothing else could do. And when this happened, it was hard to tell which had the cruelest blood coursing through their veins, the killer Indians or the Indian killers.

William watched the men work themselves into a frenzy, vowing to tear apart the first Indian they saw. He was equally concerned about Rebeckah and the children. But the safe thing to do was ask questions first then seek out the wicked.

The men began to relay the happening of the night before. "A woman and a man were killed in their cabin near the Seneca landing. The savages, if that was who did this, went along the waterway burning barns and houses and killing who ever happened to be there, mostly slitting them in the back and around the neck. Probably came upon them without warning."

William knew that was the mark of the savages. The stories of burned out houses all up the Seneca gave him concern as to what he would find when he returned home.

He turned to Thomas. "Rebeckah will be out of her mind with worry if the news has come her way. If what this man says is true, it would put my place in real danger. Could you keep my wagon and go claim my plow at the blacksmith's tomorrow?"

It had been Thomas's plan to get an early start back home tomorrow morning. He did not like being away so long, but because the danger seemed to be closer to William's place than his, he felt an obligation to be the one to wait around for the plow.

William pulled a handful of monies from his inner pocket and handed them to Thomas. "Here is the remainder of what I owe on it. Deliver it to

93

your barn and I will come for it. I hesitate forcing you to reach Martha and the children at such a late hour but—"

Before he could finish his sentence Thomas had waved his hand, "Go—go. Martha would never forgive me if I refused."

Once away from the tavern without the wagon, he was able to give the horse full rein to the road, but the rain had left the pathway muddy. It would be well into the night before he would reach home. He had brought his small pistol with him in case of wild animals, but that would do very little to defend himself from any savages. His eyes searched the woods near the creek as he approached. Crossing this late would mean he would probably be alone and this made the crossing risky at best.

By now, what sun was left had fallen down behind the Sugar Loaf Mountain, and William was feeling hungry. He stopped to let his horse graze. Just before leaving the ordinary he had stuffed a biscuit from the cook's kitchen into his saddlebag and now took it out to eat. What seemed to be a sound coming from somewhere behind the tree line made him nervous. He decided not to wait around to see what it was and reached down for the reins of his horse with one hand and reached into his side pocket and gripped the pistol with the other. The sound stopped each time he stopped. Someone was watching him from the dark confines of the forest undergrowth. He turned around in every direction but saw nothing. Anyone in the deep woods this time of night was nothing but fodder for a savage's playtime.

He slowly turned the horse around so he could see what might be behind him and quickly mounted. The drizzle had stopped and a hint of the moon dodged in and out of the clouds. He was almost to the Great Seneca crossing. It would be slow going in the dark, but he would be to the Sittlers by the time they got up for chores. He would stop long enough to eat and get the news. Then he could be to his place before Rebeckah would have to send the boys out to the barn. If John had not been working on the road with the Birdwhistles, he would have worried less. But at least he knew White Horse would see to their safety.

The moonlight was short-lived, and before he could cross the creek there were signs of a storm building. He stood on the bank watching it approach, trying to decide if he could beat it across. As he turned his horse toward the water, a bolt of lightning streaked in front of him, and he quickly pulled back to find safety. It would mean sure death if he tried to cross during the storm. There was no choice but to bed down here for now.

He took his blanket from the back of the horse. Shivering in the cold, damp air, he tied the horse to a tree branch. It was going to be a rough night to sleep. What he would give for his own bed. Even Rebeckah's cold feet could be tolerated over this.

William felt the mud ooze in around his blanket. Rebeckah would surely have a different description of his appearance than her praise of yesterday morning.

The lightning flashed across the sky, leaving threads of vengeance, followed by thunder so close you could feel the earth shake. William felt only one consolation as he watched the battle in the skies, "It will be a good planting season with so much thunder so early this year." That was a given, or at least the old timers in the area always put stock in the saying.

The exhaustion of the trip and the afternoon tankards of cider played into the hands of sleep. When he awoke the rain was gone and the sun was just off the earth's edge. He rolled over quickly and grabbed the blanket, rolling it as he went to untie the horse. In a sudden moment of horror, he realized the horse was not there. The storm must have frightened him, and William, in his deep sleep, had not heard him pull free. His words were loud and real. "What else could go wrong on this trip?"

The horse could have gone anywhere on this side of the creek. As he walked, he checked for hoof prints, but they had been washed away by the rain, telling him the horse must have pulled free not long after they had stopped for the night. He made his way along the creek whistling for him to come. This usually worked but still no sign of the horse. Then he heard a whinny and with relief he turned to see his rein caught in a briar bush. This was the kind of miracle that would send him to church to offer up thanks.

The sun was up by the now and he felt secure in finding a cabin where he could ask for food. Not familiar with the families living on this side of the creek, still there was one family by the name of Seibert that would work the crops for the Birdwhistles. The old man had told him where his cabin was, and if he was not turned around it should be close by. He stopped to scour the horizon for a sign of smoke leading from a chimney and was about to move on when he spotted a thin stream of smoke coming from a short stack.

The horse stumbled, almost falling on the rutted road, giving William the feeling no one traveled this way often. It was obvious there were not many comforts among these meager surroundings. He hoped his asking for a meal would not be a burden to their table supplies.

William surveyed the old cabin with its rotting roof and crumbling chimney before calling out. The old man Seibert must have fallen to poor health to let his cabin go to ruin like this. The size reminded him of the first cabin he had built for his family. It had been a one-room shed with no floor and a lean-to for the cattle. That was a lifetime ago.

The fire in the fireplace told him they surely would have food. He called out again, "Seibert, it is William Littlefield," and again, "Anyone home?" The word home stretched the imagination when he looked at the old place.

There was still no response. He turned his horse and was about to go back to the main road when an old woman slowly opened the door to peer out. William was quick to explain, "I've been traveling all night to get back to my family down near the Seneca Mill. I would be much obliged if I could have a bowl of mush or whatever you and your husband could spare from your table." The woman looked William over before she pulled her gun from the door. "Tie your horse over there," she said, as she pointed to a post by the small shed. "My husband is long dead, and I don't have much to interest the likes of you, but you can come sup if you're hungry."

William did not stay long, just long enough to eat a journey cake made from a coarse wheat mixture, stale with age. This poor woman just barely had enough food to make it until crop season. The lack of life made him that much more thankful for what he had eaten. He would get his fill when he sat down again at Rebeckah's table.

While William ate, the old woman began telling about a man stopping by her place yesterday. He had told her of several families murdered somewhere on the Seneca, and their children either taken or slaughtered as well. He felt a shiver all over at the thought of Rebeckah and the children's safety.

The urgent need to be home was all he was interested in. He called back to the old woman that her kindness would not be misplaced. He gave full rein to his horse, vowing to send John back with food to keep her through to harvest. What good German stock that old woman came from. She just wouldn't give up and let herself die.

By now the road was nothing more than an old Indian path, making it dangerous for a horse and rider going fast. He kept his eyes open for anyone that might be coming his way but saw no one. This worried him, considering most of the farmers would be starting to plant any day now. A good farmer always took the necessary trips for supplies just prior to the hard planting time. Did this mean something? Had the Indian raid sent everyone to their cabins for safety? A sick feeling hit his stomach. What would he find waiting at his own door?

The smell of smoke filled the air. William was worried about getting home and decided not to stop at the Sittler's house. By the end of the week they would be to his place to start planting.

He pushed his horse on faster now until he could see his own chimney as he came down the hill. Everything looked just as he had left it early yesterday. Relief came over him. His eyes searched for White Horse who somehow always knew when he was coming, long before he was close enough to see. The old Indian would wave him home then go back into the woods. William wondered where he could be on this morning. When he got to his own yard no one but the dogs came to greet him, and they did not bother to bark. He climbed down from his horse and tried to open the door. Strangely, it was still bolted from the inside this time of day. He pulled himself up to look in the window and came face-to-face with Rebeckah pointing the gun straight at him. She burst into a mournful sob when she realized it was William and ran to unlatch the door.

"Oh, William, thank God it is you. I have such sad news to tell you."

One look into the eyes of Rebeckah and his children, William knew something terrible had happened.

When he asked what had happened they told first about going to find White Horse as their mother had asked. "When we got home the sun was not up yet."

"I heard a scratching on my window," Rebeckah told her husband. "It was the boys trying to get my attention without alerting anyone that might be waiting to attack if I opened the door."

William by now was trying to figure out why Rebeckah was sleeping by the door while the boys stayed away so long, or who was waiting to attack. "What were you two boys doing out so late?" Anger filled his voice for causing so much concern to their mother.

Not being able to hold the gruesome news any longer, Rebeckah cried out, "Oh, William, it's the Sittlers. They have all been killed. And White Horse is dead." She again began to cry as the children watched with wide eyes. Nothing this horrible had ever happened to them and they did not know how to accept the news.

William sat down on the bench in disbelief. The Sittlers had worked for him for years. He had seen their children grow up and helped lay to rest Mrs. Sittler's father who had come from Germany just last winter.

William wiped his eyes with his sleeve. Who has done this dastardly deed and why? But it was the news of White Horse that had caught him the most unprepared. The old Indian had the eyes of a wise hunter, always alert to what was happening even if the white man was unaware. How could this happen to him; this loyal friend who never asked for anything in return. It did not seem possible.

"A man came to the door late on the night you left," Rebeckah told him and began to unfold the horrid story of melee. "He said the sheriff had sent them to get you to help hunt down some killers. The next morning I told Absolom and young William to tell White Horse I needed to see him. And when they went to find him, they came upon some men down by the creek. The boys hid in the trees for fear they were the men that had attacked the family the sheriff had told us about. We had no idea it was our own Sittler family."

Absolom, waited for his mother to finish her part of the story, feeling older than his twelve years by now. Then he began to tell the scariest part of the story. "I told young William to keep quiet. He almost started crying because he was so scared, but mother said he did real good for someone still eight years old. He stayed brave most of the time."

William reached out his hand and patted young William on the back.

"We watched the men from where we were hiding in the tall grass by the creek." Absolom continued to tell the story. "One big man laughed and said the Indian had done it. They meant White Horse because they were pointing to his cave. They acted like they were trying to decide on a story."

Young William could not wait to tell his part of the story. "We heard them say that the Sittlers had all been murdered just in front of their cabin as they were leaving in their wagon. Absolom told me he remembered you had said they were going to Fredericktown to buy the corn for planting."

"What happened to White Horse? Are you sure he is dead?" William asked his sons.

There was pain on Absolom's face as he recounted the murderous sight. "While we were still lying in the weeds, we saw White Horse coming over the hill. He was covered in black soot. They didn't wait to talk to him and just shot him right there. White Horse let out a real loud cry, you know like the Indians do, then he just fell on the ground. Those men got back on their horses and circled around White Horse as he lay there on the ground. Then they rode off fast."

"They were talking real excited like, but we couldn't hear much of what they were saying."

Young William looked at his father with tears in his eyes. "We ran over to see White Horse after those men rode off. He was just lying down and we couldn't see him breathing. Absolom tried to talk to him, but he didn't move. We got some water from the creek and tried to wash the blood off him where he was shot. Absolom said that is what you would have done. He did a real good job. I didn't want to touch him, but Absolom said I had to help. But he still died. We didn't see him move at all."

"Did you boys bury White Horse?" William asked his sons, almost reverently.

"No, sir, we did not. We wanted to wait so you could see what they had done to him, and besides we thought maybe we should hurry home to see if Mother was all right."

Rebeckah spoke up, "Tell the rest of the story, Absolom."

Absolom shook his head and just sat there a moment trying to decide how to say what happened next.

"Tell him, Absolom," young William prodded, watching his big brother with wide eyes.

"We started home but then we heard someone coming. I told young William to run and hide, but before he could get under the brush, some

Indians with their faces all painted up came across the creek a little ways down. There was no place to hide, so we slipped into the creek next to the fallen tree trunk. It was the one you said probably would be a good place to fish because the fish like to hide around the tree trunks," Absolom told his father.

Young William, eager again to talk said, "And we had to stay there until after dark because they didn't go away. It was so cold, but we were afraid if we moved they would kill us, so we had to stay real still."

"They were drinking from a jug like the one Mrs. Sittler used to carry her molasses in at the candy pulls. You know the one with the speckled colors on it and the broken handle," Absolom explained to his father. "When they fell asleep, I had young William follow me, and we waded down past where the Indians were, taking one step then stopping, then another one so they might think the noise was just a turtle climbing up the bank. After we got a ways down we crawled up the bank on the other side."

"Then the big thunder came, so they couldn't hear us," young William remembered.

"And we could run faster because they couldn't hear us. It took us a long time to get home. It was so dark, and we thought we heard them coming behind us one time."

For a long time, William listened. By the time they finished, he turned and looked at Rebeckah. She thought he was going to scold her for having them go find White Horse. Instead he reached out to take her hand. "You'll miss Mrs. Sittler, Rebeckah." He got up and without anymore sentiment said, "We better be burying White Horse and maybe the Sittlers if no one has seen to them."

Several weeks passed and Benoni Dawson was paid to pick up the wagon and plow at Thomas Thrasher's place. William stood at the top of the hill watching the hired hand work the shiny blade into the dirt and move to the next row. It had been a long day in the fields. The tobacco plants did not want to wait. Next week they would work on the cornfield. Life in the colonies depended on each crop, each tender seed that came up. Year after year, William had sent the hired hands farther down the hill to clear the trees from the ground to make way for more crops. And with each year, his dream of a plantation equal to the land he had come from in the mother country was getting closer. This spread was a far cry from the one hundred acres he received when he first came to these parts. After the purchase two years ago of the 1,371 acres next to his first land, which he had chosen to call *Resurvey of William and John*, he could say with pride that he had given his family a secure legacy. As secure as any could be with the changing rules being set by the British royal lords.

William started for the cabin then stopped. From up here he could see the rooftops of Thomas Dawson's buildings. The last streaks of pink stretched across the sky and all seemed well for planting. Taking in a long, deep breath, smelling the freshly planted tobacco, he bent down and straightened several plants. He never had to do that when the Sittlers planted his tobacco plants, never in all the years they worked for him.

William could still see Zadock Sittler even now, working the ground with his big hands, standing and straightening his tired back, stretching out the stiffness, and bending down again to check the direction of his rows. That old man and his Sarah knew how to make a crop grow. There was just something about them and their son Eli—the way they worked together.

The loss of the Sittlers was painful, but did not weigh up to the loss of the old Indian.

"Oh, White Horse, what really happened to you?" William said in despair. The boys had pointed out the place where White Horse's body had fallen. But when they reached the site near his cave, he was gone. Nor could they find any evidence of a recently dug grave. Finally they had to resign themselves that wild animals had dragged him off and devoured his remains. A painful thought crossed his mind. Could someone have taken his body as a trophy?

At the bottom of the hill, William reached out and pulled the gate closed behind him as the last sliver of light slid from the day. He paused as he had done for weeks, searching the edge of the earth in hopes of seeing the familiar figure coming toward him.

But again, the old warrior did not come.

Chapter 9

April 1764
Seneca Creek

Rebeckah stomped her foot in disgust. Her spinning wheel was tangling the thread and she was frustrated. There was never enough time to get her work done before bedtime, and to now have the spinning wheel refuse to take the thread was more than her patience could handle.

"Nancy come help hold this contrary wool string tight." Rebeckah, wiping her forehead with her sleeve, called to her daughter who was sitting outside the door working a crewel sampler to place on the wall over her bed.

Nancy put her sewing into the basket and begrudgingly came into the hot room where her mother was working. "I saw a cloud of dust rising from the road just over the hill. Do you think it is Mr. Dawson coming again?"

Since William and Thomas had been sharing the plow, not only did the crops get set earlier than if they worked with the worn out plows, but Thomas brought news from the other families across the creek.

William got to the house just as Thomas was coming up the path. He stopped to pull the door closed to make sure they were not interrupted in their talk.

Rebeckah stopped the spinning wheel trying to listen.

Thomas was telling William about some Indian sightings. "I was told there have been more Indian sightings—some serious enough to set out the call to surrounding settlers to go to Cresap's fort for safety."

Rebeckah went back to spinning when she realized the sightings had been on the other side of Fredericktown and were little threat to her family.

As in other visits, ever since William had brought news back to Thomas of what had been rumored at Dowden's Ordinary a few weeks back, the news of the sea port found its way into their conversation. Thomas Dawson was the one man William would confide in when it came to finding less than praise for the King and his Parliament. Not that Thomas always agreed with William, but he did not cause a fuss like his brothers-in-law.

Rebeckah again put her hand on the wheel to stop the spinning to try to hear. William's voice had become sharp.

"What does Grenville think we will use for monies if we cannot afford to ship our tobacco because of his outrageous rules. Sometimes I wonder why I bothered to clear more land if I cannot afford to sell the product."

Thomas was saying something about Dowden's Tavern and waiting for the papers with King George's seal on it to make it official. She listened as best she could with the door shut.

"The rumors proved to be factual on the last news," William reminded him.

"So you think the tobacco that we will ship this year will first be ordered to go to a British port?" Thomas asked.

"That is what they are saying and it means they will deduct the cost of paying the British duties from our payment."

"I'll fight it, William, I'll fight."

"I don't like it either, Thomas. I've always been a loyal supporter of King George, but this may be too much."

Rebeckah could hear the voices rise and fall in the discussion but could not make out all the words. She whispered to Nancy to open the door all the way, but to not disturb her father's talk. She did not tell Nancy it had only a little bit to do with the heat and everything to do with the hearing.

"I can just hear them now. Let's tax the colonists. After all, we had the war for them." Thomas railed on. "I fear we are on the hard road to the mountain, William."

William was quiet for a moment, then told his neighbor, "King George has always seemed fair in his dealings with my interests. I guess I choose to wait for his answer to the charges."

There was silence. Then Thomas asked, "What happens if there is an uprising? Do you think the parliament will back down?"

William lowered his voice when he spoke. "Probably not. Grenville seems to be in control of the young King. Cannot say I like our King to be so weak, but I guess he will not be asking me how I feel." With that last comment the two men chuckled half-heartedly.

The men went on to talk about something of no interest to Rebeckah, and the next thing she noticed was the squeak of the wagon as Thomas Dawson lifted his body up onto the seat.

No sooner had Thomas gone, William appeared in the open door, his eyes set on his wife. "Rebeckah, you know that was men's talk and I thank you not to listen in. Don't deny it. I saw Nancy open the door wider."

"William, I have the same greeting, thank you very much, not to tell me when I might open my door wide. If you men had to work in this hot room you would not be so concerned with who was speaking about what. Seems to me it is fair enough for anyone to hear if you stand within whispering space of my door."

Rebeckah Littlefield was not about to let her husband refuse her speaking rights, like so many of the husbands did. William Littlefield knew her spirit before he married her.

William gave her a long hard look but did not challenge her words. When he turned around abruptly and walked out the door, she knew he would not be back until the next day. This was the way it was with him. She had overstepped her boundaries but did not call out for forgiveness.

Once the older children had gone up the steps to the bedchambers, Rebeckah sat in the dark room, the door still open as a testimony to what had constituted the argument. She looked down at baby Mary nursing in her arms but could not bring up the feelings to sing to her this night.

The anger she felt with William had not visited her for many years and her thoughts simmered there through the evening. William's old ways could hurt. Maybe it was the way he had been raised without a mother or grandmother in his life to teach him how to treat a woman. It had happened before, once when they first married and she still held the numbing pain of the rejection in her heart.

The sun was coming through the open door as Rebeckah opened her eyes. Why had she felt so brave to leave a door open through the night without William at home to guard them? Anger was a strong deceiver of wisdom, she reasoned, and she had allowed it to take the place of common sense.

When Rebeckah put the scrapple on the table for their first meal, William walked in the open door, but said nothing about where he had been. In fact, he did not talk at all. After he finished his meal, he left the house to do the chores. The boys followed their father, as was their routine. Mad or not, chores would not wait.

She cleared the table, all the time angered by what had happened. She was determined not to let the children be affected by her husband's ill temper and forced a hymn to her lips as she often did when anger threatened to get in the way of a good day. Nothing but the tune came at first. Then gradually she allowed herself to form the words. She sang *Come thou fount of every blessing* in a slow determined meter like they did at the big church in Fredericktown the few times she and William were able to attend. The minister had explained it was a new song some parishioner had brought from England on his recent trip. She had hummed it all the way home until William said he had enough of church for one day. But right now she needed a blessing so she sang it over and over. And it must have worked because by the time she finished the indoor chores the rift was all but forgotten.

This morning Rebeckah had left young William with the sleeping baby. She had grabbed the hoe in one hand and a basket of seedlings planted earlier in clay cups and called to Nancy to come with her to the garden spot.

Solomon followed them with his bucket to pick wild berries. All winter long, each time she looked out her window, she had planned the way she wanted her garden to look. "Nancy, do you remember how Aunt Rachel's garden was laid out last spring? I believe it had the cabbage in the center and the other small herbs planted around it." The sisters had been in a contest for years, each trying to see who could plant the prettiest display of vegetables. Last year Rachel had won the vote for her "cabbage stars" as she had called them, surrounded by different colored basil, watercress and parsley, then outlined by beans and squash and even a few potato plants with their dark green leaves mixed in.

"Rachel knows how to make a pretty garden. She learned it from your grandmother. The plants just seem to bloom prettier the way she sets them out."

"Mother, have you always loved your little sister so much?" Nancy asked.

Rebeckah turned to look at her daughter. "What are you asking, Nancy?"

"I was just wondering if I will love baby Mary when she is grown up, like you love Aunt Rachel."

Rebeckah thought a moment. "Well, first, Aunt Rachel is not that much younger. It is just that she did not marry and move away. That makes her belong to all of us more."

"Will poor Aunt Rachel ever get married?"

Rebeckah laughed at her daughter's concern as she pushed open the garden gate. "Now, we will put the cabbages over there next to the fence and the spinach in front of it, close in color, but one stronger than the other."

The two worked close together. Rebeckah would dig the hole, and Nancy, on her knees, would plant the tender plants then cover it with a handful of straw brought from the barn. The nights were still too cold in Maryland to leave them on their own.

It was midmorning by the time the two had the plants in the ground.

She gave Nancy and Solomon the job of gathering water from the creek to water the tender plants and went to the cabin to feed the baby.

In just a few minutes Nancy came running in, pulling the arm of a scared Solomon, all flushed and out of breath.

"Mother, some men are coming this way. I couldn't see them but I heard them crossing the creek down by the Seneca Mill. They were shouting and hollering about something."

Rebeckah sent young William to the field to get his father and Absolom. Then she gathered the others into the kitchen and got the gun down from the fireplace.

When William came he scoffed at Rebeckah. "You know better than to bring me from work just for the notion that some fun-loving men are going to come for you. They are probably just getting a head start on the fair in Fredericktown."

This was the one time of year that all thoughts of work were put aside. "Oh, Papaw can we go, can we?" Solomon squealed. The children were all jumping up and down, begging to see the fun.

"Father can we take the kite we made for the contest? John has been working on it ever since you told us. You saw it fly, it flies real good," Absolom begged.

William said nothing until he was back outside the door. "We have work to do. Besides John is not back from the road crew work."

The boys knew better than to ask again. Nancy quietly went to her mother's window and looked out toward the road. She wished she belonged to her Aunt Martha's family. They always went to the fair.

The day wore on and the work seemed heavier when balanced with the thoughts of the fair. It was past the noon mealtime when William came back to the cabin. "If you boys will see to extra chores, and Nancy, you and Solomon help your mother prepare the food, we will leave before light tomorrow morning. If John comes home tonight then you can take the kite." They each let out a yell of anticipation and sprang into action. Nancy pulled the frying pan from its hook to help prepare the extra meal they would need for the traveling day.

William picked up his hoe and headed for the field with his boys. "Do you think you boys can hold up to get us ready?"

Young William spoke what they were all thinking, "We need White Horse to get us ready to go."

Chapter 10

April 1764
Going to the Fair

The old oxen stumbled to a halt at Seneca Landing giving a jolt to everyone in the wagon. Rebeckah looked up from her half sleep, now aware of the sun trying to poke through the trees. She could see people moving about, waiting to load up and move across the waters.

William climbed down from his seat and called to John and Absolom to help lead the animals into the line. Crossing the sometimes-deep waters was a dangerous job and Rebeckah cautioned the children to keep quiet. William was always weary of this junction anytime he was trying to handle the oxen with the wagon. Normally on occasions like this, he would have brought the horse team, but this was foaling season and he did not wish to disturb nature. Horses were a luxury that many could never hope to afford, but William had been fortunate to find a good mare whose colts were strong. Now he protected them with his life. The oxen were the real workers, so it had probably been wise to bring them, Rebeckah thought, but she always felt so proud to have people see their wagon being pulled by their fine horses. It was a foolish thought, she knew, but one she could not seem to put aside.

The heavy coverage of trees beside the creek, gave their wagon a sheltered place to stop while waiting to make the crossing. Rebeckah decided it would be a good time to feed the children. She handed baby Mary to her daughter and took the cold corn bread and fried fatback strips from the pouch she had brought. When she looked up, she noticed the wife of the mill owner coming toward the wagon.

"Who is that woman, mother? And where is Mrs. Owens?"

"It's Mrs. Pelly." Rebeckah told her daughter. "Her husband bought this landing from the widow Owens."

Mrs. Pelly's words spilled out fast like she knew there was little time for conversation before each wagon moved on. "I've been intending to meet up with you since my husband took over this place. I hear tell Sarah Owens was a good woman, always keeping you women notified of the news, bless her soul. I dare say the men folk never give you a wink of news."

Nancy and young William giggled at the way Mrs. Pelly expressed herself.

Just as Rebeckah started to tell Mrs. Pelly how much they had loved Sarah Owen, the wagon started to move. She had to grab hold of the siding to keep from falling out of the wagon.

Mrs. Pelly waved her on. "I'll send for you and the children to come sit with me some hot day this summer. The children can swim in the creek by the mill." They had moved passed her words, leaving no time to accept the invitation. Rebeckah returned the wave, as a flood of memories came in around her. She remembered how nice it had been to have a dear friend like the older Sarah Owens. She had come to sit with Mrs. Owens and the two had talked about all that had come before them and what was expected of her as her children got older and moved away. Widow Owens had a lot to say about that. And sometimes the widow expounded on life in-between and fearing the children of the day were not prepared for what lay ahead of them.

By the time William climbed back onto the wagon seat, his leggings were wet and muddy from leading the oxen into the water. He leaned over the side of the wagon to watch the oxen's heavy bodies sink into the water. After he was sure they were getting a footing, he reached back and took a quilt from the top of a stack of quilts and began to wrap his wet, dirty feet.

"That is my best quilt you are fumbling with; here take this old one," Rebeckah scolded as she threw him the old quilt the children had been sitting on.

William grumbled, "Then why did you bring the good one if it wasn't to be used?"

"Because that is what you do with your nice things. How else will anyone know what I have. We are so far out no one ever comes to see me."

William paid no mind to her comment. His mind was still on getting the wagon across the creek. "I inquired of Mr. Pelly as to what he had heard about the safety of bedding down on the side of the road tonight. He told me there had been news last evening about a sighting of some roaming Indians down by the point of rocks."

John climbed up next to his father after pushing the wagon through the muddy bank. He hung on every word his father spoke, especially when the talk was about the Indians. It was his favorite subject now that he was older. "Is there going to be an Indian uprising?" John's eagerness reminded William of his own, once youthful, outrage over anything that offended the people he lived around. It was that same outrage that had brought him to the colonies from the countryside of his England. Oh, how he wished he could give John the insight to decide between a truly worthy cause and an overheated one.

By the time the oxen pulled the wagon from the waters on the other side of the Seneca Creek, the warmth of the sun was a welcome feeling. The older boys had jumped off the wagon to help a woman with a load of children who was having trouble getting her oxen to follow the line.

Rebeckah sat with her back against the front of the wagon, next to William. She held baby Mary close, her eyelids just beginning to close. Nancy was leaning against the side of the wagon with Solomon in her lap, both warmed by the afternoon sun and lulled into sleep by the sound of the creaking wheels and the sway of the wagon.

In a rare moment, William began to make conversation with his wife. "Mr. Pelly said the travelers had been talking all week about how the Monocacy has been holding very little water for this time of the season. But one thing I've learned these fifteen years since I came to this part is that the Monocacy can play you for the fool, especially in the spring rains. Remember, Becka, that boy that was on his way to his own wedding, and just as he got halfway across the river, it started rising, and before he could get to the other side it swept him away? They found his body a full week later wedged in a tree trunk all dressed proper in his wedding suit. Well, that was right about where we will be crossing. You just can't trust this river if a rain has come." After that they rode on in silence and Rebeckah knew he must be thinking about the rain that had come two nights ago.

William tipped his hat to one of the men in another wagon as they passed. He would reserve his conversations for the courthouse square. But he did pause long enough to ask of a traveler coming from the Monocacy River about the condition of the cross over and was much relieved to find the Ferry was in use on this day. "What a pleasant day to be going to the fair," one lady shouted to them. In return, William tipped his hat and agreed, "Life is indeed good at this moment."

The day wore on with nothing more than a slight delay waiting on the ferry to make a return trip across the Monococy. As the sun began to set, William tried to rush the slow-footed beasts with sharp cracks of the whip.

Finally, the wagon began descending the hill. Young William was the first to spot the path that led to the Thrasher cabin down in the valley. "Oh, William. Look!" Rebeckah shouted as she stood up, holding the side of the wagon. "Just look how those tulip poplar trees have grown so much taller since we were last here. I've never seen the beech trees and white birch and ash trees mixed with the colors of the white dogwood and redbud so magnificently like this before." Then she announced as if about to break into song, flinging her arms out wide, "They are all decked out just to welcome us."

William chose not to answer the poetic descriptions of his wife as she pointed to mother nature's good form. "Rebeckah sometimes you send strong signals of being someone I do not know when you pull out the big words from somewhere." There was only a hint of softness to his voice but she knew he did not mind her jovial mood. Not wanting this exposition to get out of control, he yelled back to the children. "Remember we leave at sunup tomorrow. Be at the wagon early or be left."

As they rode closer, they could see Martha through the open door standing in front of the fireplace stirring something. She turned to run out when the dogs began barking. They all laughed at their Aunt Martha for being so excited, standing in the front yard waving both arms and doing this crazy little whooping dance with her children.

First Rebeckah had expounded so eloquently about Mother nature, and now this wild dance Martha was putting on gave William to imagine this wildness must have come from the Lee side of the family.

Before the guests got to the end of the road, Martha rushed back into the cabin to stir the pot one more time and quickly tore the roasted chickens from the spit. Then she lit more candles. By the time Rebeckah was climbing over the side of the wagon Martha had come out to greet them.

"I just had a feeling someone would be coming to the fair. She rushed over to take the baby from Rebeckah. "Oh, my sweet baby. Did you know you are named after your grandmother?" she said, with a questioning eye to Rebeckah. "Mother would have been so proud. Rachel sent word about her birth by Thomas. You know he went to court to render his name to the sureties for Father's will filing?"

"Marthy, these people have been traveling all day, and filling their bellies makes more sense than a lot of talk," Thomas reminded his wife.

As the two sisters put the food on the long table, they wasted none of their precious time in silence. Before they could serve the dinner, they heard the dogs barking at someone coming down the long pathway to their door.

Robert Lee gave out a shout to be recognized in the dark. Elizabeth and the children spilled over the sides of the wagon and ran into the cabin, hungry from the long trip.

After the meal, the men settled into their routine of filling their pipes and discussing the recent crop failures. The women sent the children to find a place to play their games, with the older ones watching the babies. Once the chores were finished and the bones thrown to the waiting dogs outside the door, the women sat down at the table to spend the evening making sure all the family news was covered.

"Ann Hughes was here for a night before going on to give Rachel advice about the inventory," Martha said, making a funny face when she said it. "She and John Hughes had been to the courthouse to check on Father's will to see if Rachel had been in to file it on time. They still think she doesn't have sense enough to carry the work to completion." Martha stopped talking when she noticed Elizabeth had gotten up and was staring into the fire, obviously distressed about something.

"Libby, you are mighty solemn this night. Is there a cry within you?"

Elizabeth looked at both women, being careful not to speak so the men could hear her. "Robert is saying words about moving away."

Rebeckah gasped, "No, not for one moment would he leave his land." Elizabeth, with tears running down her cheeks, shook her head as she put a finger to her lips.

Before they could say more, a log fell off its irons and sent sparks flying, catching Elizabeth's skirt on fire. She managed to wad the blazing skirt into a ball, but not before she had burned her hands. Robert ran to find the water bucket, as Martha pulled the lard from a shelf and began covering the red blisters with the slippery grease.

Nothing more could be said tonight about the plans for moving away, but that did not quiet the questions in each woman's head. If Robert and Elizabeth would move, then who else would want to follow? This was the land of their families, and their dreams had been formed here. Every woman had seen the lost look of a woman sitting beside her determined husband as the wagon train slowly made its way to a new life. All the things they had ever owned were left behind for someone else to set a house with.

For the first time, someone had broken the sacred union of togetherness and spoken the cruel unthinkable words "move away from here."

And now in this very room, without a word spoken further about it, they realized it could be any one of them seated on that wagon with no say as to what was happening.

Chapter 11

April 1764
At the Fair

The outer roads leading into Fredericktown were cluttered with wagons. Some had a cow tied to the back hook, making the trip from the Thrashers longer than usual. Going to the fair was about the biggest excitement a family could have in western Maryland, but William Littlefield was determined his children were not going to act like the others around him, yelling and screaming and jumping off the wagons.

As he reined his oxen team through the streets, he wondered what his grandfather would have done if he had acted in this heathen manner on the streets of London during fair time. Maybe this had something to do with expressing the new found freedom in the colonies. But for his children, they had been taught by the old country's standard of manners, and they would not dare act in such a way.

William was forced to slow his wagon to let a mother duck and her ducklings waddle across the street in front of him, and before he knew what was happening, he could hear children yelling at the top of their lungs—his children. They were straddling the sides of the wagon. The next thing he knew, they had jumped off and were running into the crowded street.

When the wagon rocked to a stop, only Rebeckah and baby Mary were left. And Rebeckah was acting almost as heathen as the children. Only, slightly with honor, her yelling was an attempt to keep Solomon from running after his siblings.

"Solomon—Solomon, you stop right now. Wait, wait for us," Rebeckah yelled.

Before Rebeckah could crawl over the side, Solomon disappeared with a group of young children. If he could not find his siblings would he be able to find his way back to the wagon among all the strangers?

William yelled back for her to sit down as he cracked the whip to move the wagon along. "Rebeckah, I hold you responsible in the training of my children and you have neglected to control them."

The field was crowded as the Littlefield wagon pulled into the area set aside for the fair goers along the banks of Carroll Creek. When he finally found one for himself and one for Robert's family it was near midmorning. He wanted nothing more to do with this situation and focused on finding a gathering of men with news from the latest ship to arrive from London. His voice had a gruffness to it when he spoke. "Rebeckah, I'm going to the courthouse square to hear the talk. When Robert and Thomas come, tell them they can find me there."

"William, what about Solomon? That poor little thing will be scared to death alone out there."

He turned, and in a tone much too impatient, he called back, "Rebeckah you fret too much about that boy. I'm going to capture the news. When his belly is empty, he will start looking for us."

Rebeckah watched him walk away and stifled the urge to call out a protest to his decision. Instead, she stomped her foot in defiance. She had learned a long time ago not to argue in public about her husband's reasoning.

As William hurried down the path a wagon pulled into the place she had hoped to save for Martha and Thomas. He climbed down and started toward town. Rebeckah could not help but wonder what power the news held over men that made them forget about their good senses. If women acted this way to hear the latest news about a new color in calico or the number of thread chains in lace, the men would be quick to put a stop to it.

There was nothing to do but try to get the fire started. She gathered up her skirt and crawled under the wagon to find the shovel William kept stored underneath.

At least one blessing was to her favor. This morning she had gathered enough small sticks from her sister's yard to start a fire. As she suspected, they would be too late to buy from the young boy that always came to sell kindling before each meal.

She could hear baby Mary beginning her slow whimper and by the time she could get the firewood laid, she was demanding her feeding.

Rebeckah climbed up into the wagon to feed the baby and thought she heard someone moan, but when she looked around she saw no one appearing to be in pain.

Again, she looked toward the roads for any sign of Solomon. Should she grab the baby up and go through the crowds calling his name? But what if he came to the campground to find them?

Again she noticed a strange odor coming from somewhere nearby, and she wondered who might have left their food out to spoil.

If she did not get the fire going there would be no hot noon meal, and William would grumble the rest of the day. Her thoughts mingled between William's leaving her to do the work alone, to wondering if Solomon could find his way to their wagon.

Rebeckah wiped her face on the hem of her apron and pulled the heavy wooden bucket from the hook at the end of the wagon. There was just enough water to fill the kettle. While waiting for the water to boil she took the meal bag from the basket of foods she had brought and scattered handfuls of meal into the bubbling water, then began stirring it vigorously. Mush could lump so fast if you did not stir it quickly. And if there was one thing William would not tolerate, it was lumpy mush. He always said he could understand that on busy days she did not have time to go kill a bird or fish the creek, but he expected her to make the mush without lumps. She caught herself laughing out loud at the thought that maybe this was the day she would leave a lump just to protest his lack of help.

Sometime before the next meal she would need to find the market tent to buy the necessary foods. That was part of the joy of coming to the fair; shopping the different booths set up to handle the needs of the fair goers. Most of the foods, depending on how warm the weather had been, were brought in daily. And of course, there was a large supply of dried foods set aside to sell for this event.

Rebeckah's thoughts were interrupted by the sound of her brother calling to her. He had stopped his wagon just as they were coming into the field to let his children climb orderly over the side of the wagon. Robert's oldest girl had taken the younger children's hands, and then proceeded to walk calmly toward the festival street. Rebeckah could not help but notice how well behaved they were today, compared to her own children. Maybe it was just as well that William had gone on ahead. Somehow a lecture on how well mannered Robert's children were was not what she wanted to hear just now.

"Over here, Robert," she pointed to the spot she had managed to save for some of the family by putting her milk jug at the entrance. She could see Elizabeth's hands were still wrapped in the rags. The burns had been ugly and red blistered this morning and the heat of the day must surely be making the pain worse.

When they had settled the wagon into the spot, Rebeckah called out for Robert to bring their skillet over to her already hot fire. "Elizabeth, should not be that close to the heat with her hands. It makes no sense in having two fires, anyway," she said, trying to be careful not to offend her over her infirmities.

The morning wore on as the women sat together, Rebeckah stirring the food while Elizabeth held baby Mary. Finally, Rebeckah approached the subject left unfinished from the night before. She did not face her sister-in-law, afraid of what she might see on her face. In a hushed voice spoke what they all feared. "Do you really think Robert would really give thought to moving away, or is this disagreeable talk?"

Elizabeth took in a painful breath as she began to explain. "Robert gets upset with me for starting rumors, but ever since father Lee died, Robert has talked of nothing else. The travelers that stop by our place on their way to Carolina tell of fresh new land that grows the blue dye plant in big fields. Robert has been told at any given morning you can see the long line of ships just waiting to come into the dock. They've come from England for one purpose only, and that is to buy up all of the blue plants as soon as the crop is harvested. Rebeckah, your brother says we could all fill our pockets if we go." Elizabeth shook her head sadly, then added, "I've tried to tell him money cannot take the place of our families, but he will not listen."

Rebeckah continued to stir the mush for a time. When she spoke, it was with barely a whisper. She reached over and gave her sister-in-law a consoling pat on the back. As a way to change the subject she picked up her water bucket, "Stay with baby Mary while I go to the water well."

Elizabeth fanned her face with the edge of her apron as she watched her sister-in-law go down the road to the water well. The sun beat down on her head and made her feel lightheaded. But more than the heat, a horrible odor penetrated the air, leaving her with a sick stomach. It seemed to be coming from the next wagon. Finally, she put her apron to her nose. It smelled like spoiled meat or something dead being left to rot. Who would have come to the fair with something like that in their wagon?

Elizabeth heard someone moaning in pain and climbed up into the Littlefield wagon to see if she could see into the man's wagon. To her horror a young woman was tossing around in obvious pain. Her feet were covered with flies eating at the flesh and it appeared she had not held her food for sometime, which added to the odor. As Libby stared at the girl, an old man clutching a big stick staggered up to the wagon. He had brought what looked like a bucket of food to the girl. When he saw Elizabeth looking in his direction, he spoke, "It's her feet. She stood on a red ant bed and got her feet and legs all bitten up by the pesky creatures sometime ago. There's been lots of puss for about a week now."

Elizabeth shook her head in sympathy and resolved to offer help when someone came back.

William and Robert, followed by the children were just coming down the road when Rebeckah returned from the water well. She quickly set the bucket down and ran to meet them, "Did you look for Solomon?"

"Rebeckah, I've told you to stop fretting about that boy. The child will come back on his own. And if he does not, I will find him and he shall remember from now on to stay with his family."

"William, you do not know what they do with small young children?" Rebeckah, close to tears, turned to her sister-in-law, "Elizabeth Dawson said she had heard they kidnap them and take them on ships to sell in some far off port to anyone looking for cheap labor. And who would not love to have my sweet precious curly headed baby scrubbing their front steps?"

Young William looked down at the newly bruised knot on his shin and wondered if that sweet blond-headed baby his mother was talking about was the same Solomon he knew.

Finally, William agreed if he did not show up after the meal they would all scatter out and search the town.

A wind had come up and sent the stench in the other direction, and with the excitement over Solomon, Elizabeth had forgotten to mention giving help to the poor girl in the wagon.

After the meal the family went up and down the streets calling out Solomon's name. No one had seen the boy, or at least had paid him any mind. All the crowd was interested in was the news going around of how Col. Cresap had come from his fort in the up-country and how he had fought off some Indian uprising or killed a bear at his gate. Even the Cresap's old Indian companion, Nemocolin, caused more excitement than the story of a lost child.

After searching every busy street of the town, Rebeckah and Elizabeth returned to the wagon in hopes of finding Solomon waiting for his dinner. With so many wagons, could a child so young remember what his wagon looked like?

When the two women rounded the road, Elizabeth yelled out, "Oh, it's gone—a good thing else we would have all had to move our wagons." Rebeckah looked puzzled, and Elizabeth explained about the conversation she had with the old man. "His poor daughter, judging from the smell, may have been near death." She took hold of Rebeckah's arm. "Oh, no! Do you think the poor thing died?"

Before the two could speculate as to the fate of the girl, a young boy yelling to the top of his lungs was coming toward their wagon. "Aunt Rebeckah, Aunt Rebeckah—we found your Solomon, Aunt Rebeckah, we found Solomon." It was Martha Thrasher's son, eleven-year-old Benjamin. "We just rode across the creek and there was Solomon standing with some other boys throwing rocks into the water. Mother, couldn't see you standing close by and she told me to catch Solomon and come find you," Benjamin said, pulling the loudly protesting Solomon up the path by his shirt collar.

Rebeckah, under her breath gave a moan of relief, but outwardly she scolded, "Wait until I get my hands on that spiteful child." She could not let Solomon get away with having his own mind as to when and where he should go. But before she could bring her threat to place, Solomon broke loose and ran to his mother with outstretched arms. "Mummy, I found two new friends. And I got to ride a pony that belonged to one boy."

By the time the others came back to camp, Solomon had told of riding a pony and playing on the creek bank with the new boy. "His name was Michael."

Solomon's eyes widened as he retold the story to his family how his new friend was the grandson of the famous fighter Cresap. "He has only one ear. A big horse came up to his house and bit his ear off. He said it hurt real bad but he didn't cry much because he has Cresap's blood in him, and they don't get scared of anything." His audience of cousins and parents laughed at Solomon's innocent reasoning.

"Whose pony did you ride?" Young William was more interested to hear about the pony than the ear being bitten off.

"Oh, it was just some boy's pony. I think he would let you ride him. Come on, let's go see."

"Hold on," William said, reaching out to catch his youngest son as he was about to head for the road. "I think it was Francis Key's young son of which Solomon speaks. They live on that big plantation we have heard so much about that sits close to the Pennsylvania border. I believe they call the land *Terra Rubra*. I suspect it is the horse they had down by the water well earlier."

Solomon piped up proudly, "My friend's name is John Ross Key."

William turned to explain to Robert, "The boy's horse is an offspring of one of the British General's horses that was injured in the last war."

"Are you talking about Horatio Gates's horse or Braddock's horse? I've heard the story of them bringing the injured horses into Fredericktown to sell," Robert asked

"Yes, well, this is an offspring from both those General's horses. When I was talking to Francis Key today, he said they suspect one of General Braddock's spirited horses had sired a colt with one of Gates's mares. After Braddock was killed, they brought Gates's horse into Fredericktown to sell. So this must be one of their offspring, like you say."

"There are those who will pay a pretty price for the honor of the name branded on the rump," Robert surmised.

"The way I see it, someone is going to take advantage of the French and Indian War even if it has to do with standing around looking at horses born of a hero's horse. War is war and it will continue to hold the fascination until the next one comes around," Robert said.

"All the same a good horse is a good horse, no matter whose name it comes under," William said as he watched Solomon glory in the fact that the older cousins were now all asking him about his time with the horse. "What did it feel like—did he turn real fast?"

Solomon beamed with excitement over this attention and began talking fast before someone else could take over his story. "And they are going to take him in the big parade—he is a brown horse with a big star on his nose."

The children all laughed at his description. "You mean on his forehead, Solomon."

Solomon did not like to be teased and stood up to punch his cousin, but was stopped by Absolom.

William began telling the others, "Seems to be a favorite among the fair goers at the parade, I've been told. Look for a small boy riding a dark bay horse with a high step" he laughed and added, "with a star on his nose."

After all the excitement things settled down to be just plain talk among the women while the children noisily went into the road to play tag with the children from several near by wagons.

But for William and Robert, they wanted nothing more than to sit on the ground with their backs leaning against the wagon and talk about the news they had heard that morning, mainly the Indian raids.

"Did you see Cresap?" William asked Robert.

"Seems they still have to press the fort into service from time to time because of raids. Some of the Indians set a trap for the people along the ridge. Cresap managed to calm the Indians down before they killed anyone, but then more Indians became upset at him for not having enough corn in his fields to feed their horses."

"Nemacolin and that other Indian boy—what's his name?"

"Indian George."

"Yes, Indian George. They are always by his side."

"Did I hear you say that the Indian living down on your creek had been killed?" Robert asked.

William answered only with a nod. He did not want to talk about White Horse today and moved to a new subject.

"Have you been by the church door to see what new postings might be on the dockets for next month?"

"I did not pass by there. Remember your boy took up our morning. That Solomon is going to be your spirited one. Robert paused then remembered, but I did hear some news that might interest you. We had to wait a long spell to get over the bridge and some men were talking next to our wagon."

William turned around to look at Robert. "What news?"

"Well, for one thing the Mason Dixon line was a topic of interest. You told us some of it at Father's burial time. They said Cresap is looking forward to the line getting as far as his place. He is tired of being dragged off again to Philadelphia each time he builds onto his fort. They say that line is almost impossible to read in all that wilderness."

117

"Is that all the news? I thought coming to the town would give us something we have not heard from Dowden's place."

"You heard about the land Parliament has promised to Governor Sharpe?"

"Yes, that was news awhile back. I was not planning on going that far west anyway."

"But it could mean that anyone hoping to buy there, will now come up our way to look for more land."

"Well, you are right to worry. I have not seen a fresh piece of land for sale in several years."

"You know Parliament says he is to have ten thousand acres?"

"Ten thousand acres!" The tension in William's voice rose to a new level. William kicked the dirt with the toe of his shoe in protest.

"I know you do not see eye-to-eye when we speak against the King, but he is making it hard on us. First our ships must go through the English ports so they can collect the duty, and now they are holding the land from us. How long will it be before they tell us exactly what we can plant in our fields?"

William did not have a rebuttal for once. He reached over to pull a long blade of grass from near the wagon wheel and stuck it in his mouth. The men seemed to be deep in thought. Then Robert spoke again, this time just above a whisper. It was obvious he did not intend the words to go beyond their side of the wagon. "They say there is a sure profit just waiting to be made in the crop of indigo down in Carolina."

William continued to chew on the grass until he finally broke the silence. "I will give thought to your words."

"Be sure you do not mention it to the women, or we will be chained to the barn door." Robert said. Both men gave out a lazy chuckle but both knew the seriousness of the statement.

Slowly the men forgot about moving and turned their thoughts to the upcoming events of the fair. By now Thomas Thrasher had joined them in the talk.

The most anticipated and final event of the fair was the parade, followed by the horse races. If you came to the fair you made sure you planned on staying for this big event. And if you had a fast horse you entered the race. The purse for winning could give you a head start on your monies supply for the year. Mostly adults took part in these, with exceptions of a few young people experienced in handling a horse.

But that was for the final day of the fair. For now the children were excited about a new event had been added. It was the kite making and flying competition and a time when the young people could show off their creation. The fair promoters had set aside a goodly amount of monies to the kite that could fly the highest. It was all the young boys could talk about. For them it was their chance to be someone special.

For the Littlefield, Lee, and Thrasher crowd it was John and Absolom's kite that captured the attention.

It had been William who created the interest in the boy's minds to enter the contest when he came home from one of his meetings at Dowdens with the flyer announcing the prize. Now it was time to test their skills.

The hot afternoon sun beat down on William and Rebeckah, as their brood, along with aunts and uncles and younger cousins, all walked together to the grassy knoll just outside the campground. They had come early to make sure they had the best place to watch the contest.

Ever since stories of Benjamin Franklin's success at capturing the lightning with his kite several years earlier, the interest had been big.

William pointed out where John and Absolom were standing.

"John seems to be counting up the other entries." Thomas Thrasher jested.

Absolom was busy unraveling the last of the long tail, trying to keep it from getting tangled. You had to be ready to move fast when the call came to send your kite airborne. For several weeks they had gathered up the scraps to add to the tail, trying to decide how many tails were too many or too few, always testing it when the slightest breeze came up. The kite itself was made from an old piece of muslin once used to diaper Solomon and who knows how many other children in the family before that. The material was worn thin from the many washings in the strong lye soap, giving it a lightness that should make it easier to catch the wind, maybe even better than any new piece of printer's paper, which was out of the question. No one but the very rich would have monies to spend on the expensive paper for something so unnecessary as a kite.

The fact that they had no monies to spend on their kite was not lost to the boys. Life was hard, and on any given day it could be harder. But it did not keep them from hoping their best efforts could win the prize. They had worked for days searching for weeds to dye the cloth shades of purple. When it was finished they had taken it into the treeless field back of their cabin and their father had come to watch. It was then he had anointed it with the words, "Not much to look at, but it sure can catch the wind."

Now it was time to see if it would be the best kite. Rebeckah put her hand over her eyes, shielding the glare from the bright sun as she waited for the starting call to be announced. She wondered what lessons her son's had learned—what lessons they would learn from this experience.

The group watched their older cousins from a spot just behind where John and Absolom were standing. They were as eager as if it had been their very own entry. Benjamin Thrasher, just a year shy of Absolom had already told his mother that he was going to make a kite for next year. So much pride rested on John and Absolom to make a good showing, not only with the surrounding challengers, but with their aunts and uncles and cousins as well.

The wind was doing its part sending the puffy clouds across the sky, beckoning the young flyers to send one on up. Finally, the boys received the order to stand on a mark with their number, keeping in mind to stay within the distance set aside so not to tangle with another kite.

The crowd shouted as each team let their kites begin on their upward journey pulling to the heavens, up then down, causing the kites with too much weight to dive straight to the ground. John held the string tightly wrapped around his hand while Absolom kept the tail free of any ground brush. Slowly they eased it into the currents of the wind and watched as the camouflaged diaper-clad frame pitched and jumped. There was no time to glance around at the other participants. Nor did anyone notice the big cloud hovering at their backs. All they heard was the cheering crowd getting louder and more frantic. Someone must be winning. Only a few kites were left in the air when Absolom turned loose of the last tail, a remnant of their mother's lace trimmed petticoat. He then had time to look around. He yelled at John, "We might be winning." Their kite was so high now that they could barely see it. As the thunder got closer, the cheers seemed to get louder, muffling out the approaching storm.

It all happened so fast. The crowd made a scramble for cover as the sky split open with crooked fingers of light. It was all John could do to keep the wind from whipping the kite out of his hand and he yelled for Absolom to help hold onto the string. But nothing could help. They watched helplessly as the currant caught the offering and twisted and pushed it through the air. It gave up the fight and viciously made a dive for earth.

After the storm subsided, the children went back to look for their twisted and broken kite. Absolom was the first to point it out. The rain had washed away the carefully dyed bright colors leaving nothing of their glorious creation. Dangling from a tree branch for all the fair goers to see was the well-used diaper with a big yellowish-brown spot squarely in the middle.

Their father stood looking up at the kite and in one of his rare moments, spoke, using his truest Shakespearean tongue. "Be ware of glorious creations that doth put on the face of new paint, while surely their destiny bespeaks their humble beginnings." The time in jest with their father was far better than any prize they might have gotten.

On the night before the parade and horse race, which signaled the last day of the fair, Robert Lee's family and the Thrashers gathered at the Littlefield's wagon to share the evening meal and join in on the ritual of prayers for safety. William read the scriptures, as he always did, pronouncing the words in his thick English sound of thees and thous. When he finished, he closed the heavy leather Bible and set it on the wagon seat.

The lamps from a hundred or so wagons sent a soft glow into the night sky and the sound of someone singing from a near by wagon filled the air. The singer was so skilled no one wanted to move for fear of disturbing the singing. One song after another offered a moment few of the fair goers had ever experienced. The light from the fire pits worked a story of its own on the faces sitting nearby. The last one this night was a favorite of William's. It had been brought over with every Englishman aboard the ships sailing across the ocean. William was not a singer, but tonight feeling somewhat free of his inhibitions, sang along with the music.

The song started quietly, almost a whisper. "For when I go, I will not come—Forbid me not to stay—My heart, my love, is in the land where my spirit has not trod, where my spirit has not trod." The song's melody started on one note, going two notes up and working around until it ended where it had begun, telling the story about those leaving their homeland knowing they would not return, and always begging for the blessing of those left behind. It meant the same for every singer, old and young alike, leaving the countryside of their beginnings. It was a farewell song to home.

When the last note died away, there was silence. Only the cry of a baby in a far-off wagon and the mournful howling of wolves at the edge of the darkness lingered.

William did not know how it happened but he was stuck with Solomon for the morning. After giving the child a harsh warning not to run off, they started off for the festival street leaving Rebeckah to shop the markets. He heard his wife call out a greeting to Libby just as he rounded the curve in the road.

"Oh Libby, what a beautiful, bright day it is and just made for our liking." Rebeckah called to her sister-in-law who was coming across the road toward the wagon.

"I do surely agree, Becka, and I'm here with some of my brood to take to the streets of this fair city." Both the women laughed at the freedom they were feeling as they started down the path to pick up Martha Thrasher.

Martha was waiting outside her wagon at the end of the road. She handed three-year-old John to her daughter Mary, while she carried Keziah on her hip.

121

Last nights rain had made the roads a slush rut but that did not bother the group. Nancy and her cousins, Annie and Milly Lee and Mary Thrasher ran ahead to look in the windows. "Oh, mother, come look," the girls called out. "It is one of the dolls they call *Fashion Babies*. Remember Eleanor and Verlinda Dawson told us about them?" Nancy excitedly told her mother. She came back to pull her mother's hand to come look.

Rebeckah shifted baby Mary to cradle on her arm and went with Nancy to look. "I think you are right," she said. She turned to show the doll to Elizabeth and Martha. Both women were struggling to keep their toddlers from getting too far behind while jostling their babies on their hips. "Libby, you and Martha come look at these dolls all dressed with clothes we should be wearing."

The women stood at the store window looking at the doll propped on a shelf as Rebeckah explained to Martha, "Libby and I have a neighbor, Elizabeth Dawson, who has a relative that on occasion goes to London. They came home with glorious stories of seeing these dolls in the store windows. It seems the store owners dress them in beautiful dresses as a way to make the people passing by want to have one made."

"Mother, you would look real pretty in one like this. I would help you stitch it. And Father would say you looked good too."

"Why, Nancy, where would I ever wear something that fine?"

All the while the women protested the elaborate dress, they still could not stop studying how it could be made. "That looks to be made of heavy silk. You would need at least ten yards to make the skirt alone."

"I imagine Mrs. Carroll has ordered something like this before." Martha said. All the women regarded Mrs. Carroll, the widow of a rich landowner who lived next to the Lee's cabin, as the most fashionable person around, whether it be in her dress or house furnishings. Mrs. Carroll was the picture of refinement for the entire county, even if she chose to stay homebound most of her time. If she had a certain lace on her sleeves, you could be sure it was what every woman wanted. Sadly, few women could come up to her standards.

"Mama, mama, wait for us," Benjamin Thrasher yelled out to his mother. Just as the women thought they were free from the older children Benjamin and Ruth and Elizabeth's, James and Richard followed the others, running to meet up with their mothers. Before Rebeckah knew what was happening, Young William and Solomon came from across the street. The children had been standing on the street corner playing tag while their fathers talked and had spotted their mothers coming. As the playful children followed behind their mothers, they paused at each window to cup their small hands over their eyes and peer into the stores along the street, sometimes giggling at what they saw.

When they got to the corner of Counsel Street, the children had run on ahead but stopped abruptly, horrified at what they were seeing. "They are getting ready to hang a man."

The women ran to whisk the children away but were relieved to see it was not a hanging. Two men were being punished by putting their heads secured between two locked strips of thick wood, and his hands placed in slots next to his head, forcing his body to try to conform. Martha turned to the children an explained they were held in the pillory for some mean deed they did. They put a paper with each man's charges around his neck with a rope so everyone can see how mean they were. "Children, see what happens to you if you disobey the law?" At that suggestion Solomon ran back to his mother and hid behind her skirt, pulling at her to hold her back from going closer to the sight.

"Oh, look," Elizabeth pointed, "They are blind you know?" The women watch as the woman lead her three little children across the street. "Robert told me about her when he was on jury last November. She was there petitioning for expense money."

"I remember him telling about them and how she wanted to have funds to take them to Pennsylvania," Rebeckah recalled.

"Robert said she brought an issue of the *Maryland Gazette* with her to show the courts where a doctor said he could heal blind people."

"Oh, yes, I remember now," Martha said. "Thomas told me the courts said they could not be responsible for her problems. I thought to myself, if any one of those men sitting in the court chairs had to lead their blind little children around, day in and day out, then they would have another thought about what responsibility meant."

"What caused all of them to be blind?" one of the children asked.

Young William stood transfixed, watching as they tried to feel their mothers skirt."

Finally, Rebeckah was forced to go back and take his arm to pull him from the torment. "It is time we start back to the wagon or miss the parade this afternoon."

With that threat the children let out a cry with Solomon leading the protest. "No, no, I can't miss the parade. John Ross and Michael are my friends and they are going to ride their horses. Father said he will take me up close to see them." The child pulled at Rebeckah's skirt and then went back to push young William. "We need to go fast."

When the men turned on the corner of All Saints Street, they could see others already standing at the door of the All Saints Church reading from the long sheet of paper nailed to the church door. "Anything important pertaining to the court cases?" one of the men asked. This was a spot where all men came to look for their names. If your name was on it, it meant you were destined to go before the judge, either to be judged by him or to sit next to him in the jury box.

The man who had just finished reading the sheet said, "Well, if your interest is in a hanging, then you'll have satisfaction. It says here, a slave by the name of Toby murdered an eleven-year-old Linchcom boy. They have ordered that the slave be hanged."

"I've heard some really mean ones are being brought over ever since someone has been kidnapping the slaves at the overseas ports and bringing them over to sell."

"Whose slave was it?"

The man turned around to read again, "Says here, the owner was Benjamin Hall."

"I venture to say I do not know him. What does it allow about the slave?" William went to read from the list for himself. *Not having the fear of God before his eyes on the 25th day of December 1763 upon Eli Linchcom did shoot said Linchcom.* William turned around and told them, "He was worth fifty pounds."

"Must have been a big strong slave to carry that much worth. Dealing with slaves isn't worth the loss you have to take when they get in trouble," one of the men yelled out.

"Too bad for Mr. Hall's pocket book," Thomas said.

Before the conversation could go any further, young William and some of the other children were running toward their fathers.

"Mother said if you were going to the races it is time to come get your food."

As usual, it was Solomon that was unafraid when it came to persuading his father by tugging at his coat.

Solomon, followed by young William and Absolom, was the first to reach the field where the horses were lined up with their riders. He pointed to John Ross Key who was just mounting his pony. "There he is, Absolom, I got to ride on that horse. I did, didn't I, young William?" Solomon unabashedly wanted everyone to know about his new friend and his horse. He turned to the man standing next to him and proclaimed proudly, "That is Brad—what's his name, young William?"

Absolom, who by now was getting tired of this attention concerning the horse, answered in a tone less than interested, "Solomon, how many times do we have to tell you his name is General Braddock."

Solomon was not phased with Absolom's lack of interest and continued to brag, "Braddock's horse is that horse's grandpapa. That big boy, whose name is John Ross, told me so." Solomon stopped to look around to see who was listening, then proudly declared, "And I rode it."

A crowd milled outside of the field, restlessly waiting for the riders to start the review parade. The main event would come shortly after the parade, and by now those placing wagers had selected their horses. This year's purse was enough to make everyone nervous.

William, Thomas, and Robert, were standing together at the starting gate when John Seager came up. The men exchanged greetings with John and wasted no time on family or foreign business. The concern of the moment was how much of the allotted wager to put on which horse and as to how much the purse contained if you won.

The women with their children stayed a safe distance away in case a wild horse broke through the gate and ran into the crowd. This was the first year John had been allowed to take his place near the front with the men. Rebeckah could see him from where she was standing and watched with a sense of pride as he talked with the sons of some of the fine people of Fredericktown. She wished now that she had packed his better shirt. The way his worn out linen fell limp from the dropped shoulder revealed they were not accustomed to this type of social exposure.

Baby Mary started to cry from too much sun. Rebeckah wished for the cradle back at her cabin. Her back ached as she rocked Mary back and forth on the hot hillside. She called out to Absolom and young William, who were standing closer to the parade line, to be sure and keep an eye on Solomon. She smiled at the thought of how good this outing had been for her children. They had a hard weeding season ahead of them and maybe the sweet taste of jolly times would help get them through it.

All eyes were on the high platform built for the occasion. The announcer lifted his speaking horn to his mouth. Before each function the honored allegiance was chanted. "Hail to the King, King George the Third, long live King George, long live the King George!" As the chant echoed across the field and died out, the trumpeter stood up and held his long, flag adorned herald trumpet into the air. The crowd stood transfixed in silence.

With one shrill blow of the trumpet, the horses pitched and side stepped, eager to line up. And then the parade was moving.

The rider on the lead horse carried the union jack flag with its cross bars of red on white linen. The next rider carried a bright blue flag with red stripes that flared in the wind, adding to the pageantry of the occasion as the crowd cheered.

"Look, Mother, here comes that little boy Solomon met," Nancy told her mother and pointed to John Ross Key and his special pony. Rebeckah stood up to see. The children felt a sense of pride to know someone riding in the parade and waved excitedly as it moved in front of them. Rebeckah turned to the woman standing next to her and pointed to the pony, "That horse is an offspring of General Braddock's own horse, you know?" No sooner had Rebeckah uttered the words, she felt a red flush come from her neck all the way to her forehead. She had never been so bold as to brag of knowing someone special and to speak of it to a stranger.

Earlier in the day when the families were walking together to the racetrack, William had pointed out to Rebeckah the horses that had been winners before. She had kept an eye out for them as they passed her place and had spotted the surefooted shiny black horse with a star on its forehead. It sidestepped and pitched, showing its anticipation of being turned loose on the track. According to William, it had won the purse last year and a big purse it was too. The races were what brought most people to the fair, and William had allowed that this year's entries looked very promising.

And now as she stood watching the prideful owners and riders, William's other words had come back to her as well. "Maybe we should enter one of our colts in next years races, Rebeckah" She still felt the shock of his words. Had the excitement of the social outing taken a hold of his senses?

Rebeckah watched the riders turn at the top of the track, and caught a glimpse of someone, a child probably, darting in and out of the crowd on the other side of the field, in pursuit of the parade. The horses obviously noticed it too, several becoming unruly, prancing and rearing up and pawing in the air, some breaking out of the parade entirely.

Suddenly, the announcer with his big speaking horn stood up. "We demand the parents of the boy who is responsible for this outrage to come get him immediately."

And in horror she caught sight of William in pursuit of the boy, and she knew. She just knew.

Chapter 12

April 1764
A Long Trip Home

William sat stolidly, looking straight ahead and not saying a word—not one word. In fact, so humiliating was the event that ended the parade and almost the race, that no one was saying anything. They had left without even saying good-bye to the Thrasher's or Robert Lee.

All the children had to take the punishment, as well as Rebeckah in her own way. She felt sure of one thing, and William had already said as much, they would never be asked to go anywhere with him again. Rebeckah wondered what the future held for them. Oh, they would see the church reader when he made his round every six months or so, but that was only for the time it took to read the scriptures and say a prayer, then he would be gone.

John was fifteen. He could go out on his own by now. Nancy at thirteen would grow up without even the slightest idea what other women were learning. That thought made her want to burst into tears. It was bad enough to have only a few trips when time allowed, but to be disallowed because of something someone else did was so unfair. But if she spoke out against it, William would become even more stubborn.

Rebeckah leaned over the back of the wagon watching the wheels imprint the soft ground. Her mind was sinking into despair with thoughts of defeat, thoughts of giving up, thoughts of—William dying. This last thought brought her out of her silent mood with a suddenness that scared her. The thought of his death as a means of escaping his anger was disturbing. How could she think such an unforgivable thought. Tears flooded her eyes and she tried to stop them with the sleeve of her dress. But not before the children saw their mother's distress, and Nancy and young William moved closer to put their arms around her. John and Absolom said nothing. They were too old to abide by the innocent, freely given love of girls and children. Solomon was asleep next to Nancy. It had been a hard day learning the difference between excitement and control.

The day dragged on. There had been so many travelers going into town to the fair that the road was nothing but one big rut hole. The road crew would be sending for John to help smooth them out. The thought held some consolation to Rebeckah. At least, he would be given the opportunity to see new faces and know what was happened outside the *William and John.*

Maybe she could work on the road. That thought made her laugh out loud. The children turned to see what was happening that made their mother dare to utter a sound with their father so mad. The break from anger made her feel better.

The day had been cloudy and sunset came early. They were still too far from home to go the distance, so William was forced to find a place to stop the wagon for the night. It would have made him feel safer had he seen someone the last few hours to ask about any Indian sightings. But they had mainly traveled alone for a big part of the afternoon.

William climbed down from his seat and secured the oxen for the night. He had heard one of the wheels squeaking more than before and sent John and Absolom with the grease bucket to dab a stick full of thick grease between the wheel and the rod. So far on the trip, the wagon had not broken a wheel and the bottom still held them above the ground. Tomorrow could be another story when it came to repairs for the wagon.

No words were passed between Rebeckah and her husband even as she handed him the quickly made journey cake. Nor did he talk to anyone else but John when he handed him the second rifle and told him to bed at the end of the wagon. He put his bedroll at the front on the hard ground and was not sure they could survive the night if the Indians came upon them.

William awoke to the sound of thunder in the distance leaving him ill willed and more than a little anointed at Rebeckah who had run out of grain last night. She could only offer them each one cold journey cake left from last night's meal. She quietly told the children to not complain. She would make a decent meal just as soon as they got home. He yelled at John to begin loading the supplies back into the wagon. It had been a cold night and sleeping on the ground had left his back stiff with pain. Pulling the reins tight, he drew the whip back and let it go with a crack. The wagon gave a jerk and started rocking into the rutted path.

No one was one the road. Everyone that had been going to the fair had made the trip in time for the races, and no one but the Littlefield's had left before the race. But then they did not have a Solomon in their family. The scorn William felt of yesterday had not changed, and he vowed to not let it be forgotten. He swore between clinched teeth, "How could my name have been so disgraced." His temper boiled easily and this embarrassment had surpassed anything committed to his memory.

The wagon hit a large rock, disrupting his thinking momentarily. The wagon tilted precariously to the side. This only added to William's annoyance and gave him reason to raise the whip. The oxen bolted. He vowed to give his family enough work to drive any thoughts of "fun time at the fair" out of their thinking. If his family was seen as being well disciplined and God-fearing, it would help restore his name among those that knew him.

Once they arrived home, William handed out orders that everyone was to be up one hour earlier than before, and they would not be allowed to bed down at night until all the chores given to them were done.

It had been well over a month since the family had returned from the fair in Fredericktown, and Rebeckah had not found a moment to do anything but work.

The days and nights were consumed with fixing the meals for the few hired hands William had used. And if there was any time leftover, William expected her in the field beside the others. Nancy took care of baby Mary and kept the kitchen garden tended. And Solomon had to rake the barn each morning and clean the hen's nests and gather the eggs. And if he broke one his father gave him another job to do before he could eat that night. As if work was not enough, William set out the schooling books and tablets. He insisted his own children would know how to read and write and do the numbers. So while the children ate their meals, he would render the numbers to them. Even Solomon was made to repeat the lessons, even though the meaning was lost to him.

Rebeckah stood beside the table rubbing her aching back, listening while William gave the rules for the day. She dared to complain in front of the children. "William, the way you are working us, I'm not sure I will live long enough to see you get your good name back."

Before William could finish the assignments, the dogs began growling outside the open door.

William walked to the door to see who was coming but there was no one around. The dogs had settled back down. Satisfied no one was there he turned to go back to the table.

With the assignments finished, William and the boys left for the day. It was just barely daylight, and Rebeckah already felt tired to the bone. Feeling faint, she sat down on the bench. Was it the work that had caused this dizzy feeling or the green apple she could not help but bite into last evening. The craving for the sourness was more than her common sense could withstand.

William would be expecting the water for the new plants he was setting in the ground. She did not know which was worse, the thought of his scolding or her dizziness. Again, the lightness in her head warned her of something.

She wearily pulled herself up from the table and started outside to pick up her water buckets. "After I take the water to your father I will be in the apple orchard this morning. Bring Mary to me when she is ready to nurse."

She started down the path, then turned back to remind Nancy to not be afraid to blow the new horn William had made if danger was close.

William had hollowed out the horns of a big bull, and if you blew into it in the chimney, it could be heard all the way to the field. Rebeckah and the children knew it was not to be used lightly but for only extreme danger.

All morning Nancy worked at the jobs her father had set out. Besides taking care of Mary so her mother could work the fields, she watched the pot of stew for the midday meal to keep it bubbling and started to churn the butter from the milk her father kept outside the door in the big wooden barrel. Not every house in the colonies had butter, but her father had a cow that gave enough milk to wait for the cream to come to the top. Butter making was something Nancy liked to do. The time spent pushing the paddle up and down gave her time to dream about her life outside of this cabin and all the places she would go. It was one of the few jobs in the kitchen that didn't require attention.

But even now, her dreams were interrupted. Baby Mary had been fed early that morning and now was demanding something more. She cried a lot of late because she would not take the milk from the feeding bag her father had made out of a gut of the cow. He had done this so her mother could get more work done in the fields. And today Nancy had forgotten to save out some milk for her before she made the butter. Nothing would stop her crying this morning.

Nancy gathered up the baby and started for the apple orchard to find her mother.

Just as she passed the barn on the path that led to the orchard, she heard someone getting ready to come out of the barn door. She could not see who it was but he was. And it was not her father, she had just watched him go into the field. She ran as fast as she could, carrying the baby to her mother.

Rebeckah was standing on the ladder picking off any bug infested apples to keep them from ruining the entire crop. When she saw Nancy running toward her the first thought was that something terrible had happened to the baby. She climbed down and ran to meet Nancy.

Nancy yelled out the warning to her mother. "Someone is in the barn. It isn't Father or the boys."

"Did the dogs bark?"

"No. I think I saw them follow Father to the fields."

William had taken the rifle and Rebeckah decided they should go to him for safety. But to get from the orchard you had to either go by the barn or forge the creek. This time they would take the creek in case someone was hiding in the barn.

Rebeckah grabbed the baby and together they began to climb down the muddy creek bank, full of thick tangled vines just ready to catch your step.

They lifted their skirts as best they could, always fearful a snake twisted somewhere under the murky waters and would wrap around your leg. When they reached the other side and started to climb the bank, Rebeckah looked up. Her heart jumped in shock. Nancy reached out to her mother in fear. Standing at the top of the bank, partially hidden by a tree, was White Horse. Or, at least it looked like the old Indian. He did not utter a sound nor did he move.

Rebeckah's heart began to race with fear. She had never before been afraid of the old Indian until now. There was something strange about him. Not wanting to scare Nancy she did not say what she was thinking. He looked the same as when he was killed. Obviously that had been a misconception. If this was White Horse, then a cruel lie had been laid upon the family by their longtime friend.

Very cautiously she called to him. "White Horse, is that you? Absolom and young William saw you die." She stood waiting to see what he would do or say. But he made no response. Finally, he turned and walked back into the trees.

Nancy spoke in a whisper, "Mother, what is wrong with White Horse?"

"Go tell your father. I will go back to the house with the baby." Rebeckah now felt fairly sure it was the old Indian who had been in the barn earlier and why the dogs had not barked.

Later, William and the boys searched for White Horse but did not find even a trace of the old Indian. He was a sly one and could hide his tracks if he did not want to be found. But why did he feel the need to hide. That was a more serious question to William than where he had been all these weeks.

There was nothing else to do but wait for him to come back on his own.

Night after night, when William had taken his rakes and hoes back to the barn he could not help but ponder what he should do next to find the Indian. He needed him. Always before when his tobacco crop looked sickly, he had only to ask White Horse and he would pick up a yellowing leaf and tell him exactly what would stop the withering if it was not too late. No one knew better than he did which crop to plant first after the frost, or predict the growth of a tobacco plant. Nor could anyone cure ailing cattle like he could.

Now today, William thought about what Rebeckah had said last night. At the time it had caused his back to stiffen in argument. As much as he did not want to admit it, her thinking held merit. He was losing valuable time when he insisted that only the children should bring in the crops on this side of the hill, all just to show the neighbors he was in control after the embarrassing incident at the fair. The jesting from those that heard the story had finally stopped. Now all they said was to point out that his crops were

131

slow in coming this year. Rebeckah had as much said, if he failed to bring in his crops it would do nothing to save his good name.

William closed the barn door and looked back out into the fields. Maybe it was too late to regain his name among his neighbors. Even he was beginning to feel no matter how much he worked the family, or how many extra bails of hay they stacked, it would do nothing to help his honor. The thought of starting over was working at his mind. This morning he resolved if Robert Lee still had plans to move to the Carolinas, he would consider moving as well.

Chapter 13

July 1764
Lower Seneca Creek

For weeks, each time a wagon was heard rattling down the road, Rebeckah caught her breath. Rachel was here. But each time she came away from the door disappointed.

Just today she had gotten her hopes up when they saw the dust flying. But it was a man from somewhere down by the Seneca Crossing. He had come to ask William to look up a meaning in his Bailey Dictionary. This was not the first time a neighbor had come for help. It had started when they first moved to the *William and John.* Somehow word had passed around that William had brought a big book from his home in England with all the words in it. So through the years, it was no surprise when someone knocked on their door and asked him to look up a word. This morning William had found the word and explained the meaning so the man could understand it. Evidently, it was not to the man's liking. He had asked a question of William, then showed his emotions by repeating the word and spitting on the ground in disgust. For those who came to question, some words just did not say what they wanted them to. The man had climbed on his horse and laid the whip to its flank all the way down the path. That was the end of the visitor, no news, no thank you, just a spit on the ground. William only shook his head and reached over to pick up his rifle. "Let's go boys, our work here at the house is finished for now—the fields await."

Rebeckah watched her husband and sons head for the fields and went to the table to look at the list he expected her to do before midday. As she turned to go she noticed William had left the dictionary on the table. She knew he would be sorely upset if she had not put it back on the shelf by the time he came back. He possibly cherished his dictionary more than anything in the house. The thick book had been given to William by his grandmother after his grandfather had died. He had used it through the years of his tutoring. When he came from England, he had brought the dictionary as proof to anyone that he and his brother were not indentured servants brought over to work off a crime or debt of passage. A free traveler was allowed to carry extra baggage, unlike an indentured man. And William was a very learned man, so it was expected of him to carry a book like this on his person.

She picked up the thick book and ran her hand down the black leather spine. The words *BAILEY'S DICTIONARY* were spelled out in big bold gold lettering. She tried to remember the word the man had come to hear that morning. All she could remembered was that William had turned to the front of the book to find the word.

She always tried to remember the big words she heard so she could prove to William that she could learn new things.

Rebeckah opened the book to a page close to the front and let her fingers run down the words, but could not find the one called out this morning. She saw one William had used before and sounded it out, A*l-le-giance*. She tried to read the words following it as best she could. *Obligation of loyalty,* it said. William knew about loyalty. He was very loyal to the King and to his old country, that she knew.

She rubbed at the water spot on the page and remembered William saying he had left the book open while teaching some children traveling to the colonies on the same boat with him. A big splash of salt water was caught by the wind and lashed up on the pages. What had it been like to get on the boat in a country you had known all your life and go over all that water, then to walk off in a brand new country? As she closed the book she noticed a string hanging down from the insides and out of curiosity opened it to the pages to see what William had marked. It was between a page with the words all starting with the letter P. A listing at the middle of the page caught her eye. It showed a title. William had taught her what a title was. It said something about it being a proverb. She liked the proverbs that God had put in his Bible because she could understand what God was meaning to say. She read the words out loud. *"Little Pitchers have great Ears"* She started reading the smaller print slowly, picking her way through the meaning. *"This proverb is a good caution for parents and others, not to use too much freedom in discourse before children. For that their sense of hearing is not only so quick or quicker than that of older people, but also because they have long tongues as well as wide ears and their innocence often divulges what their elders would have kept secret."*

She had never heard God's verses being in the dictionary or that he spoke of children as little pitchers with ears. She would have to admit to William that she had tried to read his book instead of doing the work if she was to ask him to explain if these were really God's words. William liked for her to learn, but not when he had given her work to do.

Just one more word, she decided, then she would put the book away. She wanted to find something she had not tried before. She played her game of shutting her eyes while holding the book closed. Then she opened it to a surprise place and let her finger find a word.

Rebeckah opened her eyes and did as William had taught her to do. She began to pronounce it as the markings showed. *Il-le-gal.* She read as best she could from the definition. It said *Forbidden by official rules.* This was fun. She had been successful in finding a good word. Just one more word and she would put the book back on the shelf. She spotted a large word with lots of markings. *Il-le-git-i-mate.* She pronounced it again, reading out loud the word, then read the meaning, *Not legitimate; born out of wedlock.* Her pulse raced as she stared at the book.

Quietly, almost reverently, she closed the book and took it back to the shelf and stood for a moment at her window, transfixed in her thoughts. She quickly grabbed the garden basket and went down the path. Falling on her knees in the early morning dampness, she dug her hands deep into the cool dirt. With each weed she pulled, the word seemed less painful.

By the midday meal she had cooked a table full of garden helpings, including freshly caught fish from the creek and a pot of squirrel stew.

William looked at her meal with surprise. "What caused this much work today. Have you received word of company?"

At first Rebeckah made no effort to give a reason. Finally she offered, "I guess I was just hoping Rach would come." But she knew the reason had nothing to do with her sister.

Dust was again seen coming with a rider but it still was not Rachel. Thomas Dawson, returning from the Dowden's tavern, had stopped by to give William important tax news. He had gone straight into the field with the news.

William had later explained to Rebeckah that the tax news Thomas had brought was something he had heard the man named Graves McIlvain speak of when he was at Dowden's a couple of months ago. The enforcement was just getting as far as the province. The tax was on the sugar they used, along with some small items that did not mean much to their lifestyle. Since the Province of Maryland did not make rum to sell, it would not affect their tables that much.

Rebeckah could not help but think how she liked the sweet gentle taste of the white sugar in her puddings and cakes. For now though, she chose not to worry about it. The cone shaped sugar loaf sitting on her shelf had barely begun to wear down.

By the end of the week, Rachel had sent word as she always did by way of the Madden brothers or her own brother, John, when they had traveled the Fredericktown road. They would drop the letter off at Dowden's Ordinary. And in turn Mrs. Dowden would hail down a traveler coming past the Littlefields road trusting him to deliver it. And if no one was coming that way, Mrs. Dowden would just hold it until someone came. It was never known how many messages fell to the side of the road for lack of interest in carrying it all the way. This time William luckily happened to come by the ordinary on the day he took the oxen slings into the blacksmith shop for welding.

When he handed the half-torn-off paper to Rebeckah she knew it was from Rachel because of the small flowers neatly drawn and painted with flower dyes all around the border. And it was just like Rachel to not waste the costly paper by sending a full sheet. The message said, *Wil not hav tim to cum to ur place on wa to cort hous.* Rebeckah tucked it in her sleeve and went back to dunking the wash up and down into the kettle of boiling water. Her thoughts were the same as before when she had expected family to come; they never had the time to drop down this far off the main road just to visit her.

July was not half over and the crops were looking dry. If rain did not come soon the family would have to all go to the creek and carry buckets of water to try to save as many of the plants as they could.

William looked at his crops that evening and wondered if he could leave long enough to go into Fredericktown. Word had come that a committee was submitting a petition for another place of worship closer to this county line and all votes were needed. Because of the distance, most of the families in this part could only get into to All Saints once or twice a year at best. And the scripture readers sent out from the church could not possibly visit all the parishioners. This need for a new church was twofold. The ministers wanted the monies the parishioners would bring in and the landowner had to have the credit on the church rolls. Without a man's name on the church roll the landowner had no right to a voice in the making of the laws for the province. That was the rule; no excuse a person might give could undo the ruling. This fact alone made William and his neighbors make the trip to add their name to the petition.

William had another agenda as well for going into town. It had to do with the schooling of children. He had heard that the governing assembly of the state had decided book learning was a good thing in moderation. It was his understanding that the land was to be in Fredericktown. That was fine and good, but he wanted to let them know the children out here in the far edge of the county had learning needs too.

If he offered to give enough of his land to the county to build a school he thought they might listen to his petition. He would offer himself as the teacher. That was how William Norris was chosen as the teacher of All Saints Church School. Of course, it probably had a lot to do with the Reverend Thomas Bacon who had been so supportive of education. Now with the new rulings of the state, William hoped to be considered.

The monies from teaching could pay for someone else to oversee his farm. After all, he had been trained in England for just such a cause, and it was time he used his skills for something more urgent than a good corn crop for the pigs.

William finished writing out his letter offering his skills and set the pen in its holder and put it back on the shelf.

"Rebecky, where did you put that letter I had telling of my schooling experience?" William called out, all the while rummaging through the trunk Rebeckah kept next to the window. By the time Rebeckah could get to him, as was his practice, he had thrown out everything to the bottom of the trunk.

"William, I don't keep it there. It is on the shelf with your dictionary. Now what mess you have dealt me," she scolded as she began to pick up the clutter of strewn baby clothes, old mittens, and a fur piece she had saved to make a collar. A half-rolled yarn ball slid loose across the floor, and she ran to retrieve it before it unrolled all the way. She picked up the portrait of the new King George III, painted shortly after he was seated on the throne. It had been sent from England, by the lawyer William's sister had used to settle the family affairs. She looked at the picture for a moment, then turned to her husband, "William, if the next baby is a boy, would you like that we called him George after the King?" William took the picture from Rebeckah and looked at it in the candlelight, then handed it back to her. "I will let you know—I prefer to wait and see how they plan to treat us before I commit a child to wear the name."

Rebeckah went on piling the plunder back into the trunk and closed the lid softly as if to protect her prize possessions inside.

William had found the letter on the shelf and sat down at the table to review the contents. This was the first time he had been this close to something so important since he walked onto the boat to come to the colonies. Learning was close to religion to him. And it was time to practice his learning.

He finished reading, then stood up stretching his arms out and announced, "Tomorrow I will go to Fredericktown to deliver my papers."

When he put the papers in his satchel for the trip he turned back to his wife with a puzzled look. Rebeckah, what did you just say? Something about the next baby being named after George, after the King? What are you telling me?"

Rebeckah, not knowing if it was true or if it was the hard work that gave her reason to suspect it, she simply said, "Time will tell," as she continued picking up the mess William had made. The possibility did not come with rejoicing. Especially after the way William had been treating them all like slaves, although he had begun to mark through some of the chores, leaving them more time to rest.

The sun was going down by the time William reached the edge of Fredericktown. He turned at the Market Street and headed to the ordinary to take a bed for the night. But to his surprise the sign said the building was now occupied with James Dooley's chair shop.

William guided his horse down the dusty street and could see a woman scolding some children throwing rocks at her door. That was one nice thing about living in the country, you didn't have to bother with the neighbor's boys. His horse tired of being reigned in, began high stepping, ready to break into a run. William pulled harder on the reigns and the horse began side stepping in protest. Finally, he gave him what he wanted and they moved swiftly through the town. At the corner he slowed down when he almost ran over some young lads hanging together in the street. As he passed, one of the boys yelled profanity in his direction. He paid them no mind and just kept riding. But it did bring to mind the actions of the minister at All Saints Church, and how Reverend Bacon had been so upset he went to the courthouse to appeal for a law to put a stop to evil speaking. Evidently, whatever decision the courts made to stop it, had not reached the ears of this rowdy bunch of young men.

The sign on one of the buildings, advertising he was a Peruke Maker caught William's eye. He climbed off his horse to look through the windows. His interest went to the wigs, each secured to a blockhead and lined up on a long table for showing. Rebeckah had been complaining about the one he was wearing and he had agreed to look for a new one. If by chance he was to receive the teaching position, a new wig was essential.

Next door to the wig maker, William noticed some women coming from what was obviously a boarding house and he remembered Rebeckah telling him he should look up Rachel who would be in town for another court appointment. He quickly got back on his horse. The thought of encountering Rachel made him anxious to move on. She would surely expect him to handle some business for her, and that was not why he had come to town. Besides she was probably retired for the evening, fearful of getting out on the streets after dark.

A few adventuresome children ran into the street to take chase of William, while a boy walking on tall stilts came crashing down just in front of him causing his horse to jump, almost throwing him from the saddle. William stopped the horse, pointing at them, and yelling out, "Be gone with you or I'll pin your ears back." Nothing had been lost when it came to William's authoritative voice as a teacher. The children ran quickly to their own front stoops, thinking someone important had come to town.

He turned his horse around and started back south after finding no tavern. The houses were even few and far between here. He had hoped to hear the town crier. Now it was too late. Thomas Dawson had been by his place over a week ago to give him the news of the Sugar Tax. Surely by now other ships had come into the ports with updated news.

The sunset scattered brilliant orange-red colors across the western sky, probably forewarning rain by morning. If the tavern on Carroll Creek had a space on a bed, he would take it, otherwise he would have to pull the blanket from the back of the saddle and sleep on the ground, rain or no rain.

A number of horses and some with wagons still hitched were crowded around the small tavern. He stopped to look for a tree he could sleep under or other protections from the elements. Once inside William took his place with the other men at the table for a filling meal of mutton and baked squash and enough sweet apple cider to wash it down. As always, he complained about the cost of a meal but was willing to hand over his hard earned monies in the end.

Finally, he wiped the last of the cider from his mouth, feeling invigorated about coming to town and the purpose for which he had come.

He went to the pipe rack and selected one, then took his place with some men leaning against the mantel of the now empty fireplace. The talk so far had been about the savages causing panic in the wilderness section where Colonel Cresap made his fort.

Much to his disappointment, he heard no news of the British.

By now the room was filling with smoke from the heavy smelling tobacco. As William stood for a time, sucking the last draws on his pipe, he could not help but notice a man sitting with a somewhat younger fellow at a corner table in the dimly lit room. Between swigs of cider, the older man had been ranting on about something with Benjamin Franklin's name tucked between oaths.

William looked around for a table, exhausted from his long trip. All he wanted was to think in solitude and make some notes before he met with the trustees. As he passed the table where the man had been carrying on, he met the eyes of the old man, but William did not speak. The man kept talking to the emaciated form of a boy seated across from him. Then unexpectedly he yelled out to William, his tongue heavy with drink, "This is my boy, Henry. He sits with me sometimes. We've been studying on how the wagon got broke up. Old man Franklin took the wagon, you know." The old man spit on the floor while waiting to finish his complaint. "Drang him, he took all the wagons."

William said nothing, hoping to sit in silence, but it was not to be. The man turned his head around and addressed William again in a much louder voice.

"I just told you old Franklin took my wagon. What do you have to say for that?"

Not wanting to get involved with the man, but feeling he needed to set the facts straight, he addressed the question. "It has been my understanding Mr. Franklin just asked for volunteers, that is all." William did not realize how much he was getting involved by speaking up.

The old man struck his fist on the tabletop. "Ben Franklin came to my place and took my wagon. Said he needed it for that general's war. Said he was fighting the French. Frenchmen, that's who we were fighting. And Henry, here, thought he needed to find some patriotism." It took the old man three tries to get the word right, but that did not stop him. And with disdain he spoke General Braddock's name. He began to cry shamefully through his drunken stupor as he said, "They got my boy struck senseless, they did."

During the conversation a man William had heard addressed as Isaac, walked over to William's table. Appearing to be of means, the man was dressed in a green-colored high-pocketed coat, which he had unbuttoned on this hot July night. He tapped the table where William was sitting to get his attention. "I was standing right here watching General Braddock and George Washington converse the war."

Isaac wiped the table with the back of his hand, enjoying his notoriety by telling what he knew of the story. "They had their papers spread out on this table making plans for the battles."

The man paused for a big gulp from his tankard, then continued. "George Washington was not much over the twenty year mark, still just a boy, just about the age of this boy." Isaac pointed to the poor young Henry sitting next to his father. "Braddock chose George Washington to be his aide-de-camp. Guess you have heard the story." He did not wait for William to answer. "And I would say we all agree Braddock took a good choice." The man looked around the room for agreement before he cleared his raspy throat with another drink. Now that he had an audience he walked over to lean his arm against the mantel. "General Braddock was a man of vicious words. Never once that day did I hear him say words of praise for his men." Isaac shook his head slowly emphasizing his own words.

William listened, not wanting to encourage Isaac to continue, but afraid of how he would look if he tried to stop him. The recent French and Indian War was dear to the hearts of these colonist. Before he knew what was happening, other men began crowding around to be a part of the telling. Gradually they forgot about the old man and his simple-minded son, leaving both to mumble through their thoughts.

A man of lesser refinement stood up. "I was here that week. 1755, April it was. Came to Fredericktown thinking to buy a new rifle, but not a rifle was left in town. Ben Franklin was in charge of gathering up the supplies for the British and he got them all."

Another man yelled out from across the room. "We were standing at the edge of town as the wagons went by and we stopped counting them after 150 wagons rolled on the road. Some of the wagons were so loaded it too four horses to pull them up those steep mountains."

The men continued to add their thoughts on the subject, jumping around the room from one person to another, making it hard to tell who was voicing what.

"We couldn't even get enough wagons to carry in the supplies to finish the courthouse. Guess you all remember that? The shortage was bad, real bad."

"Before General Braddock ever got to Fredericktown we had been forewarned about all the soldiers coming."

One man proudly bragged, "When the ships came in my brother's boy, Zeke, happened to be over at the Virginia port of Alexandria that day. He heard someone yell out, 'The Englishmen are coming' and he looked out at the water's edge and there was a procession of big ships with their sails full of wind for as far as his eyes could see. No one knew what was going on— at least not those standing next to Zeke."

From the man's story the men in the room heard how Zeke was powerful frightened to see all those men in one place dressed in their fancy red uniforms marching off the big ships. "He said they sounded like a herd of wild horses tramping over a bridge. It took a lot of supplies for each soldier and before it was over each carried off several trunks apiece. Someone said they all were full of those fancy uniforms. When the soldiers started lining up to march, Zeke took off running so he could tell everyone back home to go out to the main road to look."

William listened as several men told how it took several days to march all those men to Fredericktown, each with a different story. Some came through Rock Creek while others split off and some came up by Clarksburg. The roads were just too narrow and marching single file was too slow.

A man just coming through the door wanted to be part of the story, "I'm from Winchester over in Virginia and some of them came our way in their flashy red uniforms. It was quite a show they put on us with those long rifles over their shoulders. Just about blinded a person when the sun struck the barrels just right."

William at first had no intention of joining in and started to read a paper he had picked up at the front. But when someone called out to ask him if he was living here at the time of the war William was forced to join in. "I live over on the Great Seneca not far from the banks of the Potomac. I like you, loaded up our wagon to participate in seeing the King's troops march through Clarksburg. I have to say it was a proud day for an Englishmen. I have never seen such precision marching. They never missed a step." William went on to tell how the people saluted the soldiers, some by removing their hats and placing them over the heart. "One woman standing beside us started screaming out with joy when she spotted her brother marching passed. Seems he had stayed back in England when his family moved to the colonies some years before. She said she didn't even know he had joined the King's army." William kept thinking of more things to mention as the crowded room listened. "The sound of the chanting *long live the King, long live the King* was contagious that day. Most of the women and children brought gifts of food to give to them. With such honor bestowed on them, is it any wonder they felt free to ask for our help with the wagons and horses. There was no demanding that I could see. Some of the people followed their hearts there on the spot that day and turned over their wagons. We had to make several trips back to the place to take them all back to their cabins after that."

A man in the back rudely yelled back, "If you were so proud to be a part of that, why did you not give them your wagon?"

Then someone else yelled out, "Let the man speak. I like the way the way the man is talking."

William stood up to defend his actions. But before he could speak, a man with a commanding attitude took a step forward. "And I felt the same pride as that gentlemen over there," he said pointing to William. "When I saw the several hundred tents sitting on the hillside near Clarksburg near sunset. I had come to deliver food my wife and other women had made that day for the young men fighting for our cause. It had been an unusually hot day and I was rightly afraid a storm might be brewing. I noticed the clouds forming to the north."

Another man just waiting for his chance to speak said, "I saw it too, I was only a short distance from there when I met up with my friend Zopher. He had been at this very tavern some hours earlier and had witnessed General Braddock sitting at a table making plans for the war. I guess the General just did not think of how the weather could change so quickly out there on that hill, else he would have put them down in the valley."

Another man eager to talk picked up the story, "We stood a little distance from the camp and watched the soldiers work like ants swarming a colony. Every tent had its own campfire. None of them seemed to suspect the approaching weather. They just sat watching the lazy smoke from each campfire. The need for kindling was so great that before they pulled up camp most of the underbrush had been cleared for miles. Maybe if they had known about the weather coming they could have gathered larger pieces. Kindling won't warm that much."

The stories continued. One man said he brought enough pork to feed them, and told how the mill had set aside a days grinding to give them enough meal to make their journey cakes. "I remember how one wagon after another pulled up with jugs of cider to give them something to drink. The men were real friendly and talked a lot about the war plans and how they were going to beat those Frenchmen into the ground the first day out."

The man with the friend Zopher again managed to break in. "Well as I was about to tell you before someone took my speech—" The men laughed knowing how hard it was to keep the floor when everyone wanted to talk. "It was sunset and we thought we better bed down in a farmers barn, because it sure looked like bad weather. Sometime before morning the freeze came. By the time we got back up on that hill to take the road home, we heard that those men of Braddock's were turning blue in the cold. I heard one man froze to death when he fell into the creek while fetching water to make breakfast. That wind was blowing ice with it."

"Friend, I know of what you speak." A new man just coming in spoke now. "I was here in this tavern when the General got the news that his men were freezing to death out on the hill side. All he did was just wave the messenger off, unconcerned like. We couldn't believe he would feel that way about his own men."

The cook at the tavern had come from the kitchen to clear the leftover's from the table, all the while listening to the men talk.

Finally, hearing enough she stood up straight and wiped her hands on her apron, looking squarely at the man talking. "I saw them, too. A bunch of complainers they were. That big fat one they called the General was a pain in the behind." The men laughed at her unlady like talk. But then they expected it of her, as she had worked at the tavern for years and knew how the men talked. "He came to town thinking he was the high and mighty. I say, 'an arrogant bug is a cocky roach'—that's what me says. He called our boy, George Washington, some really bad sounding names. And I didn't set with that. Then that man you called Ben Franklin rode his horse into the back real fast. He was in some big hurry. Brought his son with him too. Seemed like nice enough boy. But he didn't have much to say. The three of them—Braddock, Washington and Ben Franklin had plenty to say." The cook took the cloth from her shoulder and wiped up the droppings on the table while she continued to talk. "They messed around with my tables putting all these cross bars marks down with some chalky stick. I heard them tell someone that is where the soldiers were to line up when they got to the fields. I had to cook some real fancy food with the pigs roasting all day, and every time they needed something I had to stop and bring it to them. I worked all day getting the food ready just to the fat man's likings. When I brought it out to the men, that man you call Ben Franklin just turned his nose up at it. He said he didn't eat meat anymore. So I had to go house to house around town to find something besides meat to keep his belly filled while he was here. Real strange, I said to meself. Not eating meat seemed real peculiar." She bent over and picked up a large load of dishes and waddled to the kitchen. The men went back to sucking on their pipes.

An unusually tall man had come through the door unnoticed. He leaned over to William at his table and asked if he might sit down. William pointed his hand to the chair as a way of inviting him to sit, not minding the interruption of the war talk.

"I've just come in, but I surmise they are talking of the late war?" the man said.

William told him it had all started when the man had complained about the wagons being taken.

"I can see how they felt." The man reached out his hand and introduced himself. "I'm called Johann Jacob Brumbaugh, but mostly find the name Jacob fits comfortably."

"By your German calling name and accent with which you speak, I surmise you were not born in the colonies. I haven't seen a lazy German come to these colonies yet. You people do a fine job with your farms. Do you live amongst us here or are you traveling through?"

"I was orphaned at an early age, so decided to follow my aspirations and came to the colonies about the 1750 mark." Brumbaugh went on to explain he set up his farm close to the border near Pennsylvania, and on this day was headed to the warehouse at Georgetown to pick up supplies.

"So you live close to what they are calling the Mason Dixon line?"

"Ja. I live near the mile of where I am told they will bring the chains." Before the two men could discuss the land any further, they were caught up in the conversations still going around the room.

A man standing at the fireplace noticed Jacob and pointed to him. "Don't I know you? Were you the man that bedded down the General and Washington up near the Pennsylvania line? I was guarding the General's trunk. We were bedded down at your house for several days." The man talking turned to address the men in the room. "This man was one of few men I saw that could get the General to stop bellowing out orders." Then he turned back to Brumbaugh "You were building a big house with fireplaces at each end and you had heavy oak doors and floors, almost like a fort they were so thick.

Brumbaugh answered in his deep voice, "Ja, I have thick doors." Jacob laughed and added, "Ja and two big fireplaces."

The man again turned to address the room, "We were almost starved by the time we got to this man's place and he butchered two hogs so we might fill our bellies." The man turned back to Jacob Brumbaugh, "There wasn't a wife as I recollect rightly, so you did the cooking."

"Ja, I had no wife."

"Your German was still so fresh on your words." The man turned back to his audience. "We thought the General had to stop talking so he could make out what Brumbaugh was saying. Couldn't understand him very well." The men in the room laughed at the thought of the General stopping to listen to a German man. "Didn't the General try to get you to join up with him?"

Jacob addressed the man's question. "It was because of my belief to religious teachings that kept me from fighting."

"Yes, but you did go as a packman and bring in the supplies we needed." The man turned back to the room. "General Braddock could be so hard headed about what he wanted and he refused to listen to Washington on how to route the army through the mountains. Washington being a surveyor knew what the wagons could handle. But the General always came back with the answer that he knew how to move the army better than any colonist soldier." The man turned back to Brumbaugh's direction "But let this Brumbaugh speak his word, and the General listened. There was just something about his soft speaking I guess."

"I just gave him what he needed," Brumbaugh said.

"This man takes not the credit he deserves. It was because of him many of us were saved. Just too bad the General did not pay that close attention. Maybe he would not have taken the bullet. After the battle that killed the General and so many were injured, this Brumbaugh single handed set up a place for the wounded to come get their strength back. He fed them and housed them and what ever else they needed, he tended to."

Jacob Brumbaugh laughed softly, half-whispering to William, "It was because I cannot hear too well that I talked softly. Had nothing to do with my disposition. I can be as hard headed as the rest." He stood up. "I need to be getting on down the road tonight. If you are ever up to see the new state line coming in, take a meal with my wife, Mary Elizabeth, and me. By then the cradle should be filled."

William watched Jacob leave, then went back to listening to the others still haggling over who did what in the war.

They were talking about what a smart man George Washington was and how the arrogance of General Braddock is what got him killed, along with hundreds of the colonist boys as well.

"The British figured colonists to be untrained fighters, when in truth it was the Englishmen that knew nothing about fighting the Indians."

A man sitting unnoticed in the dark corner of the large room stood up, his large gold buckle caught the candle light when he stepped forward. William noticed he spoke in a deep educated voice. "We lost many fine horses that did not need to die. The General knew nothing of our high mountains and what it took to take the over loaded wagons up those inclines. Once a horse lost its footing it was gone."

The men agreed. "I saw big strong horses collapse and die trying to pull those cannons up and down the mountains."

Something in the talk must have triggered Henry's simple-minded head because he acted like he was back on the mountaintop with the General's men. Sitting across from his father, he began to yell out, "Yes sir, yes sir—I'll get this horse up the hill, sir—he's my horse, sir—don't die, oh please, don't die, Old Red, don't die, don't die."

The men watched the young boy as he began to fight that fateful day all over again. It was evident his horse had been overcome with the heavy load and died, just as the man had been describing. The boy began to convulse through his cries, "It was too heavy—the cannon was too heavy—don't hit me—don't hit me—my horse, my horse." The boy put his hands up shielding his head against what he remembered. "Don't hit me." After this last outbreak the boy fell out of his seat and his head hit the floor with a thud.

Several of the men stood over the boy not knowing if they should lift him to his seat or let him lie where he had fallen. His father looked at the men standing over his son, "I told you; he's gone senseless."

What was once a burning desire to tell the story was now just a flicker of interest. A few men agreed with what Henry had been reliving. One man watched as several men carried Henry outside to lie on the ground and turned around to tell the others, "All the troops could do when the horses died was unhitch them and push them to the side and keep marching.

William decided it would be a good time to ask the owner about renting a bed, but just as he got up another man he had not seen before walked over and stood where William was intending to go.

The man that pointed out Jacob Brumbaugh to the men stood up. "There is another deserving person we have failed to give honor to"

"Who—who are you talking about?" one of the men asked.

"We have spoken of many men tonight worthy of our credit, but no one has mentioned Doctor Craig." The room seemed to all recognize the name and stopped talking. If you were among the injured you would remember him. He tried to save the General Braddock from his wounds—he doctored him for three days, but no instrument he had could save the general. Over nine hundred men fell during that battle, and Dr. Craig took care of most of them. He kept Washington alive as well. It was a miracle Washington did not take a bullet. It was close though. Four of his horses fell dead with shots intended for him. After Washington said the funeral sermon for the General he began to get real sick. Some speculated he had picked up something from the stench of all those wounded men. We thought Washington might die right there on the battlefield the way he was bending over with the shakes. Dr. Craig took him in a wagon back over to Brumbaugh's big house—that's the house of the man with the heavy doors. Brumbaugh and Dr. Craig just would not let him die. And to this day Dr. Craig is George Washington's doctor. I know because he lives on the land next to mine. I still see him loading up his wagon from time to time. Sometimes he tells me he is going to Mount Vernon to check on General Washington's health. I cannot say if he doctors Martha, ah, Mrs. Washington, or not—probably not."

The talk seemed to die away with this last story about the Doctor. So again, William got up to go ask for night quarters. He spotted a boy sitting in a chair at the far side of the room. The boy raised his hand shyly, wishing to be heard. Unlike the others, he did not stand up to talk. And on this hot night he had a blanket over his legs. The voice was so weak William wondered how he hoped to get the attention of the rowdy traveler's. But it was his demeanor that made the men stop and listen.

"I know all about the Dr. Craig"

With a voice turned old; the boy began to talk. The story appeared to be about the beautiful traveling coach owned by the Maryland's Governor Sharpe.

At first, the men in the tavern were not sure how this story related to the boy doing the talking, but they listened. Some in the room agreed they saw what a fine coach it was, having been on the same road when Governor Sharpe would be out for a ride. And one related how he had been in Fredericktown the day the Governor had met with General Braddock at this tavern.

The men listened intently to talk associated with such a fine spectacle of wealth. "It had curtains you could open and close, and it sat up high on shiny wheels. Lanterns hung from the front to light the way and the inside was lined with green velvet. Some thought it was surely the King George himself riding in it because it was so fine."

"General Braddock let it be known that he wanted that as a gift from the Governor," the boy told the men.

Another man called from the door, "I heard Braddock tell the Governor that if he would give it to him he would see to it the King would give him favors in return."

A man sitting next to William leaned over and whispered, "I don't know if that is a true story or not, but the men like telling it that way." William nodded his head at the man but did not reply. He was more interested in what the boy was saying.

"By the time the King's soldiers pulled their tent stakes from the ground to move out, it was General Braddock who was seated inside enjoying his new travel arrangement. The coach was so heavy it took six to eight horses to keep the wheels rolling, depending on how high the mountain was."

The young boy started coughing and someone found a tankard still half full to help his cough. After a gulp the boy went on.

"The General had us colonist soldiers walk behind it. We soon found out he had us there so we could lift the coach out of the deep ruts, or when the driver had to go under a tree, the limbs would catch the top and we would have to put the coach back on the road. The day the General decided the coach was not going to make it over the mountain without tumbling down the side, he abandoned it and took to a fine horse. That was when he made us shield him with our lives."

William asked, "You mentioned knowing the doctor? How did that come about?"

The young man defiantly ripped the blanket from where his legs should have been, revealing only the dirty rags covering what was left. The Indians helping those Frenchmen came upon us and took their tomahawks to any part of our bodies they could hit. They got the heads of the first three in front of me and almost got my head, but I moved in time. He got both my legs with one cut. They said my blood filled the rut I was standing in. The man behind me pulled me off the path. I still know the pain. Dr. Craig came to my side and had to take the legs off right where I was lying. Oh, it hurt. He took a knife and cut the flesh away from the bone, then took a hammer and knife to break the bone away. That is all I remember. They tell me I yelled so loud the men on the other side of the mountain could hear me."

William felt sick at his stomach when the man, really just a boy not much older than his son John, finished telling the story. He went over and picked up the blanket and put it back over the dirty bandage. "You are brave, my boy, and we are proud to hear your story."

After that, the men seemed to have had enough of the war. William felt the need for fresh air and walked out into the night. After a time he pulled the blanket from the back of his horse and leaned up against a big tree down by the creek. Sometime in the early morning hours, he finally found sleep.

Chapter 14

July 10, 1764
Fredericktown

Rachel waited for a wagon to pass, then stepped onto Second Street on her way to the courthouse. By now, Thomas Betterton would be waiting for her at the front doors. Breakfast at Miss Phoebe's boarding table had been slow this morning, making her late. Oh, how she hoped Thomas would wait for her. Thomas would be in the middle of harvest now. If she did not get there he just might think she had not come, and leave before he could vouch for her integrity of the possessions of her father's inventory.

Maybe after today she would be released from this taxing duty. The family had worried over her every move since her father died, almost giving her the feeling they were afraid she might withhold something from them. Oh, the sisters, well most of them, had not questioned her, it was the men who were worried. John and Ann Hughes were probably at the house even now, waiting for her to return to get what was coming to them. On the last visit Anne had tried to copy the list the appraisers had forgotten. The thought almost made her laugh. Anne or John neither one had good skills at writing.

Rachel wondered if the family would have treated her mother in the same way if she had still been alive and handled the will papers as her father had written. As long as Rachel could remember, Mary Lee had never protested when something went wrong. She had held her feelings to herself. Her response would usually be, "Life is short. Don't waste your breath disagreeing." Her mother would smile her quiet smile when something had crossly been directed at her, usually by some family member, and reach out and pat the person on the arm, then walk away rather than cause a fuss. Oh, how she wished she could feel her mother's hand on hers just one more time. But she was on her own now, and what she had been taught had to hold her up.

Running the last block to the courthouse, afraid to keep Thomas Betterton waiting, she could see someone pacing back and forth in front of the door. It was Thomas Betterton's brother William waiting, not Thomas.

She was more than a little upset that he was the one to come and her voice showed the displeasure. "William why are you here, I thought Thomas was coming."

He took a long look at Rachel. "It is about time you got here. The court has been open for a time. If the family sent you to do the business, they have the right to expect you be here on time."

William Betterton was obviously taking his brother's place of which he was no match. Thomas was tall and well cared for by her sister, Eleanor. And William on the other hand, was William. And he found no reason to set himself up as anything other than the rough cut person he was. Rachel just plain did not like this man. He was arrogant and sarcastic. And why, she did not know. She remembered when he first came to live with Thomas, it was rumored his wife had died and he seemed to resent all woman. Even Eleanor had suggested William was hard to understand.

"I told them not to expect you to do anything with the will," he gloated.

Rachel was sure it made no difference to the courts as to who came to vouch for her trustworthiness. It just had to be someone that knew what was going on at the Lee farm. But if she had the choice she would have told him to leave. His coming made just one more unpleasant thing for her to deal with. She straightened her shoulders and looked this man squarely in the face. Her voice held an edge to it.

"William, your inconvenience does not match what I have had to go through since Father died. My not coming on time was not of my own making. I came as soon as I could." Rachel did not want to give him another reason for sarcasm so did not tell him she had to wait for a later than usual breakfast to be served. But she did leave most of it on her plate to get here.

William shrugged his shoulders and changed the subject away from her excuse. "Are there any other family members here that could handle this? Thomas heard Alexander Grant was bringing a stray horse in to be registered. Have you seen him?"

"My brother John delivered me here late last evening and we were advised by a stableman at the ordinary that Alexander had been by there earlier. That is all I know. I have not talked with any others outside of the boarding house today."

"So if John is here, why did you think Thomas should come? I did not have time to waste to come in for nothing."

"William, I am truly sorry for your time. Dennis and Anastasia Madden had planned to bring me but his father was overcome with the hot sun and they had to tend to his needs. Dennis came by to see if John could bring me. We had already sent word to Thomas some time back about coming, so John thought there was no reason to stay. He left just as soon as he set my bag down on the doorstep, and I suspect he is halfway home by now," Rachel explained.

"Well how in the blazing sun do you hope to get home? I guess John Hughes was right when he said you do not plan ahead rightly well."

Rachel tried to control her feelings against this man but it was still with sharpness in her voice that she corrected him. "William, I consider that my business, and I can do without your judgement of character. I would appreciate it if you would leave these decisions to me or at least my blood family. It just so happens my brother John or Dennis Madden will come for me in three days. I shall spend my free time here shopping for supplies."

"Oh, so you are going to waste more of your family money with shopping. Each time you come to town, staying in a fancy place like that Miss Grave's boarding house costs monies."

"And pray tell me William, where would you have me stay?"

William did not take the time to answer that question but went on to add to the accusation. "The men in your family are concerned they all will be shorted their monies if you don't stop this foolishness," William said with a slight twist to his mouth.

"I have a list of necessaries. But as long as I have to be here I just as well enjoy seeing what new things are becoming of interest," Rachel replied in defiance. By now, Rachel realized others standing around were taking note of the disagreement.

"Buying up all sorts of new wardrobes, maybe? Well, dearie," William paused to smirk, "I've been asked to help find a husband for you, so consider how much of a dowry you will be expected to bring to the wedding."

Rachel stopped abruptly, her mouth open. Had she heard his last comment correctly? She turned quickly, face reddening, to look at Thomas's brother. "You what?"

William looked puzzled at her response, then laughed. "The men in the family feel you will be having to come live with them if they do not take control and see you get help with your father's farm. A spinster just can't handle the work."

Rachel had lost all her fears of making a scene, something until her father's death and her need to handle the affairs, would not have happened. "How dare you try to decide what I can or cannot do. I plan to hire good help just as soon as I finish up with father's will."

"The families reputation has to be considered. It does not look proper for you to be left alone with a hired hand," he said as he walked away from her toward the court house door.

Rachel's response was frozen in her throat. So this is what the men had been planning? She had wondered why those that had come around her cabin since her father's death had taken such an interest in the land. They were planning on making a deal to some man and all under the guise of protecting the land. She could just hear them say, "You take her as your wife and then you get a good piece of land, with a cabin in return." That is why none of her brothers-in-law had tried to buy the land from her." To do that would mean she had no place to live and would have to come live with one of them. It took the complete arrangement if they were to be protected. She had bought *Maiden's Folly* that joined the portion of the home place her mother and father had given to her, with the hopes of arranging her own life as a farmer woman. This was to be her protection from unforeseen trouble. Now her own family was attempting to chart her future.

Her thoughts fumed in her head as she reached for the door handle, and in her frustration she stubbed her toe on the top step, almost causing a fall on her face. She steadied herself and realized she had better get control of her thoughts before she met with the clerk or else they would think her incompetent to handle the will.

As before, a pinch-faced man seated at the front door inquired as to her name and the meaning of her business. As she gave him the information about the inventory, she had the unnerving awareness that this man was surveying her entire body before he spoke.

"Very well, I propose you should be at Mr. Bowles table." He sorted through a number of papers, then wrote her name on the long sheet. "They are very busy today, and you can wait over there."

William followed her into the room, and deciding it was too hot inside, said, "I'm going back outside."

She took the fan from her pocket and began to push some air over her face, all the while reviewing the conversation with William Betterton. The anger that rose within her made it seem hotter than it was. The realization that her family was trying to manipulate her into marriage was more than infuriating it was heartbreaking.

She wanted to cry at the thought of how her family was willing to discard her. She could not shake the words William had imparted to her soul. He just as well have declared her the most unloved of all the family.

A woman came to sit next to her and began to talk, giving her something other than the pain to think about. As they talked, the woman complimented Rachel for being so well fixed. "For me, I do good just to get dressed to come to the street. No time to fix up."

The woman stood up to leave, making it necessary for Rachel to stand up to let her by. She caught a glance of her own features in the reflection of the window behind her. She still had all her teeth, and at thirty-four that was somewhat of an accomplishment. Her dark hair was pulled back with a slight puff to it, and she had let an unruly curl hang loose to the side, like a woman she had seen at the Carroll's house just a few weeks ago. She was fortunate to work on occasions for a woman that entertained such finery. How else would she know what was going on in the outside world?

When she again sat down she took pains to smooth the skirt of her new blue and white dress. She probably should not have tired to make it for the trip with so many chores to do. But Mrs. Carroll had unexpectedly sent over some left over materials ordered from the West Indies or some place like that. Mrs. Carroll always ordered her materials from far countries, and when they came, she usually had bought more than was needed. Rachel had worked for Mrs. Carroll since she was a young girl, so knew she could count on the leftovers, but she sometimes had to wait for several years between dresses until Mrs. Carroll's seamstress finished making the Carroll family wardrobes. Today's garment was an especially favorite one because of the color. Rachel's mother had loved the color blue, and she smiled now as she could hear her mother's words, "I feel so lively when I see blue."

A sudden thought crossed Rachel's mind. Maybe she should have worn a dark dress, seeing she was coming to the inventory of her father's death. A black dress would have been good. But even if she had thought of this before, she had no black dress.

The courtroom was filling up fast and Rachel watched the court clerk discuss the court business being filed today. There were suits concerning unforgotten debts, suits for trespassing on properties, beggars wanting a handout, stray horses being registered, and a few vouchers requesting monies for jobs done on court business. There were even new rulings being posted for the public to read.

Several items caught her attention. A man named Thomas Reynolds was being paid for a long list of jobs he did for the court. She almost laughed. The thought of this man running up to the front of the court house to cry the case and then running back down to begin mopping the floor and before he could finish someone called out to tell him he needed to beat the drum. What a busy man he was and tired too by the end of the day, she imagined. They were paying him four pounds and that seemed like a lot of monies.

Another man was filing for money because he had built the gallows, made the coffin, and dug the grave. Another very busy man, she thought to herself.

The next man to come to the front was a downtrodden man of unkempt appearance. He fairly swaggered up to the clerk's table. The crowd began to chuckle at his manners. The clerk shook his head as if not knowing what to do with this man. Before the man could plead his case the clerk stopped him from speaking. "I suppose you are here for more pension monies? Where's your badge? I warned you the last time not to come without it penned on your shirt. You know that is the rule. How else can we tell you apart from others?

The man made an attempt to explain. His use of words gave the feeling he was used to making excuses and getting by with them. "I looked under my bed for it but it was gone. My wife did the washing last year and I never saw to it again. If you give me another one, I'll tell her to leave it on my shirt so I will have it when I come to you. But you know, those tin things really do hurt when you roll over on them." It was obvious the man did not take his badge as serious as the courts would like. Again there was a response from the partitioner seated around the room.

The clerk reached in his drawer and handed a shiny new badge to the court usher. The old man was doing some kind of jig like he was being hurt as the court helper attached it to his shirt. The old man was not shy in putting on a show and turned to the others and bowed. Everyone applauded.

The clerk, not taking this case as serious as some, called out to him, "I'll be watching for you, and you better be wearing it or I'll take your pension away from you."

After the man left things got serious again, revealing some filings that were not so lighthearted. Rachel listened intently when the case of a white woman named Tessie Blaylock was being entered into the books from an earlier meeting with the courts. Rachel watched the young woman standing before the clerk, hugging her baby who was still too small to walk. A man with a long wavy white wig stood by the table and read from a paper. The people in the small courthouse had stopped talking and were intent on what was about to take place.

"After much talk about this case the clerks all came to the conclusion that the wench's skin is lighter than this child's is, so that being, we had no choice but to reason it was born from a slave living on the place where this woman is indentured. This mulatto baby-child is to be sold to the highest bidder at twelve noon this very day." The woman erupted into a scream as the man forced the baby from her arms and dragged her from the room. Don't take my baby from me—no, no—no." Rachel put her hands over her ears in an attempt to shut out the cries of the small child with its tiny slightly brown arms reaching out for its mother. Rachel was forced to remember again the pain she felt the morning the indentured little "want-a-bes" left in the wagon with Miss Lucy. Even after several months their sad eyes still haunted her dreams.

A man stood up to address the clerk, but before he could say anything the clerk asked a question. "Why are you here again? We paid you for the last hanging you handled."

"You owe me for the hanging of that last slave that shot that boy."

"What? What are you talking about?"

"I think his name was Toby something. I hung him like you wanted."

The clerk stood up, obviously upset. He pointed his finger in an accusing manner. "You are trying to charge for something that has yet to be ruled on." The clerk turned to a man sitting next to him responsible for scripting the entries in the large book on the table. The two conferred as the scripter flipped hurriedly through the pages in the book.

Rachel turned to the man on her left. It was so unlike her to make conversation with strangers but she felt comfortable to do so in this place. "What are they talking about?"

The man began to explain that the slave named Toby was found guilty by the court, but before he was to be taken away the court judge had deliberated about the ruling with several witnesses. Because of Toby's reputation of being a good person from the heart in so many people's eyes, it was decided to send the case papers up to Governor Sharpe to make the ruling. The most honorable Mr. Dulaney, himself a friend of the Governor, was carrying the papers to the Governor.

Rachel watched as the man in charge of hangings was irate by now and all but yelled at the clerk. The voice sent fear through Rachel. But why?

The clerk sensed the man was trying to unlawfully get money and told him to leave his courtroom.

The man began to swear.

The clerk stood up abruptly, his voice harsh, "That will be enough. There are women in this gathering."

The man again told Rachel that the man causing the trouble was hired to take care of the bodies of the men they hang. "I've seen him before. This slave, Toby, they are calling out about, shot an eleven-year old boy named Eli Linchcom by placing a gun to his ear. I was here when they brought him in and I'd have to admit he was of good manners. His owners came in and told the clerk he had nothing but good things to say about the slave." A woman on the other side of Rachel, having heard the conversation, leaned over and confided to Rachel, "Of course, what else would they say. They stand to lose a lot of monies if their slave is hanged."

Rachel raised her head again as the clerk yelled out to the man. "We will deal with you at the next court. Now be gone with you."

Her eyes searched out the man as he was leaving the courtroom. Who was this man with such a rude, gruff sounding voice? Where had she heard this man speak before?

The lady next to her again whispered "I've been seeing this man on the streets of Fredericktown many times in the company of some unsavory characters. Someone said he might be associated with another man that went around stealing slaves." The woman pursed her lips together and shook her head as if affirming her knowledge of the story.

It was not just the story the woman had told but something about this man that gave her such an uneasy feeling. Her thoughts started considering all the places she had been of late and who might have spoken to her in this gruff voice. It wasn't anyone around Chestnut Ridge. And she had been nowhere else but to Fredericktown in the last year.

The clerk called for the next entry and Rachel began to look around at the crowded courtroom aware her name was surly coming up soon. She could hear the woman sitting next to her tell another person that the boy up front was her neighbor's boy, and she felt so sorry for his mother not having him at home. Rachel turned back to listen to the clerk. "John Campbell will be an indentured servant to learn the art, trade, and mystery of a weaver." The word art struck Rachel, and she stifled the sound of shock. That was where the voice came from. Her mind quickly forgot about the case being entered and began reliving the afternoon she walked past the painter's sign. That was who it was. It was the portrait painter or at least someone that visited his place. He had knocked her down when he came out the door of the shop. Now the next question in her mind was why was this man so interested in carrying out the punishment of the slave and to do it without a witness as he had been instructed? He had used the same rude, gruff, accusing voice that he had addressed her that night and again as she and Elizabeth were walking to court that day. She wondered how a person could make a living out of hanging people. And why did he not have a witness as they required?

Rachel felt a tug on her sleeve. The lady sitting next to her was motioning to the front of the room. "I think he is pointing to you, miss." She looked up to see the man at the desk pointing in her direction. Rachel jumped up so quickly she dropped her fan and had to stoop down to retrieve it from under the bench. How inept she must look to the others in the courtroom. Flustered, she walked to the front of the room where Mr. Bowles was seated next to the large side window. It did not seem to help to cool the room down, but at least you felt if a breeze was out there somewhere it could find its way in.

Mr. Bowles had begun to shuffle through some papers, leaving Rachel to awkwardly stand before the filled room. She brushed at her skirt to push out the wrinkles, then nervously pulled her hair tighter into the knot on top of her head. She felt the color creep up her neck and face, but there was nothing she could do to make it stop. Finally Mr. Bowles looked up at her face with suspicious eyes and pointedly said, "What's your name?"

"Sir, I'm here to present my father's inventory as you requested." She handed the inventory that Andrew Heugh had left at her house and started to explain that it had been left, but then stopped. She was beginning to feel more in control of her business and if this man needed to know why it was she who was presenting them, then he could ask.

Mr. Bowls looked through the list, "Have you anything else to add to this inventory of your father's possessions?"

"Yes sir, I found these items that had been missed, as far as I can tell. I tried to read Mr. Heugh's report and didn't see them scripted in." She handed the clerk the piece of paper that in the last few minutes she had nervously managed to roll into a tight tube.

Mr. Bowles took the paper and preceded to unroll it then looked up at Rachel. Eyeing her for a moment, he looked down at the paper. "I say, Miss Lee, there is nothing to be nervous about. You will find it not unusual to come back with recent findings." He looked at her writing for a moment then asked, "You found a parcel of beans—and some lumber—and what is this word—a small bett?"

Rachel felt the color come up her neck again. In front of all those sitting in the big room of the court, it was obvious to them that she could not scribble a legible word. What had possessed her to think someone could read her scripting? If only she had taken the time to go to William and Rebeckah's before coming here he could have written the words out from her list.

"That word is bell—the kind you ring—a bell—a small bell." She made a ringing motion with her hand, then realized how silly she must look. She again started to explain in a rush of words in one breath, "One of my sisters had stuck it in the crevice of the cabin after the meal at the burial. We were all laughing about how our mother always made us take it to the field. My sister wasn't trying to hide it. It just fit in that place, so they had left it there." She suddenly stopped. Who was this man anyway but just someone that wrote down the facts? But she did repeat in a loud strong voice to make sure he heard it this time. "A bell—it is a small bell," she said, emphasizing "bell" as if to say it was his eyes, and maybe his ears as well, not her writing that was at fault.

To her surprise Mr. Bowles seemed to lose his boldness. "Miss Lee, ah, please, won't you sit down here," at which time he got up from behind the desk to push a chair over to her. "Now, let us go forth over the items one by one."

After the marking of the inventory, Rachel gave a sigh of relief, as she watched Mr. Bowls lift his pen to set the date of 10 July, 1764, to the bottom of the page, then add the word Tuesday after it. When he looked up he had a serious frown on his face and she wondered what could be wrong.

"Now about the debts listed. Did you bring the papers from the debtors saying they have been paid?"

Rachel must have looked puzzled, because Mr. Bowles went on to say, "You do know the estate cannot be closed until all debts are paid and you bring a paper from—" He stopped to look at the names again listed at the bottom of the paper. "A Mr. Thomas Cramphlin and Mr. John Peters, stating they have been paid?"

The room seemed to get hotter and Rachel opened her fan and began to force the air across her face.

Mr. Bowles called for one of his aids to bring the water bucket around to his table and offered her a drink.

As she took a sip of the tepid water, she awkwardly began to explain "No, sir, I was not told. I thought I could pay out of the receipts after it was settled as long as I had their agreement."

"Since that is not the case, how do you plan to deal with the debt?"

"I—I will find a way. My father no doubt was unaware he still owed the monies or they would have been paid. The Lees have always pay their debts."

"Very well, I will set a new date for the final hearing of the inventory and will send you word. It is wise to take care of it soon. It is not the policy of this court to let things to go unsettled. And one more thing, who do you have coming to vouch for you aside from the ones who signed for the sureties?"

"My brother-in-law, Thomas has sent his brother, William Betterton to vouch for me."

"I see." He called to a young boy waiting by the door and told him to go outside and call out Betterton's name.

When William came in he was all kind and nice to Mr. Bowles, like they knew each other from a long standing acquaintance. It was as if he forgot that Rachel was the one doing business here. And when he had finally signed his name, he left without making a motion to even show he knew Rachel. Rachel watched as Mr. Bowles added his signature to the bottom of the page. She held her breath for fear there would be another shock coming, but to her relief Mr. Bowls put the papers inside a large brown leather bound book and stood up to shake her hand. She wished her brothers-in-law were here to see this. This would show them that she was capable of handling the affairs of the estate just fine without a man telling her what to do.

As she was about to go, the clerk called her back, "Miss Lee, this is apart from the records, but one advice I feel you should know about. It concerns your debts to Mr. Peters. He has been known to take the land for an overdue debt. Just be advised not to let it linger any longer."

Rachel thanked him and smiled for the first time during the inventory reading. Not so much because it was over, but because she had handled the family issues to satisfaction.

Once outside, the heat of the July sun hit her face and almost took her breath away, but she could not let it deter her. She had to do the shopping today for the next few months in case John or one of the others came back for her by the end of the day. Her list was long, but she had already decided it would not be prudent to try to carry back everything in one wagon. She would see if one of the other family members would carry some back to the home place at a later date. Today she would order the farm tools she would need if she were to work the new strip of land. This season would be a good time to try some of the new seedlings that Mrs. Carroll had offered. She was told they had been purchased from the English country catalog that was sent once a year to their plantation. How glorious it would be to surprise the men in her family with some never before seen crop. But that was dreaming, and she had no time for such foolishness.

She wasted no time window looking but reached into her side pocket for her list and began mapping out in her mind where she needed to go.

First on the list was the part for her old spinning wheel. Jacob Grubbs came around to the farm each summer to repair things. He did a good job of keeping her wheel turning, but last year he had warned that it would not stay together another year. She needed to have the part ready for his next visit.

Next on the list was Greely Hite's Clocksmith Shop. It set two doors down from the spinning wheel shop. It was a quaint little house that you knew owned clocks, because of the sound, even before you opened the door. Mr. Hite was a short little man with a long white beard and a friendly smile. He had come from Germany in 1733 and still talked German to those coming from his homeland. As she entered the shop, she could smell the sweet smell of oiled wood and hear the soft ticking of time from all sides of the room. And everywhere she looked, tables held small parts and pieces of clocks laid out ready to assemble. There was something so pleasing about coming into this place. Maybe it was because Mr. Hite and her father had conversed well together the time they had come in many years ago. It brought back good thoughts of that visit.

She introduced herself and explained she was in town to file her father's inventory. "I just need something to tell me when it is time to start for the church readings or when to make dinner for company—not that I have that much company, but I always like to be ready." Mr. Hite suggested one from the wall display that had a mellow chime that would not scare her each time it signaled the hour, but one loud enough to be heard from her garden. Mr. Hite assured her it would be ready to be picked up when she came again to court.

Rachel had turned to take the road back to the boarding house when she remembered she needed to go to the potter's shop on Church Street. She would not forgive herself if she returned home without a milk vessel with a good lid. The one she bought on her last trip had a crack in it.

As she walked through the long narrow shop, pottery of every shape and color and size faced her from shelves on every wall. She knew she would have a hard time deciding which one to buy or how many she needed. There were at least twenty shelves full of beautiful pottery in many different styles and textures to choose from. She chose three and had the owner pull them down to set on the table. They would deliver it to the boarding house that afternoon. The first one was to replace the favorite jug she always kept her maple syrup in. It had been sitting on the floor next to the table the day Rebeckah's sons, William and Solomon, were chasing Robert's children around the cabin during her father's dying days. What a mess they had made when it broke. It must have taken her sisters half the day to clean up the gooey mess, and to this day she still felt her foot attach when she stepped there. It had been her best jug and the one she could lift up on the shelf without a struggle. She chose carefully the next two. A smaller one to keep the butter in after she finished churning and the last one needed to be large enough with a tight fitting lid so she could store the buttermilk in the cold creek water and not have a possum fill his stomach from it.

Rachel hurried out of the shop intending to go straight to the boarding house for the noon meal, but thought better of it. If she was to get all her shopping done before someone came for her, she better forgo the meal and collect the dress she had the seamstress make for her on the last trip. She had been so excited to have a dress made from the blue calico but now wondered if she had been too hasty and frivolous. Now that she had made the one from Mrs. Carroll's scrap material she did not need another one. But she had already paid for it, so there was nothing to do about it. She dreaded what the family would say when they heard she had two new dresses, especially two blue ones. There would be no peace concerning her monies after that.

As the seamstress took it out of its covering, Rachel felt a rush of excitement just like the day she had selected the material. Turning to the lady, she realized she must sound foolish when she said, "I'll never hope to get another dress as nice as this as long as I live."

Once outside the shop, the sun was placed well past high noon and she suddenly felt hungry. Maybe if she slipped in and they were still sitting at the table there would be some leftovers that would satisfy the need for food. But she would not ask to be served properly. Miss Phoebe had been reluctant about renting to her after the ordeal of the indentured servant children, and she had promised not to make trouble again. The thought in an odd sort of way almost made her laugh. What would her family have to say if they knew their obedient shy sister had almost been kicked out of a boarding house, even if it was to protect the children? The brothers-in-law would feel they had reason to take her away to one of the asylums built for funny people.

When Rachel arrived at Miss Phoebe's, three older women, two introduced as sisters, were just being unloaded at the front door. Miss Phoebe invited them to come to the eating table as soon as they deposited their belonging to the rooms and she would see that the cook brought the food out for them. Rachel shifted her packages and helped carry a satchel up the steps with her free hand, giving reason to escort them back down to the table. Miss Phoebe, not wanting to scold out right, raised only her eyebrow as Rachel sat down beside the well-dressed women. Rachel began talking about what a pretty dress one of them was wearing, leaving Miss Phoebe and her eyebrow unheeded. The one thing Rachel had learned on these trips was that she did not have to accept the scolding of anyone but herself—and maybe the court clerk.

After the meal, Rachel quickly washed her face and tightened her hair before going back to the shops. Time was short, and she must finish marking off her list. It was essential to buy the supplies on this trip, because you could not trust the weather to be agreeable to a wagon wheel or family to have the time to shop for her.

She headed for the end of Church Street where she had been told she would find the bridle and saddle shop. Once inside she explained to the owner that Mr. Heugh had just taken her father's inventory and was told she should buy a new harness for the plowing, as the old one had rusted from the rains. While standing at the front waiting for the man to figure a price, Rachel was almost overcome by the smell of wet leather sizing in the tubs in the back room. She put her handkerchief to her nose to hold the strong odor away. It reminded her of going to the Maddens when Dennis was sizing the leather for his shoe cutting. She never could understand how Anastasia could stand being around it when she was counting off the first days before a baby was born. But as always, dear sweet Anastasia always tolerated anything her Dennis could do.

Rachel paid the monies and gave instructions to have the harness delivered to the boarding house that afternoon. Out on the street again, she crossed the small bridge over Carroll Creek, and had the urge to stop and dangle her feet in the cool water. Her tight fitting shoes had again blistered her feet. Oh, how she wished she could go barefooted like she did at home, but a lady had to keep up appearances when in public. Or, that was what her sister, Anne had decided. She had issued the rules before Rachel ever started on these trips. From her talk to Rachel, she seemed to often feel embarrassed at the lack of properness by her sisters.

Two boats were trying to dock along the edge of the slippery bank, and Rachel paused to watch. She enjoyed seeing what was being brought into the different town shops. Her thoughts wandered to her lack of monies to spend on things other than the necessities of the farm. Her mother and father had given her the land and enough monies to get by on. And now it was up to her own dealings to make things work.

She checked the crumpled list in her pocket once more and looked around to see the blacksmith shop. She had been told it had a very good smith that could repair the old door latch. She braced herself for a rude encounter. It was a place dominated by men, and they did not take kindly to a woman intruding into their world of welding broken plow handles, wagon tongues and other pieces of equipment waiting for the hot coals to make them new again. Talk was the only thing that interested them on this hot day.

She shielded her eyes with her hand to see through the smoky darkness. The men standing around the room, idling their time away with no good, began to make throaty responses at her presence. Rachel pulled the courage from somewhere and asked in an authoritative voice, "Is the owner here?"

A voice behind her said, "Homer, there is a woman in here needin' your ex-purr-tese," and the others snickered as if his statement was an inside joke. A large man appeared out of the darkness, wearing a shirt that resembled the black of the fire well, with his ragged shirtsleeves rolled up to his arm pits. He had massive arms that could hold a hammer to the fire with no trouble. "I'm Homer. I can take care of you." The laughter spilled out of the dark smoke-filled caverns of the shop. Rachel had the urge to turn and run out of this horrid place, but the truth was, if she was to work the farm, she had to hold her own with unpleasantness such as this. "I've been told by the blacksmither near Rock Creek you are possibly the only shop that still would bother to repair the old fastener my father placed on the door of our house. It is a very old piece once owned by my grandparents, and I wish to keep it in workable condition."

The man listened to the description of the hinge before saying rather bluntly, "Sounds like it isn't worth the bother. You'd do better to have a new one forged."

"I'll tie the door shut before I will put a new latch on the door," she said, turning to go.

"Now hold on here. I didn't say I couldn't fix it. Bring it in. I've blacksmithed harder than the sounds of that."

Thankful to be finished with this man and his friends sitting around the sides of the room, she turned too quickly and ran into a plow handle being repaired. She stumbled, falling with her hands spread out to catch her fall. A roar of laughter erupted from behind her. Enraged at their lack of manners, and the way they made offers to help pick her up, she quickly stood up and wasted no time in finding another street out of their sight.

Thankfully, that had been the last shopping she had to do on that side of town and decided to go pick up supplies at the candle shop. She usually saved the fat from the slaughter to make her own but the wicks always burned down so fast. Anastasia said she had tried the wicks bought at the candle shop and they did not burn down so fast.

Rachel stood for a moment at the street corner trying to remember where she had seen the sign cut out like a candle holder with a white candle and even painted to look like the flame flickering from it. You could not misjudge what that was supposed to depict. It had fancy scripting on the bottom that said *Candles by Susanna.* When she came to Counsel and Record Street she could see the sign hanging from the roofline of a house.

Once inside the shop, she could hear someone talking in the back room. Rachel had remembered her mother talking about buying candles from Miss Snively when she had come to town on the few occasions. She remembered because her mother had commented about her having such a good shop that her mother and sister had come to help her make the candles. One look around made Rachel wonder what had happened to the neat lace curtains and well-polished furniture that her mother spoke of. She saw nothing about the place that was neat. There were candles melting in the hot sun, and through the kitchen door, she could see food still on the table. She called out, "Susanna—anyone—I wonder if I could bother you for a purchase?" Still nothing. She was sure she had heard talking from the back room when she came in. As Rachel left the shop, she couldn't help but puzzle over why Susanna had left her shop unattended, not even her mother or sister were there.

Once outside she realized this was the street where the Portrait Painters Shop was located, next to the Millinery Shop. As she was about to step off the porch her eyes caught sight of a movement across the street. Two men had come out of the Painter's shop door and were talking angrily to someone inside. She recognized one as being the man who this morning had tried to collect for hanging the slave who was not yet dead. She could see he sure enough was the one who had knocked her to the ground that first trip into town. He spotted her as she was looking in his direction.

He started toward her. Fear, as before, gripped her throat and seemed to squeeze all the breath from her. Unwittingly she had gotten caught up in this mystery by being at the wrong place and she wanted no part of his story. Quickly she sought the safety of a group of shoppers going toward Second Street. When she turned back to look again, the men were gone. How could they have vanished so quickly?

Rachel desperately wanted to talk to someone about this and what she should do to protect herself. Oh, why had her brother left her here by herself? Tears of fear were close to her eyes. A steeple of a church being repaired was visible from the corner and she headed in that direction. It would ease her fears if she could talk to the minister and see what he suggested. Her fear was of knowing too much, although she was not sure of what she knew or what crimes had been committed. Maybe she would just ask of the rector prayers for safety and then leave.

The heavy front door was open and she went inside. The interior was not ready for services but there was the beginning of an altar. She decided to go to the front to look for the minister. The sound of workmen hammering in the room behind the altar gave her some sense of safety. At least she was not walking into an empty building. As she looked around, she felt a calmness come over her as she repeated the prayers she had learned at her own church. Oh, to be home again within the safety of her own walls.

A commotion outside the church contrasted with the peace within the wall of this place, even with the construction going on. At first she was afraid the men had followed her. To her relief the ruckus had nothing to do with the previous incident. A crowd was following an old man in a wagon just pulling up to the front of a house. When she looked at the sign on the house it said *Dr. Brand's Medicines—a cure for all ailments.* Two men came out of the house and lifted a young girl from the bed of the wagon.

Rachel, feeling secure in the crowd, walked over to the edge of the see what was going on. She quietly asked a woman standing next to her who the white-headed man was that was attending to the girl.

The woman proudly told all she knew. "Oh, that is Dr. Brand and the other man is his helper with the sick."

Someone in the crowd yelled out, "What's the girl's name?" The attendant called back, "This is Isabel Miller; she's been coming to Dr. Brand since back in April or May. Now move away and let us take her in."

Rachel could see the young girl's badly swollen blackened feet dangling lifeless as they picked her up. Another man yelled out, "What's wrong with her?" The doctor paid the crowd no mind as he waited for the men to carry her inside.

The old man who had brought the girl in, seemed to feel important of sorts and spoke up. "The doctor s'pects he will have to cut off her feet. The infection has been eatin' on her for sometime now, and the doctor cannot think what to do for her but cut her feet off."

The crowd groaned, "Why did her feet get rotted off?"

Again the old man, eager to converse, called out. "She stood on a red ant bed and they crawled all over her feet, bitin' her something fierce like."

All of a sudden the attention shifted back to the sick girl who was vomiting up a greenish slime. The doctor turned to the crowd and yelled, "She's real bad, may not live through the night."

Rachel started for the boarding house, feeling like an intruder into this poor woman's awful predicament. She could see a man sawing short planks of wood and taking them to a small shed at the back of the Doctor's house. As she got closer, she realized he had begun to nail them to the form of a coffin. Suddenly her insides began to quiver. The Doctor was having the coffins built out back as he brought the patients in the front. It reminded her of her brothers-in-law digging the grave for her father before he died.

Rachel looked back at the milling crowd and remembered all too well how serious infections could be. Her mother had lingered only a little while from the infections of Small Pox. But never had she witnessed someone having their feet cut off because of it. She could not help but wonder how long it would be before they bought Isabell Miller to her coffin.

Rachel excused herself from the breakfast table and went to the front door of the boarding house to look down the street for what seemed the hundredth time. It had been several days since she had met with the clerk at the courthouse, and she was beginning to wonder if her family had forgotten to come for her.

The constant chattering of Miss Tuckman, Miss Porchia Greer, and Mrs. Summers, the three ladies of age that had come to the boarding house two days ago, was about to drive her senseless. The first day it had been fun to listen to stories about the people they knew, like the woman who found weevils in her floured hairdo and the one yesterday they had labored over. It seemed Mrs. Summers had a brother whose wife was "hated out" as they called it.

Mrs. Summers had clicked her tongue and proceeded to say, "My poor brother Zachariah had a wife that was mean without even trying. She would on purpose not rinse the lie soap from his bed clothing just so he would break out in a rash and leave her alone. My brother was a fine man and we fixed her, my sisters and I, we did for sure."

The other woman could not believe the cruel intentions of the act and laughed at the solution.

Rachel, unaccustomed to the ways of the in-town people innocently asked, "What did you do?"

Mrs. Summers loved telling these stories and began to explain. "Oh, we hated her out—that's what we did. That is how you deal with someone doing the act. We just told the family and neighbors about it and we all just turned our back on her every time she came around us—wouldn't say a blessed word to her—ever! Yes, sir, we hated her out."

These stories and many others had turned sour and Rachel decided if this is what the townspeople did, she was glad to live in the country. And just now they were discussing one of their favorite themes of the older set. "I says, 'tis a disgrace to me'self to be taking a bath like the such of some women." Miss Porchia, the older of the women spoke up, "If you ask me, it's the evil of seeing one's self naked is what is causing the sins of the heart."

Rachel had left her fan in the dining room that morning and had tried to slip back in to find it, hopefully unnoticed by the women. But it was not to be. Miss Porchia saw her enter and addressed her on the topic of their interest. "Oh, Miss Lee, we were just talking about the neglect of so many young women now as to their lack of decency. You appear to be an intelligent woman; what are your thoughts on bathing?"

Rachel realized she had been set up for this when she walked in and to not answer would appear to give rumor that she was a loose woman. Being careful of her words, she cautiously said. "I am very careful to bath only in the dark of night so not to disgrace myself." The answer seemed to satisfy the women's curiosity for the moment, leaving them to select another topic of disgrace.

Rachel quickly made excuse to leave the house for some fresh air. The heat was not so stifling at this time of the morning, and she chose the path toward the creek, staying a safe distance away from the portrait painter's street. It was still early and everything seemed so calm and lovely with the dew still resting on the grass. It made her miss her own place. She had always found it satisfying to take early morning walks.

As she walked, she could see a crowd had already begun to gather at the courthouse door. What a relief that she did not have to return there until she paid her father's debts. What the clerk had said gave her some concern. She had decided when she returned home she would ride over to Georgetown to see Mr. Peters personally.

Rachel was so engrossed in thought, she had forgotten to stop after a couple of blocks and had passed Patrick Street and ended up halfway down to the Carroll Creek. She could see in the distance the road leading into town. There were oxen pulling carts, filled with produce and surrounded by the farmer's rowdy little dirty-faced boys, all excited to be bringing their wares to town. As she stood watching, a farmer passed with squealing, smelly pigs being carried in an old cart with its sides about to break loose. She could see the women in this part of town were already hanging their wash on the sides of the houses, giving her a feeling of safety, enough to go on just a little farther to the creek for a quick look.

Only a few boats were in the muddy water downstream a short distance. One was a larger boat unloading a large wooden box. The boat must have come from the outer waterways of the province and worked its way up the Potomac to connect to Carroll Creek by way of the Monocacy. It was a good thing the rains of this spring had filled the rivers, otherwise, a boat of that size could not have stayed afloat.

She watched the water lap onto the bank as two men tried to move the cargo. It reminded her of those summers after the chores were done when she and her sisters and John would run down to the cool waters of the Sligo

Branch to catch crawdads. She had never learned how to swim but had learned the art of skipping rocks better than her sisters and brother or the Madden boys next door. What a disgrace, they thought, and they had refused to compete with her again. Rachel stooped down and picked up a rock. She wondered if she could still skip one across. Just as she let the rock slide across the water, she felt her footing start to move, and before she could steady herself, she was slipping toward the water.

The muddy water closed in around her as she tried to gain a footing. She came up after her first dunking to the sounds of the men in the small boat next to her having a good laugh and pointing in her direction. She grabbed for the bank but nothing was there to help her. She felt the water start to engulf her body again. She was going under and could do nothing to help herself.

She did not see the man from the small boat jump in after her. She only felt the strong arms close in around her and pull her to the side of the creek, and another man pulled her up on the bank.

"That's no place for a lady," the man said as he placed her safely on the bank. By the time she could stop spitting out the water and wipe her eyes enough to see, the man had walked half way back to his boat.

Rachel squeezed the water from her skirt and pulled the dead leaves from her now dirty yellowish-brown blouse. The humiliation had dissolved her into a swell of tears as she walked back to the boarding house. Oh, how she wished it was the middle of the night.

The three old women were still sitting in the parlor room when she tried to slip in. Miss Tuckman put her hand up to her eyes, shielding the sun so to get a better look at Rachel. She clicked her tongue. "Miss Lee, I can't believe you would go out in public in such disarray." Miss Porchia simply shook her head. But it was Mrs. Summers who gave the worst indictment in a most scolding tone, "Miss Lee, it is most disgraceful the way you allow your form to show through your garment that way."

As she started up the stairway, Miss Phoebe called to her, eyeing the water dripping from Rachel's dress and pulled a handkerchief from her bosom to wipe the droplets of water from the floor. "It has been five days since your brother left you here. I will be needing the room you are in for other guests who had made arrangement earlier. I had no idea your family would not come sooner."

Rachel wanted to cry. "I'm afraid something might have happened to my brother on the way here, and I have no way of finding out," she said. But her unspoken fears were more of the nature that they simply had forgotten about her.

Leaving a trail of water behind her Rachel reached her room and changed into her night slip. Never had she felt so alone. Was her family trying to say they could not be bothered by her schedule in court? On the next trip, she would simply ride her own horse and hope to make the trip safely.

Embarrassed at being abandoned by her family but even more afraid to trust her life to a stranger, she dressed and went out on the street to listen for someone that would be going toward the Potomac to Martha's house. She did not have enough monies left to pay for a ride back to *Chestnut Ridge*.

Chapter 15

Late July 1764
Chestnut Ridge

Home never looked so good to anyone as it did to Rachel on that late afternoon, one week and two days after her brother had left her at Miss Phoebe's boarding house. Even the sagging roof and the old gate that was threatening to fall from its hinges, looked good to her. They were on her list to fix sometime this year. The weeds had grown up around the front door just in the time she had been gone. She would take care of that tomorrow.

Rachel turned to wave good-bye to Miss Millicent Sanderfurd and her driver. Miss Milly, as she liked to be called, was in no way like the other three older women at the boarding house. Having stopped over for the night at Miss Phoebe's, she was on her way to the Annapolis port. When the next ship came she would be going to London to stay a year with her family.

Miss Milly had invited Rachel to ride the distance on the way to Annapolis with her after Miss Phoebe had explained the plight of Rachel Lee being abandoned by her family. And the sweet lady had even insisted they had plenty of time to take her all the way to Chestnut Ridge. In fact, she had made it sound like it was to her pleasure. "I get so lonely on these long roads" she had told Rachel.

The good luck of having Miss Milly come this way was a true miracle, as the ride to Martha's place did not come about, and no one she trusted was going in that direction. Next time she had to go into Fredericktown she would ask in advance for more days than she could possibly use so not to be pushed out again. She learned that Miss Phoebe could be a mean-spirited woman when it came to running her boarding house. When all efforts failed for Rachel to find a ride, Miss Phoebe had no choice but begrudgingly accommodate her. She had set up a bed in her sewing shop in clear sight of the front door and of the boarders as they came and went from the dining room. And because Rachel's funds were limited she had asked her to work with the kitchen maid to pay for her dinner.

Miss Milly had been so quick to befriend Rachel it made Miss Phoebe look cold hearted, and the other boarders took note as well. But no matter how embarrassing the last few days had been, still it was a safe place to stay and she would have to stay there again. But Miss Phoebe had very directly

169

told her she would be expected to pay for the room in advance of taking her satchel up the steps.

The last few days had made up for the painful times, and the trip from Fredericktown with Miss Milly had been a pleasant one. They had spent last night at Miss Milly's sister's place near Clarksburg. All the way home she had looked into the faces of those passing their wagon for any sign of family. Once she thought she saw her sister Eleanor's husband, but if it was Thomas Betterton, he made no effort to answer her wave. Maybe William Betterton, had gone back home with a less than kind word about her, leaving Thomas to disavow her. But that was so unlike Thomas that she decided it must not have been him on the road. Rachel wanted to say an ugly word at the thought of William Betterton, but she was not raised that way. Instead she took in a deep breath and tried to think of something pleasant.

Rachel opened the door and found a basket of stale bread on the table. She recognized it was Anastasia's basket. Why had the family expected her home days before if no one had come for her?

Later that evening after the chores were finished she sat down to unpack her satchel and unwrap her purchases. If what William had announced was finalized by her family, even against her protest, she might not ever again have a say so as to what she bought. Any man she knew that was of her choosing was already married, and her brothers-in-law would only give consideration as regards to who could successfully run the farm. At her age she could not presume to marry a man for love. All it would be now was an indentured contract for her land and to see how much work she could do to keep him from the poor house, and nothing more. When she was young, like Martha or Rebeckah had been when they married, she would have rejoiced to call a man, husband. And that had been her plan the time she was once courted by a boy. But there was now no reason, as her mother used to say, to cry after you spilled the milk. Her life was cast long ago when her parents had needed her to care for them, and that was all there was to it.

Rachel had been home only three days when she heard her brother's wagon lumbering over the hill. It was late afternoon. What would bring John at such a late hour?

"Rach, you here?" John yelled from the road. "I've just come from Thomas Davis's Ordinary over by Rock Creek Road. They had a letter waiting for you from the court house." He handed the folded paper to his sister and began to scold her for not coming over when she had gotten home. "I thought surely you and William, maybe Rebeckah too, would come over when you got here."

She took the folded piece of paper with the wax seal on it, and slowly read the ornate script. When she spoke again she worked to make her voice sound cheerful, "Oh, I have to be back to the courthouse to close out the will on the first day of August. They had led me to believe I would have more time. How will I ever get my field ready for fall planting?"

Rachel worked hard to conceal from John the worry she felt after reading the letter. The fact was, she was hurt and too proud to say so. He had just let her sit in the town without as much as a letter to instruct someone to pick her up. She knew he had his chores to do, but surely he could have sent word as to his intentions.

Usually after a trip into town she had all sorts of exciting stories to tell. This time she sat in her chair just looking out at the road and answering in few words what he asked.

"Something is bothering you, Rach, what is it?"

She told him how she been forced to be "put up" by Miss Phoebe in the first floor sewing room in sight of all the patrons to see her dilemma. "I had to beg a ride home with one of the boarders."

"Why, pray tell. I sent word to the Littlefields." John went on to tell how Mrs. Carroll's servant came by one evening to say he was going to pick up some visitors coming across the Potomac at the Seneca Landing, and I decided it was good for William Littlefield to take his turn at helping us out. I copied a letter and gave it to him to deliver. He was rather rushed so must have forgotten to stop by their place. I'm certain Rebeckah would have made sure you were picked up if she had known."

Rachel just smiled and patted her brother's hand. "I suppose you did what you had to do." There was nothing else to do now that it was over. The mail delivery service was never reliable. Next time she would take her father's old horse and hope for safekeeping.

Once John was gone, Rachel hurriedly went to the monies box to count how much she had saved to pay the debts. Only a few coins rattled at the bottom. She would need at least that much to pay the men to "prize" the small crop of tobacco she had been able to raise between court filings. Then more monies would be needed to roll the hogshead to the warehouse if there was to be a return on the crops.

Rachel had planned to ask for work from a few of her neighbors before going to see Mr. Peters and Thomas Cramphlin. No one in her family could afford to give her a loan. Well, maybe Anne Hughes could, but Anne would expect to be given the land in return for the favor. All the others had children to feed and clothe, or sick husbands to secure medicinals for. She went to the table and began to set down the figures she needed to live on. Anything leftover could be used to pay the debts.

Her mind began to jump from one solution to another. Maybe if she checked her father's record book it would show someone owning him, as well.

She pulled her father's book from the shelf where it was kept next to a stack of writing paper and pens and sat down in her rocker to begin going line by line through the pages.

The words of the early years were faded and hard to read. She turned the pages carefully so not to crack the edges of the old book.

23 April 1718 Bought land from Capt. James Greenfield called Wards Pasture beginning in main north branch of Deep Creek bounded chestnut on a barren hill containing 60 acres.

Rachel looked at the land description her father had voiced out so it could be entered. It had been so long ago. Her mind wandered from the task at hand, to thoughts of what her father and mother must have looked like back then. Her brothers, James and Robert and sister Elizabeth, were just babies when they had bought that land.

The words *sold land 23 November 1732* were scribbled in the margin next to the entry.

She turned to the page that gave the date 23 November and looked at the description of the land that had been referenced earlier and slowly began to sound out the letters.

> *November 23, 1732 I, James Lee received 4000 pounds of tobacco from Thomas Wall for land lying on branches of creek called Deep Creek. It had been surveyed for Murphy Ward now dead. He had given the land to his son whose name was also Murphy Ward. This Murphy Ward sold the land to Thomas Busby. Mr. Busby sold the land to Capt. James Greenfield. Mr. James Greenfield sold it to me 23, April 1718. It was known all along as Wards Pasture. It begins in the main north branch of Deep Creek bounded chestnut on a barren hill containing more or less 60 acres.*

Rachel's finger circled the 1732 numbers as if it could make the image of her mother and father appear as it was on that day. She had been only two years old when her father sold the place and did not remember if the house was small or large. Did it have pretty trees like the Chestnut Ridge? She read the entry again, and noticed the names of Ninian Beall and Samuel Magruder. They had been called in to witness the sale. Those names had been familiar to the family for as long as she could remember.

Rachel looked back down at the writing.

Mary went with me so she could release dower.

Rachel wished she had asked more about the earlier home and the stories of those living close by. She would have to ask James Jr. if he remembered the place.

Reminiscing was not getting the debts paid she chided and turned back to the book, this time choosing the middle pages to search. The old writing drew her to spend time in their presence. Rachel tenderly turned the pages, reading out loud what had been important to her father.

Bought Chestnut Ridge 10 July 1741 from William and Alexander Beall and James Edmonston.

The last date she read caught her attention. *July 10.* It was the same day she had gone into court last week with the list of what earthly effects her parents had saved in their lifetime. She wondered if they had known that their life would be a mere memory twenty-three years later, would they have done anything differently? She could almost feel the cockleburs she had picked up in her feet that hot day she helped load the wagon for the move up to the ridge. That was the time her father had wanted to burn a load of books her mother had added to the plunder. Rachel had never before seen her mother speak up to her father, but that day she had told him, "I have a right to treasure my own books, James Lee."

Rachel thought about the old book Rebeckah had brought up from the cellar, the one with the love notes in the margin. It must have been her mother's book. The notes in the margin must have been from a boy she had known. Had he loved her mother? She slowly spoke the words "I came to love you late." Was this a secret her mother had held in her heart all these years? Was her father's jealousy the reason he wished to rid his house of the books?

She looked back at her father's record book. If Mr. Peters did feel it necessary to take the farm for a debt then all her father had toiled over meant nothing but a bad name in the end. And so far the records had shown no one owing her father monies.

She looked back at the record book, drawn to what had been written, maybe not so much to find monies owed but now to relive a time when her family had been there to care for her. Now she was the keeper of their memories and the things they had worked so hard for. She must pay their debts.

Spring 1743. I bought one brown cow from Mary, Benjamin Thrasher's widow.

Rachel remembered when her father had made plans to bring the cow over from Mrs. Thrasher's house. Even then, long before she was old enough to have a boy friend, Martha had begged to go with her father in hopes of seeing Thomas. She would say, "He is so good looking. Someday I'm going to marry him." They had all laughed at her insistence, but on her nineteenth birthday, she had indeed married him. It had rained all morning, but that did not spoil the excitement. The neighbors came anyway. Rachel remembered how pretty the cabin looked after her mother scrubbed it clean and dared the life of anyone that made a mark on it. They had brought newly budded blossoms from the field to place in a basket. Rebeckah and Eleanor had gathered wild lilacs from their mother's bush next to the house and braided the lavender buds into Martha's pretty long hair. Martha always did love flowers. Maybe that is why she loves living down close to the Potomac point of rocks. Their pasture is always so full of pretty blooming trees in the spring. Rachel smiled to herself, remembering how pretty Martha had looked standing before the gathering with Thomas by her side.

Rachel sighed and went back to searching the entries.

August 1744. Finished paying off Thomas Clarke for attorneying—

Although her father could not even write his name he still had learned to sound out enough letters, or to memorize the looks of a man's name to know what he was looking at. On this occasion he must have seen something he did not like because he had marked through the word so fiercely the pen point had torn the page and left a blob of ink over it. Rachel set the ledger down. That had been a very hard time. Her mother had cried uncontrollably that day. They had all cried at their mother's feet as her father's old wagon passed over the hill with their sister sitting up so straight on the seat next to him. They fully expected her to return home with the customary lashes to her bare back. The thought made her shiver even now after almost twenty years to the month.

Rachel skipped to the later entries where William Littlefield's fancy English scroll was obvious, and even some less carefully written lettering of her brothers and sisters scripting. She still remembered her father calling to one of the children, saying "come set the record for me" as he handed them this book. It must have been difficult to have to trust his children's better skills to his own bookkeeping pages.

March 1749 Mr. Robert White goes to court to ask for the use of the old road through our land so he can get his tobacco to Bladensburg warehouse. The court rules in our favor. Mr. White has gone away.

She could not help but laugh when she read the entry recounting the little old man standing out by the gate with his long train of horses pulling the hogsheads full of tobacco. Mr. White would stand there and yell—he just kept yelling—for someone to let him through the gate so he might take a shortcut to the tobacco warehouse. Her father would go out to the road and tell him he could not come through, and Mr. White would argue he had always been allowed to cross through. But ever since James Lee had bought the place there had not been a road through the land to the other side. The old road had even been planted over with crops, but that didn't stop him from yelling. Finally, Mr. White went to court to force the road to be reopened. Rachel read the last line again.

Court rules in our favor. Mr. White has gone away.
April 23, 1752 Went to Fredericktown to register the black gelding. It was a stray.

Rachel noticed someone had scribbled on the side of the page,
a very fine horse smart well trained

Bad crop year end of 1752 need monies
Year 1753, 4ᵗʰ Day of May to be exact. Gave home place to Rachel and John. Shan't have to worry about them when I'm gone. Mother is to live here in her own house as long as she lives.

Rachel skipped down to the last entry.

1756 Feb. 29, Needed to hire off some of the work. Hired some of John Madden's sons for the crop season.

Her father had been talking about his head hurting most days and said he couldn't even pull the horse into the barn he was so weak. His breath would be gone before he got up the hill. Her mother had fretted over him until he finally agreed to get help. Dennis Madden was hired to help bring in the crops. That was the last time her father had left the place, and he called his will out to Mr. Butler just a few weeks later.

Dennis Madden and his wife, Anastasia, had been so good to help her aging parents. It was a natural thing that they would be the ones to buy her brother's land. It bordered *Chestnut Ridge* on one side and close to Father Maiden's old home place on the other side.

At first the family had all tried to talk James Jr. out of selling *Batchlor's Purchase*. He had bought his land on the same day her father had bought *Chestnut Ridge,* and it always seemed like one big place with not even a fence between them. The family had laughed at both men as they rode off in her father's wagon to go register the deeds. One of the sisters had called out to them, "Be careful you don't mix up which land you are buying."

James Jr. had married Anne and had babies on the place. Then he bought the new fresh land farther west in the county. The decision to move just as his father and mother were getting so frail was hard. But the land was so much better to raise his tobacco crop. Rachel remembered her mother crying as she watched the last wagonload leave over the ridge with their plunder. "I'll never see them again" she had cried. But she did—twice."

The Madden's had tried to make up for the loss. They were hard workers and shared their crops. Even now since her parents were gone, it was nothing unusual to find a basket of ripe blackberries or newly picked beans, waiting at her door. Not to speak of the shoes that kept her feet shod, even though the fit caused blisters. Dennis made good shoes in his shop; it was just her feet that did not like them much.

The prospects for paying the debts were no better, she thought as she placed the record book back on the shelf. But just reading the entries gave her a sense of well being. The same love that had gotten her parents through the hard times would sustain her now.

She went to the window to look at the hillside in the distance. From somewhere in the crevices of her memory, she was reminded of the words read by the rector, "I will lift up mine eyes unto the hills from whence cometh my help." Her father used to look out this window for long moments at a time. Was he looking for wisdom to solve some problem?

The sun was sinking over the edge of the ridge in a ball of heat as she walked toward the barn to check on the cows and old Thunder. The crickets from beneath the bramble bushes announced her coming as she walked through the long shadows that stretched out before her.

After closing the barn door for the night, she had walked down the road in the moonlight hoping to think of an answer to her debt. One thing she did know was she would have to go to the Glassford Company and hope to talk to Mr. Peters about selling him her own land, the *Maiden's Folly*. Strangely, she thought, what was bought as a security against her forced marriage, now was a security from failure.

She returned to her own yard and stood looking at the sky full of shooting stars and slowly lowered herself to the ground next to one of the big chestnut trees that had birthed the name Chestnut Ridge. The prayers she had been repeating to the Almighty all evening were still on her lips as she slipped into an exhausted sleep.

The next thing she knew was the brightness of the early morning sun hitting her face, and feeling stiff all over from sleeping on the hard ground. Before she could sit up, a voice from behind caused her to awkwardly clamor to her feet. It was Mrs. Carroll's son, Daniel. "Oh, Mr. Carroll, how embarrassing to have you find me sleeping on the ground like a common drunkard." She started to explain as to why she had been sleeping there but decided better of it. That far away faint whisper of her mother's words of training reminded her that there are times it is better not to talk so much.

"You gave me a start. What a pleasant surprise to have you visit," she said, as she tried to smooth the wrinkles from her skirt.

"Forgive me for startling you, Miss Rachel. Mother would be so ashamed of my manners. Here, I've come upon your land so abruptly. But I was on the road going back to my home in Upper Marlboro, hence the early hour. I saw you were already in the yard and I thought it a good time to bring my mothers request to you."

"Oh, my! Is something wrong with your mother or your sisters?" Rachel asked with concern in her voice.

"Oh, no, indeed not. We will be having a number of guests joining us when my brother, John, the archbishop, entertains a group of his church officials. Mother fears the chairs are in an overused state. She desires you to find the time to make new covers out of the heavy embossed materials like those you fashioned before," he said, as he pulled out a hand full of coins. "Mother always prefers to pay in advance."

Rachel could hardly contain her relief as she quickly set a date to go to the Carrolls. "Tell Mrs. Carroll I will be free to come to her house week after next."

She watched Mr. Carroll make his leave, and then unfolded her hand. The coins were not monies just now. Instead, she saw them as symbols of an answer to her prayerful cries. She turned her eyes toward the ridge of hills on the other side of the road and softly said in a whisper, "From whence cometh my help."

A nervous pain in her stomach reminded Rachel of her responsibility as the wagon took the final turn to Glassford's Company. It was just as her brother had described it to her. He had told her, "When you reach the well used and smoothed out road you will know you are getting close and there will be a sharp turn in the road just before you see the warehouse." He had also explained that Mr. Robert Peters worked as the attorney and manager for the owner.

As the wagon rounded the road she almost fainted at the sight of this building. It had to be the largest building she had ever seen. It was situated right at the water's edge and was so large it almost covered that side of the port.

And again in this moment she felt a renewed thankfulness to her neighbor, Mrs. Carroll. She had just last evening sent a message by her most reliable slave, Tuck, to insist that he accompany her on this trip. It happened after Anastasia Madden had delivered new shoes made by her husband, to each of Mrs. Carroll's daughters, and on that day Anastasia mentioned Rachel would be going to Mr. Glassford's to settle a debt. Rachel smiled at how Tuck had delivered the message so serious like. "Miz Carroll says she is insistin' I's go with you on yore journey on the morrow, Miz Rachel. She allows to not feelin saf for you's to go by yo'self."

177

Tuck was a trustworthy young boy that professed religion and had always been a good example for the other slaves.

And now that there were fresh rumors of Indian uprisings the last few days, she felt safer traveling with him. Although, she knew if Indians surprised them, it would not matter if she was alone or with ten slaves.

But even without the threat of Indians it had been a good thing he had come. If it had not been for Tuck's strong back to push the wagon through the high waters after yesterday's heavy rain, she might have lost her brother's wagon. Poor old Thunder was not much of a horse now and even pulling a wagon on dry land was slow going.

It was obvious that Tuck was in awe at the sight and just sat on the seat with his mouth open, unable to move the horse from the spot. She found it necessary to speak up again, "Tuck, you can hitch old Thunder over there and wait while I go in to do business." Her voice gave off the sound that she was accustomed at doing official business but the flutter of her heart told a different story.

She crawled over the side and began to straighten her shirtwaist, remembering the warning from Mr. Bowles at the courthouse. Mr. Peters could take away her land if she did not present her case just right. She decided a well-kept appearance would give him confidence in her abilities to work.

Rachel had spent most of the trip trying to decide how she would approach Mr. Peters after she realized her monies might be short by just a tad bit from what the court note said. She had to convince the proprietor that she could be trusted to send the balance due. She wondered if this Mr. Peters would even take the time to listen to her.

"Tuck, while I'm doing business, keep an eye open for any unseemly characters that might steal you away. And you are under no circumstances to go with any other person. Do you understand?"

The wide eyed slave shook his head and began to watch the surrounding area as if someone was waiting in the grasses to whisk him away.

It took all the strength she had to force her weak knees to support her body as she climbed the wide steps and pulled open the big oak doors in the front of the building. The musty sweet smell of tobacco assaulted her nose, and her eyes began to water as she entered into the largest room she had ever seen, much less walked into.

The room was surrounded with big windows hung high to the ceiling, leaving storage space below for crates of every size. Another set of big doors at the back was opened to a waiting boat.

There were barrels, hundreds of barrels, filling the center of the large room. She stood by the door waiting to ask someone where Mr. Peters could be found, but no one paid any mind. She cleared her throat hoping someone would notice her. A man loading a crate onto a low-slung wagon finally looked in her direction and said, "Lady, get out of here. This is no place for a woman."

Rachel managed to control her voice as she spoke. "I've come to do business with Mr. Peters."

The man looked hard at her before he spoke in a rude sounding voice. "He's back by the dock. Watch where you step and don't break anything on your way back there."

Rachel stood for a moment selecting a pathway before starting to make her way through the maze. She was forced to stop every few steps to redirect her path. Some of the crates had words she could read, while others words made no sense to her. They must have been shipped from other countries that did not write the English sounds. It was like watching Mrs. Carroll do her yearly shopping from her big catalogs from faraway places. There were bolts of silk from London, at least that is what the crate said, and there were several crates marked China Dishes along one side of the wall, and something for the church at Georgetown, probably new hymnals or prayer books.

Some of the crates projected out into her chosen path and when she moved passed one, her skirt caught the loose edge causing her to lose her footing for a moment. Once again her actions were a reminder of just how clumsy she had always been. Her mother used to say it was because she wanted to move her life too fast. Rachel quickly looked around to see if the man who had warned her so strongly was watching. And in the process of checking, she bumped into a large basket that held small chunks of marble. The pure green, pale blues, azure, and amber nuggets spilled all over the floor. What was it about this place that made her so awkward? As she bent over to pick them up, her skirt snagged the side of a rough crate. She would be lucky to get out of this place not owing more than when she came. As her hand swooped up the little nuggets she noticed one marble piece that reminded her of the beautiful rock her father had given to her mother when he had gone courting. She could not resist the urge to put the rock into the sun. Just as she did she heard a man clear his throat. She jumped and almost lost her balance. Standing before her was the dirtiest man she had ever seen. His words were choice cut and not kind in any way. Determined not to let his vial talk upset her she defiantly put the nugget to the sun. After all, her father would never allow anyone to talk like that to his daughters so why should she stand for it now. It was with an air of sophistication that she spoke, trying to sound like some big plantation owner. "A fine piece of marble they have shipped," she said as she continued to pick the light through the nugget. The thought of convincing this man that she was a well to do woman that had come to order from the catalog gave her strength, and she moved on past the man without saying a word. She could hardly wait to give an account to her sister-in-law Elizabeth. Betsy always liked to hear about the outside world.

Rachel worked her way through to the back of the warehouse. She could see several men, dressed in fine silk suits with lace bibs and wide lace sleeve cuffs that hung over their wrists. Each man wore black leather shoes with big shiny silver buckles and they were clean of any outside mud. They must be buyers because they would call out questions about a crate to a number of slaves unloading the boat. The man in the middle was wearing one of the very fashionable wigs like she had seen in the wig shop in Fredericktown and was told only the very foppish men wore that one called macaroni. His vest was brocaded with silver threads making him appear to be a very important person. She assumed he must be the man in charge. Rachel stood listening for anything that would tell her who might be Mr. Peters. Finally, one of the workers called out, "Mr. Peters, where do you want this crate? Doesn't have a number on it." Rachel waited for the instructions to stop and then quickly raised her voice. "Mr. Peters, Mr. Robert Peters?"

Robert Peters turned around, annoyed. "Yes, I am Robert Peters and who might you be?" He spoke with an edge to his voice. "This is not a suitable place for a woman."

Rachel had to dig deep within her soul to keep her voice from quivering. "My name is Miss Lee and I have come about my father's debt."

He looked questioningly at her as he walked closer. "And there is not a man in your life that could have come to address these matters?"

For the second time since she had walked through the door, she had been told this was not a place for a lady. "Sir, it was the intent of my late father that I should be the one to take care of his affairs."

"Very well, follow me to my office but watch your step. I cannot afford to allow you to break something."

Rachel followed behind Mr. Peter's swift step, clutching her skirt tightly in her hands as she walked. When they reached the side of the big room, she could see a door secured by big locks just like the front door. Again she realized the great need to protect against thievery.

"Did you say your name was Miss Lee? And who was your father?" Mr. Peters sat down in a big chair behind a table and motioned for her to sit down on the bench by the door. He took a big ledger from a shelf and dropped it on the table and preceded to leaf through the middle of the book. "Lee—could that be Daniel Lee or Thomas Lee?"

"No, sir, it was James Lee. I am Rachel Lee, James Lee's daughter. My father owned a portion of the *Laybrinth* called *Chestnut Ridge*. I am not certain what it was he ordered, but there was a bill with no markings of paid on it. When I turned it over to the court assessors, they told me it would be necessary to pay it before we can close out my father's estate. Can you help me?"

"Now how can I help you if you don't know what it is you owe for or how much? If these men would not make it so hard by thinking a woman can handle these matters. It always forces me to study the matter."

Rachel handed the paper to him with the big scrawling letters "owed to Robert Peters five pounds of tobacco or equivalent of monies." It was signed in big script with clear handwriting *Mr. Robert Peters Oct. 1755.*

Mr. Peters took the paper from her. "Well, speak up woman why didn't you tell me." He studied it for a long period then leafed through the book several more times. "How much did you bring to pay for this debt today, Miss Lee?"

"That is what I would like to discuss with you, Mr. Peters. Due to my father's illness, we were unable to get as much from the crops as in former years, and I have not had the opportunity to make up the difference. I am bringing with me monies to pay a large portion of the bill and offer the promise of my good name that I will return and pay you in full. It will be necessary for you to mark out a paper saying you agreed with the arrangement so I can take it to the courthouse. They will finalize the closing of the estate if you agree."

Rachel felt flushed after giving her explanation, and when she finished, she looked up and noticed Mr. Peters was actually smiling.

He looked down at his books again, then back at Rachel. "Just how much did you bring with you, Miss Lee?"

Rachel reached into her side pocket and retrieved all the coins Mr. Carroll had paid her and handed them to Mr. Peters. She watched as he stacked them one on top of the other like he was playing a game of some sort. She held her breath as he reached for the last stack, still counting out loud.

"You are short by just a few monies, Miss Lee. How do you plan to pay the remainder of the debt?" Mr. Peters looked up in time to see her begin to fan her face.

"I plan to put myself out for work just as soon as I return from the courts, allowing you sign the papers favorable to pay later."

Mr. Peters looked again at the book, running his finger down the columns as if counting the numbers, then back at Rachel. When he spoke, a serious tone entered his words. "I am a fair man, Miss Lee, although some do not always think me so. You seem to be trusting in your word—willing to work for what you get. It is not often in this day that such a tribute can be paid."

He reached into his drawer and took out a sheet of paper, lifting his pearl-handled quill pen and began the twisting motion just like William

Littlefield did before letting the words spell out on the page. When he had finished, he blotted it with a heavy gray matte paper and handed it to her.

"I have given you consideration for your caring for your father and your willingness to work for the debt."

She opened her mouth to say a proper thank you but he continued on as he handed her the paper, "Most women do not try to read so let me assure you it says—"

Before he could finish she broke in to defend the training her parents had tried to give. "I have been reading since childhood, Mr. Peters."

"Miss Lee, I have to confess, you have brought a smile to a normally quarrelsome day. Your father chose wisely."

Still a little put off about his remarks about the ignorance of her gender she looked down at the paper he had handed her.

Overwhelmed by the words, *Paid in Full*, she dropped any pretense she had given and began to thank Mr. Peters profusely.

Once outside she felt like shouting with relief. She could not believe she had brought this account to a close so promptly. Particularly after her brother had warned her Mr. Peters most likely would force her to pay more because of the delay. And not one of the men folk had to assist in the transaction. Maybe this would convince her family she did not need a husband to do her business.

They had ridden for several hours in the heat, old Thunder getting slower and slower and Rachel became worried he might drop dead at any time. It was getting too late to make it home before nightfall, besides a bank of clouds had begun to darken what sun there was left in the day. What she did not want was to be on the road with Indian threats and a slave that was jumpy. She had been told to stop off at the house owned by an acquaintance of the Allison's who was overseer of the land Dann, close to her father's cabin.

The house was plain without the finer curtains or furnishing of Miss Phoebe's place, but it had beds for rent and a secure barn where Tuck could sleep.

They had left at dawn this morning, trying to reach home before mealtime. But Rachel had finally been forced to send Tuck to a farmhouse just off the path in hopes of finding leftovers on the table, even though the hour was well past midday. After he was out of sight, she stood up in the wagon and stretched her stiff body. Thus far the trip had been uneventful, if you called spending the night in a stranger's house, sharing a bed with a croupy child and an old woman that snored so loud she could not hear the birds sing at daybreak, and Tuck being bitten by the owner's dog, uneventful. Now all she wanted was a bite to eat and her own bed by nightfall.

Last night's clouds had given no rain but now the sky to the north gave a hint of rain, and from the smell of it in the air it might be close. What a welcome relief that would be for this stifling heat of late July. Wiping her face with the dress sleeve, she turned around to look for any signs of people coming in her direction. There was a line of men climbing along the ridge some distance away, probably returning back to work after the midday meal. But it seemed a trifle late for that. As she watched, she could see it was more than a gathering of men; there were women with children slowly making their way up to the top of the hill. Then she noticed the two men carrying a small wooden box and she put her hand to her chest to stifle the moan. "Oh, how sad. A mother has lost her baby."

It happened every summer when the suffocating heat played evil tricks on the young and on the old. She wondered what it must be like just now for this young mother walking behind the box, knowing she would never again hear the cry of her baby or sing a lullaby to its once warm, soft body. Rachel watched the procession stop at the top of the hill, lowering the small box into the ground. Babies died all the time. It was a fact of life, and a mother giving birth knew it full well. She would be blessed of God to see her baby live to its first birthday. But still, the mother's pain was just as real.

She heard Tuck coming and called out to him, "Did you hear the family's name called?"

"Can't say I know his name rightly, Missy Lee. But I know one thing, they were all standing around watching a sickly baby. They said it was the summer sickness. The woman said babies have been dying everyday now." Tuck quickly changed the subject from death to food with his glance to the bucket he had brought back. "I told them your pappy's name, and the woman said she thought she had heard of him but didn't rightly know of him going on to his rewards."

Tuck was becoming increasingly more interested in the contents of the bucket. It was up to Rachel to make the talk. He patiently watched Rachel for a signal. She offered him a piece of pork, but he reached for the over burned journey cakes, either feeling he was supposed to leave the meat for her or honestly desiring the taste of the cakes.

After they had finished eating and Rachel had tucked the leftovers in her satchel to save, she noticed Tuck nervously shuffling his feet, wanting to speak but afraid to try. He did not look at her when he spoke his question. "Missy Lee, I heard Missy Madden tell that yous goin to the big city sometime soon. I'd be proud to see you safely there and back home again seein's you spoke of being afraid to take the trips. I never set eyes on that many buildin's at one place before, ever, ever."

She looked at him for a moment, smiling at his choice of words. He was so intent. "I'll speak to Mrs. Carroll about it. You have been very well behaved on this trip, Tuck, but Fredericktown is a big place full of dangerous men just waiting to cause trouble for a slave. I don't know if it is wise to take you there by myself."

Secretly Rachel wondered if this could be the answer to her traveling woes. Her pride still hurt over the lack of communication in the colonies. John swore that he sent word by way of Mrs. Carroll's servant to William Littlefield, who in turn had not received it. If Rebeckah had known Rachel needed a ride she would have made sure someone would come for her.

When they reached home and Tuck walked the horse into her barn Rachel assured him she would approach Mrs. Carroll about the trip to Fredericktown.

The question was, how did a spinster show a man of his color the town without bringing attention to the fact she was entertaining a slave? She would have to be very discreet in dealing with him.

Rachel stood at the window looking out into the darkness, defined now by the freedom of a handful of late evening fireflies, darting here and there as they so pleased. She wished for a freedom of her own. She had been tethered first by sick parents and now the fixing of the will. And it was not over until she plead for one more debt.

For as long as Rachel could remember, Mr. Thomas Cramphlin had visited their cabin at the beginning of each new season to enjoy the latest news. She remembered her parents dressing for the funeral of the first wife, Mary Cramphlin. After his marriage to the widow Bowie, everyone had welcomed her as a friend as well. When Mr. Cramphlin's son, Thomas Jr. began to take over the responsibilities of the mill, he also took over the debts owed to the family. And when the elderly Mr. Cramphlin died, no one had mentioned the Lee debt. When Rachel received a notice from the court clerk saying a member of the Cramphlin family had filed papers it was her first to hear of such a debt. And there was no mention of what the debt related to.

Surely, Thomas Jr. would allow her to arrange for a payment when her tobacco crop was harvested. Or if not, maybe she could handle it in the spring when the wheat was harvested. She again felt a sort of panic at the thought that this might not be agreeable, and then she could still lose the farm. The younger Thomas had always been a friendly type, but he had not attended her father's burial. Did the Cramphlins hold the debt against their friendship because it had been so long? With only a few days left before being expected at the courthouse, it was necessary to visit the Cramphlins quickly.

The heat of the late July sun made Rachel feel almost dizzy when she stepped over the last stone. She looked back down the hill at the Cramphlin's ford she had just passed. As a child she and her siblings had played all through this land with some of the neighboring young folk, and never before had she realized how steep it was and how many big stones there were. Could it be that the years were taking their toll?

Rachel watched from the gate as the widow slowly made her way to unlatch the lock, all the while clutching her cane tightly. The effects of the hot summer had left Mrs. Cramphlin looking frail. It reminded Rachel of her father's illness, but she had heard nothing about Mrs. Cramphlin having an illness.

"Mrs. Cramphlin, I've a need to see your son if he is on the place at this hour."

The older woman looked at Rachel strangely as she led her into the cabin. Then she spoke. "Are you here to try to marry Thomas's boy? He is needing someone younger who can bear him a house full of children. Age is not on your side, Miss Lee. Keep your proposals to yourself."

Rachel realized she was serious about the concern. The feebleness had done nothing to dull her protection to her family.

"Mrs. Cramphlin, I beg to disagree with your account as to why I have come. The court clerk gave me a notice that you have filed a debt with the courts against my father's estate, and I've been given the duty to settle it out."

Mrs.Cramphlin eased herself into her chair again and relaxed her face. "Very well, you know a person cannot be too careful with a son's future. My late husband Mr. Bowie told me that about our son, Allen Bowie, and I have remembered it well with Mr. Cramphlin's son, Thomas Jr."

As Mrs. Cramphlin talked, Rachel was reminded again of this Mrs. Cramphlin's life. Once when she had attended her mother's quilting table Mrs. Cramphlin had told the ladies she was Elizabeth Pottinger before she married a Mr. John Bowie. Then when he died she married the late Thomas Cramphlin Sr.

"I would dare say, I have fought off the young women that have had his money on their minds. I took on the task of raising his son just as he took to seeing after my Allen Bowie," Mrs. Cramphlin said proudly.

Rachel approached the subject of Thomas Jr. again as to his whereabouts.

"Thomas Jr. and my own Allen are both down beyond the Sligo Branch. Early this morning someone came to ask the boys to help establish the boundary for the *Discovery*. I guess you knew my late first husband, John Bowie—oh what a fine man he was. He was the one that laid out the *Discovery* boundary years ago." The older woman clucked her tongue with pride. Before Rachel could make a comment, Ruth Cramphlin, the stepdaughter of the elderly Mrs. Cramphlin walked into the room.

"Did I hear you say you are looking for our Allen Bowie?"

Rachel sensed a hint of defensiveness at the thought that maybe she had come to call on Allen. At first she was puzzled by Ruth's concern for her stepbrother, then sensed this girl had affections for him. This brought a new wave of awareness of how life had moved on. The last time she had seen Ruth was as a child accompanying the first Mrs. Cramphlin to her own mother's quilting table.

"Miss Rachel, have you seen the fine lap desk Allen made for me?" Ruth got up to bring a small wooden box over for Rachel to admire. Ruth lifted the lid so she could see where Allen had made little places to hold the paper and even a place to put the inkbottle.

"Oh, Ruth this is very remarkable—he must care for you to make something so fine." Rachel had a feeling that is what Ruth wanted to hear by the smile on her face.

"Allen is so dear. He does things like this for me all the time." Ruth was about to begin another story when they could hear the horses coming down the back path.

Thomas Jr. had come to the house to eat a meal after several hours in the hot sun, and was polite, but in no mood to haggle over the small debt. He began to frown when he asked his stepmother how this bill ever got to the courts. Then he turned back to Rachel, "It must be something about the mill, and that has been closed for several years. Whatever was owed by your father to my father has long been forgiven, and I have no account of the amount. I am sorry that the matter has called you out on such a hot morning." He pulled a paper from his sister's lap desk, much to her dislike, and hastily wrote out a note dismissing the debt. Then he turned to his stepmother and with a determined tone said, "There, that should take care of the matter." Rachel had the feeling there had been harsh words about the topic before this morning.

Chapter 16

July 30, 1764
Going to Fredericktown

The first hint of day appeared through the clear blue-pink streaked horizon as Tuck led James Lee's horse, Thunder, from the barn and hitched it to her brother's old wagon. Rachel heard him coming and quickly read over what she had just written on a piece of paper. She would buy a new record book when in town. It was time for her to set down her own farmer dealings and retire her father's book to the keeping chest.

> *Today is July 30th. Goin to Freriktown to Cort hows.*
> *Takin Tuck with me brother John told me where to stay with*
> *famly just befor I cros the Makockocee The name I do not*
> *kno but brother John Lee dos.*

Rachel knew traveling with Tuck would not be easy. She had been warned that slaves would try to get together for a "gathering." And it was at these occasions that the slave snatchers would slip in and kidnap the strongest and healthiest slaves and would take them far away to sell. The kidnapping was so bad now the sheriffs were given new powers to arrest slaves found in the presence of each other without the owners there. Rachel had no desire to return home only to carry the news to Mrs. Carroll that she had lost her valuable slave.

Tuck had been lectured by Mrs. Carroll about the possibilities of being kidnapped, and Rachel had secured Tuck's word that he would not cause her grief. Not that a promise given would stop any slave from running away if he so desired and the opportunity came. But Tuck was unlike most slaves.

The morning wore on. Rachel leaned back against the side of the wagon, dozing for a time. She trusted Tuck's handling of Thunder and had told him to sit up on the seat by himself. The trip was uneventful until they came upon a pack train and were forced to follow slowly behind it on the narrow road. The mules at the front of the train were staggering under the load of leather hides. Other mules behind were loaded down with big brown bags strapped to their backs, while the horses in the far back pulled two stone sleds loaded with big wooden crates. Rachel thought she recognized some of the crates as the ones at John Glassford and Company's warehouse in

Georgetown. For the first time in her life she realized with pride she knew something about the outside world.

At the first sight of the train, Tuck was nervous and overly excitable to a degree Rachel had not seen before. He began to tap his foot real fast and sing in a high pitched sound something she did not know. She tried calming him down by engaging talk.

"What do you suppose is in the big boxes, Tuck? Looks like some nice plunder for someone's house."

Tuck did not speak. He jumped down and took the reins in his hand almost pulling Thunder along. Then he started to do a funny little nervous dance and suddenly Rachel realized she did not know how to handle this big slave. What would she do if he bolted and ran away in fear of some unknown spook? Maybe a different approach to his thinking would help. She climbed up on the seat but did not ask for the reins. As long as Tuck was holding onto the horse he was not as likely to run.

She began to talk calmly about his family. "Tuck, where did you come from before Mrs. Carroll's husband bought you?"

Tuck did not answer at first and Rachel pried again. Maybe if she gave him a lead into the conversation it would help. "I first saw you at the Carroll's house when you were but a small boy but I don't remember ever seeing you with your parents."

"My pappy and mammy were done dead when I got here." Rachel continued, "What happened to them?"

Tuck took a deep breath before he started to unravel a horror story of cruelty and greed. "They died in the box—they put us in a big box with no holes in it."

By now Rachel was so interested in the story she had forgotten the reason for the conversation. "What do you mean—a box?"

"On the big boat they had a big box. We were all just taken away one night. Men came up to us whiles we be standin' in the street back in our old country. They told my mammy we could have some nice plunder for our house if we would just come over to look at it. Our Mammy said for pappy to go look. When he didn't come back we all went to look for him. Those men trapped us and pulled up us onto a boat. We didn't have any vittles. Our mammy died early on, and then my bubba and sissy died. Then pappy went. I's could hear em others cryin' to get out, so I knows we was on a big slave ship—the one we'd been warned bout. I's couldn't breathe cause the stink. The mean devil men took the big whips and tore open my back and made me help push them that were dead off into the water." By now Tuck was talking so fast that she could hardly keep up with what he was trying to say. He let loose of the reins and old Thunder stopped. Tuck had taken a step toward the ditch. "There was nothin' to eat but some wet biscuits that were full of maggots and—" his words stopped, and Rachel could hear him begin to heave at the side of the road.

Realizing she had let him go too far with his story, she desperately tried to change the subject, "Tuck, do you have a wife and children?"

Finally, from somewhere in the bushes she heard him say, "No'em."

There was silence but when he walked back to the wagon he simply said, "Alyce says she will step over the broom with me as soon as Missy Carroll says she can." He picked up the reins and began to lead the horse down the path.

Rachel watched the young slave and wondered what it was like for him, knowing he will never have any control over his life, always at the mercy of his owner. In Tuck's case, he was in kind and considerate hands, being owned by Mrs. Carroll. But that still did not give freedom to do as you pleased. Rachel thought for a moment about her own life and the hard times she had experienced and sometimes fearful of what was ahead. But knowing she was free to make her own choices made her life okay.

They went on in silence with the hot afternoon sun beating down. By now Tuck was slowing down his pace and Rachel felt it was time to give him reason for rest. "Tuck, you can stop over there under that grove of trees." She knew he preferred to walk rather than ride but they were not making fast enough time. She would insist he take the front seat to continue after she sat out the meal. After they ate she told Tuck to unhitch Thunder and take him to the creek to water. The heat was surely working on the old horse's heart by now. Maybe that was why Tuck insisted he walk the horse. Slaves knew about things like that if they were good slaves.

As she waited for Tuck to return she watched a wagon traveling fast from the direction of Fredericktown. She could see a man with a woman and some children in the back, slowing down like they wanted to tell her something. The man began pointing to Tuck and began to yell a warning. "You better not let that slave out of sight like that. The word is out that a gang is snatching up slaves all along this way. We heard at least twenty have disappeared."

Rachel yelled back a frantic appreciation for the warning as the strangers raced their own wagon on up the road. She turned and yelled at Tuck in a demanding voice.

"Tuck, bring Thunder now—hurry." For the first time she gave out an unmistakable command to the slave, in a tone unlike her nature. Tuck turned around in alarm as if to wonder what he had done wrong. She pointed to the strangers wagon almost out of sight by now. "A man in that wagon just told me we could be in danger." There was no way they could make it to the house her brother had suggested and she began to look around at their location and realized they had already passed the crossroad going to her sister's cabins. The Willis cabin might be closer but Elizabeth did not take kindly to being put upon by anyone now that Richard was so ill, so she decided to cut through to the Betterton's place. Besides, they had the safest barn in which to keep Tuck. She could always expect the Bettertons to stay close to home as they had a larger farm and more chores than the others aside from the Littlefield's much farther down on the road.

It would be late evening by the time they could get to the Betterton's cabin. What she did not want was to be out in the dark forestlands with a slave after dark. Someone could grab them before they had time to run. Her fears were churning in her head about the gang. She had heard of men seeking out unsuspecting owners and their slaves. She knew the stories of the Paxton Boys lying in caves to shoot Indians as they rode by, but she had never heard of them stealing slaves. It must be another gang.

Thunder's pace slowed to almost a limp by the time they reached Eleanor's cabin just as the sun disappeared from the sky.

The Betterton's dogs signaled their arrival long before they reached the door. Thomas Betterton, carrying a lighted torch, was already halfway down the road to see who was coming.

"Thomas, it is Rachel Lee. I'm on my way to Fredericktown to handle the will and I have a slave with me."

Thomas Betterton yelled back to his wife with a touch of excitement in his voice, "Eleanor, Rachel is here."

Immediately Eleanor ran out to greet her, carrying her youngest child, little Joseph, and right behind her were the other boys. Joshua tugged at her skirt, wanting to be picked up in the presence of this stranger in the night. The other Betterton children were less shy and James and Thomas Jr. ran over to pet Thunder.

It was young Thomas who noticed something wrong with the horse and called out, "Aunt Rachel, is Thunder okay? He is sweating awful bad." The boys all knew and loved this old horse. They had ridden behind him and on him every time they visited their grandfather's place.

Eleanor could not wait to talk to her sister and rushed the children to the barn to tend to the horse. "Oh, Rachel, you're here at last. What a wonderful surprise to have you come." She looked at Tuck still standing there, waiting for Rachel to tell him what he should do. Your slave can go to the barn with the boys. I'll bring out some food for him." Then she whispered to Rachel, "What's his name, the slave, I mean?" she cut her eyes in the direction of Tuck. "When did you get him?"

"Oh, Eleanor, he is not my slave. Mrs. Carroll insisted I bring him along to keep me safe."

"I see. That was right nicely of her."

Rachel went on to explain, "He has been such a help, probably the best slave in all of Frederick County." Tuck was having a hard time keeping his smile off his face after the kind words of the two sisters. He was not used to this much attention. "Tuck, this is my sister, Eleanor. You might have seen her at Father's place on visits." Tuck set his eyes on the floor for lack of knowing what to say or do in this moment of being brought into the conversation, saying only, "yes'um, yes'um."

Once the meal was over and the dishes done, Eleanor could not wait to have a long uninterrupted talk with her sister. It was the first time to have her visit since their father had died and she had so many questions to ask. "Father loved that place better than any place I know. Remember how he used to take us out to the edges and point out which trees set the boundaries? I think I could still find the chestnut that had that secret hole in it. Father said Elizabeth had made a hole in the tree side and put a marble in it. Of course, in a few years the hole had grown over, but I remember we could still see a tiny bit of the color showing at the opening. What fun times we had living back there."

Rachel was still touched by her father's death and the fact that she was struggling to keep up. "It seems I work from sun up to long after sundown, and I still can not make the farm produce by myself. Sometimes, I do not know if life is worth all this work. Maybe—" she started to say something then let the words drop.

"Maybe? Maybe what? What were you going to say, Rachel?"

"Maybe, if I had something to live for it would be different. There is no one that cares if I come or go—well outside of keeping old Thunder alive, I guess."

Eleanor dried her hands on her apron and went to the shelf over the back wall. She took down a rolled paper tied with a scrap of one of her old dresses. "Here, look at this," she said as she shoved it into Rachel's hand.

Rachel took the paper, holding it near the fireplace to read. "I'm not too good at reading this kind of wording."

"Well, try as best you can," Eleanor said.

The word London was written in big elegant lettering at the top, then some printed words with spaces to write something in between. It said First day of December, 1729."

Rachel looked up at Eleanor. "This was before I was born."

Eleanor nodded her head, "I know, and I was only three years old."

Rachel looked again at the partly printed and partly written in long hand words. She could read, for five years, written in long hand filled into one space, then other spaces were filled in with the age as sixteen and the name Thomas Betterton signed to the bottom. She looked up at her sister. "What is this Eleanor?

"It is Thomas's indenture paper. We keep it close to remind us that life can offer up a fair amount of joy if we set our dreams in the right places. When he was just a lad of sixteen, he made the decision to come. Sadly, when he went to the ship clerk to buy the ticket he was told his pockets did not contain enough monies to pay for it."

Eleanor brushed the paper with her hand and continued to tell the story. "Somehow a man heard that he was wanting to come to the colonies but was lacking the ticket. Thomas remembers the sound of the man's voice to this day. He had come to Thomas with a proposition that he would be willing to give Thomas the monies in exchange for hard work for a number of years. Thomas was so excited. Then he remembered the warning by the family living next door when he was a child. Their sons had come to the colonies as indentured servants. Thomas remembered how the boy's parents had sat around the table and each evening talk about the mistreatment their sons were having at the hands of the masters in the colonies. Some of the boys were beaten so badly they could not walk for days. But the one story that frightened Thomas the most was the boy that wrote back telling of several servants whose masters refused to give them enough to eat or clothes to keep warm, and they had frozen to death one snowy night."

Eleanor got up to dip her hands in a bucket and splash her face to relieve the sweat on her brow. Rachel wondered if it was because of the heat, or was it from thinking about the pain Thomas experienced. "Now there was Thomas standing before the man with a hand full of monies with which to buy the ticket and the sound still in his head of the old couple around that table crying over their sons. Should he become an indentured servant in order to have a better life? Would he truly have a better life than what he could get in Cricklade, Wiltshire? That's in England you know."

Rachel looked again at the date on the paper. "Did he decide right then to come?"

Eleanor went on with the story, enjoying the telling of it. "He said he looked back at the long line of men going to the work and knew that what he wanted in life was not to be found in those jobs at the factory. He signed the paper with the man on the boat and came to America. For five long years he did just what the Mr. White told him to do without anytime to play as he pleased."

Rachel broke in to ask, "Is that the same Mr. White that tried to get the courts to make Father open up the road through his land?"

Eleanor thought about it a moment. "You may be right. He was hard to get along with. I know that from Thomas." Eleanor went back to the story. "Finally, when he turned his twenty-one year he was set free. But the work was not much easier then either. He had to work hard just to feed his stomach. But he made it happen." Eleanor took the paper from Rachel and pointed to the words Five Years. "After five years he had his freedom. Of coarse, he likes to tease me that a wife was not part of his freedom agreement." Eleanor laughed her goodhearted laugh and waved the paper. "Like I said, Rachel, he keeps this on the shelf." Eleanor carefully rolled up the paper and tied the old ragged cloth around it and slid it to the back of the shelf. "When things get really hard—when we do not know what is going to happen, we take the certificate down and he reads it to me. We call it our freedom certificate."

Tears were at the edge of Rachel's eyes as Eleanor finished her story. "That is so sweet. At least you have someone to share your life." And for a time she said nothing, but the thought was there.

When she spoke again her voice changed to a somber tone. "I did not want to expose what your brother-in-law, William Betterton had the nerve to suggest, but I feel I can not hold it in any longer. Has your Thomas told you the men are planning to force me to marry so the land will be cared for? William in his sarcastic way told me the men were afraid I would have to come live with one of them if I did not get a husband to keep me away. They are thinking of someone to watch the farm."

Rachel began to sob, taking in deep breaths each filled with pain. "Eleanor, I spent the last years of our parents life caring for them. Not once did I demand the men to come help if they did not want to. Why is it now I am so unwanted?"

Eleanor shook her head in sympathy. She reached down and picked up the quilt from the top of the trunk. "Let's go outside where it is cool so we can talk."

She spread the quilt on the ground. "I've heard some talk," Eleanor continued. "I tried to tell them all it was not right. But with Thomas and all of the men, even our brothers, it is hard to be heard over their set ways."

"You knew about it and did not tell me?"

"I did not think it would happen. They worry about how much it takes to keep your cabin fit, the taxes paid and the fields harvested. The monies— well you know all too well what it is like. But they would never agree between themselves on the right man."

Eleanor tried to sound as convincing as she could. Her hands were tied. She trusted Thomas too much to tell him what to do. Besides, Rachel did need someone to help her. She just was not going to tell her little sister that. Besides, she was sure about the men never agreeing on someone. That seemed to satisfy Rachel's questions for now.

They sat down back to back like they had done when they were young. Eleanor changed the subject to something they both could enjoy talking about.

"How is it Mrs. Carroll trusted you to take such a prized slave to town with all the problems they are having with the slaves these days?" Eleanor asked.

Rachel began to tell her the story of how John had left her in Fredericktown on the last trip to the courts. "He thought his letter to William and Rebeckah would get to them in time, but it did not. I had to take a ride with one of the guests from the boarding house."

"Oh, sweet Rachel. How could John do that to you? He knows how unreliable a letter delivery is."

"When Mrs. Carroll said I should take Tuck, I took kindly to the idea. Tuck behaves very well. I don't expect any trouble from him."

Eleanor shifted herself on the quilt and declared, "No more talk of other people. Tell me what I have so much wanted to hear—I want to know your thoughts on Father's last hours and the burial. I still grieve over not being able to go. I have talked to Anne, but you know how indifferent she can be. The story always has to go the way she wants it to go. And by the time I saw our sisters Sarah and Elizabeth to ask, they had other things on their minds. Everyone forgets I need to hear all the words," Eleanor said.

Rachel told her all about her father's last days and what it had taken to pay off the debts, being forced to go to the Glassford's big warehouse, and the amusing episode with Mr. Cramphlin's widow. "And to think she thought I was paying a visit to fetch her son, Allen Bowie, or the stepson Thomas Jr. as a husband." They laughed so freely and it felt good. It had been a long time since Rachel enjoyed the company of her sister.

The conversation went from one family the next. Then Eleanor told the obvious, "I guess you noticed there is to be another Betterton to grace this fine home. It should be born about the end of the year. Thomas is so good to me, Rachel. He treasures all he has, maybe even more than most of the men in the family. Okay, that is enough about my family, now tell me about the shopping you did in Fredericktown."

Rachel began telling her about mishap at the blacksmith shop and how she had fallen into the creek. She was about to tell the story of the rude man knocking her down at the face painter's shop, but Thomas came around the side of the cabin after finishing his chores.

"Well ladies, it sounds like you have just about shared all the stories. I could hear you laughing all the way to the barn. I hate to make bad news a part of your visit, Rachel, and I have not fretted Eleanor with the news as yet either," Thomas said.

"Oh, Thomas, you make it sound so serious. You are scaring me," Eleanor said.

Thomas began to describe what he had heard, and the women knew it was, indeed serious. "A man on his way through my field today told me about something he had heard a little after midday. There has apparently been an Indian massacre in the direction going into Fredericktown. This man reported he had come by the way of the schoolhouse and spotted a party of Indians coming from the road to the schoolhouse. These Indians had blood on their bodies and arms. The man telling the story had not heard the ending to the story. But with a schoolroom full of young ones in such an unprotected setting, the story would not appear to have a happy ending. I think you had better leave a little after sunrise so not to be traveling after dark tomorrow."

Thomas went on to give Rachel more instructions and then abruptly changed the subject. "I do not like worrying you more, but I think you better take one of my horses tomorrow. Thunder just won't make it all the way to Fredericktown. He is just too old for that much work. I'll see that the boys rub him down good each day and he will make it back home when you get back."

She had seen the way the old horse was limping by the time they got to her sister's cabin. That was good news for Rachel and she thanked him several times over the evening.

Rachel slept very little that night, haunted by the stories of Indian's possibly killing schoolchildren and her concern over Thunder.

She called for Tuck to bring the wagon around early. And like Thomas had suggested, one of his horses was hitched to it. Again she thanked Thomas for his care toward old Thunder. Thomas gave instructions on how to cut through to Monocacy River Bridge. It would take longer and the road was not as good but it was safer. "I wish I had the time to go with you, but the planting is in the middle now." He turned to Tuck and began to warn him to not listen to anyone but Miss Lee.

By the time the sun was at high noon Tuck was coaxing the horse along the muddy waters of the Monococy. They would be in Fredericktown late afternoon. Suddenly, a movement along the river caught Rachel's eye. A horse with a rider came out of the thicket below the road and motioned for others to come out. It looked to be about ten men in all, gathering in a clearing, waiting together but not talking. Her heart began to race. She noticed they all wore the same colored neckerchiefs. The warning from the travelers the afternoon before—and Thomas this morning had said the slave snatchers were traveling in a group like this. Were these men tracking the gang or were they the gang themselves? She called quietly for Tuck to turn around and listen carefully to her instructions, "Tuck don't leave my side no matter what some one might tell you. Listen only to me. These are dangerous men in this place and they will want to take you away to harm. Do you hear me—Tuck, do you understand?"

"Yes 'em, Missy Lee." Tuck nodded his head—his eyes wide with fear.

The rifle lay beside her in the back of the wagon. She had always been a good shot, but that was in unthreatening times. If someone came at her could she steady the gun enough to shoot?

The men had begun to move around nervously. She stiffened, tightening the grip on the gun. If they were up to no good she would be in trouble. There was no other part of the river shallow enough on this day to cross. The men were at the bend where their wagon would come up on the other side.

She had started praying under her breath for protection when she heard a horse coming up behind her. Seized with fear she turned to see who it was.

Overwhelming relief came over her as she realized this young man, in the twenty something years and very strong, was her nephew. She called to Tuck, "Pull over. It is my sister Elizabeth's son. "Oh, my soul, William Sierra, you are a sight for sore eyes. How did you know we were on this road?"

"I just took mother over to Aunt Eleanor's to help her pickle some of her garden, and they said you had left just a short time before. We got there shortly after you left. Uncle Thomas told us you had the slave with you. Mother sent me on ahead to see that you didn't run into trouble. There is talk among the farmers that a gang is traveling together, slipping up behind unsuspecting slaves and whisking them away. I'm on my way to see the sheriff about it, right now. Someone took our mare night before last, and we think it was these men that took her. There were about ten horses we tracked on the road near our house. It looks like this could be the gang." William looked around to see if anyone would be crossing with his Aunt, but they were all alone. "I'll stay with you 'til you get across then I need to run on ahead to catch the sheriff. On the way back home you might be better off to cross the Monocacy down past Aunt Martha's place and take the Ferry across in case the water comes up."

William turned to Tuck and addressed the problem. "You have to watch this River. It will fool even the best prepared. I've seen it rise several feet in a few minutes when there has been a rain." He turned back to Rachel. "There is a man named Daniel James farther down on this river. He runs the ferry at high water times. He is also the gunsmith for these parts, so no harm would come to you with that kind of fire power available—just thought I would mention it." William motioned for them to follow and started across the bridge.

Rachel motioned Tuck to move quickly onto the bridge. She kept her eyes cut in the direction of the men but without turning her head toward them. To her relief she saw another wagon approaching from the other side. The gang of men must have seen it too, because they quickly moved up the bank into the trees. But before they passed from sight, Rachel saw one of the gang point to her wagon. Had they singled out Tuck as a possible victim for their taking? Her heart did not stop bounding until they had safely crossed the waters and caught up with several other wagons going to Fredericktown.

When they reached the boarding house it was time for the evening meal. Never had she been so relieved to see the extremely plain face of Phoebe Graves. While Tuck waited at the back door for his food, Rachel gave her things to Miss Phoebe's new girl, Moriah. She would wash up for the meal just as soon as she saw Tuck safely locked in the shed at the back of the boarding house. It was necessary to lock him in for his own safety against any kidnappers.

Rachel could barely keep her eyes open during the meal as they passed the smoked fat back bacon and corn pudding. After eating some, she was ready to excuse herself from the table, and retire to her room. But before she could leave, one of the guests began recounting the same gruesome story that her brother-in-law had spoken of the night before. The woman did not spare anyone's stomach in the account. "The little boy that didn't die said the children were all just reading their books, and no one had noticed the Indians slithering under the outside windows and coming in the back door just as one big one jumped in up front. He grabbed the school master from behind and slit his throat real fast and the children were screaming and jumping up to run, but there was no where to go. The Indians in the back caught them one at a time and split them in two with hatchets. A few lived to tell the story but nine bled to death by the time a parent heard the screams and came running. And then that poor distraught mother fell over faint and couldn't help a one of them they said. My biggest boy was one of them that went over to the schoolhouse and found the room full of dead ones. We sat out in our wagon and watched as those that belonged to the children came to pick them up—all wrapped in blankets most were. You ever see anything like that?" the woman turned to Rachel and asked.

Rachel shook her head no. All of a sudden her own fear of seeing the slave snatchers gang seemed a lot less frightening.

Sun was coming through the lace curtains when she finally opened her eyes the next morning. She could hear the rumble of the wagons on the street below. They were already bringing their wares into the market. Horrified that she had slept so late she quickly reached for her dress. Tuck would be waiting for his breakfast. She rushed around gathering up what she needed to carry to the clerk and stuffed the papers in a small cloth satchel she had made before her first court visit. Now it was showing the wear of all the business she had carried on the last few months. Her thoughts raced ahead to what was needed this morning. She remembered to find the shopping list and tuck it in the satchel as well. Hopefully this was her last trip to Fredericktown for a year, as her crops had suffered because of them. She was forced to leave Tuck locked in his shed and hoped the heat did not make him sick. After the noon meal she would take him with her to do the shopping.

Rachel had planned the trip over and over. In order to keep her promise of showing the slave what the city life was like, she planned to have him follow behind her and carry the few items she could afford to purchase. That way no one would question what a white woman was doing walking around town talking to a slave.

When Rachel walked into the dining room for breakfast, the clock on the wall chimed a quarter passed seven. A new boarder, a much older woman that looked to be a plantation owner, was the only one sitting at the long table.

Moriah brought in the meal just as the new boarder was about to speak. "Was that your slave in the shed last night?"

Rachel turned toward the woman, "Yes, well actually he is not mine but was loaned to me by his owner. I needed help on this trip. Why do you ask?"

The woman looked up from her plate. "I'd watch him real close. I put the two I bought yesterday, out there. Sure hated to have to do it. A man at the courthouse said there were rumors spreading around of some slave snatchers in Fredericktown. It seems to be a front for that gang they believe to be down by the Monocacy."

Rachel felt sick at her stomach with fear. Her mind raced just thinking about what could happen. Maybe she should send word that she could not come to the court today and take Tuck down to her brother-in-law for safekeeping. Thomas would watch him for her.

She quickly rolled what was left of her mostly uneaten breakfast into a napkin to take to Tuck. There was no time to have a proper meal and she rushed out the door to the shed. It was obvious the slave was relieved to see her, and he eagerly grabbed his breakfast. She moved closer to the small opening in the gate and whispered to Tuck. "You and the other slaves must be very quiet if someone comes around." She hurriedly explained about the new danger he was in. "I will be back to take you with me shopping just as soon as the court clears my father's will."

Rachel rushed out to the street. Would it be better to go all the way down to the end of Second Street and take Record Street to the courthouse, thus avoiding all the venders and their wagons just setting up their wares, or just go straight down Public Street as she usually did? She retied the slipping bonnet to her head and started to cross the street just as a wagon piled high with crates of chickens turned from the side street and all but ran her down. "You almost ran over me," she called in vain over the noise of squawking hens and squeaky wagon wheels.

By the time Rachel reached the corner the decision of which street to take was decided for her. A crowd had gathered to watch two men fighting in the middle of Public Street.

As she came to the end of Second Street a man was standing between the two houses at the end. At a first glance she thought it was someone she had seen before. She had spent so much time in Fredericktown she likely had passed him on one of the streets. When she looked up again he was nowhere in sight.

Rachel picked up her pace. An uneasy feeling struck at her. She could almost feel his eyes calculating her every move from his hiding place between the houses. The feeling worked on her mind, warning her senses.

Several people were already in front of her when she opened the door to the courthouse and gave her name to the man at the front. Again she had reason to regret sleeping so late. She could not help but listen to the gossip of those around her as they talked about the massacre of the children and the latest news relating to Cresap and his Indian friend, Nimocolin. Another man was arguing with someone about what was happening with the ships sitting in port waiting to be loaded. He was getting heated about his dislike of the duties the people "over there" were making him cough up. Rachel thought about the ship at the Glassford Company. She was glad she was not a man being forced to deal with the likes of ships going back to England. As long as those at the warehouses would buy her tobacco she was not going to complain.

A man stepped out from the big room and called out Rachel Lee loudly. "There is an empty table next to the window," he pointed.

She bent down and gathered up her satchel with the papers. It was very hot in the big room, and a woman at one of the tables must have been overcome from the heat, because a group of men had gathered around her to help put her in a chair. Thankfully, the window by the table was letting some breeze in. The man sitting at the table looked up at her, "Miss Lee, you have come to finalize your father's will, I hope?"

"Yes, sir."

Maybe it was the heat that rushed the business along, but as soon as she handed him the papers she had brought from Mr. Peters and from Thomas Cramphlin Jr. signifying she had paid the debts in full, he only glanced at them.

"You are now free to release all provisions to be divided in the will," he said, as he took a stamp press from the drawer and slid the paper between the design leaving an imprint of the official emblem of the county. The words, spoken with a complete lack of interest, gave meaning to how he carelessly threw the papers into a basket. Nor did he look up when he dismissed the case by saying, "Next," looking past her to the person waiting by the door.

She made no move to leave. She couldn't. Her feet had become feet of clay. After all these years her father had been the main one in their family, the one everyone looked to for the decisions, and now—now he was dismissed with the word, "Next."

James Lee's life was over. He owned nothing. All that he had worked for now belonged to someone else, and at the bottom of his balance sheet, only the word "memories" appeared. Why had someone not warned her about what to expect when it was over? Her mind was overwhelmed with emotion as she walked through the outer room and pushed the big door open to find only the sad eyes of unknown faces waiting to hear their fate.

Rachel walked from the courtyard and turned slowly toward the creek to be alone. The shops along the way had once captured her attention but now held no interest whatsoever. She walked past the open door of All Saints Church and could hear the organist practicing the pump organ for the Sunday services. It seemed to invite her to come, sit, and meditate. Slipping into the back pew, she sat with her eyes closed. The words to the music were those she had heard many times at her own parish church when she sat with her family, "Oh, God, Our Help In Ages Past, Our Hope For Years To Come." Her emotions yielded to the words, never before seeking the true depth of their meaning. She wept quietly until there was no more need for her tears. The still small voice of God had spoken. It reminded her of the verse her father used to quote when she came upon troubled times, "Be still and know that I am God."

As she walked from the dark church the sunlight seemed to renew her spirit. She looked back at the open door and spoke softly. "Oh, God—only you holds the 'next' for my life."

Rachel started back toward the boarding house past the big barn in the middle of Market Street. It was crowed at this time of morning. She walked through the filled stalls. The street around the barn was crowded with horses and wagons. The children ran in and out around them playing tag. It was like a big family gathering. She picked up a strange looking squash and thought this would be a good year to try something new for her garden. She knew Mrs. Carroll would be eager to share some of her seeds she ordered each season from the catalogs. Yes, next year she would plant. She smiled. There was that word "next" again.

From the vegetable stalls she could see people bargaining for their goods. At the same time the children were playing ball with the apples from someone's basket, and a man carried a large wooden box of potatoes to a wagon. It was a happy place to be. She stopped to select a few new things she could carry home with her. A nice looking man in one of the stalls had just helped a woman load her wagon with a basket of the nicest green beans she had seen all year. When he came back she asked for a small basket as well.

"I'll take enough for a small meal," she told him.

"Oh, now, surely your husband can eat all of these. How about I put a few extra in for you," he said smiling.

Rachel thought to herself what a convincing salesman this man is. "Oh, I'm the only one that will be eating them," she admitted and strangely wanted to tell him there was no husband but caught her words before blurting it out.

He placed the beans in a basket and told her to have a good day. Then he turned and went to the water barrel, taking care to fill the gourd dipper with water and handed it to an old woman sitting at the back of his stall. Rachel decided she was probably his mother or grandmother. It was hard to know. She looked old, but old could be anything. Was this what she would be like some day? Her nieces and nephews would simply call her their old Aunt Rachel. She laughed at the thought, at the same time it was painful to think about. She remembered the conversation with Eleanor. It was true, if the good life was to come for her, it would have to be out of her own courage. No one else could make it happen.

It must have been obvious to the man that Rachel was being curious when he looked up again and saw her still standing there. He did not say anything but there was a slight frown on his face. Rachel's face flushed with embarrassment. She had been taught not to stare. But this man was so kind to everyone he helped, why would she not notice? She imagined what he must be like with his wife and children at home.

She rushed on. Maybe this afternoon she could come back to buy the goods when she brought Tuck out with her.

She ate her dinner without the leisure of talking to anyone at the table and called for the provisions for the slave. She gathered up her shopping baskets and went to the shed to fetch Tuck to help carry the goods.

Tuck so much wanted to see the town, and in honesty she needed him to carry her goods. At this point she did not care what others thought, and her thinking surprised her. When she had first come to Fredericktown she would have worried about what others thought. But now it was her business, and no one need tell her how she should conduct it.

When she went to get Tuck, he started doing his fast jig again like when they were on the road. But this time she knew it was because he was happy. She had never seen anyone this excited to experience life in the big city as much as this slave. As they passed the courthouse she took time to explain what she had done there that morning and even showed him the window she had sat by. Tuck just nodded his head. From there she hurried him along to the stores.

By the time her list had been marked off, her monies were almost gone. The last purchase was new sheeting at the material store.

As Rachel handed the wrapped purchase to the slave, she noticed a worried look on his face. "What's wrong Tuck...you look sad?"

"Missy Lee, youse said somethin bout me seein the big churches."

Rachel remembered telling him about the times she had gone into All Saints Church and how the organ sounded so pretty. "You are right I did promise that. And just as soon as we deposit these purchases to the boarding house, I will take you to the church."

By the time they got back to the church where the organist had been playing that morning, the afternoon sun was beginning to sink. Rachel opened the door to the church, and noticed Tuck pulling back, appearing to be afraid of something.

"What's wrong Tuck? This is what you wanted to see, isn't it?

Oh, Missy Lee, I'd be thinking the Lord won't sees me in such a fine place like this, causin he'd be having so many other good things to look at."

"Tuck, the Lord looks at the heart and I think your heart is just fine."

They went in and stood at the back of the church for a few minutes and Tuck began to weep. "Oh Missy Lee, I's think I's gone to heaven."

As they left the church Rachel could not help but think how the simple faith of the heart would always find approval from the Lord.

If they did not hurry she would miss the evening meal and Tuck would not be fed, as well. The sun was past the roofs of the houses when they walked back by the Courthouse Square on the way to the boarding house. People were starting to gather around the large illumination fire as the flute player and fiddler began warming up.

Rachel stopped to watch. Tuck started to clap and shuffle his feet with the rhythm. It reminded her of the dances they once had in the summer time on Chestnut Ridge. Her older brothers and sisters had let her watch when she was younger. She loved the neat steps of handing off to the next partner. By the time she was old enough to do the dances everyone had left home and there were no more dances. She wondered what it would be like to experience her feet moving so fast, she could almost fly.

As the crowd grew larger around her, a man dressed in a bright colored bloused shirt with a scarf tied to his neck danced past her and took her arm, pulling her into the lively dance. She was passed from one partner to the next so fast she hardly could catch her breath. The excitement was infectious causing her to laugh freely with the rest of the dancers. When the music died down she was surprised to find herself left in the hands of the man from the market place. He stood back and in the dim light of the setting sun said, "It's you again. I saw you at the market place this afternoon."

Somewhat flustered, she laughed, half out of breath and half for the excitement of dancing and set back that he remembered her face. "I never learned to dance much."

"Well Missy, for some one not dancing much you certainly seemed to be quick on your feet," the man said, eyeing Rachel with interest and a smile on his face.

Rachel laughed at his words.

"And a fine laughter you have as well," the man replied with a smile. "Do you live in this town?"

"Oh, no, I'm from the country. I've just come to settle my father's will." The words did not fit her actions just now. What must he be thinking of her dancing while possessed with grief. "My father died in late January and he had set aside my name to speak for his will."

A frown had come over the man's face as he said with a touch of sarcasm, "That is a most serious task and you find the time to dance as well?"

Rachel was about to tell him she was here to finalize the inventory so he would not think so harshly of her actions. Just then a gun went off in the street. Two men had started a fight. The crowd turned to see what had happened, and the man Rachel was talking to ran toward the fight. Rachel quickly turned back to where she had left Tuck. Panic struck her heart. He was gone!

She raced to the street, frantically calling his name and begged of the people nearby, "Did you see a slave standing here? Someone has taken my slave." Her panic began to swell around her and everyone seemed to realize the gravity of what had happened. One man called out above the crowd noise, "There's a gang working the town looking for slaves to snatch away."

The crowd swarmed the street yelling, "What's the slaves name? Where did he come from? What happened to him?" They made their way down the street checking out the buildings along the way. Some of the men had torches and the lights popped up and down between the buildings. But Tuck had vanished in the dusk light.

By the time the crowd reached the creek, Rachel decided to turn back to the boarding house. If Tuck had gotten scared he might have simply gone back to the safety of the shed. This time as she passed the court house there were only a few people still standing under the trees. She stood for a moment at the corner to take one last look around as the sun slipped completely out of sight.

The man at the market, and the same one whom she was dancing with when the gunshots were fired was walking in her direction.

His voice held anger. "What kind of a slave owner are you? What could you have been thinking to leave an unwatched slave in the middle of this crowd while you danced?"

For the second time that evening Rachel started to explain to him that it was not her intent to leave Tuck unattended but she had been taken in by one of the dancers. Before she could explain he turned to walk away. As he did, he aimed a few hurtful words over his shoulders.

"I thought to myself, now here is a kind woman looking after her father's final wish. How wrong I was. You are nothing but someone out to frolic."

"But I was—" The explanation fell lamely at her feet.

As much as she wanted to change this man's image of her she realized she had no time to deal with this rude man. What mattered now was going in search of Tuck. She turned and frantically ran to the boarding house to seek help from Phoebe Graves. Miss Graves knew people and maybe someone could suggest what to do to find Tuck. After still more running from corner to corner to ask about Tuck, she told Mrs. Carroll about losing her fine slave and went to her room to quandary about her fate. She had cleared up her father's debts without having to sell her land, but at this rate she would become an indentured servant to the Carroll's for the remainder of her life. Never had the sweet sleep of death seemed so much an escape as it did now. Finally, in exhaustion, she closed her eyes to a restless sleep. Only once did she think about the man who had danced with her. And it was not a pleasant thought. Why were men like that? So quick to accuse— always right about everything, or so they thought.

Sometime just before dawn Rachel heard a frantic knock on her door and jumped up as the pounding continued. Miss Phoebe rushed in not waiting to be invited. "Oh, Miss Lee, you will never believe who has just come to our door—the sheriff—he's here. I had gone to get his help last evening while you were searching. Go down to the door." The woman was so excited she could barely relate the news. "It so seems they went out looking for the slave." The woman turned to leave, then turned back to rush Rachel along. "Come see what he says—hurry on."

Rachel slipped her dress over her head and took the steps in bare feet while she twisted the loose hair that had been released the night before. When Miss Phoebe unlocked the front door again, Rachel saw the sheriff waiting rather impatiently.

"I'm Rachel Lee. Do you have word of my slave?" All the time she was talking she had the feeling she should explain the fact that Tuck was not her slave but that of the rich land owner that lived next to her. But then fewer words seemed better. She just hoped the sheriff would not think she was trying to tell an untruth.

"Well now, Miss Lee—that depends. We found a slave that says his name is Tuck and is the property of a Mrs. Carroll. I believe Miss Graves here, said the slave you lost was named Tuck as well. Is he the one you said was taken by force?"

Rachel wished she had not introduced herself as the owner. Now she would have to explain after all. "Yes sir, he was loaned to me by Mrs. Carroll from up on the Sligo Branch. I'm most anxious to return him safely to his owner."

"We do have him so don't fret so much."

Rachel impatiently broke in not wanting to wait for the sheriff to explain, "Where did you find him—is he alright—when can I get him back?"

The sheriff took his time unraveling the events of the night before and how it was they had found the slave. "I've been watching on occasions a group of men as they tried to slip into town in the dark of night. At first I didn't think much of it—it has been going on since maybe the turn of this year."

Rachel tried to break in but the sheriff continued. It was not until the sheriff spoke the name she feared the most, did she become spell bound by his story.

"They would go straight to the face painter's shop, then leave with large objects wrapped in what looked like some hides. Sometimes they pulled a wagon, it was so big. Guess you wouldn't know, but the shop on Second Street has a big root cellar in the back. I went there last night to watch after Miss Graves properly came to report the slave missing."

"Was it the portrait painter that seized Mr. Carroll's slave?"

"Seems to me Mr. Wolstein is the one calling out the rules alright, but he had other gentlemen of sorts doing the mean work. And what's more, we suspect they were all part of what we have begun to call the Painter boys, working in slave sales. They steal them, then take them to another region and sell them. Seems to be making a good business out of it."

The sheriff told how these men would start a fight to get the attention of the crowd and then other men would surround the slave and move him out of sight. When no one was paying attention they would move him to the painter's house.

"These slaves are just too scared to make a fuss, because they were being threatened of harm. You know how a slave can be whipped if he makes a fuss over anything. So most likely the slave will do what he is told. We have been suspicious of the Portrait Painter ever since he set up to paint face pictures a couple of years before. I always knew something was going on wrong there after I saw some of the pictures he tried to paint."

"I cannot tell you how relieved I am that you have found Tuck," Rachel said. But the sheriff did not seem to hear her. Instead his mind was still on the case.

"There is still one more question to be answered." The sheriff let the thought linger in the early morning dampness. "We now have to question what the candle maker has to do with the operation." He turned to go but then turned back to add one more thing for the already stunned Rachel to think on. "Your slave led us to the whole story. I'll keep him in the jail for safety until you are ready to go."

Rachel rushed upstairs and packed the baskets and called to Miss Phoebe for her breakfast and vittles for Tuck to eat on the road. She would make the decision where to stay tonight after they passed the noon hour. It was time to go home for the last time.

Chapter 17

Feb 1765
Seneca Creek

Another crack of thunder split the sky as Rebeckah screamed with gut wrenching pain—then dead silence. William tried to block out the surroundings by focusing his eyes deep into the roaring fire. It was taking too long. She had been in the borning bed for two days. Elizabeth Dawson had come from the next farm to assist. Finally, she had come down the steps to say another midwife was needed. He had gone to ask if someone from the William Hawker's place could come as well. Now both were telling him that it would be a miracle if Rebeckah or the baby lived.

What would he do if Rebeckah succumbed in the birthing? There was a numb feeling in his head. His first thought was that the young children needed a mother. Could Nancy handle all the chores and prepare the food and see to little Mary, just shy of walking, and this new baby also? Nancy was only thirteen—or was it fourteen? At fourteen some girls were already getting married. Could she handle Solomon and his childish spoiled ways? The thought of this baby, if it even lived, and its need to nurse— Maybe he could take it to another nursing mother's house until it grew used to the cow's milk. He knew nothing of taking care of babies.

Another thought crossed his tormented thoughts. The brothers would insist Rachel be brought to his cabin as a way of escaping having to deal with a continuing looking for a man for her. There was no way he could ever train her to fit into his beliefs. His life was the way he wanted it. Rebeckah had learned to abide by his thoughts and ways. The thought added more pain to the moment.

The children sat quietly looking into the same fire as their father—waiting for any sound that their life was going to be safe from desolate times. With every sound from upstairs they looked up but said nothing. Little Mary could not understand why her mother did not come for her and cried endlessly. Nancy picked her up and tried to quiet the crying. Solomon sat on the floor watching Absolom spin the top on the hearth, trying to throw spit wads to make it stop. He would laugh excitedly each time, seemingly unaware of the gravity of the situation.

It had been almost one year to the week since they had waited for baby Mary to be born. That had turned out all right, but this time it seemed much worse.

Rebeckah screamed again. William wondered if he should send word to Robert Lee's house that the family needed to come stand beside them in the deathwatch. William got up, too restless to think inside. He pulled his heavy bearskin coat from the hook by the door.

With his hand on the door he called out to his children. "Absolom, you keep the boy occupied until I come back." Then he reinforced the order with a tap of his foot on the floor. "I mean that Absolom. And young William you share the hornbook with Solomon if he wants to draw. What your mother does not need is to hear a fight downstairs." Young William was sitting at the table working on his lessons, but mainly making little scribbles on the hornbook, trying to keep his mind off of what was going on upstairs.

William needed John to be here to feed the cattle and wished he had not let him go away with Benoni Dawson the day before yesterday to work on the roads. If only he had White Horse to help him.

In a completely exhausted voice, Rebeckah called out "Oh God, let me die—please just let me die."

William pulled the heavy latch on the door. The cold February rain drenched his face and neck but it did nothing to deaden any thoughts of what was about to happen. Not even his old dogs followed him on this day.

Alone, standing on the creek bank, a deer watched him move closer before bounding from the bank.

Rebeckah had always loved the sight of a deer in the woods, William thought. He walked to the water's edge and let his body sink to the cold wet ground. For what seemed like an eternity, he watched stick after stick float by on the swollen creek. A freezing wind replaced the rain on his back as if God was dealing out the punishment one strike at a time, shrouding his cold form.

Where would he bury them? Would she want to be put in the ground here on the farm as a constant reminder she had been here? But then the Monocacy church had a nice enough cemetery and it was close to take the coffin within the daylight hours. Would she want to be buried there? Strangely, now he realized they had never once discussed the need for a burial place in their years together.

William pulled himself up and started up the hill. Exhaustion took over his body, and after a few steps he stopped, emotionally unable to return to the cabin. His body felt older than his forty-seven years. Living in the colonies was extremely hard work. Tobacco could be good one year and wiped out the next by a worm or bug or lack of rain. You could lose everything. Maybe it would be easier to keep food on the table for the children if he took them back to England. He could find a tutoring position at the academy. Thoughts of his early life among the fine countryside surrounded him for a moment, then just as quick it was replaced with the reality there was no one left there to go back to. His parents and grandparents had been dead for many years. He wondered if his sister was still living. There had been no answers to his letters for years. He let his mind wander. He thought of how much effort it had taken his aging grandparents to see that they were reared with enough determination to survive, knowing they would not live to see them grown. "Fight if you have to," they had said, "and if you lose, get up and fight again, but know which side is right" William remembered there was little room for sentimental feelings. Was that why he had such a difficult time showing his emotion? As a young man any show of kindness made him angry because it played to the tender side of his heart and he had learned early that tenderness would not fill his pockets. But that was before Rebeckah—Rebeckah with her funny little sayings and the ways she always tried so hard to please him.

The old anger that brought him and his brother to this new country began to surface. Cruel treatment stayed with a man.

William looked around at his land, cleared by the strength of his own back. From the time he had patented this land he had worked his life into it, knowing he was free to work as he pleased. For sixteen years he had pulled the stumps from the forest and put the crops in. At first there had been only one cow. Now the hillside was spotted with a full herd. And his sheep gave as much wool as Rebeckah could use to clothe them. His eyes came again to the cabin sitting at the bottom of the hill, near the road. He could see smoke softly curling from the chimney, belying all was well inside. But he knew better. Nothing could bring death away from his door.

It was so easy to shed the blame and resent wrong treatment. There was no one else that could change the outcome but Rebeckah herself. She was letting him down.

William let out his vengeance the only way he knew and yelled from deep in his throat, "Damn you Rebeckah, it's not a good time to die."

The realization of what he had just proclaimed left him shocked, and sickened his very being to the core. How could he be so calloused toward her? It was her life in the balance this very minute. He was acting as if she had planned in some vindictive way to make his life miserable. He sank to his knees and in great sobs began to beg for forgiveness. The first cries gave way to a distress call. "Oh God, Father, Almighty, the giver of all life, forgive me. I am guilty of the meanness unlike any other man."

The man that had been so proud of who he was, now crumbled to the earth hardly able to breath as one enormous cry went into another. Never had he felt this much contrition. Before he stood up again he had asked for forgiveness for everything he thought to be a misdeed in his life. But the sin he most begged forgiveness for was the grievous sin of making Rebeckah's life miserable. He wondered what contemptible evil dwelt within him?

William had put the blame on her for the embarrassment dealt by Solomon when he scared the horses at the fair. His thinking had been as childish as Solomon had been. What kind of a person would not allow her to leave the farm all these months? His grief was of his own hands and now he prayed, "Father God, forgive me my most loathsome sins. It is not Rebeckah that must suffer for what I did."

He got to his feet, stripped off his coat and as a symbol of remorse, walked determinedly into the cold creek, letting the icy waters painfully scourge his sins. He knew of nothing less to do.

Rebeckah gave him a daughter. At the first look she seemed pathetically created with a flattened head. He could not help thinking it would have been better if the child had died before her first breath was taken. Rebeckah clung to life by some force that only William could recognize now. God had heard his prayers. That was all that he had asked for. Late one night as he stood over the bed where his still very ill wife was sleeping, the unnamed baby next to her, he was overcome with grief. He could not help himself as his tears said the words his lips could not say. Reaching down he picked up the sleeping baby and gently traced the contours of her soft face. The show of emotion was so unlike William. The baby's tiny mouth formed a delicate smile as she slept, softening the spirit of William. He did not know where the words came from, they just came, and he looked into her tiny face and said, "Little Lucy Luce you are going to be alright." As he put her back in the arms of his sleeping wife, he whispered, "Becka, I think we'll just call her Lucy."

By the time spring came, Rebeckah slowly was finding the strength she needed to keep the life that had been given back to her. And to all their relief, baby Lucy's head had recovered from the hard and long birth. Even William admitted to Rebeckah, "I think maybe she is your prettiest offering yet."

On the first day after the danger of frost Rebeckah begged to let young William leave the field early to help see to the babies while she and Nancy could have this time uninterrupted. And to her surprise, William did not object.

Rebeckah called for Nancy to come with her to their garden, and the two of them began digging the hard, untended ground together. The dirt felt good in her hands. There was just something so satisfying after a hard cold winter to feel the soil sifting between her fingers and sense the promise of new growth.

She handed Nancy the seeds and picked up the hoe to work a trench all the way around the garden. This was Rebeckah's favorite garden, the kitchen garden, because each morning she could see from her window the little sprouts peeking out from the ground.

Rebeckah loved this time alone with her oldest daughter. Their conversation went from the seeds and how to lay out the design of the greens, to the future marriage chest they would start preparing for her this summer. At fourteen, Nancy was becoming a young lady with beautiful curls falling from her cap, and Rebeckah knew it could happen all too soon that her daughter would find the love of her life and move away. She wanted to have her prepared for a house of her own just like her own mother and sisters had done for her.

Rebeckah stood up to look at what they had done. "Nancy, maybe we should have put the cabbage over there in the center to make a bigger color."

Nancy sighed, "Mother it does not matter now because no one ever comes to visit anyway."

Rebeckah knew she was right. The contests that once sparked new designs in gardening were a thing of the past. But the thought that her daughter was giving up making things pretty disturbed her. "Nancy, that talk will defeat. It is enough just to have something pretty for your eyes alone."

As they were finishing the last of the planting Nancy pointed out a cloud of dust rising on the main road. A rider was wasting no time getting to where he was going. Rebeckah stood up to watch. You could never count on it being good news when someone rode this fast on their path. Rebeckah hurried to finish covering the last row of seeds that Nancy had set down and then grabbed her daughter's hand to run quickly to the house.

By the time Benoni Dawson got to the house he was yelling, "Where's Mr. Littlefield? Father sent me to deliver news."

Rebeckah pointed to the field just over the hill. Benoni spurred his horse and rode on to relay the urgent news. And just as fast, he had gone on to the next neighbor to carry the message.

William quickly gathered up his tools and called to John to come with him to the barn. "You are sixteen, and it is time for you to come with me to hear the news of the future."

Once he was at the barn door he called to Rebeckah. "Go roll up a meal. I'm taking John with me. We will go first to Dowden's Ordinary to hear what the travelers are saying there and then on into Fredericktown if need be. I hope to meet with anyone that has the latest news from the ship docks." William put the bit into his horse's mouth and threw John the harness for his horse. "It is important we get there quickly and the wagon and oxen are just too slow."

Rebeckah ran to see what was causing her husband to be in such a rush. "What is it, William? Why are you taking John with you—what is going on?"

He turned back to answer Rebeckah. "Benoni said a man on his way to cross the Potomac brought news of a bulletin being circulated along the road. It concerns word given to the officials at one of the docks coming into the New York harbor. It was from the parliament and it sounds disruptive to all of us. He said all along the road people were talking of nothing else. John is well into sixteen and needs to be informed as to how to do business with the men, so I am taking him with me. Absolom will work in the field close by while we are gone in case you need him.

William led the horses from the barn and yelled back to Rebeckah. "Pack my suit as well and something for John. I do not entertain him looking like a country hired hand coming to town."

On the fourth day William and John had returned as quickly as they had left. They went straight to the field after putting the horses to pasture. It was obvious to Rebeckah that William either did not want to admit it was all a hoax, or it was so mean he did not wish to alarm her. She could only rationalize that it was a painful revelation concerning his homeland.

By late evening she had cleared away the dishes from the table and lit the candles for the scripture readings, but still no talk. If she asked again, he would admonish her by saying, "Rebeckah, you do not need to know everything a man must deal with." She had memorized his speech from other times she had pestered for an answer. That was one thing William did not do was to talk a lot. He found no time for simple chatter, as he called it; he never had and she suspected he never would.

When Rebeckah finally placed baby Lucy in her cradle, and pushed her shoes under the bed, she turned to say something to William. Her words received no response. He had fallen asleep. As it always was after an encounter over his homeland, William restlessly turned from one side of the bed to the other, pulling her share of covers with him. She could hear him sigh and mutter something under his breath, then fall back into a tormented sleep.

Sometime after she heard the two o'clock chime from the room below, he sat up and said, "Rebeckah, something very bad is about to happen."

She sat straight up. "William, what is it, who is here?"

"I speak not of someone at our door. It concerns the future of the colonies." He spoke with annoyance in his voice, like she should have known what he was feeling.

She put her head back on the pillow, for once relieved no one was at her door.

William had put his feet on the floor, his head between his hands, and began a troubled talk.

"Rebeckah, you know this of me, I have always been true to my heritage. I even went so far as to denounce some of our neighbors for speaking out against the ruling of the parliament. I trusted reasoning, even when the ruling was hard to swallow."

"That is true of you, William," Rebeckah said, not sure what he was getting at but willing to listen.

Slowly he moved from the bed to the window, looking out into the night. Then he turned and started down the stairs still talking as if to invite Rebeckah to come listen to his grievances. At first she just wanted the comfort of her bed but knew this was a new side of William, willing to talk to her and she did not want to disappoint him.

He poked at the dying embers in the fireplace as he began to talk. "Five days ago a ship docked at Annapolis that left London three months ago. A passenger brought with him an arm full of newspapers and began passing them out. The pages were full of accounts of the rioting taking place on the streets." William dropped his poke and said disgustedly, "They are upset that the colonists are not paying for the war."

"I remember you explained the King was taking the Frenchmen to war because they kept trying to take over the British held lands. So why are we expected to pay? "

"You are right, Rebeckah." William said, as if he was proud she had remembered. "They have forgotten it was for their own purpose they fought the war. And now the people riot to make parliament pass a rule that we have to pay for it—or at least what they consider our share. I can see how some would think that. But have they forgotten it was our soldiers that fought along the side of the British? We lost our men, our wagons our horses, just like they did."

"And we fed them our beef and pork," Rebeckah said defiantly. "I know I had to give up three pigs when they came around asking for food."

William went on, "Because of us King George can now boast of having more land than any other ruler. He has what the French once owned over here. Now more goods are being sent to England, and in return England collects more duties. In time the war debt will be paid by the extra duties the mother country will collect. It is a simple method of return."

William was quiet as he contemplated all that was going on with his homeland.

Rebeckah thought he surely had run out of words and she could go back upstairs to her warm bed. But instead he turned to her and almost in a whisper made a shocking confession.

"I say this with the trust you will not spread my thoughts on this matter to any other. What I do not need is to have someone think I have sided against my country." He looked at her for an answer. "Well, do you hear me?"

"William, when do I ever have visitors or go to sit with anyone?"

"Very well. My worry has to do with the youthfulness of the third King George. I cannot tell what his reasoning is. One of those London papers had been brought to the ordinary when I was there, and I read an editorial by one of the writers I have agreed with in the past. It cited a gentleman that referred to the colonists as the footstools to their great nation. In the next line he said we only had little farms compared to the large estates of the British. I have to ask myself, do they really consider us Englishmen any longer? It has the sound of orphan children made to clean up the crumbs after the masters have left the table."

Rebeckah let out a gasp. "William, is it really that bad?"

"Would I be going on like this if it were not? I do not know of many Englishmen that do not consider they are British to the core. No different than if we still took our water from the Thames. Now the people on the streets of London make light of our farms and consider us to be lesser than their own."

Rebeckah realized she could never remember him talking to her at such length about anything, adding to the seriousness of his need to confide in someone he could trust.

"Is that why they tax us so much?" Rebeckah asked.

"Partly, yes. I paid little attention to the taxes when I first came over. I felt so privileged to be on new lands of promise. Then I started paying attention to each new tax. But we needed to help pay the bills for the parliament and their security. I have no quarrel with that reasoning. Their fine old buildings and the King's palace are expensive to maintain. We have no expenses to that grandeur in the colonies.

But it was the recent Sugar Tax brought me to thinking how it was putting some people out of their trade."

"I remember you told me to watch the sugar loaf, making sure we saved more maple syrup for our sweetening," Rebeckah said.

"We do not make much with the sugar cone but in New England they use much sugar to make the rum. That is what parliament is eyeing. The British rum makers do not like the competition so they set out to make it hard to afford to make the rum over here. Now if we need rum we have to buy it from old England."

"What about the laces they taxed for?" Rebeckah wanted to know. "I have no lace on my new gown because of that tax."

"There again they want to keep the trade to themselves—lace is their specialty. The more we make to sell, the less special their lace is."

William stood up and poked the fire again before he went on. "By the time John and I got to the ordinary the latest tax on paper was on everyone's mind. But no one seemed to know what it was all about. At the time I felt it was something minor and we could figure out a way to refrain from using so much paper. It would hurt our practices more than our pocket books."

"Why did they decide to tax paper and not something we use more?" Rebeckah asked.

"Yes, the same I was thinking. Most households do not keep a supply of paper stacked on their shelves."

Rebeckah felt proud that she had thought the same thought as her husband and smiled to herself.

"Not satisfied with the information we were hearing, John and I decided to go to the port at Annapolis to see if any later ships had arrived. And as luck would have it, we could see the full sails of a ship just off shore, ready to dock within the hour. A swarm of people were thinking as I did, wanting to hear what the parliament was intending. The news almost caused a riot on this side of the ocean as well."

"William, what are you saying?"

"A stamp will be attached to everything we use that is paper. Not just the blank paper we have on our shelf, but everything made of vellum. Grenville has outdone himself in his devious thinking. He made sure we would pay money to the parliament this time."

"Can we not make our own paper and not have to use their fine product?" Rebeckah asked.

"Rebeckah, you do not understand what I am saying. It is not the paper itself; it is the stamp that will have to go on it if it is to be official. That is where the hostility begins."

Rebeckah was not sure of her understanding on how this tax would hurt the colonists. "Can we not pay for it?"

"That is not the point, Rebeckah. Sure we can pay for it. It will take considerable monies from our pockets, but we can manage it. At least we can; some cannot. The real problem is how they went about sneaking in such a tax without first letting us defend our position."

"Then how will this effect us?" Rebeckah asked, trying to understand the gravity of the rationing.

William's voice rose, frustrated with how little a woman knew about taxes. "They are putting a tax on paper, playing cards, our documents we make with the courthouse, even my letter writing. Oh, and the newspapers that we read at the tavern. One of their special stamps will have to be placed on it before it can be printed."

Rebeckah pulled her shawl tighter around her shoulders in the damp night air and waited for her husband to end his tirade and go back to bed. But he continued, unable to put the tax out of his mind for the night.

"I am not saying that we should not pay our fair share for the war or for anything else we need from the parliament. My complaint is that our ideas should have been considered before they put it into practice. It is the principal of our freedom that has been attacked. Now, to have them declare us separate and apart is disturbing."

"What is going to happen?"

"I do not rightly know, Rebeckah. But according to a man returning home on the last ship after being in London for a year, it seems the young King has only listened to the voices on that side."

"Is that why you and John were so upset and would not talk when you came home?"

William did not answer her, instead carried on with his thoughts. "The men at Dowden's Ordinary are rightly calling it taxation without representation; pure and simple it is." William took in a short breath like a pain had come to him.

"William, some men get chest attacks when they get upset. You are not so young as to have one. Maybe you should set your worries aside until you hear more news."

"Rebeckah, I do not need you to ride this down. It is a serious matter and if you do not want to listen I will take it to Thomas Dawson on the morrow. I thought you would want to know."

"Oh, I do William, but not at causing your heart to pain."

"My heart is okay. It is my mind that is not."

"Very well" she said almost defiantly, "If your heart gives out over this heated talk I will say it was because your beloved King killed you. Then you will be mad at me for blaming the British and come back to life." In the end she dared to tease, hoping his spirit would calm down.

He took a deep breath and she thought for a moment he was going to scold her, but surprisingly he played the game with her but did not turn to look at her. "Well, if you insist, I will come back but only so I can prove my beloved British did not kill me."

They were quiet for a time. Then she suggested, "William, on occasions of having to speak before my family, you have said such fine words. Could you go before the Assembly and tell them how you feel?"

"I'm afraid it has gone too far for that. Grenville has hired some of our own colonists to be the collectors of the stamp monies. He thought if the man was chosen from our own neighbors, we would not find it so offensive.

He should know deception never works. A man at the docks showed us a sign in one of the windows and said Grenville had already rented that house to be the official stamp office. They intend to be close so to watch each ship unloaded. He surmises they expect a large smuggling ring will try to confiscate the stamp and make a profit by selling it on the sly."

Rebeckah could not help but yawn from time to time. It had been a long night but one she would not give up just for sleep.

"As John and I were on the road back home, we met up with a man just coming from the courthouse the day before. They cannot file a single deed if the paper does not show the repulsive stamp. Not only deeds, every document will need a stamp to be valid." His voice became angry as he said, "We can not even collect a debt unless we have first bought the stamp for the paper. Do your realize how many debts will go unpaid just because it will cost more to get the stamp than the debt was worth in the first place?" Again he resorted to naming all the items of grief. "All bills, all insurance papers written up to protect our losses," he said as he turned to look at Rebeckah as if this would be on her mind. "Even when we send our boys off to school we will not be able to proudly display their diplomas unless it has that ugly stamp on it."

Rebeckah could hear baby Lucy beginning to cry and put her hand out to pat her husband's arm as she took to the steps to feed the baby. It was not long before her husband followed her up the stairs and crawled into the warm bed.

For as long as Rebeckah had known William she had never heard him place blame on his monarchy—argued yes, but always loyal. But now, this was different, his old beliefs were being betrayed.

After a long silence she asked the question, knowing it would hurt, but unable to leave it unvoiced. "Now are you ready to agree with my brother James, that England does not care what happens to us?"

William was so quiet she turned to see if he had fallen asleep.

Just then he took a deep breath and began to speak in almost a whisper. There was such a yearning in his voice, torn between his distress and the love he had always felt for the country of his birth. "Rebeckah, you ask more than I am ready to admit. England is my heritage—my lifeblood. Without it, the good and the bad, I am but the outer shell of my former life. You know not that side of me before I came to this country. "

William took a deep sigh before he went on.

"When my father died I was too young to know but was told mother took us back to live with her parents, and before many years she died. It took the last strength of my grandparents to see to my sister Anne and brother, John and myself. Few were the times with them, but I learned to admire Grandfather's wisdom. He was an old cloth maker and believed in being stern. On the occasions when Grandfather needed help unloading the cloth, he would take us with him."

William's voice sounded like he could almost laugh at what he was going to say. "Once when he had taken us into the city with him we saw a parade coming down the street. He stopped the wagon and let us get out. I was but a wee bit of a child, not much older than our Solomon at the time. I remember the bright red uniformed soldiers marching along the cobbled street. My heart swelled almost out of my chest with joy. We could hear a commotion up and down the street and the crowd began to cheer. I asked Grandfather why were they cheering, but he did not hear me. A little girl standing close by said 'Don't you know that is our King?' Everyone began to chant as he passed by, hurrah for King George, hurrah for King George! Then the little girl ran out and handed him a rose. I will never forget the feeling of standing there. The King had his driver stop and called the little girl over to his carriage and handed her a coin."

William did laugh this time as he remembered the child-like hope that day.

"I wanted a coin like that so badly, I wanted to be liked by my King just like she was. I know it was a childish reaction, but I was a mere child. When I got back to grandfather's house I pretended the King was handing me a coin. Over and over again, I would pick a flower and run to the road with it when I heard someone coming, hoping it was the King coming by our place. As a small child I did not know he would never come out our way. But I vowed then and there, to be a loyal subject."

Rebeckah spoke softly, not really wanting to be heard, but needing justification, "And you wondered why Solomon ran after the horse at the fair?"

William did not hear her and continued talking. "Grandfather did not spend time outside of work with us. He was too old and we tired him. But on cold evenings, he would sit by the large stone fireplace, and if we asked the right questions about England, he would give us answers and call it our teachings. But we could tell it was because he loved to talk about his country. And if the servant girl had failed to clean the ashes out of the fireplace that day, he would spread some of the dust on the hearth and draw a map to show us how big it was. Sometimes he would pass down the stories of long ago, of men like Sir Francis Drake, knighted by the queen for being the first Englishman to sail round the world. His ship, the *Golden Hind* was so revered that when it was no longer seaworthy they took some of the timber from its side to build a service table for one of the big churches in London."

William took a deep breath, as if now the stories were painful to remember or the times too endearing to recite, but then he continued.

"Grandfather must have had a good life in his early years. I remember how he liked to tell the stories of going into London to hear a play written by the famous Shakespeare. Even then he remembered the lines of the famous plays. In his frail voice he would recite some line he wanted us to hear, using the same eloquence of the deep voiced actor on the stage." William's voice softened, "I remember we liked the words from one play better than the others. He was probably trying to teach us to be truthful. When he spoke them you could almost feel you were listening to a great actor recite his part." William paused. Even Rebeckah felt she was listening to the far off voice of his grandfather as he spoke, *"This above all: to thine self be true, and it must follow as the night the day, thou canst then be false to any man."*

William repeated the words softly, *"to thine self be true."* There are so few memories of my grandparents and none of my parents. If you argue England does not care about its subjects, it is to say my grandfather was misguided in his love for his country. England is my ancestry, Rebeckah."

William again stopped. Then something in his thoughts turned hard. "Then grandfather died, and the courts said I had to have a male guardian because that is the law. They chose William Dawes because he could teach me the cloth milling trade—like Grandfather's trade—to mill the cloth for the clothiers.

The guardian demanded Grandmother must stay away as she was too kindhearted. He said I needed to become a man. He did as the courts dictated and saw to my education as Grandfather wished. I would have to say there is no meaner, nor harsh guardian and overseer than William Dawes. Since John was eight years older than I there was no need to see to his care. But John came to work for Dawes, never telling him he was my brother. I think it was John's way of checking on my well being."

Rebeckah knew these memories were getting hard for William when he reached over and took her hand. "After my education was complete and my age advanced past needing a guardian, I went to work for Dawes because it was the job I could get. John and I worked in the woolen factory from before sun-up until the early hours of the next morning. It was hard work with very little to no pay. And Dawes's temper got meaner when it concerned his business pocket book."

William took another long sigh and muttered something about it served no good to keep these memories alive. But before he went to sleep he remembered the question she had asked about agreeing with James that England does not care what happens to us.

"Your brother James has only colonist dirt under his nails. He does not know how a birth born Englander can feel about his country and his royalty."

The next day Thomas Dawson had come, and they had spent some time talking about the same thing as he had told Rebeckah last night. She felt good that for once he had brought her into his life before sharing with a neighbor.

That night before he pulled the covers up to go to sleep she asked one more question.

"Are there no good memories, William?"

He did not say anything at first. Finally, just as she thought he was asleep he said, "I suppose I could say there are." He made no volunteer to offer any at first. Then slowly as he had the night before, he began to talk. Rebeckah wondered if this was his way of saying good-bye to his past—as passing on of his memories for safe keeping to another.

"Once when John worked for Mr. Dawes he called John into the mill office and told him he would have to take the cloth into the clothiers, as he was too sick to make the trip. John asked if he might take someone with him to help unload the cloth more quickly. It was when I was still under Mr. Dawes's guardianship. Of course, John chose me to go with him.

After we delivered the cloth to the clothiers in London, we were told we had to wait until they had time to check it over for any flaws. The owner must have noticed what eager boys we were and told us to come back at the end of the day to get the monies. We walked all around London, sometimes hitching a ride on a wagon going by, but mainly we walked, stopping to look into the store windows. Becka, I had never before seen so many things to make a life with than were being sold in one place. And on one corner there was the most magnificent church I will ever see. Once, before my grandfather died, grandmother had taken me back where I was christened, and I thought that was the most beautiful church there could be. It was said to have had the highest spire in all of England. But this church in London was larger and more magnificent. Someone was playing the organ and we went in to listen. As the organ pumped, the pipes all across the back wall sounded the notes in rich and full tones. Our organs here in the colonies sound like they are made of tin inside, compared to that organ. I wish you could have heard that one.

As we were leaving London we got down from the carriage and led the horses across the bridge leading out of the city just so we could watch the water of the Thames flowing underneath."

"Do you think you will ever see your brother again, William? Will he ever come this way?" Rebeckah asked, already suspecting the answer would be no.

"John just did not like staying in one place for a long time. If someone said the land was better in another state, then he had to go find out if that was so. And he threatened to change his name from Littlefield as he thought it sounded unimportant. He could be living down the road, for all I know, but with a different name. Maybe he took a ship back to England. He loved the city more than I did, I suppose. I remember after another visit to London he did nothing but talk about how tall and big the Tower of London was and how he wished he could climb to the top."

William did not say anything for a few moments as if holding fast to old memories.

"John was always an adventuresome fellow. He could be depended on to keep our sides splitting." William turned to Rebeckah, and in the dim light of the moon just coming into the window, he spoke like he was letting her in on a secret. "Becka, they say that tower is ninety feet high and on a foggy day you cannot see the top. There is nothing that tall in the colonies— nothing. Every night at dusk they perform the same ceremony that has taken place every night for over four hundred years. The red uniformed British guards march in, surrounding the Yeoman Warder as he carries in one hand the large lighted lantern that swings with each step, flinging shadows against the giant tower wall. And in the other hand the Warder carries the special keys. You could hear them jangling on his heavy key ring. It looked like there were a hundred keys on that ring. But then I was just a young boy— everything looked enormous back then. They took one of those keys and would lock the ancient tower door where Queens and ladies and men had been put before they took them to be hanged or their heads cut off on the tower hill. There were people like Anne Boleyn and Lady Jane Gray and Sir Walter Raleigh, all taken to their deaths from that tower. So many executions for something that did not seem all that important, at least not to be beheaded for."

"How can you know all of this, William?"

"These stories fill every corner of our being from the day we were born. It is our heritage, Rebeckah. And if you ever saw them you would remember too."

"I would like to have been there with you to see that tower."

"John and I visited the tower at night once, and I got an eerie feeling standing in such a place where kings and queens, and commoners alike, have stood—on that very spot for centuries, where we stood that night. Those people that were housed there before their death had to listen to the same deep clang of the clock chimes filling the streets as I was hearing, knowing each night could be their last. Sometimes at night after a rain, I will hear the drops falling slowly, methodically from the tree branch onto the roof. It reminds me of the guards filing past us in the dark that night, each step clicking in perfect rhythm to the next."

William again stopped as if listening again to the sounds. When he spoke again his voice had changed. "Yes, my brother John might have returned back to England."

Each time William told these stories of his homeland, Rebeckah realized he went a little farther back in his memory, telling more of himself than maybe he ever intended, but she was grateful he had included her. She could only imagine the places of which her husband talked. Even her visits to Fredericktown could be counted on her fingers. To visit such a city like London made the colonies pale in comparison.

"What were you like as a young man, William? Did you sport a beautiful lady on your arm when you strolled down the street?"

Rebeckah waited for him to answer, but he had said his piece and now he slept.

The moon on its way to the other side of the cabin filled the window with light, giving definition to the sharp cut of William's face lines. His graying hair only added to his distinguished appearance. She reached over and lightly patted his arm. How was it that a poor country girl such as herself had found such fine husband?

Chapter 18

Late July 1765
Seneca Creek

"One more day and the hay gathering should be finished," William told the field hand standing next to him as they watched the workers slashing the last of the tall grass with the scythe. A few men raked up the last of the yield to the remaining stack poles. His eyes went back to where John slowly guided the horses round and round an almost finished stack. The fields looked good. It had been a better year than last with the extra workers. At no time would he admit to any other that he had been wrong to try to win back his pride by making just his family handle the farm. His crops had suffered because of it, even if the children learned valuable lessons. William pointed to the field. "The hay stacked up right nicely this year." The two men were looking at the stacks of hay with the thatched tops, giving the appearance of a well-set roof, tied down to hold against the wind. It looked like a village of neatly placed huts. The neatness was something he had been made to practice while under the care of his strict guardian. Not that it had been something he enjoyed learning, but it had paid off. His fields gave a well cared-for look to the *William and John.*

William would be glad when the task was finished. It was a dangerous job. Already once this season young William had fallen off the tall stack when the horses failed to heed John's command to halt. If you did not keep your mind on what was happening, a horse could bolt when you tried to start them up before the man sitting on top of the stack finished forking the hay from the wagon. William had seen even long time farmers fall, if the horse bolted, and be pulled under the heavy wheels of the wagon or even worse, be speared by his own fork when falling.

After seeing that the hands were doing their work, he turned to go to the barn. Farming was not what William had intended to do with his life, but if he wanted to feed his family that was what he must do, regardless how much schooling he had. Even the latest King George had been a farmer before becoming King. But to William the schoolhouse was never far from his mind. He would teach young lads and lasses to read and write and become better farmers and maybe have a chance to go onto something grander than making neat hay stacks with thatched roofs.

He remembered his broken rake and went back to pick it up. It had been the deciding breakage to force the repairs of the box of broken tools. The barn door was slightly ajar when he got close. Surely Rebeckah had not let Solomon convince her he was old enough to slide down the pole. She knew he did not approve of the child being left there alone. Who knew what else he would get into.

William looked around for the box he had left on the bench by the door, but it was not there. A sudden exhausted anger began to well up in him. The thought that some of the workers had borrowed tools without asking was unacceptable. He turned to go back to the field to ask who might have taken them when his eye caught sight of the tool rack on the wall of the barn. The broken tools were neatly hung from the hooks in the exact spots he always kept them. The handle of the small handsaw no longer wobbled and a new stick had been rounded out and inserted in the hole of the bed wrench used for tightening up the ropes on his bed. He picked it up to examine it. He had made this tool after seeing one at the blacksmith shop. When you twisted the rope just right and tied it in a knot you would have a good bed. If there was one thing he could not live with was the backache that came from a sagging rope holding up the mattress. He examined the tool again before he put it back on the hook. Someone had fixed it that knew how it was supposed to work.

He pulled each tool from the pegs and realized they were in perfect repair. Even the ones he had decided could wait until he had more time were ready to use. It was another of the strange happenings of late. It had to be White Horse doing the repairs. He was sure none of his sons had repaired them. They did not volunteer work easily.

William called to Rebeckah to come look. Maybe she had seen something.

They stood together looking at the repaired tools hanging on the wall. "I wonder if we will ever find out what happened to make the old man hide from us?" William lamented.

"How old do you think he is? The years must be getting to him by now," Rebeckah said.

William only shook his head as a response. He needed to find the Indian and persuade him to give a reason what had caused him to fear them so much. They had never done anything to show they did not consider him their friend.

When Benoni Dawson brought a letter left at Dowden's Ordinary from Alexander Grant asking him to meet the others in Fredericktown, William eagerly made plans to attend. He had hoped for the chance to again attend the church services at All Saints in Fredericktown. There was something so invigorating about the minister's educated sermons.

Also, this would be a good break for Rebeckah and the children to be dropped off at the Thrasher's cabin, even if it was for just a day and two nights.

As William and Thomas pulled away from the Thrasher cabin they could hear Rebeckah and Martha both yelling one last instruction. "Be sure you get some word about Rachel while you are there." Both men looked at each other, knowing all too well if peace was to prevail, the news they would come home with was not news they would dare share with their wives. At least, not yet.

The closing prayers at All Saints Church in Fredericktown had just ended, and William Littlefield walked out to extend a hand to some of the parishioners. To his disappointment the Reverend Mr. Bacon had not been there to deliver the sermon. Instead a local reader was assigned to stand up while the Rector was away in Annapolis writing the church papers. William had hoped to speak to the Reverend Bacon about his thoughts of setting up a school in the Seneca area but now it seemed unlikely he would have the occasion. The word had also been passed around that that Reverend Bacon was not well and would not be able to meet with anyone in the foreseeable future when he did return back to the parish. In fact, the news was that he might be forced to resign if his illness prevailed.

As William waited for Thomas who was caught behind two women talking in the aisle, he spotted John Seager just coming down the street, his horse still wet with lather from the hard ride. William whistled to get his attention.

"Over here, John."

"What's so important that Alexander would call meeting on a Sunday?" John asked as he dismounted and tied his horse at the rail.

"It concerns Rachel's care I'm sure." William said it loud enough for others to hear, when he knew full well it had more to do with the news just delivered from London this week, the same news that Thomas Dawson had sent Benoni to deliver after coming from the port. William did not want anyone to suspect something more. A family gathering was not considered a sin, but a business meeting on the Sabbath would have signaled an arrest by the sheriff. Their words would have to be spoken softly so not to arouse the attention of the authorities, which might not be an easy thing to do, considering how some of the brothers could get rather distraught at times. Especially, if John Hughes was in attendance.

"I guess you heard I've bought some of John Wofford's land to help him fulfill some debts," John Seager told William.

William's response was what it always was. "Why was I not told so as to have a chance to bid as well?"

John Seager tried not to show the anger he felt at William for something that had happened on other occasions. "What gives you the need to always buy up the land, William? The rest of us need to make crops too," John asked with a more than a testy exchange.

Maybe the exchange of words between the two in-laws could be attributed to the heat this time. But any weather brought cause if someone bought a choice piece of land before someone else could make a bid on it.

By the time all the brothers gathered at the tavern known by the local peoples as Washington and Braddock's meeting place, the heat was stifling. William himself had been here just last year and he wondered what ever happened to the old man's son that fell from his chair that night.

The men tried to stay cool, dressed only in their breeches and bloused shirts. Occasionally they would go to the water's edge and douse their faces in the sun-warmed waters of Carroll Creek. The big oak trees did very little to help cool the air in the hot August afternoon.

Alexander Grant reached for his jug and took a swig of cider, then spoke in a soft voice. "I've called you here to talk about the recent—" He abruptly changed the topic when he saw one of the local sheriffs walking down by the creek within earshot. "I've called you here to talk about our dear sister Rachel—she is in need of volunteers to help with the fall crops."

What was to be a short topic took up more of the afternoon than the men had planned.

John Hughes had words to say. Rachel was making them all look bad. At least that was the feeling of some. The others sensed a confrontation developing.

William Littlefield wrote the notes on his paper as he always did at the meeting. Among the grievances were weeds almost to the door, no crop planted, barn roof gone on one side. Robert Lee stood up and said he had heard she was letting the graves become overgrown with thistles.

One of the men queried John Lee, who had been given the second half of the home place by their parents. "John, you must be worried about the likelihood of lightening striking a fire in those weeds and it coming over the ridge to your cabin," one of the men called out.

John agreed with the men about the risk of fire being bad. But he would not be one to lay blame on his sister. "I've tried to help her out, but I have more work to do than I can handle unless I hire some hands. And there don't seem to be any available right now—I've been inquiring."

The issue of finding a husband for Rachel was now considered to be more urgent. "It is going to be hard enough finding someone to marry such a woman out of her prime much less if the farm is all run over," Alexander said.

Finally, John Wofford told the group that it was hopeless finding someone that would consider the farm a good trade for marriage to Rachel. "At least someone we know that we could trust with the land."

John Hughes again spoke. "Taxes are coming due again and you know what that means. You better dig in your pockets for some extra or the land will belong to the courts."

"If any of you have any more ideas I would be glad to write them down," William told the men. They all shook their heads in frustration.

"We could put her up for auction. I'd be happy to take the land off your hands," John Seager said.

The men laughed, knowing John would be just too happy to have the land at the same time knowing they would not do that to Rachel—maybe just wishing they could if they had to pay her taxes.

"Well, if any of you hear of someone, you better act on it or he will slip away like the others," William instructed the men.

By now the sheriff had moved away and they felt free to go on with a more regular meeting.

Alexander went over to his coat and pulled a letter from the pocket and was about to read it when Thomas Thrasher broke in. "Before I forget it, we need to agree on the holding of the tobacco price."

The men listened to Thomas Thrasher bring up what was perceived to be unfair trade on the tobacco this year. It concerned every planter and you better stick together to hold your prices high. "They need our tobacco, and at least we can give it a try."

"It appears this is a most urgent matter," John Wofford agreed, "but if I cannot find some hogsheads to roll it there, how can I help hold the price?"

"I have five hogsheads left over from what I have ready to roll. You can use them," Thomas Thrasher volunteered.

Thomas Betterton jumped up with a wise crack. "Just don't leave any bad tobacco in the bottom," he jokingly retorted. That comment brought a round of laughter from the other men. They each remembered how some years before Thomas had gotten in trouble with the officials and was almost hauled off to jail. They had charged him with purposely trying to sell bad scorched tobacco by putting it in the end of the hogshead after the barrels had been checked.

The men, anxious to hear the important news, called to Alexander to hurry up. "The sun will be sinking before I can get home as it is," Robert called out.

Alexander waved a letter for all to see. "An acquaintance has given me a letter from his brother living under the King's eyes. He cannot verify his concern at the time of this posting, but I expect when we meet again it will have been made public."

A few men in earshot of the brothers became interested in the letter and moved closer to hear.

Alexander carefully looked around for any sighting of the sheriff before he peeled away the partially broken back seal of the torn watermarked letter. The sweat on his forehead dripped over his eyelids blinding the words. He wiped his brow with the gray sash from around his waist.

"It will not be surprising to any of you that the King has allowed parliament to impose a new act of tax on us. As far as we can tell it was to be passed during the next session. They said even our fine debater Ben Franklin could not persuade Grenville's men to cancel it. This letter has more information on what to expect."

Alexander picked his way through the first few words. "*Dear brother, I entreat you to judge me not for my word scripting. Thy messenger nary learned as yours ever, so I have asked my son to write it to you with me doing the talking.*"

"Get to the point, just tell us what the message says." John Hughes again showed impatience as he paced back and forth behind the others along the bank.

"Well, it says here, *my friend's brother witnessed the boxing of all sorts of stamps.* Here, William read this. My eyes read a little poorly of late."

William took the letter from Alexander and held it up to read to himself, first trying to make out the scribbled words. Then he explained, "It seems this man has seen the stamps for himself and is writing to give a description. He says, and I am reading as best I can, *Some stamps have the words One Penny written on it with a crown sitting on top and a number 8 next to it. Another one said America over the stamp and Half Penne under it.*" William looked up and said, "—another crown on this one as well, but larger." He lifted the paper closer to try to make out the words. "—*and a number 143 pressed on it.* The last stamps says, *II-Shillings-VI-Pence* with America at the top." William let the letter fall to his side. "It seems they have used the crown on every one of them, as you would expect. The man goes on to give the account of seeing the stamps with his own eyes because he was friends with the man that was boxing them up in wooden boxes to ship to the colonies. The man said his friend thought we should know what to look for."

John Seager let out a yelp. "Like we would not find out for ourselves when we are forced to use them!"

William handed the letter back to Alexander and sat down on the side of the bank. It was hard not to show the displeasure he had felt the last few days after Benoni had brought the news from the docks. He did not like the turn in the attitude of the parliament. But more than just disagreeing with them it was the way his freedoms were being suppressed with each new tax. But if he spoke out now against it and the parliament backed down and he took up their side again he would be called a traitor for stepping from one side to the other.

A man not related to the brothers' group, but that had been listening, stood up to offer something the others had not heard. "Just this morning I met up with a traveler on my road as I was coming here. He had just come on a ship from England two days ago and allowed that he was standing in front of the Parliament door when a group of governors came out, and he heard them being braggadocios about putting the colonists in their place."

Alexander stood up and spoke as one with extreme concern, "Gentleman that is exactly why I called this meeting. We need to be heard. This affects us all. Just remember when you go into this tavern and call for your newspaper, in a few months you will not have that pleasure without a price. Nor will your deck of cards be fresh and unmarked. They must have the new stamp on it and that will leave the establishment's balance sheet in red. The King is robbing us.

"Right, right!" most of the men shouted. No one as yet had started the chant "down with the King!" But it could be just a matter of time if this oppression continued.

William had not said much, if anything, during this meeting, but he could not let it pass with out trying to reason with the men. He put his hand in the air to quiet the crowd. "Before we go blaming the Parliament let us look at why they are demanding a tax. Agreed?"

The crowd began to protest, leaving William to his own speech. John Wofford leaned over to William, barely able to be heard over the squabble, "I think we are outnumbered in the allegiance to the King." Both men wished William Wofford still lived among them. Before going to the Carolinas he had all but controlled the crowd for the British rule.

"We have few true Englishmen left among us," William said as he turned from the crowd. "But as long as the rebel colonists control their actions, I see nothing that will disrupt the trade. Sure, a few stamps will be sold, then the colonists will stop buying the things needed, and Grenville will know he has been defeated. Simple as that. I've seen it happen before. If we act civil about this tax, the colonists do not need to worry, and we will keep the kings favor."

"But, it merits watching. I do not feel comfortable with England cutting off our trade with other countries unless we come through their ports. That bothers me," John said.

William again raised his voice to the crowd with a new approach. "Instead of fighting with the parliament, why don't we think about our future right here. Find as much land as you can, and have the deed filed before they send the stamp."

"That is not enough and you know it, William," one of the men yelled back.

Only a few men living near by had stayed around to talk as the sun started the slant downward over the mountain ridge to the west. Their voices could still be heard rising and falling in disagreement over when this stamped paper would arrive and on which ship.

Finally, when the smell of the leg of mutton roasting on the spit in the tavern's kitchen began to reach the creek bank, they forgot about the British and considered the needs of their stomachs.

James Lee Jr. stopped in front of William's table to issue some advice. "William, I feel you are showing more of a strong alliance to England than is needed in the light of the arguments we have heard today. Father always said you were strong-minded when it came to British rule." He tapped his finger on the table. "It would be wise to hold your thoughts to yourselves in the public place."

William was not one to be told how to think. He had walked away from the mother country because of someone trying to dictate his thinking, and he did not intend to sit by and let someone tell him what he should do now.

"James, I respected your father because he was Rebeckah's father, even though I did not always agree with his thinking. But I will not be told by you or any other man here as to how I should act, much less how I should think."

Thomas Thrasher overheard the conversation. He turned to Robert Lee. "This heat is more debilitating than any I remember. I suspect a fight could break out before the evening is down."

A more prophetic statement was never made as a group of men started making comments around the persons of James Lee and William Littlefield.

Rebeckah sat with Martha on a bench outside of the Thrasher cabin enjoying the first breeze of the evening. The children were all playing a game of tag along the road. Even Martha's son John, a year younger than Solomon, had been allowed to join in the game for the first time. When the children let out a whooping yell that their fathers were coming, both women ran to meet them, anxious to hear news from the other families.

Still some distance away they yelled, "Did you hear any news of Rachel? Is she coming this way soon?" Rebeckah called out.

But one look at her husband told her he had already talked too much, and too freely.

She shook her head and turned to look at Martha. "Well, I would say they had an eventful meeting." But to herself she could almost hear the saying he considered his very own mantra, *To Thine Own Self Be True,* circling and settling somewhere over his black eye.

Chapter 19

Fall 1765
Seneca Creek

The commotion coming from the barnyard sent Rebeckah out the door with her broom. Something was attacking her chickens, and she was ready to do battle.

"Get away—get away from my chickens," she yelled as she ran to the barn. In utter terror she stopped. For weeks there had been a rumor among the neighboring farmers that something was killing their livestock, and now she was face to face with the big cat. Her broom was useless against this beast. Its blazing green eyes angrily pierced her soul. She stood frozen in place all the while the cat hissed his displeasure at her being there. Its sharp teeth were ready to tear her throat open, and huge claws were ready to pull the flesh from it. Suddenly, yesterday's news of the old man and woman being found with their flesh torn from their bones flashed before her. That had happened on the other side of their creek. Could this bloodthirsty animal be the same one that did it? She dared not yell for help or run. One leap and he could overtake her. As she stood motionless, a new more terrifying thought struck at her heart. What if little Mary toddled out the door to find her? And Nancy would surely come to check on her. She felt sick at her stomach and the surroundings seemed to sway around her.

The cat crouched, positioning itself to pounce. Suddenly an object descended so fast from somewhere above her she had not seen it coming. The big cat let out a wild scream and dropped in a dying fit at her feet.

She was dumbstruck. An arrow was wedged deep into the ribs. She dropped to her knees crying and shaking,

"White Horse—White Horse, you saved my life—you saved my life." She looked around for the old Indian but as usual there was not sign of him. But in her heart she knew that it had to have been him. There was no other that could shoot that strong and so accurate.

William had dropped his scythe when he heard Rebeckah scream. By the time he got to her she was still standing next to the dead cat, crying uncontrollably. He pulled her away and sent her to the cabin, then he went into the woods to look for White Horse. What could have happened to White Horse to make him still watch over the family but at the same time be afraid to come close?

William followed the footprints until they reached the creek, all the while calling White Horse's name. There was no answer.

For weeks the children sat spellbound as the stories of the cat were told over and over again. Solomon wanted to go out and see a big cat. He would wrestle him with his bare hands. The others laughed at his belief that he was so strong. William just watched him and remembered how much this child had always gotten himself into trouble. But to Rebeckah, this event had shaken her more than she wanted the children to know. Life in the rugged country of the western part of the province still held the threats of wild beast, and ravaging Indians, and if that did not put you down, some disease was always waiting to test your ability to hold on. It was life and death, pure and simple. You could only hope to survive, and all the worrying you did would not change one thing. Maybe her mother had been right. You just have to go on, believing you will be here tomorrow.

Rebeckah wiped her face on her apron as she watched the last ears of corn bobble in the boiling water in the cauldron. If it were not for the outdoor fireplace she would have surely melted away by now. "There, that is the last of the corn for this year. I have enough drying on the roof to feed us until mid winter. If we can't find some to buy we will have some mighty hungry children come January." She turned to frown at the men in her family who were standing by for their supper. "Seems to me you had better take into consideration how many mouths there are to feed when it comes to planting time next year."

Solomon started spieling off the names. "There's Mummy, and Papaw, and John."

Nancy broke into the recitation. "John's getting married."

Everyone in the family stopped what they were doing and began to question her. John sat at the end of the table, saying nothing but looking like he wanted to be any place else but at that table.

"You are only sixteen years, John Littlefield and I will not hear of it. How can you afford to feed the poor girl?" Rebeckah was the first to scold. She turned to her daughter. "How did you come by this story, Nancy? Your brother seems to not be willing to talk."

Nancy, feeling embarrassed at the attention placed on her for the announcement, began to explain. "Gretchen Stringer told me John had kissed her sister, and now John is promised to Betsy Stringer because her father caught him kissing her. I promise that is all she said."

"I kissed her only once," John said, looking sheepish.

"Once is enough to get you married. You better go to Mr. Stringer and apologize, else we may have one more mouth to feed as your mother so aptly pointed out."

That was the end of the discussion but enough that William decided it was time to have the fatherly talk, as was the custom.

Maybe it was her fragile condition after the episode with the big cat, but now talk like this brought Rebeckah to question her life. The thought of her children marrying and moving away tore at her heart. She knew the time was coming when John would find a girl with which to share his life. That would be the start of the empty house, and the thought of being alone broke her heart. What would she do? Would she shrivel up like the old woman living down the road that sat in her chair all day, crying because she had no more children to grace her table? Rebeckah thought about that and felt sentimental and close to tears. When William looked up from the table where he was entering words into his ledger, she asked, "William, after they are all gone from my table, will you still love me?"

William, looking puzzled at his wife's question, spoke in a passive voice, "Might as well Becka, might as well." That was all that was said between them, but Rebeckah knew that was all he could give. He had never felt free to express his affections to anyone for as long as she had known him. Sometimes she wondered if it was part of his growing up without parents that caused him to be afraid to give of his heart.

William did not wait for her to speak foolishly again and changed the subject. "Rebeckah, do you recall if there was a cabin already on the land your father bought at Chestnut Ridge, and was it in 1741?"

Rebeckah turned to look at him for an explanation as to why he needed to know this detail just now, but William had his eyes on the paper he was writing. She turned back to the pot she was stirring on the fire. "We had to go to Elizabeth's house while father built the cabin." She became silent, not wanting to remember anything about living under the same roof as William Norris, her sister's second husband. When William pressed her to tell him a date she said, "It was in 1741."

"How can you be sure?"

"I am sure, William—very sure." She walked outside to stand in the night air. The thought still upset her to this day.

William continued to write the entries onto his paper alongside the roughly drawn out map he had committed to memory from visits to family gatherings. He was determined to document all the land deals that had gone on with their families and not let the rest of the family buy up more than they should.

"Did I tell you that Elizabeth Northcraft has filed poor Edward's will? I saw him about a year ago at Dowden's, I think it was, and he looked poorly then. I suspect Elizabeth will be wanting a good price for the land when she decides to sell. They say she is smart with the affairs of the courts so won't be taken in by any sweet-talking man for a cheap price. John Seager has probably already approached her about selling."

"Is that where the Buxton family lived?"

"Yes, it is next to Alexander and Sarah so they should buy it before John can get his hands on it," William said, laughing.

His ink pen scratched out deed for deed as he recited the words.

"Ninian Beall buys from Abraham Neighbors, wife Rebecca signs."

He looked at what he had just written and wondered why the Neighbors brothers had sold to Ninian Beall instead of some of the men living in the area. He didn't know Abraham Neighbors that well but remembered he had witnessed William Norris's will.

William set his pen down and allowed the thoughts to creep back in of when he had first met Abraham. Most of all, he remembered the night that Abraham had found the schoolmaster lying in the creek. It was in January and a snowstorm had come down suddenly. Norris was trying to get home from the schoolhouse and had fallen into a creek while trying to take a short cut after sending the students home early. If Abraham Neighbors and his brother had not come along it was clear William Norris would have frozen to death right then. He had known nothing of the death's door experience until Elizabeth sent a farm hand to deliver a message to the schoolhouse saying he was needed at once at the Norris cabin. Those were the days he had shared the teaching responsibilities in different schoolhouses in order to make a living. It didn't take much to live back then—no wife—no children. Just his blanket roll with his beloved dictionary tucked between the covers.

That night they thought William Norris would die and he was needed to write out the poor friend's last will and testament. When he got there the half frozen headmaster was gasping for every breath like it was his last. He had pointed William in the direction of his desk and muttered get a paper. What he had found while searching for the paper was something that still puzzled him to this day. It was really none of his business but that did not keep the thought from pestering his mind. Over the long sessions they had had he thought he knew the schoolmaster well, and never once was something out of the way mentioned. It had happened when he searched the desk for a clean sheet of paper and had reached in between the cubby holes and pulled out a document tied with heavy cord. On the outside were the words, *Paid off Bastardy Court Costs of 2000 pounds of tobacco.* Whose case was this anyway? Maybe one of the schoolmaster's family had gotten himself in trouble and Norris had come to his aid. That was just like him. Never a finer man had he met since coming to the colonies. Two Thousand pounds of tobacco was a lot of money, even back in 1744. He remembered how much he wished he could see what that was all about but knew it was none of his business, unless William Norris volunteered.

William started to ask Rebeckah if her sister had ever spoken of this to her or her parents, but Solomon had come up to beg something of his mother as she ironed William's shirts.

His thoughts returned to William Norris and that cold night. William Norris had called out his will gasping for every breath. Abraham Neighbors had witnessed it, along with Stephen Hampton. Abraham had left for his own cabin, but Stephen stayed with him to wait for death, not wanting Elizabeth to wait alone. Poor Elizabeth, he remembered how distraught she was. She kept crying, "I'm sorry, I'm so sorry," as she rubbed his cold hands. It didn't seem like Norris would live past the hour. But to everyone's surprise he had lasted through the night and almost through the year. But the rattling sound to his breathing never got better all those months.

William dipped his now-dry pen into the ink well, shaking his head, and said out loud, "I can't afford to do so much thinking back or I'll waste all my ink."

Rebeckah looked up when he spoke, wondering what had taken him so deeply into thought.

Looking closer at his map, William followed the Middle Seneca along its path as it meandered upwards in the county and put a mark where David and James Trail's lands were located. William would often see James Trail in the company of James Jr. when the two would ride away from the meetings at the ordinary. Both of their lands were at the beginning of the head spring running into the Seneca. William found the spot on the map and made a note next to it. Then he drew in the town of Clarksburg, sitting almost half way from Fredericktown and Blatensburg.

He continued to write even though his candle was nearly burned to the holder.

He wrote on into the night, even after the children had gone to their beds, filling in as much as he could remember. Rebeckah sat quietly, mending the socks the men in the family continued to wear thin.

John Seager buys from John Hughes land called John's Purchase from a tract of Wm. and John.

There had always been confusion when giving directions. So many of them had bought land off of the large land holdings that the old generation Woffords had originally owned. It was also named William and John like his own land, and the outsiders always had trouble finding the right farm. William started laughing out loud.

Rebeckah looked up at her husband, "What is it you are finding so comical at this late hour, William?"

William turned. "Becka, do you remember the time John Hughes paid the warehouse to deliver his supplies by pack train to his house and told them it was at the *William and John* off of Seneca? It was the same man that had delivered our shipment a few months before. And they brought John's load to our place instead. We were not at home so they just left it by the barn. We returned home and found his name on it, and I had to go up to his place that week to tell him to come get it. Old John Hughes was one sore talker over that one." William began laughing. Not often did Rebeckah see this much fun in her husband's life. "He has made everyone else's lives so uncomfortable most of the time, it felt good to see him have the other shoe dropped," William said wiping his eyes and went back to writing. He finished writing for the night, and while he put away his papers, she blew out what was left of the candle. As they started up the steps, she said, "It is a good life if you can laugh with your husband." He patted her on the head as his way of agreeing.

The morning was unusually hot for this time of the year. Rebeckah wiped her forehead with her apron and went back to rolling the leftover mutton in a cabbage leaf. She pulled a jug from the shelf and placed the rolls into the jug. "Young William, take this to your father and brothers in the field. We will never be ready to go to Rachel's if your father does not get his crop pulled in time." The crops had been slow to come in this year, and a poor crop it was. It had been a bad year in her orchard as well, and she had spent the morning cutting the rotten fruit, trying to save what she could. Now it would take all the special care she could give them to make sure they had enough fruit to keep them supplied until next season. What made all this work bearable was the thought of going to see Rachel. She would describe to her sister the design of her herb garden this year. Even though it did not produce well, it was pretty while it lasted. She knew Rachel's would have an excellent design and would be expertly laid out and still producing. After all, when you were given the seeds from Mrs. Carroll's catalog collection you could be sure they were the most healthy of any sold.

By early afternoon the last of the bundles of clothing and quilts were loaded into the wagon. William had checked the wheels for the trip and hooked the grease bucket to the back of the wagon. Absolom and young William had carried the water jug out for their mother while she followed with a baby on each hip. "William, if our family gets any larger we are going to need a bigger wagon." She looked at her son John and laughed. "Do you hear that John? We would not have room for your wife and children."

Nancy caught the words her mother had said and began to tease her brother about being a papa. A tossing game started, with first one child, then the other throwing apples at John from the basket meant to be taken as part of the food supply.

"Stop that," William yelled, "You'll scare the horses." At the same time Rebeckah chided, "Now go pick up the apples lest you have empty bellies down the road."

The trip was full of joyful excitement as they sang together all the songs they knew and waved at neighbors along the way. A brisk breeze felt good, keeping the sun from burning. They would be staying the night with Rebeckah's sister, probably Eleanor, since they lived the closest this side of the main road. What they would not do is go to James Lee's place. After the fight at the last meeting in Fredericktown, he and James had avoided each other like the plague. "Mother, when will we get to Aunt Rachel's house?" Nancy asked. Do you suppose Aunt Rachel will still be as much fun with us as she used to be when Grandfather was there?"

"Nancy, why do you think she would be any different?"

"Well, I heard Father tell you that Rachel was not keeping up with the weeds. She must be having to work real hard."

Rebeckah gave no answer, only a sigh, knowing too well that just might be the case.

Sometime after they crossed the first crossing of the Great Seneca, near Robert's place, William began to notice the changing clouds coming from the eastern shore. What was once a clear blue, with just a few low hung clouds, was now appearing to bank across the sky. They had reached the road leading to James and Annie's cabin, and again William was glad not to be going there. By now the storm angrily defined itself in a solid blue line, coming from the ocean. Even the birds sensed something was different as they flew frantically from one tree to the next in a flurry.

William lashed the whip to hurry the horses. As they passed other wagons on the road they too were pointing to the eastern sky.

The rain began to pelt them in torrents. William was just beginning to pull into the small tributary that connected the roads.

Blinded by the rain, William did not see the rushing current that had already begun to rise to a dangerous level. The wagon dipped into a hole and before the family could get out of the wagon the sides began to tear away. Rebeckah reached out to catch the quilts and clothing she had stacked at the back before they floated away. In doing so, she caused the wagon to tilt, cracking the wheel sending the wagon sliding down stream. In all the commotion little Mary fell out of the wagon. By the time Rebeckah could get to her, the child was frantically fighting the water. Holding the child to her chest to calm her while at the same time trying to keep baby Lucy from falling out of her arms and keeping her footing in the deep water, was the worst terror she had ever imagined. But there was no time to try to control the shivering that had consumed her being.

She called for William but she could not see him. Why was he not helping with the rescue? Frantically, she began to search the creek in vain. She went to her knees in an almost convulsion of fear. By now John had realized Solomon was also missing. She caught sight of him in the partially submerged wagon. She yelled against the noise of the storm for someone to come help. Absolom jumped in and lifted his little brother, caught between the front of the wagon and the seat, and carried him to the high bank. There was a big knot on his forehead and his left arm dangled limply at his side. It was then she heard him calling out in obvious pain.

By the time she and the boys got to William the rain was pounding upon them. They could not hear what he was saying. Somehow, while he was trying to rein in the horses, he had slipped and the water carried him with such force into a fallen tree it had pinned him there. When Rebeckah and John got to him they realized he had injured his back. They could not budge him from his entanglement. No one was close to help. Rebeckah could hear other travelers calling out for help as the rain began to come down harder.

Never had she been so afraid. The tears would not stop coming.

By now the local farmers were coming out of their cabins looking for the injured. The stories were all the same. There seemed to be injured people thrown everywhere. Now it appeared a new danger threatened to take more lives. The waters were over their banks from up above on the hillside, and even small streams had become torrents. Rebeckah sent John and Absolom to get help from anyone that looked capable of helping get William up from the raging creek waters. Rebeckah could not help herself. The shock of seeing her family taken in by this disaster sent her again into uncontrollable crying. By now she realized once again they would not be going to see Rachel and the thought was only part of her grief. Now she cried just because she had to cry. Something inside of her, maybe just the fear, would not be quieted. The almighty had allowed them to stay on this earth a little longer, she did not know why or how, but the gift was accepted.

John and Absolom returned. And never a better sight to see than her own brother. James had been making his way from his cabin down to the main road, to possibly help someone in need. Little did he know it would be his own flesh and blood.

James helped his nephews roll the tree limbs from the encasement and tore one of the few remaining boards from the broken wagon to roll William onto. Pain racked every move as they lifted him up the bank and into James's wagon. Then John and Absolom mounted their father's horses and led the way through the mushy undergrowth, holding the lighted torch their uncle had brought with him.

When they finally arrived at James and Annie's cabin sometime in the night, Rebeckah had never known a more-welcome greeting than the arms of her sister-in-law. The women began rubbing hot oil onto William's injuries and put a pan of hot ashes wrapped in rags across the pain.

Four days had passed and William's back was still not strong enough to stand on his own feet without support. Rebeckah actually worried quietly to her sister-in-law that William might not ever work again.

One neighbor after another would come by with news. Finally, the fourth day news arrived of terrible damage on the far Eastern coast line, caused by what the authorities called a hurricane. William and Rebeckah counted themselves blessed when news of two families being swept away to their death only a short distance from where their wagon had torn apart. And just today someone had brought word that the Seneca Creek was still over its banks. There was concern over the condition of the rest of the family living close by and also of Rachel and John living on the Ridge. Over and over James and Annie commented that they would feel better if Rachel had a husband to see to her well being. Then they would say it did not seem likely, at least not any time soon, as there were no prospects waiting to stand in front of the minister. Rebeckah got the feeling they had discussed the matter on other occasions. Even William seemed to have thought the same thing.

Rebeckah constantly worried about Rachel. "Is she flooded out, do you think?" she had asked James until he, tired of hearing it, had agreed just as soon as the water was down he would go check on all the relations up above his house.

By the end of the week the children were restless and were ready to go home. Young William fretted about not having a wagon any more, how they would all get home, and anything else he could think to worry about.

Solomon's arm had been set with much pain at which his Uncle James had called him a big baby. This angered Rebeckah. Her brother had always been one to speak his mind, but he did not have the right to condemn how her children acted when in pain. After all James and Anne had nothing to brag about when it came to raising children. Their son Richard was always in trouble—a real smart mouth. The cousins had stopped getting along and were not really speaking to each other. Anne and Rebeckah fixed the meals almost in silence and tried the best they could to keep peace, but even Rebeckah commented to William she was feeling their welcome was wearing thin.

It did not help the situation when Richard and Susanna Watts, parents of Robert Lee's wife, Elizabeth, came to check on James's house on their return trip from Fredericktown. "I thought I better come by before going on up the hill to my house. Terrible rains all the way from the city. I hate to see what it did on the outlying lands. We had gone to the courthouse for the day, or so we thought. I had just finished signing over the deed to a portion of my land to my daughter and her husband, Brock and Margaret Mockbee. When we came out of the courthouse there was a mighty dark sky. It hit so suddenly and the rains didn't stop for three days. All the creeks around Fredericktown were over the banks. Carroll Creek ran all the way up into the tavern—you know the Washington and Braddock one—that's the one I mean. The Monococy was impassable but by ferry. I have never seen anything like it. We finally found a friendly soul that extended us a room. Had to stay three days, and even then the water was almost too high to cross. Just as he was ready to go he remembered some bit of interesting news. "You probably have not heard about the hanging? The news is all over the town."

"What do you mean a hanging?" James was the first to ask, but just as fast everyone picked up the question.

Richard Watts started laughing, "I guess anyone thinking England has a right to tax us just because she is the mother country, is simply defending the wrong side. We are going to show those buzzards just what they should do with the tax." Richard stopped for a moment, then turned to William. "Oh, William, I forgot you still believe England wraps her arms around us cause'in they want the best for us." He laughed again. "Do you not recognize they are strangling us? That arm is not for our good." Richard turned back to the others to continue his fun. "They had it all planned in Fredericktown. Really fun to watch. Everyone was laughing about it. They took a big coat and attached some breeches to it and stuffed it all up to look like a man, and they put a sign on it saying it was Zachariah Hood."

"Who is Zachariah Hood, paw?" Richard Lee asked, having just come in from rifle practice in the woods next to the cabin. True to his nature, he was ready to join in on any fun to be had. And when it came to rousting, this son of James and Anne knew how to make it happen.

James Lee frowned, annoyed that his son had broken into the story telling and now he was forced to explain what was happening between England and the colonies. "It is about those tax stamps we are supposed to be buying. The Parliament hired a man named Zachariah Hood to take care of the matter, but no one is going to support his authority. Sorry to say, some of us do not feel as strongly about our rights, as Mr. Watts and I do." He motioned with his head in the direction of William as he said his speech.

His son looked puzzled, "Uncle William, are you one of those crazy men putting up a fight about all this?" The boy turned back to his father and said, "Jacob Trindle—you know the family down by the crossroad, got in a fight about how England is the one we have to listen to. The men down there really took care of his hide, fast like."

Richard Watts began again to tell the story he had come in to tell. "Well, they hung up ole Zach and burned him in effigy right there on the streets of Fredericktown. I would have given anything to see the looks on the face of the real Zachariah Hood when he saw himself dangling from that tree. I'd wager he high tailed it back to Annapolis after that."

William said nothing. The thought of finding humor by burning an appointed official caused his temper to flair. And even if he did not like being forced to pay for the stamp, even more, he disliked the turn of the colonist in ridiculing the legal officials of the King. And maybe more than any of his dislikes he despised the way the conversation was being perceived. He pulled himself up and began putting his legs into his breeches. "We may not have a wagon to get home but I have legs and I will walk out of here today. It can't be any worse on me than staying here listening to our heritage being torn to bits by simple minds."

William was determined he was going to leave immediately and Rebeckah knew she could say nothing to make him wait to get stronger.

"Rebeckah, you will take the baby, and Nancy can ride with you and hold little Mary. And young William will hold onto Solomon since his arm is broken and ride with me on the other horse. John and Absolom will have to walk."

When they started for the door Anne sensed nothing could be gained by letting William go like that. "James, for the love of your sister, give them your wagon to get home. John and Absolom can return it tomorrow and ride their horses back home."

James looked at his wife, shaking his head in disgust. "Rebeckah, why you ever married a stubborn Englishman I will never know. Take the wagon." He turned to his nephews, "But be sure you get it back tomorrow boys—and in one piece."

Slowly they made their way across the swollen creeks and were home before nightfall. Later as Rebeckah stood by her window watching the last of the sun slip behind the hills, she thought to herself, someday she would get to see Rachel—someday.

Chapter 20

Nov 18, 1765
Fredericktown

Signs of Carroll Creek having been over the banks in Fredericktown, just as Richard Watts had said, were still causing some problems. And today, William and his son were in town just long enough to place an order for a new wagon. In the meantime, they would have to rely on the old one they had bought from a neighbor. Not far from his mind was the reason for the trip. Each time he moved it was still with pain.

William had heard while on the road coming, that the King's man Grenville had resigned and someone by the name of Rockingham had taken over. He hoped to find talk about him. They would stop at the courtyard and be home before nightfall.

Just as they rounded the corner John pointed to a large gathering of men at the square. They all seemed to be wearing red caps with long red tassels hanging from the back.

John climbed down and tied the horses to a post while William did another inspection of the wheels on the old wagon. "John come look at this," William called to his son. "We need to keep an eye on this wheel." He pointed to a spoke with a crack line already appearing and another one coming loose. "This wagon has seen a lot of hard wear over the years. I just hope it will make it all the way home."

The men started toward the courthouse to see first hand the red capped men. William asked a man crossing the street with them about what was going on with these men.

The man eagerly informed him, "Oh, those are the new *Sons of Liberty*. Cresap helped get it started here. They are just like the Sons of Liberty men in New England. They are training to defend us against the King." The man, in such a hurry to go see what was being said, walked away while still explaining what this was all about, leaving William and his son to know little more than before the question.

"What do you think that means?" John asked his father.

William had heard only a short conversation about the so-called liberty fighters when a traveler had stopped him along his road to find directions. But he had no idea it had grown to this proportion. The town seemed alive even though the regular court days were not until the next week.

John repeated his question, "Who are these men—what are they doing?"

"Can't say for sure." William told his son.

The man standing up front giving the orders looks like Cresap. I can only surmise he is still in charge of them."

Like them, others were curious and the crowd had grown even larger. The cold wind blew in their faces but it didn't seem to dampen the spirits of all the people running to the courthouse gathering.

By the time William and his son had reached the courtyard they could hear the crowd chanting,

"Down with the Stamp Act!"

"Down with the Stamp Act!"

"Down with the Stamp Act!"

William shook his head in disagreement. It was not that he liked the King and parliament putting the new pinch on his pocket book, it was the way these men were going about their protest. But if he tried to reason with the crowd they would be calling out, "Down with William Littlefield" with the same vigor these men protested the King. He would be set up as a traitor against the cause of freedom in America, and nothing could be more from the truth. After all it was in his background to tackle unfair conditions. With his added years and a more level head, it was his belief you should try to reason your case before parliament, and that is what the assembly had done when they sent Ben Franklin over to England.

William stood back watching the fury building and could not help but think of the respected citizen and well thought of colonist spokesman Daniel Dulaney, and his viewpoints published in all the papers. Even when he disagreed with many of Dulaney's points, he appreciated the manner in which Dulaney had introduced the facts. William was convinced wise thinking beat a fist fight any day. But he definitely believed in standing up for your rights and hoping to get the other side to listen. Violence only brought on terrible wrong and did nothing to introduce one's thoughts. And this afternoon as he watched Cresap's men work up to a fight, he was afraid they did not understand the difference.

Curious to hear what they might be saying, John moved closer to the *Sons* gathering. The crowd was getting boisterous in favor of the gathering. A group of mostly young men, so it seemed from the looks of them, ran past William. Out of the corner of his eye he saw a group of British officers approaching. He tipped his hat at them in a friendly enough way.

In turn, they tipped their hat and made a few words of conversation that William could not hear.

Before he knew what was happening he felt himself being maneuvered to the side, away from the crowd. At first William thought they were trying to get out of the way of a stampede but the strong grip of the officer told otherwise.

Before he could ask what the purpose was that brought on such insistence the soldier simply said, "The Captain hath requested ye speak with him."

"Why, pray tell?" William said, all the while being slowly directed away from the crowd quietly without notice.

Not noticed by the normal traveler, the house set back from the road in the middle of the block served as the headquarters for the British Captain assigned for duty in Fredericktown. It was here anyone that caused the British a problem stayed until they agreed with the King.

"One of those men," the soldier announced gruffly as he pushed William in front of the desk in the front room.

The Captain lifted his eyes to face William. "The King finds much displeasure with the likes of men striking out against him in such a display. Let me see, now. I feel some time spent in our locks will set ye thinking right."

William tried to make the officers understand he had just arrived from the countryside, and his intent in stopping was only to hear what they were saying. But no matter how much he protested that the upheaval was not to his liking, his words fell on the deaf ears of the brightly uniformed English officers.

"I am a loyal citizen of the King," he said, trying to convince the soldiers.

"Sure—sure ye are. Those are the words of the last man. Ye colonists recite the same speech. When what ye are doing is going around teaching hatred of King George the Third." The soldiers laughed at the sound of their own voices railing.

"Let us see what ye hath to say for thyself protesting now."

Once again William's temper surfaced. This had nothing to do with the taxing but had everything to do with his word. "I, of English heritage came to the colonies to escape the injustices of a few tyrannical men. It seems today I have again been taken by the same one-minded people."

The soldier looked at William, puzzling over his words. The soldier began reciting what sounded like a memorized speech. "Thee hath observed the practices ye colonists subscribe to." The officer started writing on a sheet of printed material, "And thy land holdings—what might they be called?" He looked up at William for an answer.

William thought for a moment trying to decide the best way to handle this situation. He remembered John was out in the street and if he made these soldiers mad it could cause ill will to come to his son. Besides, he had nothing to hide when they asked him to name his land.

The soldier, one of the older ones and appearing to be in charge, began to write down the title, *William and John.* The officer then pushed the paper across the table. "Put a mark there and ye are free to go." The soldier tapped his pen on the space where he wanted William to put handling mark. The soldier watched with surprise when William picked up the paper and began to read the words written at the top.

When William finished reading, he furiously turned to the officer, outraged at the deceit. They wanted him to put a mark there as a way of turning over his land to the King. And for the poor fellow that did not know how to read, it was an easy seize. His blood boiled. "As I said, I left England because of this type of tyranny from an overseer, but I assure you I did not leave because of my obedience to the King. And the King would never resort to thieving land from a British citizen."

William, trying to maintain his own control so to think clearly, slowly and with effect, ripped the paper in two and dropped it to the floor. "How dare you try this on the colonists. You are an abomination to England. Stealing in the name of the King!"

The officer summoned two of the lower ranked guards to handle the rough work. Over and over again they hit him in the mouth and lashed him until he fell to his knees, but still he refused to sign the paper giving them his land.

The soldiers pushed him against a pillar, and tied his hands behind his back.

William felt the pain of his still unhealed back injury of the recent storm. He looked around the room at the motley group of soldiers, slouched over their ale mugs, unconcerned as to how they conducted their manners. William realized that maybe even more than his physical pain it was the pain of seeing his England taken over by those that would steal and deceive. He could not believe that even Rockingham, probably the most hated man in all of the colonies, aside from the former Grenville, would stoop this low. If this was what had become his homeland, why was he so bent on defending their rulings? Had he been blind to what had happened in the years since he left the Hants?

His legs and feet began to numb, and his eyes swelled almost shut. Only once had he experienced a situation that left him in the hands of others. Just the thought of that time caused his temper to rise, as it had on that other occasion in his youth when the overseers had displayed a cruel likeness to these soldiers. Back then, the price of his freedom had been to pick up his tools and head for the door. That very situation had led the Littlefield boys to book passage on the ship to America. It had cost him nothing but the loss of a few coins in his pocket. Now, there was much more at stake: his land, his son out on the street, Rebeckah and the other children—all causes to live and die for. He thought of his neighbors as well, those who shared their plows and wagons and sweat to make life good—that was freedom. William took in a deep breath as a painful thought hit him. Could it be that he was seeing this aggression for what it was. Had his honorable mother country become a thieving government? If that was the case he now must take off the fine old coat of England and wear the threadbare jacket of the colonist struggle.

He tried to keep his mind on what was being said, as one soldier after the other came in to report to the officer in charge. With each new person there was an added sense of agitation as to what was happening. "It is treason out there. I was just standing guard at the courthouse steps, and the clerk, I heard his name called John Darnell, came out and issued a warning about refusing to do any more business as long as the British enforced the stamps. The sheriff brought a thief in to have charged but this John Carroll said he was refusing to file the papers, because he would have to put one of our stamps on it, and he just did not want to be a part of something that stunk so much. He refused right out in the open door of the court house."

"Just wait 'til the King hears about this," the officer in charge said and sat down at his desk to write a letter.

As the men continued to drink, their words became increasingly harder to understand, but William did hear the words, red caps. He could only surmise they were discussing the *Sons of Liberty* that had congregated on the square.

One soldier, standing at the window, turned around to give a warning as he made ready to take his duty. "They are everywhere ready to swarm down on us if they get the chance. Keep this door locked and your rifles ready. Before the night is over I suspects they will find out one of theirs is held."

This time the reference by the soldier as to William being a friend of the red caps did not bother him so much. Per chance that was not a bad idea after the realization his King's army, commissioned by the King himself, had turned into common thugs.

A banging on the door brought the soldier to his feet. Quickly the soldier turned to the window, "It's Beasly. Let him in."

The soldier was out of breath and rushed to convey the message as if it was the battleground on the other side of the door. "They have just locked the doors to the courthouse and refused to do any business."

"I hath predicted as much."

"What makes these colonists prefer living over here?" the soldier asked. "What doth they see in this wilderness place?"

William dared to speak again. "Freedom is what the colonists are defending. Freedom from the oppressive ways of the likes of you."

The soldiers jumped to their feet, riled at their prisoner and ready to pick up the beating where they had left off. But just as one boy raised his arm, the officer in charge looked up from his writing and gave orders, "Hold up. If you kill him, I will have to answer to the Governor for that."

After some time had passed, the officer at the desk signed his name to the report and handed it to one of the soldiers. "Burgett, I want you to take this to the official in charge at the port of Annapolis. You will find the one in charge stationed in the building by the gate. Keep this document safely to your chest. I have described to him the state of the revolt toward the stamp act. If ye ride fast ye can get there by tomorrow midday. Give him news I need reinforcements if this riot goes on farther. Be sure the officer understands that the last officer on yesterday's patrol overheard plans being made to send a delegation to New York to force a repeal to the Stamp Act. Now be off."

After the soldier mounted his horse and rode off, leaving mud spinning behind him, the other soldiers seemed to gather courage. "We'll catch them all just like ye caught this one." They all laughed a gutsy utterance and toasted the idea with their tankards.

John had turned around in time to see his father being pulled away to the house, but unable to come to his aid before the door was locked. He had proven himself to be on the way to manhood in his father's eyes that afternoon after contacting the sheriff, who passed it on to Col. Cresap as he drilled the *Sons of Liberty* gathering. They in turn marched over to the house where William was held and began kicking in the door. The officers realized they were outnumbered and without real authority to do what they had done. Quickly they untied William and let him go.

By the time William and his son had passed over the Monocacy River, William felt it safe to set a campfire and wait for daylight. Rebeckah always insisted on putting a supply of coarsely ground corn and some oil into his saddlebag each time he left the house, and tonight they tasted better than he ever remembered. It didn't matter if the journey cakes held more burned spots than William would have ever tolerated at home, especially when Rebeckah let Nancy do the cooking. They had left town without looking back and there was no time to stop for a leg of mutton.

The two sat in front of the fire watching the flames slowly die down. William felt the need to explain his feelings of the day to his son as to why he did the things he did.

"For Years I have fought hard to keep my allegiance with my mother country. It has not always been easy. I was not blind to the changes in the British rule, but stubborn. I had no plans of returning to the land of my grandfather, so why was it so hard to give up my British beliefs? I even bragged of being a full born British descendant with our neighbors and riled some family. Through the years I would let my temper be my guide. And at times that is what gave me the edge on my opponent. But it is not always the right thing to do." William's words led into the same story he had told Rebeckah the night after learning of the Stamp Tax

"When I was young I was too cocky to know that hard times can have their benefits. Hard times will make you tough, son. I did not believe this when my guardian pressed so hard on me to learn, although his was not for my good name but because he was mean. There is a difference. But he made me read and write and have a trade. And equally important is the lesson to never be deceived by the talk of others."

William stopped talking for a while and let the words fall where they may and shifted his sore body to find another place not so bruised.

"Life is hard and the sooner you learn that the better off you will be. No one will come to you with favors. You have to take your own chances at life. But you better be schooled in what is good. My brother had heard the stories about the colonies and set out to find a way for us to cross the ocean. We walked every day by the docks on our way home from work, dead tired and no hope of a better life at the mill. One evening he dared to stop and inquire of the sailors hoisting the sails, ready to depart. 'Where are you headed,' he yelled, to which the men replied, 'where else but to America.' That very evening we ran to our bunks and gathered our pillow sacks full of our belongings. I brought my dictionary because it was the one thing I never wanted to be without. The educated mind brings you good luck. We left because of oppression from an overseer, not because we did not honor our King. There is a difference, son. Since that time I have never tolerated injustices, be it upon humans or animals. But for all that injustice, I am still the same person I was sitting at my grandfather's table, loving the land and the sights I saw, but mostly the stories I heard my grandfather tell.

These soldiers today, I saw in them the same as the overseer. Over zealous trouble makers, feeding off their own self-importance. They, like the common overseer, do not stand for the England I ascribe to."

William suddenly could not contain his feeling about what England really was, opposed to what today's outgrowth of cruel behavior had been. "England is about the beautifully carved buildings and the magnificent churches whose spirals have reached up to God for centuries." He rushed on, portending to the lessons he wanted to give to his son. "It is about the courage of those sailing around the world for the first time, life times ago, or the mysteries of Stonehenge cropping up from nowhere. It is the Shakespearean sounding words you hear along the streets, unlike the grunts you hear uttered at our ports. It is the musicians, the artists, the craftsmen all doing what they do best. And then there are the simple things, like tasting fresh hot chestnuts from the street vendor for the first time. That is England, son. Not these ego-searching rulers set for the good of their own purse. Remember that, John."

John sat by the fire poking it with a stick as he listened to his father talk. Finally, he looked up, and asked, "Do you think it would be a good thing to fight for your true England by wearing a red cap of the *Sons of Liberty?*"

"I cannot be saying, John. I do not know what the outcome will be after this afternoon. This I am sure of, I will listen more closely to the colonial reasoning of the news. Time shall be our teacher."

William let out a moan as he tried to stand up. The afternoon beating had been hard on his body. He climbed more slowly than usual into the wagon and wrapped himself in his blanket to find some sleep. John was left to ponder all that had been talked about as he sat watching the last of the embers slowly die out.

After another trip to Dowden's Ordinary, William was convinced he was fortunate that the Sons of Liberty had come to his defense on that day in Fredericktown. More and more stories circulated of ill treatment to the colonists at the hands of the British soldiers. After a boy living close to their farm had been blinded at the hands of an over zealous red coat, John had asked his father if he might be allowed to join the *Sons*.

Each night the family sat around the fireplace after the scripture readings, and their talk usually came to the possibilities of war making its way once again to their countryside. Nancy had innocently called the stamp a silly little stamp, no bigger than a thumbnail. But the effects from it encircled everything they had or hoped to have.

William knew trying to get Rebeckah's approval, if he should be compelled to join, would be a worse war than the British would bring. One colony after another had put up defenses ready to do battle if it came to that. Someone had begun writing in big bold letters on the tavern walls the names of those leading the fight for freedom. New names had appeared each time William went in, verifying more men were now willing to risk their livelihood over speaking out against the King. It had first started in New England when the big shipping merchant John Hancock protested, then he was joined by Samuel Adams and a little known man they called a false teeth maker, by the name of Paul Revere. The cause came through Pennsylvania where Benjamin Franklin wrote the headline news for his paper and on into Maryland where Daniel Dulaney kept the spirit alive with his much read, well written pamphlet. By the time you got to Virginia they had more than one complaint. Money was so tight, and the King did not show any sympathy for them. Add that grief to the stamp tax, and you had reason for revolting. So it was no wonder when a new member of the House of Burgess, named Patrick Henry, got up to speak, the people listened. At only twenty-nine years of age, he showed the promise of being a voice of authority when he denounced Parliament's taxing plans. Farther down in the Carolinas the voice of Christopher Gadsden was making a difference. And you could always expect John Adams and Thomas Jefferson to be mentioned as someone willing to risk all for the colonists. The names on the walls just kept growing until one whole wall was filled with names of aristocrats and commoners willing to stand up for the colonies. But on another wall there was a list of equally famous names. Names like Grenville. It had been marked through, and the name Rockingham written in but now barely recognizable. No one dared to list King George the Third in big letters but if your knew where to look you could find it. That was where everyone that frequented the tavern practiced their dart throwing.

On the last trip William had brought home a newspaper from Dowden's Ordinary and sat down by the firelight to read it.

Rebeckah could hear him laugh out loud ever so often. Finally, she could not stand being left out of the story and said, "William, for goodness sake, read it out loud so I can have some frolic too."

"Oh, alright, but just don't stop me when you don't understand." He looked up at his wife and tried to explain what the reason was for this writing. "The editor at the paper—the Maryland Gazette, has found a way to sell papers by writing something most of the colonists would like to see. It is about the stamp that we all have complained about. And the editor is doing this to sell papers. You do understand that, do you not? They call it a spoof—you know like a book that makes up a story. Now do you understand before I read it out loud?"

Rebeckah looked annoyed but for the second time said she understood what the writing was all about.

It says here,

"Mortal Wounds to the Stamp Act"

"It is talking about after the Justices at Frederick County closed the Courthouse. Remember John and I told you all about it. Well this editor in jest told all about the funeral of the stamp and what I am reading is an account of the make believe funeral."

William read on. Rebeckah found it hard to follow what he was reading but did not dare to ask questions.

> *"First they showed the colors of the Town company then the Drums went by and next the banner was displayed with real big words written out so all could see Constitutional Liberty and it gave the dates 22 Nov 1765. Then the Conductors went by and next the coffin. They had written on it also, and it said, 'The Stamp Act had expired of a mortal*

*stab received from the genius of liberty in Frederick County
court...aged 22 days."*

By now John had come into the room to listen to the account and was laughing at the reading.

*"Words of Tyranny, Military Execution, Fines,
Imprisonment, Ruin, Slavery taking possession
of America, were tacked onto the coffin."*

Rebeckah sat very still as she had been told. But her mind was churning with thoughts of fear over this kind of mockery aimed at the monarchy. What if it riled up the soldiers and they would come after anyone that showed an interest in this means of story telling?

William continued to read.

*Zachariah Hood as sole mourner, carried in an
open chariot. His countenance pale and dejected
his dress disorderly, unsuitable to his rank
betraying great distraction of mind, being
scarce able to stay on his seat."*

William stopped at this point in the reading to remind Rebeckah and John that this was the Stamp Official that had been burned in effigy, a fact that William now found uncomfortably amusing. After the beating he had gotten at the hands of the officials he was able to see what the others had tried to point out much earlier. But it still did not feel right.

He read on,

*Next came the Son's of Liberty filing two by two
They marched through the streets of Fredericktown
until they came to the gallows erected at the courthouse
green all the while the bells of the city continued to ring."*

William put the paper down, tired of reading the story again and began to recite as he remembered it to be written. "It seems Zachariah Hood nodded off to sleep. They had dug a grave and when the drums stopped, old Zachariah woke up with fright. So scared was he, not a word could he say. It goes on to say more but you get the idea of the fun. It does not mean a thing. Just a little jest to sell papers."

As always, William folded his paper neatly and put it on the shelf. Rebeckah watched him, knowing even in this moment of jest, and he had willingly joined in, there was still pain. She saw it in his eyes.

Chapter 21

May 1766
Going to Dowden's Ordinary

William wiped the sweat off his forehead as he guided the horses up the path. He could see Robert Lee, standing beside the road, his water jug on the ground.

"It's a mighty hot day for early May," William yelled as he slowed the wagon to a halt.

"And the sun's not even to midday," Robert said, lifting his supplies into the wagon and climbing up on the seat next to William. "Elizabeth fixed some fried bread and meat for the trip. There is no time to stop for a meal."

This meeting was different. The call had gone out for all landowners to come to Dowden's Ordinary for an afternoon meeting. No one seemed to know who had called it or what the reason, but it sounded important. The messengers had put the news out, and now the roads were full of wagons headed to Dowden's.

Robert reached down and picked up his water jug, taking a swig, then offered one to William. "Who do you think is calling this meeting?"

"Must be something pretty important or they would not be calling us in just as we are getting ready to plow the fields," William said.

"I speculate it has something to do with the assembly room being locked. Guess you heard about that. The King sent word that the Governor was to lock the doors to the meeting house after he heard that our business men have refused to honor the stamp tax," Robert said, looking for a reaction from William. When it did not happen he continued to talk.

"I know you are in sympathy with the King, William, but I do not think you are blind to what has happened here. It means we do not have a voice to protest any longer," Robert said and looked up at the position of the sun. "You better give your horses a full rein, or we will miss the beginning."

William cracked the whip, and the rattle of the wagon cut out all the talk.

By the time they pulled into the back lot of Dowden's, the sweat had wilted the ruffles on their shirts and both men were red faced from the sun. "From the looks of this lot, I'm inclinable to think every landowner has gotten the word," William complained. He hated crowds. Too many voices speaking at once.

Both men stopped at the water trough and cupped their hands to splash their faces and neck before going in. As they entered the dimly lit tavern, still wiping the water from their eyes, they spotted Thomas Thrasher and John Seager standing by the cold fireplace. As the men started through the crowd they saw Alexander Grant waving his arms to signal he had come early and had a table reserved for the group.

The room was filled with unruly colonists, waiting for what they feared would be more bad news. The rumors began to take on a mind of their own, as more and more neighbors crowded in.

By the time the meeting started, all the family brothers were accounted for except Richard Willis, who Aquilla said was no better since his last attack and admitted he probably never would be able to attend again, which was no surprise to anyone.

"Hope we can hear this far back," William complained as he sat down with his usual paper in hand for note taking. He nudged Robert and pointed to James Beall who lived in the Northwest Hundred over by James Lee's old place. He had gone to sit on the small step-up floor the Dowdens had put in place for today. Next to him sat an unknown gentleman wearing what was probably once an expensive green suit; now worse from wear and missing, as best William could count, at least three shiny gold buttons.

The men all respected James Beall for the work he did to keep the colonists informed of anything important in the Northwest Hundred and beyond when it was necessary. He was most likely the man that had called the meeting.

When the room quieted, James Beall introduced the man only as a landowner from Baltimoretown.

The man stood up. No one spoke or moved about. This meeting had been touted so important; no landowner within the area dared miss the news. "Gentlemen, I sailed from England three months ago on the seventeenth day of February of this year and arrived at the port of Baltimoretown just two days ago. I bring news of Parliament that could affect all of us by the time the next ship docks. Just behind my ship another one was scheduled to depart in two weeks, as best I could tell from the departure notice on the dock. I have been asked to inform you of news I learned while on the streets of London on the morning I departed. We were told a vote was coming that morning. They were to decide what to do about our refusal to honor their directions on the stamp tax. I would have waited for the news if I had not already bought my ticket some days before." The man waited for the men to stop mumbling so not to miss the importance of what he was about to reveal.

"Gentlemen, Parliament was set to vote that morning. It would be to repeal the stamp act and leave us alone or to declare war."

When the man on the platform said the word war everyone started to talk at once. The man put his hands up to quiet the crowd so he could continue. "The word on the street for weeks had been there is no way they would repeal. After the Englishmen took the rioting all the way down to the parliament doors last year, it was understood that there was no answer to the turmoil unless they collected our monies.

Those standing by the door heard the doors lock in place, thus keeping the outcome secret. No one was privy to the vote that was to be taken any minute. Not even was it known to the doorkeepers who, for a fee, could be counted on to slip the information." The speaker took in a deep breath; his voice held the sound of exhaustion. In a very solemn tone he said, "Gentlemen, this is as close to war as we have been."

The words stunned those in the room. Not that they had not expected it, but when this man who was the most recent to stand before the door of parliament said the word war, it seemed all too real.

Finally, a man in the crowd yelled out, "How do you come by all this information concerning Parliament?"

"I can only tell you what I heard in all the pubs over the last few weeks before my ship sailed three months ago. The English are tired of paying the bills for the colonists when they themselves have so high a tax they are broke. An ultimatum seemed to have been issued before parliament that nothing less than enforcement would be accepted."

Another man stood up and called out over the noise, "We had heard the British merchants were protesting to the parliament that the stamp tax had caused them extreme lose of monies after we stopped buying their goods. Has this not made a difference to Parliament rulers?"

The man again stood up to explain. "The way everyone outside the parliament door was talking it seemed a slim chance that the merchants could win the argument. It was reported by someone close to the new minister, that Rockingham said if they did vote to go to war it would be immediately, possibly before we even got the word over here.

The colonists in the room began to shout the now familiar chant

Down with the stamp act

Down with the stamp act

By the time they stopped chanting the man in the green suit had slipped out the side door to go to his next called tavern meeting.

From one side of the room to the other, the receipt of news was causing upheaval. The colonists had hoped their revolt against the merchants would put a stop to the tax. But now it appeared all that the British government was really interested in, even going against the desires of their merchants, was to force the colonists to do what they were told to do.

"We will show those British what they can do with that stamp," a man yelled from the far end of the room.

One man standing near the door stepped forward. "We need a good spokesman in Maryland. Virginia has that new man Patrick Henry, as well as Thomas Jefferson. Pennsylvania has Benjamin Franklin. We need a man to speak for us."

A group of men sitting near the back drinking heavily seemed to have lost sight of what was being spoken and were getting louder with each swig. They began yelling out insults. "He sits on his throne and makes stool pigeons of us all." Another one stood up, swaying with the cup still in his hand. "He is nothing but a Willy Neg sitting on a soft pillow."

William watched the men cavorting and thought back on what he knew to be factual about the latest King George. By all accounts he was a high minded youth that could not possibly know of the struggles the colonists were facing over here. How could he know about struggles when he was so removed from hardships that two of his aids were actually fighting over who should have the honor to dress him each morning.

William turned his back on the crowd and began to do what always served him best. That meant looking at the factual points on what was happening. If the colonies were to survive they had to save the trade between other countries, not only the mother country. And it had already been threatened when England made their ships go first to the British coast to pay the duties. William methodically went through the points and settled on the most important one. It would do no good to use facts as a way to decide what to do, if the King would not listen to their needs. What kind of a ruler gives no voice? And that is exactly what the King had done when he gave the orders to lock the doors to the assembly halls and arrest anyone who tried to hold a meeting where they spoke out against the stamp tax. That meant no voice, no audience to the King. Even Benjamin Franklin had evidently been unable to persuade the King to listen.

And what if all of this led to war? Oh, how William disliked war as a way to resolve the differences. When he was a youth his scrappy ways had been a way to get what he fought for. Now he was older and his punch was not as effective on the opponent's jaw. It had been only a little over two years since the last war, and that had solved very little, other than to expand the borders and make the King ruler over more land.

When had the British first begun to change? The King, the Parliament, the friends on the streets of London—When did they first begin to put on the face of the enemy—deceiving the people; deceiving him?

These thoughts, these decisions were painful. Giving up his allegiance to his mother country left an empty space. A longing. He could not explain it. It was almost akin to the feeling he had when told of his grandfather's death in the night. Or maybe that day he watched his brother John walk over the ridge for the last time.

William shook his head, chiding himself over this foolish sentiment. He was educated, and educated people decided on things by looking at the reasons, then doing something about them.

How many times had he used that ridiculous saying to defend his emotions? "Feels not right to bite the hand that raised ye." The British had stopped caring for his interests a long time ago. He had to admit, although painful in the admission, that James Lee Jr. was right. England no longer cared for the colonists as their own blood.

William reviewed all the man in the green suit had announced. He knew what that scene looked like as the crowd mulled around the vendor's cart across the street, eating hot chestnuts and waiting for news from the governing powers.

His thoughts turned from the parliament to the old vendor himself. He wondered if the same one still came—the one with the daughter. She, on occasions, came to help him sell the chestnuts. As a young boy, William had imagined what it would be like if he took her for a wife. He couldn't remember if he had liked her enough to marry her. Or was it the free chestnuts he hoped to gain? William felt foolish when he realized he had a smile on his face and immediately controlled his thoughts. This time of reflection had no place in his life today.

James Beall had been speaking, and William realized he had missed most of what was said. But the last words were not missed. It was a warning.

"Go back home and prepare to defend the colonies if the next ship comes with a declaration of war."

Robert was the first to hear the fight within William. As they rode home, he admitted that his new thinking was firmly set with the colonists.

"You have come the long way around, William, and I suspect it is with an educated mind that you have made the decision. Your mind and reading and writing will prove a help to the cause."

William had not planned to spend the night at Robert's house, but when they got there they discovered several wagons had come through the land on their way to the Potomac and had stopped to water their horses.

Robert's wife, Elizabeth, had insisted the women come in to sit a spell to talk while the men helped with the horses.

The travelers were interested in the news Robert and William had brought from the meeting. When they were satisfied they were in no danger for the morrow, they were ready to answer the question Robert had posed several times. Why just now, did they decide to move to the Carolinas?

One man related the story of how several of his neighbors had gone to Virginia to buy up big sections of cheap land to speculate and sell. "We could have bought there, but I like the sound of the Indigo on down in the Carolinas."

The conversation intrigued William as much as it did Robert when the man suggested, "Besides, why buy the land we are leaving from? Virginia land is as worn out from years of planting tobacco as ours. They say the Carolina land is fresh and unturned."

William kicked at the dirt in front of him, "You are right, it would be wise to have some fresh land." He looked at his brother-in-law as he spoke, knowing this was not a new thought in Robert's thinking.

The sun was just coming up when William took his wagon back onto the road. He would stop just long enough at the mill to pick up the grain he had left yesterday morning before picking up Robert.

Jacob Waters and the men standing around the big mill stone were anxious to hear the news of yesterday's meeting. When he once again was on the road toward home, he was willing to let the horses trot at their own speed. For now, he needed time to think over what had transpired since he left home.

He was still deep in thought.

His eyes settled on the sight of the big trees that edged the Seneca Creek, dividing the field in half. On one side was the Dawson land and on the other his own place. There was something about coming down this road between the trees and past the fields he had cleared those first years. His chest still filled with pride when he saw it. It was his land, and no King or the minister Rockingham dared try to take it away from him.

Once over the ridge he could see the top of his barn. He loved that old barn. The first year out here had been a struggle. From late September and into the middle of November he had taken the ground sled down to the creek hundreds of times to load it with rocks. The thought of how hard he had worked stayed with him even now. Maybe that work was what made him feel a part of it even more. The pain in his back would never be forgotten, he was sure. One stone at a time, he had laid the grayish blue slate, row by row, until the snows came. It had taken him several years to get it as high as it was today.

He pulled the horses to a stop when he rounded the last curve. The full side of the barn with the preposterous orange-reddish door could be seen from here. William had given in to Becka's whims back then. It was just after Absolom was born. She had begged, "Things on this side of the house look so forlorn. I need a little color to give me life." He had given her permission to mix the milk paint to whatever color she could make it if she would do the work herself. He would never forget the shock that time when he came home from Fredericktown. Orange-reddish it had become, and orange-reddish it still remained. Only now, after years of sun, it had faded and one hinge had broken off leaving it hanging loosely to one side. He would send Absolom to fix it.

William spent the next few weeks plowing the fields and dropping the seeds, but his mind was not on the task. He watched the road for any sign of a rider. Absolom and young William had been given the job of repairing the rakes, while John would tend to the scythe. This was a time of farming he usually enjoyed; when you took the freshly sharpened scythe blade, letting it slice through the hay grass, gently laying it down to be raked up by other hands. Hay season was not until July and he wondered if by then there would even be field hands available if war broke out.

Surely the ship spoken of by the gentleman in the green suit had docked by now. Are we at war with the King or not? The thought shocked him. He was including himself in the question. It was the word *we* that made him know he fought for what his fellow colonists fought for. They were one and the same against the King and Parliament.

Shortly after midmorning William saw the horse coming—the one that would bear the news. The rider was unleashing the whip on his animal in a desperate attempt to rush him on as he rounded the corner and came up his path. William's heart began to pound. He dropped his hoe, leaving it where it fell and called for John and Absolom and young William to follow. When they got to the cabin Rebeckah and Nancy were already standing in the yard with the babies. Solomon was just finishing up his morning chores and ran crying from the barn, frightened by the noise.

It was Benoni Dawson, the one designated by the neighbors to deliver the news to that part of the county.

When Benoni reached the cabin, before he could speak, William yelled out. "What is it, son. Are we at war?"

"The ship came in to Newport, Rhode Island. We just got the news today." Then he shouted with glee at the top of his lungs. "It's over. Parliament abolished the Stamp Act. We are free." No sooner had he let out the yell and put both hands in the air in a gesture of winning, he turned his horse sharply and raced down the path to deliver the news to the next house.

William lifted his arms in response as well and yelled triumphantly, then put his arm around Rebeckah's waist and swung her around, "Well mother, I think this calls for a party. John bring the new wagon around. We are all going to the tavern to see the celebrations."

That night, all the way along the road, to the tavern and back, they could see the big bonfires and people dancing in merriment around every cabin. Their struggle for freedom had prevailed.

Chapter 22

Early June 1766
Chestnut Ridge

Rachel set her pen down on the table and looked at what she had just written in her mother's Bible. The old leather bound book had been used for as long as she remembered. From the looks of the worn spine and the dates inside, all written in various hand scripting, she probably had used the Bible since the first child was born. Her mother would run lift the heavy book down from the shelf and call out precisely what birth or death she wanted written down. And now, as long as there was space to write on, it was up to her to keep the pages filled in.

She reread the entries out loud, practicing her reading to the old cabin walls, the only thing that held the same memories as the old book.

> *"Borned in 1765 as far as I know it to be.*
> *John and Elizabeth Lee's baby girl named Dorcus*
> They will cal her Darkey
> *Rebecka Littlefield had a girl baby Lucy.*
> *Marthy Thrasher's little Sarah borned."*

Rachel wondered how many of the children she had missed and counted on her fingers the children of each sister and brother that were still having babies. She closed the inkpot and started to put it away when she remembered the recent news and could not resist putting a piece of news with the book until she had time to register it in her father's account book. It had to do with the news of victory for the colonies. She found a scrap of paper lying between two pages, probably someone's marker for scripture readings, and wrote *May 1766 hurd stamp tax ended. It will be a good year.* Then she stuffed it inside next to what she had just written. Now she would put up the inkpot and pen back on the shelf before she forgot it. The one thing she always did before going to the field was tidy up her cabin. There was always the hope that some of the family would come.

Living so far away had never seemed to be a problem until her father had died. Now, sadly, very few came back to the old home place. Well, Anne and John Hughes would drive by to look around but rarely did they stay to converse. Did her family think she did not crave for family news? Did they think she did not need their help even now?

Standing by the window, she watched the sun come up. It looked like a ball of hot fire ready to strike anything that dared live. Nothing but parched earth and weeds growing as high as the barn door faced her this morning. Especially now, she needed them to come.

She could see the roofless open space of what had once been her father's good barn. The hurricane had done that. She had crawled up on the lower part of the roof to pound some nails in the remaining covering. And John and his boys had helped her cover what was underneath to keep the rains from soaking the hay. That seemed so long ago and the work still was not finished.

As she looked at the barn a second thought came, maybe it was a good thing they stayed away. What she did not need to hear was someone telling her how father would be so disappointed in her abilities to keep the place from ruin.

Everyday she got up long before the sun came up and went to bed long after it had disappeared, but that still did not give her enough hours to make a difference.

And today was the same. She pulled on her dust cap and picked up the blue wooden water bucket that her mother had bought on her last trip to Fredericktown. Her noon meal would be a piece of bread she had stuffed in her pocket. Coming back to the cabin to eat would be a waste of precious time.

Once into the field she began to pull at the weeds that choked out what little crop she had managed to save during the drought. Oh, if only some rain would come, she thought as she looked to the sky.

Time after time that day she went to the creek to bring water until her back ached from the weight. If only she could afford to hire the help she needed. Her brother John had promised he would lend a hand, but on the very day he and his two oldest sons were to come, he had fallen off the roof of his barn. His leg was broken in at least two places they said, and it would be a long time before he would be able to stand on his own. And now his boys, John Jr. and Daniel, were needed at home. So instead of Rachel getting help, it was she who had gone over to John's place to help.

To make matters more distressing, John had told her of the talk at one of the family meetings and how John Hughes had said, "If she doesn't keep the place up we will bring in a man to marry her. James Lee's honor is at risk."

Then her brother had told her the group suggested they find a man who would agree to marry her. And if she could not find a husband then she should pay a family to move to the homestead. And pray tell, she thought, where was she to find the monies to pay the family? It was all she could do to keep her own mouth fed, and little it was.

That night she had returned home to try again to make a crop. If John could not stand up for her against the family, then he would have to do without her help, even with his injury. She would go again after her weeds were pulled.

Thinking back on the conversation still made her blood boil. The nerve of John Hughes words. After she had paid all the small monies her father had requested, John and Anne Hughes had given her a bill for all the seeds or supplies they had given to help their father over the last two years when things got bad. Rachel had paid them from her own money jar, leaving it empty for supplies, and had even given up the mare as part of the bill. She suspected his anger was settled on her because she had inherited the most. Did they not know how much she had given up to care for her parents? The very thought of that conversation caused her to yank at the weeds with a vengeance.

It was the same old story, "If you don't do what we want, we will force you." On the last visit, if you could call it that, Anne Hughes had told her a lot of men in the county had lost their wives and needed a wife to care for their children.

Didn't they know how much she would have liked marrying a good man and have his children? She wondered where they were looking for this husband? Not one of the brothers-in-law gave a thought of what kind of a man she would want to share a life with. Would they care if he was one that would beat her, like Sarah Crowley's husband? Or that stayed drunk like Leah Grimes husband, or one that cursed the very life he lived from sun up to sun down, like Sonya that lived at the edge of the road?

Nothing could be done about the brothers'-in-law plans just now. The best she could do was to keep the weeds pulled and the crops hoed and hope to quiet their talk. And that thought kept her going during these hot days.

Rachel pulled the last weed on the row where this morning she had found a few tender young tobacco plants still hanging on. Her knees burned from the hot sand and her back ached all the way down to her legs. She tried standing up but the strength was not there. Reaching for the hoe, she pulled herself up and wiped the dust from her worn out dress. For the first time she noticed the sun was beginning to set. Thunder would be waiting for his oats at the barn.

The poor old horse, once a beautiful specimen and the pride of her father, was sadly feeble and almost blind. The long trip into Fredericktown two years ago had started his down-fall she was convinced.

She remembered the day he had wandered into their barnyard full of spirit. Her father had gone into Fredericktown and registered him, as was the law. That was so many years ago. She remembered what someone had written in the margin of his logbook at the time, "A very fine horse." This evening as she approached the barnyard she listened for his welcoming whiney. Rachel smiled just thinking about how he always seemed to respond to her steps. But tonight there was no sound—just silence. Something was wrong. He always came to meet her at the gate.

She grabbed her chest and let out a scream. The gate was lying on the ground, torn from the rotted fence post. She ran through the field calling his name hoping he had not wandered too far. But there was no sign of the horse.

The moon was just visible up at the edge of the earth when she walked back to the now dark cabin. Her body ached, weary from the work but even more because of the despair of losing her father's favorite horse. In fact, the reason she had given Anne Hughes her father's much healthier mare to pay some of the debt was because she could not bear to part with old Thunder. Slowly her whole life was slipping from her grip and there was no place to turn for help. She ran from the hot cabin in the darkness to the graveyard. Pushing the weeds from her parent's graves, she fell face down. Her uncontrollable sobbing broke the stillness of the night.

In her outpouring of grief she did not hear someone coming down the road. A man's voice called out to her, "Who is there—are you in need of help?

The moonlight filtering through the trees did not offer up recognition nor did Rachel know the voice. Suddenly her heart raced with fear.

In the dim light he again called out, "Are you in need of some help?" His voice was closer now.

Rachel tried to think. Should she run for the cabin in the darkness or answer the man?

"Are you hurt?" he asked for the third time as the voice was very near.

All Rachel could do now was to offer the reason for her crying and trust this man meant her no harm. Still shaken and her voice weak, she said, "My father's old horse has gotten out of the barn and he is no where to be found, I've failed with the crops, and I cannot find help." She began to cry all over again in heavy sobs partly out of fear and partly because of her dilemma.

"Is their anyone I can get to come help you?"

"No, there is no one." Normally she would never have told a stranger that there was no one at the cabin waiting for her, but tonight she was not thinking about her safety. All she knew was that her life, as she had known it, was about to change.

She regained some sense of the moment and asked, "Where did you come from? How did you find me?"

"I was on my way to deliver some goods to a Mr. Madden on this road. If it had not been for the moonlight tonight I would not have come along just now."

"There are several Madden families on this road. Which one were you intending to see?"

"They called his name out as Dennis."

"Dennis lives in the next cabin straight on this road. He has a big barn near the road." Most likely it was leather supplies for his shoemaker shop, Rachel guessed.

"Will you be all right—I could help you to your cabin."

The man's kindness seemed sincere, but she hesitated to accept his offer of help for fear of appearing defenseless.

"Please go. I will be all right." Rachel tried to sound like she was over her crying spell. "Dennis Madden will be happy to know he is getting his supplies. "

"All right, ma'am, if you are sure. But I would be satisfied to help you."

"I thank you for your kindness, but it would be better that you go on to Mr. Maddens place with his supplies."

"Well, if you are sure," the man said, sounding puzzled at her refusal for help.

Rachel could hear him go back to the road. The sound of his horse gaining speed let her know she was safe to go back to the cabin.

She ran for the dark cabin and quickly lit a torch to see her way to the barnyard. As she approached she listened for any signs that Thunder had come home. But the lot was empty. She called for the horse one more time after feeding the rest of the animals and headed back to the cabin.

When she finally gave up for the night and blew out the candle, her sleep was haunted by dreams that did nothing to help solve her problems.

Rachel awoke the next morning with one thought on her mind. After she looked again for Thunder, she resolved to set a list of jobs that needed to be done. The top of the list had to be those things that would keep her sisters' husbands and even her own brothers, from taking action.

Fix ruf over my bed befor nex rain

Rachel looked down at the black spots left by mildew on her once white chemise morning dress, a testament to the leaky roof. It had happened during the spring rains while she was working at John's house for days at a time. She had sent her nephews to feed her animals but they were unaware of the leaky roof and the basket of clothes right under it. By the time Rachel returned home the mold spots had sadly colored her wardrobe.

She continued to scratch the pen over the paper.

> *if Thunder comes home put up nu gate*
> *clen fireplace and chimney*
> *clear field and plant winter wheet*
> *dig nu trench for pig pen*
> *cleer path way to grave yard*
> *go se Mrs Caroll about work*
> *talk to Maddens about selling my land, Maidens Delight.*

She had bought her land only four years earlier from Jane Edmonston after going to her place for a dress fitting. How many times had she stepped off the dimensions on her new land for the house she had hoped one day to build? Then again, how many times had she said, when Father gets better? She should have known he would never be able to live alone again.

Just the thought of giving up her land caused tears to welt up in her eyes. She loved the way the hills softly sloped to the creek where the natural seeded flowering trees had set themselves at the water's edge, along the meandering Sligo creek rocks. It was such a peaceful spot, and she had planned to bring her father down to see it just as soon as she could build a bench.

She looked down at her list. Little pools of ink had dropped over some of the words while she was distracted. Frustrated with her day dreaming, she lifted the edge of her skirt and blotted the mess, scolding herself. "Won't I ever learn? I always make a mess when I bother to dream."

She slipped her faded brown sleeveless dress over the chemise and picked up the basket to take with her to the garden just as the sun was beginning to come up. Hopefully there would still be beans on the vines for her evening meal. When she opened the door she noticed a trail of dust signaling someone was on the road beyond the gate. Who could be coming past her place so early in the morning? After last night's encounter she did not feel safe alone and waited for the traveler to pass.

The thick bank of trees along the road obscured the rider from Rachel's view, but she thought she heard more than one voice. Whoever it was, must have seen her at the door because a man called out, "Miss Rachel, this man came by your place last night and said he was worried about your well being. I thought I'd better come check on you before going to the fields."

Rachel called out. "Who is speaking?"

The question was met with a laugh. "Why, Rachel, it is Dennis—Dennis Madden. Of anyone, I thought you would know my voice. Didn't mean to cause you fright."

Rachel quickly went out to meet her neighbor and the man traveling with him. When she got close enough to see them, her mouth fell open. What she did not expect was to discover the identity of the other rider.

Sitting on the horse next to Dennis was the man she had seen at the market in Fredericktown, the one who had danced with her, and the one that had felt it his place in life to scold her for losing Mrs. Carroll's slave.

The man recognized Rachel as well. "Well, if I'd known it was you, I would have gone on by last night."

"Well, I've done nothing to cause you distress. You found it in your mind to bring condemnation over the slave."

"I saved you from drowning in Carroll Creek, didn't I?"

"You what?"

"How else would I have known about it?"

The thought of this man being the one who had snatched her from the murky waters embarrassed her beyond thinking. The memory of her muddy dress clinging to her form and her hair falling like a wet horse's tail around her face was not one she wished to be remembered by. In her embarrassment she railed in anger, "Well, I certainly did not fall in the creek to give you entertainment. I slipped on the wet bank. You saved my life and I thank you for that. But I did not appreciate the laughter in which you and the other men devoted so much time to."

The conversation had left Dennis Madden confused. "You know him, Rachel?"

"I've seen him in Fredericktown."

The stranger turned to Dennis. "My sympathies go out to you living this close to her. It must be one distress call after another."

Dennis came to Rachel's defense. "You will not find better neighbors than the Lees. Mr. Lee was sick a long time and Rachel took care of him all that time. And since her father died I have tried to devote some help in keeping up with the repairs. Since you are acquainted, I don't suppose it would be too much to ask you to hold the first board on that barn roof. I've had a right terrible time getting the first nail in."

The man seemed hesitant for a moment then said, "I've work to finish down the road, but since you did not object to me bedding down in your barn last night, I can help you with a few boards." He then turned to Rachel. Addressing her with a somewhat disapproving tone. "Did you find the horse?"

"Thunder is missing?" Dennis asked. He was acquainted with the aged horse and Mr. Lee's love for the animal.

"The gate fell from the holder," Rachel explained. "I knew the wood was rotted out. The nails I put in could not hold it, and I had it on the list to have someone replace it."

"You have a list? What else needs to be attended to?" Dennis asked.

Rachel pulled the list from her pocket and read it, omitting the personal parts about going to seek employment from Mrs. Carroll and the part about selling the land.

The men decided the jobs they could finish this morning and went to the barn to find the tools they would need.

Rachel quickly ran back into the cabin and pulled the flour bucket from the shelf. Luckily, there was enough left over from the last milling to make biscuits for their noon meal. If she fried up the fat back and hurried down to the root cellar to get the Quince Jelly she had made last year, she could feed them. Anyone kind enough to help with her repairs should have a belly full, come mealtime.

Once the biscuits were rolled out and put in the side oven and the bacon was left in the skillet far enough from the fire to not burn, she went out to finish pulling the weeds from her kitchen garden near the door. Hopefully she could find a few fresh vegetables to put on the table. There were not enough beans to even fill a good sized spoon, but to her surprise there were new shoots of growth beginning to come from the earth, giving her more hope than she had had in months.

Dennis Madden had climbed up into the loft and found the lumber that had been intended for her father's outside shade covering. He had been there when the lumber had arrived several years ago and had been there to help store it two years ago after his death. Rachel looked up from time to time as she pulled another row of weeds and could see there was more than enough lumber to make the new frame for the gate. She wondered if there would be any use for the gate now. At least, not for the horse. On any given night you could hear the cry of a hungry wildcat on the prowl for something to fill their empty bellies. And now, the once powerful specimen they had named Thunder, because of his blustering spirit, was wandering out there somewhere, incapable of protecting himself against even the smallest barnyard cat.

It was almost midday when they hammered the last nail in and fastened the latch in place.

Rachel saw Dennis coming toward her and stood up to offer them the meal. "That is right kindly of you Rachel, but Anastasia will be worried if I don't return to give her news of your safety." He turned and yelled at the man who had helped him, "The Lee women are all good cooks. It makes no sense to waste good food in this drought. A man never knows when he will be forced into hunger. You should stay and eat."

Rachel felt shy when she set the pewter plate in front of the stranger. "I didn't hear your calling name."

The man spoke without looking up from his plate. "The name is John."

There was silence. Rachel was not used to making conversation with a man and especially a stranger sitting at her table. "I want to thank you for the work, John."

He still did not look up as he spoke. "Pray tell me. How did you get yourself in such a run down state? Then he looked straight at her, and added, I mean the farm."

At first his question angered her. How dare he insult her while sitting at her table. If she had known in Fredericktown the day would come to have this rude man sitting in her cabin, eating at her table she would have—well, she did not know what she would have done. How twisted fate becomes when you are in need.

As she opened her mouth to give him a piece of her mind for his manners, she noticed a fresh deep cut on his hand. He had wiped the blood off with his shirtsleeve. It must have been cut while he was working on the gate. Maybe she did owe him an explanation; after all, he had stayed around to help.

Slowly she began to give him reasons. It was hard to tell a complete stranger, well almost a stranger, what had happened to cause this much damage.

The first thing out of her mouth was not what she intended to say, but she could not stop herself. "I'll have you know I do not beg of anyone for a hand out. I pay my dues, my taxes and repairs." She walked over to the cup where she kept the coins and felt the bottom. There was nothing there. Awkwardly, she turned back to face him. "Well, I will pay you. I can write my name—and I read some."

The man looked at her like she had two heads. "That is not what I asked. I just wanted to hear why you are always getting in hard situations. Does anyone else come to your aid?"

"Yes, I have brothers and sisters."

"And do they help?"

Her voice had turned weak against his inquiring tone and she felt defenseless to his question. "No—well not much. They all have families."

He did not speak but kept looking at her, prompting an explanation.

Finally, she realized he was waiting to hear the story. "When father took on his sickness I was already twenty-six years old. Oh, once I had an intended." For some unearthly reason she had put that in. Why did it matter what he thought about her? She felt a redness creep up her face. She rushed on to save any self-respect she could find. "My brothers and sisters had decided I should be the one to care for our parents. Mother died first from the smallpox, and father just grew weaker and weaker until—" her voice faded off.

Awkward silence again filled the room.

She admitted her pain, "They came when they could to help when father was alive. Well, sometimes they came. At harvest time they would send my nephews. My brother John mostly came. He lives over the hill."

There was nothing else to say that could satisfy the reason for the weed infested land. Rachel went to the window to look out. She wished for words to talk, but nothing smart sounding could be found. She guessed it was because they had nothing in common.

Then he asked, "Didn't you want to leave home?"

When she turned around to look at him, she wanted to tell him how many times she had wished to have her own place but was afraid it sounded too selfish. But after the first words she could not stop. Suddenly she realized he was the first person to ever ask that question. Embarrassed to seem so eager, she spoke lightly, "One night real late I was sitting up with father during one of his bad spells, and I remember standing at this window, looking out into the darkness and realizing my life was just like the dark out there. I could see nothing ahead. Once I did think father might be getting better, so I bought the piece of land next door to this land. I was going to build my own house there. I am good with my hands, and Mrs. Carroll that lives on the big place close to here asks me to work for her on occasions. I knew I could afford to keep my own house."

"Did you build the house?" John asked.

"Father did not get better. I should have known he would not. Father had told the others I was the one he wanted to discuss the will at the courthouse. But when he died I was so unprepared for handling everything. It was not my choice to go into town. And when I did not have enough monies to pay his debts, I did not want the others to know about it. They would have just scolded me for my lack of planning. Now they have the nerve to propose bringing in a—" she stopped short of mentioning the word husband. "I think they are embarrassed at how ragged the home place has become. I as well am distressed."

She noticed her guest had eaten his last biscuit and turned to dish another one up from the pan. She had told her story. It had spilled out. Now she felt strange for giving this man another reason to give her advice. Nothing could take back her words. The best thing she could do was stand up straight and look straight at this man. "I do not need your jests and ill words you have said to me in the past. I am a good worker."

"So your father had just died when you came to Fredericktown?" the man said and let the thought rest a moment, "and they let you be overseer of his will?"

"Yes, that's what I said." She wondered if he had heard a thing she had said. "As to the farm—I have tried to find someone to help, but there are no 'hiring people' to be found. Do you know of anyone?"

The man did not speak but shook his head no.

There was silence now and it was as though no more conversation could be found until she blurted out, "Are you married?"

A shocked look came on his face then his laugh broke the silence. "I'm not interested in marrying you lady, if that is what you are asking."

Rachel turned to face this stranger partaking at her table. She gathered all the anger she felt and let the big spatula she still had in her hand, drop with a clang on to the table. Her eyes pierced his smirk. "For your information I have no intentions of marrying any man—especially one with so little experience on how to treat a women, as the likes of you." The words shocked even Rachel, and she turned away to regain her composure.

The stranger stood up in defiance. "Oh, you think I'm not experienced, do you say? I've kissed more than a few." With this last exchange he threw his spoon in the fireplace and walked out the door.

Rachel watched as he walked through the gate and turned west, probably going toward the road along Rock Creek. Why did the conversation cause her so much distress? Why did this man always seem so annoyed with her behavior?

She turned back to the fire and retrieved the now blackened spoon and laid it on the table to cool.

Without washing the dishes, she grabbed her sunbonnet and stomped to the weed patch.

It was late in the evening by the time she came back to the cabin. She took a candle from the shelf and lit it. The light dispelled the darkness, but not the gloom she felt around the heart of her very being. She wondered how long she would be able to live here. Without crops growing, without food for the live stock, without monies to pay the tax collector, she knew she would be forced to sell. On this night she did not bother to boil the greens, she had brought in with her. It did not matter if she ate. What did matter was the sleep she so wanted as she sat down in her father's old rocker.

A commotion out by the barn woke her. She stood up from her rocker and was about to reach for the rifle hanging over the fireplace when she heard the voice she knew all too well. He called out to her from the gate. "Lady, your horse is in the barn—see if you can keep him at home this time." Rachel could not help but wonder why this man always felt a need to address her with such a stern commanding tone?

She could see from his torch he was walking toward the road, but before he got there, turned back to give her his final thoughts. "I've looked at your tobacco crop and if you plan to make any money with it you need to plant at least twice as much."

Why did he think his advice would be welcomed, she wondered?

"And you had better move the piglets from the mother sow or they are going to founder." After the last instruction his light disappeared around the bend in the road.

Chapter 23

August, 1766
Baltimoretown

"Absolom, stay here with our crates while I finish tending my business, then we will load them in the wagon," William told his son as he disappeared somewhere into the fog.

Absolom remembered John's warnings just this morning about watching out for any thieves ready to snatch their crates away to a waiting wagon. But more frightening then their crates being stolen were the stories of men and boys standing on the docks being snatched away and made to become slaves on a big ship, never to be heard from again.

The stories last night, told by the old dock workers as they drank from their tankards at the table next to theirs in the tavern, had relived their life on the high seas and the gangs that ruled the waterfront.

The big ship next to where Absolom sat with his crates swayed with each incoming wave, and his imagination built with the sounds going on around him. His heart raced and he turned around to see if anyone was coming close. The dock was becoming crowed with sailors going and coming off the ships and workers loading big crates, like the crates his father had brought from a ship.

The sun began to slip through the early morning fog and Absolom could see a rope maker with a hand wrench twisting long strands of roping laid out at the edge of the water. His eyes followed it all along the waterfront and up the street someone had called Aliceanna Street. He wondered if these ropes would be used for a big ship like the ship on the dock next to him. He looked up to see if the rope holding the now limp sails was of the same size.

He could imagine himself being a sailor. He was fourteen and full of spirit and high flung dreams. He would sail into the world and visit the ports his father had taught him about in their book learning. It would certainly be a better life than plowing the rest of the rock filled field back home. A grin crossed his face when he thought of his mother ringing her hands in her apron and crying out for him to come home each time she received one of his letters from a far away port. He knew she would. She was like that about the family. Suddenly, he jumped. A hand grabbed hold of his arm and yanked him around.

"Absolom, I told you to watch our crates," his father scolded and went to pick up the barrel that had rolled almost to the water's edge. "Now sit on them, while I go find John."

After his father left, Absolom went back to watching the people around him. He could see a man on the hillside above the dock pulling a sled in his direction. The man went from worker to worker selling baskets of biscuits. Another man came along after him selling something from a jug. His attention changed directions when a dog carrying something in his mouth came from behind him in a dead run. A boy about his age was running after him, waving his arms frantically. Never before had he seen a town so full of adventures, even better than going to the Fair. Just yesterday, his father had pointed out streets with familiar sounding names from London near his father's home in the Hants, streets with familiar names like Thames Street and Queen Street and even one called Shakespeare Street.

Someone shouting on the street above the docks made Absolom turn to see what it was. He shielded his eyes from the sun as he watched the people scurry off to work from their tiny houses with green colored windowpanes. He wondered what it was like to always see splashes in green when looking out from those windows and why they build all of them that way.

He turned back to watch a slave stack small crates marked Lamp Oil on top of the larger crates that smelled of onions and potatoes and strong smelling cheese.

Nothing in Absolom's entire life had been so exciting and he felt a new inner life jumping out. Neither the salt that stung his eyes and gave taste to his lips nor the water that splashed up and soaked his moccasins could dispel the feeling.

He heard someone calling his name, "Hey, Absolom—up here." It was his brother John standing with a group of sailors on the deck of the big ship.

"Are you crazy, John? Father will tan your hide for going up there," Absolom yelled back then gave out a warning, "Father is looking for you."

With that warning John took hold of the big rope and hand over hand climbed down, dropping on the dock in a whooping yell. "How is it I got stuck sitting on the crates and you got to have all the fun?" Just as he said the words he heard his father coming, having seen John climb down from the ship.

William shook his finger at the boys. Absolom looked at John and could tell they were both thinking the same thing. What they did not want was another lecture about his travels on a big ship—a big leaky ship.

"Don't you boys ever try to cross the ocean on a ship like this," William warned his sons. Neither boy said anything, hoping their father would not feel the need to tell the entire story again about his transport from his homeland to the colonies, and how the boat had leaked so much that all they did was take turns bailing out the water. But it was too late. Their father had already begun the words. "I was so sick. It afflicted me the first day out and it stayed my enemy until I stepped out on the solid ground." He looked out to the sea for a long look then said, "When I came off that ship that cold windy day, I made a vow that I shall never ride the high seas again. But that is another day of stories and we best be moving on."

They had finished loading the last crate into the wagon, when someone in the crowd several ships back yelled out, "Littlefield, wait—wait up." William whipped around, squinting his eyes against the sun to see who was causing such a ruckus. The man was making a valiant attempt to run but from the looks of it an old injury had slowed him down.

William eyed the man to see if he knew his name. His suit of clothes suggested he obviously was not an authority of the government, for which William was thankful. With all the trouble the British authorities were handing out over shipping disputes, a person felt fortunate not to be stopped. The man's clothing showed signs of having once been considered well dressed, but now well worn would be a better description.

William grunted his disapproval at the delay. He reluctantly handed John the reins to the wagon. "Get in the wagon. I will go see what the man wants."

William had no desire to spend time with this stranger, who by the time he got to him was having trouble getting a decent breath.

"I've been told by some of your acquaintances of this morning that you and your relatives are looking for a suitable husband for one of your wife's folks. Can you tell me something of her qualifications?"

William eyed the man with suspicion before asking, "And can you tell me who might be inquiring?"

"Grove Hollock is the name." The man offered his hand in response to the introduction.

The sun was well into the day by the time William joined his sons at the wagon, and the impatient boys were anxious to hear what it was that had detained their father so long.

William did not give an explanation but simply tipped his hat to the man still standing on the docks and lashed his horses for a quick start. "We will be spending some time seeing your uncles on the way home. Something has come up that needs our attention."

Rebeckah was outside scrubbing the clothes on her scrub board when William and the boys returned home, four days after she had expected them.

He jumped down from the wagon and greeted her with a tip of his hat and did a little step that resembled the quick steps of a jig. She stood back and looked at her husband with a puzzled look. "My, but you are in fine spirits today. It must have been a profitable trip."

"Indeed it has been, Rebecky—indeed it has been," he said as he started for the barn. Then he yelled back, "We have found a good husband for Rachel."

"You have what? What are you talking about, William?"

"I've sent Grove Hollock a message that we would be agreeable for him to pursue Rachel in marriage. Your brothers seem to think she would be well taken care of by him, and more importantly, it appears we could trust him with the land."

William knew he had thrown down a fighting tool and did not wait to hear her reaction. By the time he reached the barnyard, he called back to her hoping to soothe her response. "Rebeckah, his children are crying for a mother," he said, trying to let sympathy be the mediator. But before William could get inside the barn Rebeckah rounded the corner.

"How dare you men take Rachel's life in your hands. It may be okay in your eyes, but women folk deserve to be talked to about these arrangements."

William turned to see the anger in his wife's eyes and knew there would be no stopping her. "We did give her an option before this. We told her to find her own husband. It is not our fault she dallied around."

"Before—what do you mean gave her an option before? You were afraid to tell me. You knew I would not stand for it and you chose to keep quiet and let Rachel defend herself without someone to help," Rebeckah stormed back.

"Rebecky, you know Rachel simply cannot handle the farm by herself." He hoped his tone change would bring some reasoning. "Your brothers and I have been worried for some time that the taxes will fall on us, lest she lose the farm to the courts. The way the place has grown up in weeds shows she can't help herself. And besides, have you thought about her old years? She will be lonely. We are just trying to help her out." Even to William it seemed his mouth had uttered a lie, but it did not stop him from trying to convince Rebeckah that her sister needed a husband. He paused before uttering the words, "A husband and children is what she needs."

Rebeckah knew William and the other men in the family were right about the monies for taxes. That had been a worry to them all. But at this very moment she was not in any mood to agree with them. This was a cruel idea. "It is no different than the slave being put up for auction to the highest bidder," she raised her voice to his face.

As the day wore on, every time Rebeckah poured the boiling water over the wash, it was as a tool of vengeance toward men.

The truth of the matter was, the men were right in worrying over both Rachel's old age being lonely and the monies it would take to keep the farm running, and that included paying taxes. Even if this year the family pitched in to pay the taxes, what about next year and the next? But selling their parents homestead would break Rachel's heart. Rebeckah thought for a moment. Which would be worse, losing the place or having a husband chosen for her? It would be like dashing her father's dreams for his youngest daughter's wellbeing. The options Rachel could pursue seemed to dead-end over the word "marriage."

With a heart felt sigh, Rebeckah sat down in her rocker. The tears were not only for Rachel's despair, but they were also a cry for the plight of being a woman without a voice.

That night Rebeckah found William working in the barn shop and cornered him with questions. "Is he an upright man, William—how many children? Does Rachel know him?"

William turned to his wife and looked at her for a long moment, trying to think how he should answer her. What he did not want now was the wrath of his wife and her sister's messing up this agreement. "Mr. Hollock heard we had been worried about the farm, and he inquired. His wife died awhile back, and he has had a hard time keeping the children fed and doing the work to make the farm. Now Rebeckah, you know it would be improper for a man to live at Chestnut Ridge or she at his house helping out with the children and not be married by the minister. Think about it. What kind of a scandal would be on the lips of everyone? Rachel living with a man not related or married. I would not wish that on Rachel." As William talked, he sensed he was making excuses and Rebeckah knew what they were.

"Trying to put this on Rachel's reputation—how can you tell me such a thing? You men were afraid you would have to help with the crops. Not to mention seeing to her old age."

In an attempt to soften his wife's outrage, William tried a new approach. "It is hard for you to give up your sister, ah lassie?" Not often did William show his wife the tenderness of an arm, but he knew when it came to her younger sister, more than words were needed to console her. When he mentioned what he thought would set the case for the marriage, he did not expect the outcome. "Mr. Grove Hollock has ten children for Rachel to love—well, ten that I know of."

"Ten—ten children that you know of." Rebeckah threw her hands in the air, horrified at the thought. She repeated the number, shaking her head in disbelief. "Poor Rachel! How can she care for so many on such short notice? It is hard enough having them one at a time." Then she asked, "What did she die from—the other wife I mean. Hard work?" Rebeckah opened the barn door to leave. She stopped, waiting to see if William would answer. She

277

reached up on the outside wall and pulled some withered vines from the stones over the door, then walked back to William, the dead vine in her hand. She crumbled the leaves on the workbench in front of him in a declaration of fight. "Is this all life is going to be for Rachel? Will she just wither away like some old vine?"

William did not look up from his work, aware that his wife had not moved from her position.

When she spoke again there was emotion in her voice. "Tell me, William, look me in the face and tell me how long you and my brothers have sought this husband?"

William still did not look up when he answered, "Long enough to go through a long list."

"A long list? Pray tell who was on that list and to whom did you talk it?"

This conversation was teetering between all out war and a less than peaceful consideration for what was best for Rachel. William knew that if he could not convince his wife this was the right thing to do, she would send word to her sisters. They could put a stop to the agreement or at least make it so hard for Grove Hollock to say the vows that he would decide to go elsewhere for a wife.

"We thought of the best men—the finest upright men." His voice was not as reassuring as he hoped. Maybe it was due to the fact that some of what he said was an untruth, and William was not good with something less than truth. His thoughts revisited the first lists they had made and the names of some of the desperation candidates he had written down on that list. Maybe if he gave her some of the more upright names it would bring peace to her mind. "Well, we thought of Daniel Carroll. He had just lost his wife. And there was someone in John Darnell's family, but that did not work out either. We did inquire of many others.

Rebeckah, we have tried to find someone, and until now the men we thought you and your sisters would approve of have not been there. Mr. Hollock truly needed a mother for his children, and I suppose desires a wife also, and he is good with the land."

William looked up at his wife for the first time through this talk, and he felt ashamed that he had to deceive her on such a serious matter. But he knew best. Feebly, he tried another approach. "We would not hear of anyone marrying her that would not be good for her—and the land." William said almost meekly.

"The land? What does the land have to do with you wanting a husband for Rachel? If Father had thought she would be best to have a husband, he would have seen to it himself when he was alive," Rebeckah fumed.

"I cannot think of anything more important as a well cared for piece of land, Rebeckah. Without it you have nothing. Mr. Hollock is a man with a reputation for bringing in big healthy crops at the end of the season. He told me how much tobacco he had rolled to the warehouses the last three seasons and I only wished for such success. And his winter wheat—well, it was more than good."

Rebeckah still continued to harp, and it was distracting William with his work. "William, you do not care about Rachel. It is being embarrassed when you walk in the tavern and face someone that has ridden the road in front of father's place."

"No, it is more than that."

"What pray tell?" Rebeckah asked

"She would be forced to come live under our roof," William said without thinking. But it was a truth.

"So that is it. You are afraid she will have to live with us?" Rebeckah said, so sharp that it cut right through the other attempts of saying the taxes or old age were their worries.

Before William could give an answer, John came into the barn to put the tools away for the night. "Father, when do you think you will hear if Aunt Rachel has received her letter about the marriage?" John asked his father.

Rebeckah looked confused, "How did you know about this note, John? Were you a part of this ugly deception as well?"

"No, ma'am. I was there when Mr. Hollock called out to Father. But I didn't have anything to do with the talking. Then later when we went to the uncles' houses, Absolom and I just sat next to Father when he was telling them about Mr. Hollock needing a wife. And Father sent me to the tavern to post the letters to Mr. Hollock and Aunt Rachel. Then I came back, that's all I did."

Still in disbelief, she rushed to ask as a worried look came over her face, "And the seal—you did put the waxed seal over the edge, did you not?" The thought made her weak, and she sat down on the bench. "I would hate to think of someone other than Rachel seeing something so private as a marriage agreement. You know how many times you have said you saw a traveler pick up a letter and read it from the basket before it was picked up." She looked at John, questioningly. "Well did you?"

"Guess we will rightly know soon enough, won't we?" William said.

"Does it matter so little what my sister is about to go through? And then to hear it from a sweaty frothy mouthed traveler?" She got up to go.

"Maybe you would like to take some monies with us to the wedding to help with her dowry, what say ye, Becka?" William offered.

"Seems to me that would suit you just fine to have me busy myself with her dowry, William. I will indeed take your monies and do some fine things for her. It will most likely be the last finery she has in this life. Ten children—" She shook her head at the thought.

This conversation had lasted too long and William's patience had reached the end. He had tried to be reasonable, but Rebeckah was testing his authority and that could not go on, especially in front of the children, and John had seen too much.

He turned to Rebeckah and firmly put his hands on her shoulders. "Rebeckah, this is the way it is to be. I want no more talk on your part. We—your brothers and sisters' husbands know what is best. Now I do not want to hear another word about it. It will take place with or without your helping her. Now go back to your mending."

Several days had passed, and Rebeckah had given up her fight. She felt sure it was the same in all of her sisters' cabins, as well. A woman just did not have the options that a man had to fight for what was right.

Sometime after the fire had been put out in the big fireplace for the night and all was dark in the cabin, Rebeckah called for Nancy to come sit with her on the low branch of the tree down by the road. It had once been her favorite spot to reflect on some problem, make a decision, or even a safe place to have a dream in the shade of the branches. That had been a long time ago. Now she sought the place again for its quietness in the night. "Here is what I have been thinking about Rachel's wedding. We need to make something special for her for all she is going through."

"Mother, is it going to be that bad for Aunt Rachel? Seems to me when it is time to get married you should be happy."

Rebeckah put her arms around her daughter and softly stroked her hair, "Oh, Nancy, I do so hope it is that way when you find the man of your heart." At fifteen, her daughter would soon awake some young man's fancy, and Rebeckah was not ready to give her up.

Rebeckah shook her head sadly, remembering the eagerness she came into her own marriage. Now Rachel was to be denied the joy. The men had taken away any chance of choice.

"Rachel never had much given to her in the way of fancy things. And heaven knows, after she takes the vows with Mr. Hollock with all those children following behind him in the wedding march, she will be likely as not, too poor to have another fancy outfit until she goes to her final dress up."

"What do you think we should do for Aunt Rachel?"

"Let's make her a dress of white linen—with tucks and lace like we saw at the store window in Fredericktown. You can stitch the tucks while I tat the lace." Unable to say Rachel's name in connection with Grove Hollock, Rebeckah simply said, "We will have to work fast, as your father and your Uncles claim Mr. Grove Hollock will be claiming his wife in a hurry."

Chapter 24

September 1766
Chestnut Ridge

Rachel dropped the hoe and ran to see who was jangling the bell at the front gate. It might be Anastasia Madden with the supplies she had offered to pick up for her while at the market. If it was Anastasia she hated to make her wait to unlock the gate. But ever since that rude man had come with Dennis, she had begun to lock the gate from the inside. It seemed like a silly thing to do, now that she thought about it, because she was fairly sure he would never return to her place again. It still made her blood boil just thinking about him throwing her good spoon into the fire.

By the time Rachel rounded the corner of her cabin she could see it was indeed her neighbor. Anastasia was frantically waving a letter in her hand, and the smile on her face must mean she brought good news. Dear sweet Anastasia always was a pleasant person, and Rachel loved to have her visit.

"Rachel, why did you not tell us you were getting married?" Anastasia yelled with enthusiasm as she got close enough to hear.

At first Rachel thought her neighbor was jesting with her as she took the letter with William Littlefield's hand writing on the front.

She turned the paper over. There was no seal to conceal the message. Anyone visiting the tavern where it sat in the basket could have read it and probably did. "Anastasia, what on earth are you talking about. I have no man to marry."

"It is all there. Dennis read it to me. Rebeckah's William has found a suitable man that can take care of you and the land as well."

Rachel let out a moan and slid to the sandy ground, unable to speak. She opened the paper and read what had been the dreaded edict. "Grove Hollock will be coming to ask for your hand in marriage. He is a worthy husband and father. It is well that you accept his proposal." She continued to read about his need for a mother for his children and that he could build a room onto the house to make room for them. "Mr. Hollock says your land is better than his, so he will move to your place."

Rachel let the paper fall from her hands and turned to her friend for advice, "Anastasia, what am I to do? I do not desire to be married to a man I know nothing of, much less, do not love."

Anastasia slid to the ground beside Rachel, unconcerned that she was soiling her pretty pale blue linen dress. "Oh Rachel, I am indeed sorry for intruding on you with news of so great a decision. When Dennis picked up the letter at the tavern stop, he said the word was spreading throughout the whole room. I thought it was something that you had already been consulted about and were holding out a surprise about the wedding. I just couldn't wait for you to tell me in your own time. I know how you do not wish to make a scene, so thought the wedding was to be a secret. You know how I am about weddings. It would not be a pretty thing to have me miss out on giving you the full ceremony. Why, I planned it all the way from the tavern until my Dennis got tired of hearing me chatter. Now, are you telling me you know nothing of the man of which I speak?"

"I've never heard of him before this letter. It is not fair Anastasia. A woman ought to have a say so as to who sleeps in her bed."

The two friends sat on the ground for a time while they tried to think what to do about the news. Anastasia looked around at the run down conditions of the place and consoled her for what was inevitable. She tried to help her see that it would be better to marry than to have to give up her parent's gift of land. "Rachel, I do not know what I would do without my Dennis, and you could feel the same about your Mr. Hollock."

"He is not my Mr. Hollock." Rachel said in defiance. "Let William Littlefield help him out if he thinks so much of his needs," she said as she poked a stick at a little black bug that had crawled up close to her ragged petticoat hem. Anastasia in turn, joined in with another stick. "There, you mean old man. How do you like that? And that?" Anastasia said as she jabbed at the bug. The women laughed at how fast the bug retreated to a safe place under the dried up grass.

They both felt better for the talk. When Anastasia announced she needed to get back to her house, Rachel went with her to the wagon to get the basket of supplies brought from town.

She waved a last good-bye to Anastasia from the door and began to put the items on the shelf. Once that job was done she felt into her pocket for William's letter. Ceremoniously, she tore it into tiny shreds and began dropping it one shred at a time into the licking flames of the fireplace. She spoke out loud, "There, no more Mr. what-ever-your-name-is." She went about her chores as if nothing had happened, but from time to time she reflected on the visit with Anastasia. Slowly, the words of her friend began to find a place in her thoughts. Could it be that she would begin to feel comfortable thinking about marriage? Anastasia could never live without thinking first of Dennis. And their life was far from easy as long as Dennis had to work with such unpleasant odors. Tanning the leathers and stitching the shoes made good monies, but it was not kind to one's back or hands.

There must be times when she wished to be married to a shopkeeper rather than a shoemaker. But that was the life they had, and Anastasia seemed to be content as long as she had Dennis to love. Is that what could happen to her?

Rachel let her mind wander. What would it be like around her table with children and an adoring husband? But that was all a dream. She knew what it was like for most of the women that were forced to marry at someone else's doings. And if she knew her brothers and the brothers-in-law rightly, they had given no thought of what the man's appearance was or his smell or how he would treat her. All they wanted was the land to be weeded and see a healthy crop on the good earth.

The days wore on and Rachel saw no one except a neighbor that lived several turns down the road who slowed down to say a hello, as she pulled the weeds by the gate. He had said he was on the way to check on the new Mason Dixon line. "The chains are almost to the summit of the Little Allegheny. Sure will be nice to have that settled. Then I guess I will stop back by the courthouse to pay up my taxes."

Rachel watched his wagon go on down the road and thought about how it would be to just take off when you wanted to on the way to see some new thing and still have monies to pay the taxes. A pain hit her insides causing her to whence. She went back to pulling weeds. The work seemed better than worrying about the taxes.

She heard another wagon coming down her path and she braced herself as to what visitor might come next. To her relief it was her nephews, John Jr. and Daniel. They carried with them a serious look as Daniel yelled out, "Paw's real mad about you not telling him about the wedding you are going to take. He said he demands you to come right now to our house."

"Your father is mistaken making it sound like I am getting married," she said with a smile on her face. Surely John did not think she would make plans as serious as a wedding and not include him. "But I shall go with you to explain the misunderstanding."

As Rachel and the boys approached her brother's cabin she could see John sitting on the step with his leg propped up to keep the swelling from returning and teasingly called out to him "Didn't you know I cannot get married until your leg heals. You will have to stand up with the one I decide to marry."

"Don't jest with me Rachel Lee. Why was I not told about the marriage plans? I've heard it from at least three travelers coming down the road. It is all over these parts." By now, Elizabeth had heard the commotion and had come out of the house to scold her for not letting them know.

"Oh my soul, do you two not know I would never marry a man I do not know? Or, one that I have not passed before you for judgement?" Rachel said, trying not to show her annoyance at them for not trusting her decisions. What she really would have liked to do was break down into tears before both of them so they could console her and help her fight against the others for the right to be left alone. Those years were gone. She had to stand on her own two feet. And she could not cause them concern just now when John was having such a difficult time with his leg.

This settled their fears for the time and she explained about the letter from William Littlefield. "It seems it was voted on by the other men in the family, including our own two brothers. I guess they went on to vote without you, knowing your leg was not ready for walking."

Rachel stayed long enough to help with the evening meal. That gave John plenty of time to remind her over and over about how she should be saving for the land tax. On the way home, she could not help but wonder what he thought she was spending money on. There had been nothing bought since she went into Frederick two years ago, outside the few supplies she asked the Maddens to pick up for her. The fact was, there were no monies to use. Her cup was empty.

It was almost sundown when she took her path up to the gate. To her surprise it was already open and a horse was tied to the post. Someone had come but she did not see anyone at the door. She felt her heart jump to her throat. Who would be coming? Anastasia or Dennis would have not left the gate open, allowing the animals to get out. She waited to see if anyone came out of the cabin or from the barn, but no one came. It was then she spotted a mess of fish hanging on the door, and cautiously moved closer. They were still flopping on the string, so it had not been that long ago that someone had caught them. She looked toward the road to see if any dust was rising, but the air was clear. Then she saw a man coming from the barnyard. He waved his hand to her.

The blood seemed to drain from her head and she felt faint. It was almost like a conviction sentence issued, like those she had witnessed at the courthouse. She could only guess this was the man William Littlefield had referred to in his letter. She could think of no other man coming to call. His appearance showed him to be about the age or a little older than her oldest brother. He was coming toward her with a big grin on his face. She supposed he could have at one time been considered a respectable looking man, but now his beard needed trimming. He wore no wig, showing a balding head, and seeing from the few strands that had stayed put, he at one time probably had wavy red hair. His suit had been of a common cut, but now showed the signs of his added pounds. There was a tear in his breeches, probably caused by going over a fence somewhere. The buckle on his left shoe was loose. His coat was open and showed the shirtwaist was missing the top two buttons leaving his chest hairs to show. This was more than Rachel wanted to know about this man.

"I've come to court you. Just thought I would look around to see what I might be getting myself into here. The place is run down 'bout as bad as I've seen it in these parts, but I suspect I can get it in shape in no time. I'll plant a big crop next year. And the house needs repairs. I've lived in worse I guess. We will add a room for the little ones," he said, not looking at her. "Your brother seemed to approve of my plans."

"If you are referring to William Littlefield, he is not my brother." Rachel was mad at the presumptions of this crude man.

"Well, don't get upset, Missy. From the looks of things around here you are the one that should be asking me to marry you, not the other way around."

Before she could tell him to leave, he said something that brought her back to facing her problems.

"Just how do you plan to pay for this years taxes? Doesn't seem to be much way of making monies out here," he said.

Rachel quickly came back with an answer. "I can't see how any of this concerns you, Mr. What-ever-your-name-is."

The man grinned, "Now missy, I think you know who I am." The coy way he spoke suggested he knew she had received a letter from William telling her to accept the marriage proposal. He changed the subject and became a meaner person. "Grove Hollock likes his fish fried black. Let's see how you can satisfy him," he said as he took the fish from the hook and thrust them into her hand. Rachel tried to draw back. His hand lay across her bosom as he pressed the fish into her hand. She wanted to dismiss this man by pulling the gun from the hook over the fireplace, but knew she could not move fast enough. She could only try talking to him and convince him to leave her alone.

"Mr. Hollock, my brothers would never accept a man that could not mind his manners," she said. I am full aware of why you are here and even if the taxes are due I will not give myself to someone I find overbearing and crude." Rachel said this so convincingly, the man backed away from the door and let her pass through with the fish.

"I will fry your fish. I was taught by my parents to never waste the food God has provided. So I will fry the fish the way I always fry fish, and if you want to eat you can help yourself. I will not be told what to do. This whole ordeal has been without my consent and I will not be your wife or anyone else's unless it is my choice." She took the frying pan down from its hook over the mantle and reached into the grease bucket for a cup of lard. When she threw the fish into the hot pan the lard sizzled and caused flames to surround the offering. She would show him she could fry fish black. That would leave the decision open long enough to decide how much she could tolerate this man. If only there was another way out of her dilemma. At the same time she had the strong sense that there was no way out from marriage if she was to save her father's land from the tax collector. Even John had suggested that this evening. She wanted to cry out or run away. But that would do nothing to solve her problems. And pride was involved as well; if she lost the land, her family would never forgive her lack of controlling her feelings.

Rachel dished the fish out on the pewter plate and poured a tankard of watered down ale.

The man's satisfaction was obvious. He was no less the bully as when he came in, but he did resist wiping his mouth on his sleeve as most crude men did. He stood up, and Rachel opened the door for him to leave. But instead, he turned around and pulled her to him and kissed her on the mouth. Then he pushed her away. "You will do just fine. I have ten children and I'll expect to have more. You can't expect to raise tobacco with no help. Two Saturdays next I'll bring the reverend."

He had gone quickly. Too quickly for her to tell him she had no intentions of marrying him so not to bother bringing the reverend.

For the rest of the week Rachel had thought of nothing else but the unfavorable encounter with Grove Hollock. She was probably the only person in the province that wished the stamp tax were still in force. That way, maybe the cost of the marriage license with the new stamp, would be too high a price to pay.

One by one the neighbors had come by to tell of hearing she was to marry on two Saturdays next. As she had feared, the groom-to-be as he thought of himself, had gone to the tavern that night and announced to everyone that Rachel Lee had agreed to marry him. The news had spread to her family as well, and Rachel had received a letter from William Littlefield that he and the other men in the family were extremely pleased that she had chosen such an upstanding man as Grove Hollock.

It was no surprise when Mrs. Carroll's wagon pulled up out front and Mrs. Carroll herself climbed down, instead of one of her servants. She had come to give Rachel a present.

Rachel tried to tell her that it was not going to happen, but Mrs. Carroll never gave her a chance until she had heaped all sort of blessings on them. Rachel stopped trying to deny the rumors after the wise Mrs. Carroll let it be known that she had so hoped for such a marriage. "After all you could never keep this place up by yourself. My dear, it is so run down I hardly recognized it on the way over." Mrs. Carroll reached over and patted Rachel's hand, trying to soften what she was about to say. "Your father's name has been so marred by the looks of what I see here. This marriage is truly what we have all prayed for."

After Mrs. Carroll's wagon rambled back down the road, Rachel sat down on her step and cried. It was hopeless. She would have to marry Grove Hollock, Saturday next.

Chapter 25

October 1766
Chestnut Ridge

Rachel opened her eyes. All night her sleep had been tormented with phrases like, "You need a husband—the weeds have taken over the field—the roof is sagging in—a husband will keep the land—" words that had haunted her sleep since the letter had come. And just last night she fitfully tried to find a different ending when a man intimidated her and told her what she had to do. And somewhere in this dream a man had rattled the gate, coming to take her land if she did not pay.

Rachel rolled over to try to make the memory of the dream go away but it was hopeless. She opened her eyes again and the first thought was, if she could talk to Rebeckah she would know what to do. She was the sensible one. She had taken adversity and learned to find a life in spite of it. But by now she felt sure William Littlefield had convinced her to think a marriage was the best thing.

As on every morning of late, Rachel was forced to count off the days to what would be the end of her life, as she had known it to be. If the Lord she prayed to stayed on her side, then maybe this Mr. Hollock would be the man of honor William believed him to be. She remembered the encounter of their meeting last week and hoped it was only his effort to impress her as to who would be the boss of the family. Maybe he was a really nice man, but this did nothing to dispel the feeling of doom she had.

She put her feet on the floor and pulled on her faded brown sleeveless dress over her morning dress. Her hand ran around the bottom where there was once a row of pretty lace. Now she had to search for even a small piece still hanging on. There had been no time to sew for herself in such a long time, and now there would be even less with Mr. Hollock's brood to care for.

There were so many things she had put off buying that would not be possible now, unless Grove Hollock needed them. Her list had included a new pair of shoes. Dennis Madden would be agreeable to handle a trade for the price. He liked the taste of her father's Quince Apple jelly and she would take him a fair share of the jars from her shelf in the root cellar.

Another depressing thought heaped grief onto her this morning as she sat on the side of the bed, dreading to face the day. What would she wear on that day? She would not allow it to be called her wedding day. But the minister would be there to say words over them and she needed to be presentable before God. It was just something she felt she needed to do for her own respect and for her father's and mother's name.

She had one good dress left useable after the rain leaked in and molded her clothes. It was the one she had sewn while in Fredericktown two years ago. This one also had the molded spots but not as bad as the other garments. It hung on the wall hook where it had stayed since the last time she had found a need of a dress-up dress. She pulled it off the hook. If she could find the scraps she had brought home with her maybe she could cut out the molded spots and replace it with good material.

As she climbed down the narrow steps her eyes caught the sight of the bed in the corner she supposed would be taken up by the new master of the house. Why did it have to happen this way? What if Tobias had not found another, prettier girl, than herself? What would her life have been like? At least the children she would have fed at the table would be of her own birthing. Where is the man she should be marrying? The one she could love?

Rachel had spent the day carrying what few prized possessions she owned down to the root cellar, away from all those many hands wanting to touch her things. And she was determined not to let her father's book be torn apart by someone's children, unrelated to any of them. She was eleven years old when her family moved to this cabin, and that shelf had been the resting-place of the family's important items. Now as she stood back and looked at the unadorned shelf, she wanted to cry. Come Saturday next, the new man in the house would have the say-so as to what was placed there.

Rachel put on her sunbonnet and tucked a half loaf of bread she had made last evening, along with five jars of Quince Apple Jelly, into her basket. Dennis would understand how hard it was for her to come up with the monies. Possibly she could arrange to do some work for them one afternoon before—well before her life changed.

It might be her last chance to see her dear friend. The thought left a lump in her throat. She had no idea how this husbandman would work her, or if he would beat her if she did not do as he thought she should. The thought of running away came to her mind. It was not the first time to think such a thought. And again, she knew there was no place to run. To be a pauper on the streets or being bound to an overseer would be far worse than even this situation of marriage. She tried to console her fears. This way she would at least have the say-so as to her own kitchen or the roses she grew over the door.

The walk along the road to the Maddens had always been a pleasant path. When her brother James had owned this land before selling it to the

Maddens, she had walked over with her mother to see Annie and the children. Sometimes her brother John and her sister Eleanor would go along when they were all young. Those were good times. She and John had made a game out of naming the young chestnut seedlings along the road and made them characters in the stories their mother often recited to them. This morning she spotted old Mr. Blower and Miss Whistle and Little Boy Chessy. She laughed at the silliness of the names of the now overgrown trees. Those were fun carefree days; days she would never have thought would end this way. How innocent youth can be.

Today was a hot day with a touch of stickiness. The clouds that were gathering from somewhere over the mountains were puffy and white. Oh, how she wished for rain to help what little garden had survived the summer. But she had seen these same clouds everyday for weeks and nothing ever came from them. When she turned onto the path going to Anastasia's house, she noticed Dennis working in the barn. She called out to him but he did not seem to hear, so she went around to the barn door and called again. To her surprise it was not Dennis Madden, but the man named John. What was he doing in the Maddens barn? He turned around just as she was trying to walk away, hoping not to be seen.

"Well, if it isn't Miss Lee or should I say for today it is Miss Lee. They tell me you finally found a man to marry you." He spoke with such disdain in his voice it caught her by surprise.

His words hit hard. "Why do you dislike me so much you feel the need to be rude?" The interaction with this stranger pained her the most because she had done nothing to give him reason to dislike her.

The man said nothing in response. He simply walked past her and began to load big barrels of grain onto the wagon.

He worked shirtless on this hot day, having hung his white shirt on the barn door latch. Rachel could see the muscles on his back and arms flex with each heavy load he picked up. She could not help but compare the overweight Mr. Hollock. Her face flushed with color when he turned around and noticed her staring at him. Embarrassed that he had caught her gawking she turned and ran from the barn before he could send another comment in her direction.

Thankfully, Anastasia was standing in the doorway of her cabin and Rachel waved. To her surprise Anastasia did not wave. Instead, she placed her hands on her hips, ready to give her a piece of her mind.

"Rachel Lee, you have again neglected to inform me that Mr. Hollock indeed came to court you. I had to find it out from your brother's wife only yesterday," Anastasia said, teasingly scolding her for the neglect.

Rachel's response was quick. "And why did you not tell me you have that rude man working for you?" She pointed toward the barn.

Anastasia was puzzled at her question. "You think John is rude? We have seen nothing but a kind heart from him. Why, just yesterday he came to the house to give me a hand. I was tending to Richard, oh that child of mine, at two years old he is into everything." Anastasia waved her hand at the comment "Well, I didn't mean to get off on that, but John saw me and came over to finish the scrubbing. I guess I did not think to tell you about him staying on to work."

All Rachel could think to say was, "He looks good at first but—" She decided against saying more, seeing that her neighbors liked this man so much.

"Dennis is fond of him—that is enough. And he is a good judge of character. Although, he still wonders why he chose to stay around and work for a spell. Dennis asked him but his comment was not revealing. John just said he had no interest in the life he once thought he would have and was bent on forgetting his familiar place of living. We could not measure what that talk was about. But Dennis surmised it had to do with a woman friend because the other day when they were working on the bridge over Sligo he said the new neighbor's daughters came riding over and Dennis paid them no mind at all. Oh, you would not believe how much he has done since he has been here. He insists on staying busy. He is the hardest worker we have ever had, well worth the monies we pay him."

The two women were quiet for a moment then Anastasia shocked Rachel with a question. "How was it you knew John in Fredericktown? Dennis said you two were not exactly friendly at your place the other day. And why would that be so, Miss Lee?" Anastasia teased her neighbor. "Dennis said John was asking about you a few evenings ago. That was before he heard you were getting married."

Before Rachel had time to answer, Anastasia remembered, "Oh my, here I have been getting off on a subject that has no place for a woman getting married. I want to hear all about your wedding plans." You know how I like a good get-together."

Rachel told Anastasia how Grove Hollock had spread the news about the wedding without her consent and how Mrs. Carroll had unknowingly made the decision for her when she said her departed parents would have been distraught over the condition of their farm. "Oh, Anastasia, there was nothing else I could do. My family is determined that I marry. I have no fight left in me," she cried.

There was a noise behind the women and Anastasia turned around in time to see John standing in the doorway. Anastasia called to him to come in. "John, forgive us. We did not know you were standing there. Have you been waiting long?

"Long enough," John said. "You are busy. I will come back later when you and your visitor are not making wedding plans."

When Anastasia turned back around she whispered to Rachel, "He is so good looking. There must have been a heartbreak for him is all I can figure.

Now what were we talking about? Oh yes, Rachel, if only we could have helped you more, then you could have tended your place and no one would have need to find a husband for you. But as you know, we could hardly smother the weeds on our own place before John came."

"Anastasia, I would never expect such an imposition on you. Maybe if my brother John had not broken his leg, it could have been different."

"Life issues us out a heap of surprises sometimes. Accept it and make something good happen from it," Anastasia said. Although she was some years younger than Rachel, still she did like to take on the mothering tone. She began down her sympathetic path, shaking her head in compassion. "Think of those poor dear lost orphan children, left by their dying mother. It was not their fault either. Forget about Mr. Hollock as your husband. Just think of how you can love the children."

Rachel shook her head sadly but said nothing in response.

Anastasia changed her voice; this time trying to sound excited. "I will come help you get the place ready for the wedding. We will have a good time making the meals we both so like. And I'll help you bring the bedding from the barn trunks so your family will have something to sleep on. It's a good thing it is not winter that you decided to marry." She gave Rachel's hand a pat. "Something good will come out of all this, you'll see."

"Oh, Anastasia, you are the best friend anyone could have. I didn't come to fret. I came to order a pair of shoes." Rachel laughed for the first time in what seemed like months.

As the two walked to the shop, Anastasia pointed out the thickening clouds. "Oh Rachel, you must hurry. It does look like the rain will come this time." She opened the shop door and called for Dennis. "Dennis has been able to do more shoe work now that we have John working full time for us."

Rachel placed her foot on the floor to be measured, as Dennis instructed. The smell of leather being treated with tanning oils and hot irons pressing the glue in place was overpowering at first, and she wondered how the Maddens could stand being inside this room for long periods of time. Dennis took his marker from his long wooden box and marked Rachel's foot on the piece of leather. Then he showed her drawings of the choices he knew how to make. She spotted a pair of white silk, brocaded all over with blue flowers.

Dennis noticed her looking at the white silk shoes and suggested, "Those would make fine wedding shoes, Rachel."

"Oh, Dennis, never in my life would I be able to afford something so elegant."

Rachel finished the business she had come for and started for home. By now, the clouds looked like a boiling pot of milk on a too hot fire. She had always found a delight in watching the dance of the lightening as it streaked from the edge of the clouds almost to the edge of the earth and this time was no exception. As the storm got closer she began to run, realizing there was no way she could make it home before the fury hit. On the road behind her, she could hear a horse coming up fast on the trail. By now the lightening was close. She would be forced to move over under the trees to let them pass. That was the one thing her parents had instilled in their minds was to stay out from under the trees when the lightening comes. Then a voice yelled out to her as the horse slowed.

"Rachel get up here."

It was John from the Madden's house. He reached down and caught her at the waist and pulled her up behind him on the horse, giving her no time to argue. The storm whipped the trees all around them with vicious force. A limb fell just in front of them on the path. The horse reared up. Rachel grabbed John's wet shirt to keep from slipping off as the rain came down in blinding sheets in front of them. The horse began to stumble and slide into a ditch and John reached back to hold onto her. She pointed to her cabin on the left side of the road. He yelled over the noise, "I see it."

He jumped down, pulling her after him, then wrapped the rein over the post and ran to the door to help her force it open. The storm was getting worse. He stood in the door watching the hail beat the ground in front of him. "We got here just in time," he said, as Rachel handed him a quilt to wrap around his wet body and grabbed one for her self as well.

He turned to her and pointed to the trees. "Sure glad I'm not one of those trees."

Somehow the situation seemed funny to both of them and they began to laugh. Then John went to the fireplace and stoked the embers until a flicker of flame came up and he added the kindling. He stood together beside the warmth but said nothing.

Finally, Rachel took the kettle from the hook and poured water into her mother's painted teapot, and crumbled in the dried mint leaves she had grown in her garden. She busied herself taking down two of the matching cups. They were something she never used for fear of breaking them. When she looked up he was watching her. She politely smiled, remembering what Anastasia had said about him probably being hurt by a woman recently. She knew the feeling and thought again of her once intended, Tobias.

When he spoke it was without disdain. "I guess I have to say I'm sorry for the way I acted when I was here last. You just caught me by surprise that day. I'll see to it you get another spoon."

She shrugged, and spoke softly, "That is not necessary, there is just the one of me eating at my table. Then she remembered. Well for this week anyway." And suddenly her face did not hold the smile.

Between the silences, a few awkward words were spoken. Then he surprised her by saying, "You were right, I should not have let the other men make fun of you after you fell into the creek. But one look at you with your muddy clothes clinging to you and your hair in your eyes was a funny sight." He laughed at the thought. Then stopped abruptly. He looked at her again. "Guess I have been a real stubborn looser." When she looked puzzled, he continued to explain. "I've been straight set on not dallying around with any woman needing a husband. That's all I need to say about it. Just a happening that took me there."

The two drank the hot mint water and Rachel got up to add more to his cup but he waved her away. "I consider the storm died down enough to get back. The Maddens are nice people to work for, but I'm headed back to my parent's place in a couple of days. They need me."

After all the disagreements they had observed she would think his saying he was leaving would be good news. But somehow it seemed sad. She told herself it was because the Maddens liked his help so much.

John sat the cup on the table and bowed politely. "I wish you well in your marriage to Mr. Hollock. Although, why would—" His words fell silent. Then he was gone.

Rachel stood at the door and watched until he was out of sight.

All afternoon she worked in the clammy, damp cabin, mending the dress that she would use when the reverend came. Anastasia's words had fallen on her heart more than she wanted to admit. She could be a good mother to the children. If only she did not have to bed with their father.

Sometime late in the evening she noticed the candlelight flickering and realized a breeze was coming in the open door and a chill began to fill the room. Fall was in the air, she thought. She could hear the wolves howling at the edge of the trees.

She got up to close the door and stood for a moment on the doorstep thinking of the events of the day. She found herself remembering how he had called her Rachel.

When morning came, bright and clear, it seemed to soften her anxiety over the distress she was facing. The fall season with its changing colors and the cool crisp air always invigorated her. The reprieve came to a sudden end when she looked at her calendar and saw the note she had put on the page for three days from now. It said, "My life is over after today." She felt sick to her stomach and sat down in the rocker. Maybe she was coming down with the last of the dreaded "summer complaint." As much as she hated the inconvenience of the complaint illness, it would be a welcome sickness if it would keep Mr. Hollock and his ten children away. They would have to postpone the wedding. She felt her forehead. Disappointingly, there was no fever.

The first of her family began to arrive on Thursday midday, two days ahead of the Saturday wedding. One by one they came, invading her small house for the spectacle they had all been wishing would happen for so long. She felt like standing up on the barrel at the edge of the house and shouting, "Now are you all happy? Rachel will no longer be a problem to you." But she did not.

And not wanting to be the topic of their conversation, Rachel tried to stay away from any of her brothers and in-laws whenever possible. The sisters came to her room to offer advice on every subject, as if she had been living in a far away place, unaccustomed to the outside world. Did they not remember she was the one who had been well versed in city life by going into Fredericktown so many times to handle the will? And that was partly the reason they were all here. If she had not had to be away so much, she could have kept the weeds from taking over. And then there would have been no need to bring in a husband.

The days were a blur to Rachel for which she was thankful in some part. The men had set up tables outside, next to a big open pit to cook on, leaving the cabin for all the wedding preparations. The sisters had come with wagons full of food. There would be many guests coming on Saturday. They kept sending Rachel to the upstairs loft to rest. Always they instructed her to "rest," as if a curse was about to be dealt to her come Saturday. And each time they smothered the word inside a handkerchief over their smirks. Did they think she did not know what was expected of a bride on the wedding night? She had attended weddings of neighboring daughters enough to know about the crude ritual of the wedding bed by those attending the wedding. She had been there when the men in the group had passed the bottle and then took it on themselves to make sure the couple had plenty of inspiration. Personally, Rachel thought it to be disgusting, but that would not keep the men in the family from helping make a game of it. The bride and groom were at the mercy of all those attending.

She let the family come and go and instruct as they pleased. She even laughed at some of their jokes about the wedding. But quietly she kept to her plans. Rachel had already decided she would be a mother to his already born children, she would work the fields and do the wash and keep them all fed, but she would not have his children. She had quietly, without their notice, prepared a mat for herself in a secret place. Grove Hollock would be too much in a stupor with the bottle by the time the jovial celebration was over, to notice she was not beside him. And later, after they were all gone, she would learn to make excuses as to why she could not sleep with him.

Early on Saturday morning, Rebeckah arrived with her family. William Littlefield was greeted by the other men and proudly accepted the congratulations over being the one that had found such a good man for Rachel. "Well, if I had not been at the Baltimoretown dock that very day, Rachel would not be marrying this day and father Lee's farm would only get worse." He made the last remark as he looked around at the tall weeds eating at the field. "Mr. Hollock tells me he has been very successful with his crops each year and I spoke to a gentleman that lives near his place and was told the same. I think we will be proud of the place again."

Rebeckah and Nancy carefully unloaded Rachel's surprise from their wagon. All the sisters climbed the ladder to the attic room and gathered around to watch the unwrapping of the new dove-colored linen dress they had stitched. Rachel began to cry when she saw it. She ran her fingers down the front and counted all those tiny tucks edged in the fine tatting lace.

"Nancy sewed the tucks while I tatted night and day," Rebeckah said proudly. We were afraid we would have only enough lace for the front of the dress. Ever since the King placed the new tax on lace we have not bought any. I even had to unravel some thread from my under skirt to finish the tatting." She picked up her dress to reveal the bottom of her chemise without lace. "We thought we would never finish in time to come. I worked up until William said he would be leaving without us if we didn't finish. I still would like to have added a few more tucks but I guess it has enough." They all laughed.

It was Martha that jested, "Would you have really stayed home if you had not finished in time?"

Rachel held the exceptional treasure up for all to see. "I've never seen anything like it, it is so beautiful." She hugged her sister and niece then admitted, "I just wish I could be as happy as the dress is beautiful."

Rebeckah sent the others back to their chores, announcing she wanted some time alone with her little sister. They understood. Rebeckah had always been the closest to Rachel's heart.

It did not take long for their conversation to get to the heart of the grief. "Rachel, I am so sorry about this. I had no idea of the mean plans to find a husband for you. It was settled before William let on to me. If it makes you feel any better I burned his meal for the last two weeks."

The soft laughter settled in around them at the thought of William being unknowingly tortured. No sooner had the laughter come than it was gone.

Rachel began to tell Rebeckah of all the fears, and even the anger she had over the marriage. Finally, despair enveloped her confessions. "If only it could have been someone who was good to look at over the meal and someone who worked hard. I should not have to marry someone like this man. Father and Mother would not have heard to it."

Rebeckah pulled her sister close as Rachel began to sob.

They heard Anastasia coming up the steps with the warning that it was almost time for the groom to arrive. "Here let me help Rebeckah get you ready. I've brought a new comb to sweep up your hair."

Rachel, facing the inevitable, slipped off her old worn out dress and dusted her body with rose pedals to freshen up. She took the most beautiful dress she had ever seen and held it up to her body. With tears in her eyes she turned to her sister and Anastasia, "Why does it have to be this way? Why am I marrying a man I can never love?"

Anastasia hugged her friend, and tried to help soothe the anguish. "Rachel, what if it turns out you can learn to really love this husband?"

With those words, Rachel burst into sobs. "No, no, no, I do not desire to love this man, ever." She fell onto her bed and cried. Eventually she was forced to accept her fate and got up to take the dress from her sister.

It was everything that a wedding dress should be. After all the little ties had been tied and the layers had been smoothed, Rachel took a small piece of broken looking glass from behind the trunk and moved it up and down the length of her body to see the entire dress design. "Oh, it is so beautiful. Have you ever seen anything so perfect, Anastasia?" she asked her friend. Then she hugged her sister again and thanked her profusely.

The two women stood near the window, letting the light show off the beautiful stitching Rebeckah and Nancy had done. Then Rachel asked as if the question had been there all along, "Do you think your friend, John, will come with Dennis today?"

Anastasia looked at Rachel and smiled. In a voice just above a whisper she said, "He packed his saddlebag yesterday morning real early and took leave for his father's place. I suspect a wedding would be too painful just now. Dennis mentioned he said to tell you he wished you the best. Strangely on several occasions these past few days Dennis said John had pried as to the reason for your set up marriage. I guess he heard us talking that day you came to set your foot print on the leather."

A commotion outside on the road took the attention off the dress as well as the question just posed and sent shivers down Rachel's spine. Someone from down in the yard yelled up. "Tell Rachel her man is here."

Rachel froze at the announcement and asked her sister and best friend to please go on downstairs and see how they appeared to be. She waited until they were gone and then looked out to see Grove Hollock and his family

297

climbing down from the wagon. There was also another wagon with some older people she imagined to be his parents, although she did not know if he had parents still alive or not. The children looked to be from about marrying age all the way down to a baby in arms. Rachel's heart went out to the children for the loss they must feel at the death of their mother, and now to have a stranger put before them as a mother. She had no intentions of trying to take their mother's place. But it would be her responsibility to see that they grew up with some resemblance of love. No child, step or otherwise, should have to live without love.

She remembered the children that had come to the boarding house when she was in Fredericktown that cold night and wondered if these children would have been given to child slavery as well if she was not destined to marry their father.

Since it was considered bad luck for the groom to see his bride everyone kept calling up to her to not come down. Did they really think she would volunteer to come down? She watched from the window as the husband-to-be mingled with the men in the family, while the children stood shyly next to the wagon. Were they afraid to leave the supposed safety of the wagon, or had they been told to stay there? Finally, to her relief, one of Martha's girls ran over to meet them. Rachel did not want to marry their father, but she did not want the children to feel unwelcome. She thought to herself, maybe she could mother the children and leave the father to someone else. The thought made her laugh out loud.

Before long the road was full of neighbors coming for the big feast and fun. It would not be long now. She mourned, "Oh, Mother—Father, why did you have to die and leave me in charge. It has spoiled everything." The very thought of blaming her parents hit her heart. She could not help remembering the times she had sat by her parent's bed and talked with them and been thankful she was the one that could see to their needs and make them comfortable in their last years.

Rebeckah came up the stairs to give Rachel the word that it was time to put on her lace bonnet. She took the lace cap and fixed it over her sister's dark comb swept hair and tied the bow to hold it in place. "It is the one I had for my wedding. Do you remember that day Rachel? Maybe you will be as lucky with Mr. Hollock as I have been with my William. You know it could have been a lot different for me if William had not come when he did."

Rachel looked at her sister. "You did well to get a good husband Rebeckah." Rachel had said the words, and she meant them for her sister. She just could not feel kindly right now about her brother-in-law setting up this day for her.

"We had better rush this ceremony up before the groom gets too soused to say, I do," Rebeckah laughed. "I think he has had a head start long before he got here."

Rebeckah called for Martha and Eleanor to come help get Rachel down the ladder safely without catching her dress on the rough steps. They started slowly down, one rung at a time. Rachel began to cry. The feeling must be akin to what the guilty feel when being dragged off to the hanging tree in the courtyard.

When they reached the door Rachel could see those standing with the minister had begun to look around. At first she did not see Grove Hollock and for a moment wondered if he had decided against the marriage. How lucky could she be? Under her breath she began to pray, "Oh blessed, blessed, blessed, please let it be so." Just when she thought she might have been given a reprieve, she saw two men walking him toward the decorated place her sisters had made for them to stand.

The gathering began cheering and motioned for her to come out. She had one fleeting thought of running away but knew they would surely come after her and drag her back before she could get free. She took a deep breath and closed her eyes and began to walk toward the minister with Rebeckah holding her hand, partly pulling her to the altar. Once in place, the minister began to speak. It was not a voice she recognized and she wondered where this man had come from. For all she knew he was not even a minister of God. The smell of rum was strong all around her, and she had the feeling both Grove Hollock and the minister had been familiar with the jug that afternoon. If there was no escape, Rachel just wanted to do get it over and find a hiding place away from everyone, including the groom. Strangely she realized she had yet to call him by his given name and if she had her way they would remain that distant. The readings were just about over. Next would be the vows.

The minister began saying the words that would bind them together for life. "Rachel Lee. This man intends to be your husband. What say ye?"

Before the minister could finish his words someone threw a rock at the side of the cabin. "Stop right there," a man yelled out from the road near the gate.

Rachel felt lightheaded. Her heart began to pound.

Everyone turned to see who was intent on disrupting the ceremony.

John Lashley showed an anger even Rachel had not seen, and he continued to yell out at the minister and Grove Hollock. "I've just come from checking up on you on this day," he said, addressing the groom with a very determined threat. "Get out of here, you fraudulent thief, before I punch you in the nose." He turned to the gathering, "This man's claims are not trustworthy. I spoke to those that knew his friends and they reported the

299

stories of his good name have improved without merit. In fact, his last wife is just over the border into Pennsylvania. No one knows if the motherless children he claims to be tormented for even belong to him. His only reason for marrying Miss Lee was to lay claim to the land once they were married. He even had a buyer for it in order to settle his debts. Seems he has done this before." The gathering stood shocked at what was happening, leaving William Littlefield and some of the others confused. They did not know whether they should put a stop to this young man's accusations or go after Hollock's throat.

Hollock did not protest when he saw the size of the man coming toward him. All those that had come with him, including the minister, wasted no time running for their wagon.

Rachel let out what seemed like a gasp but it was her heart leaping for joy. She stood still, unable to move from the place as John came toward her.

He turned to the gathering and said without looking at Rachel, "I've known Rachel Lee on many occasions on her trips to Fredericktown, and I've been her protector each time. I could not stand by and watch this man do such a despised act. He has done harm to your reputations as good judges of character and put Miss Lee to grief of the heart.

The crowd began to all talk at once and even a few took out after Grove Hollock's wagon.

Rachel turned to John. She could not help but smile. He had been her knight in shining armor, just like the make believe stories her mother had told to her when she was young.

"You have done a kind thing this day, Mr. Lashley. How can I thank you?"

John did not take to the sweet talk when he meant business. "Rachel Lee, I have saved your life on several occasions, sometimes harshly dealing with you, but it was not because I disliked you. I was hurt by another and had no plans to ever let myself feel things of the heart again. But each time I rescued you from those annoying little situations you managed to get into, I found myself changing. Even so, I never intended to find myself in the place I feel today."

Rachel did not know what to say. She just looked up puzzled. What was this man trying to say?

"I thought I could do nothing to save you from Grove Hollock, seeing your family had their minds set. I have no monies to bring to you or the farm. But I'm a good worker and will do my part to put this place in a good working order."

Rachel put her hand on John's arm, "You are the kindest man I have ever known, Mr. Lashley."

He reached for Rachel's hand and placed a shiny new spoon, more ornate than the one he had thrown into the fire that day. He smiled his winsome grin just like she had remembered when he was at the marketplace in Fredericktown. "I brought you a spoon, seeing it would be fitting to have two spoons if you will sit with me at our table?"

Awkwardly, she began to question. "How is it this is the day I so hoped it would be, when all along I was led to believe you did not care to find a wife?"

Like a man knowing what he wanted, he leaned down and kissed her firmly, sealing their future. When he looked into her face he could see tears beginning to form but knew it was not for sadness. Her smile announced the secret her heart held so close.

Unmindful that the gathering had been watching with renewed interest as John spoke to Rachel, now both were surprised when there everyone began to cheer.

John took a step forward and spoke to them in words Rachel had never heard from him, words that sounded like a man with a head full of wise thinking. They made her heart swell with pride. Even William Littlefield did not make such nice speeches.

"On numerous occasions the good Lord Almighty has placed Rachel Lee in my path to protect. I consider that an honor from this day onward. She has given her answer that she will sit at my table as my wife. If you question my working abilities please inquire of my qualifications from the Dennis Madden family." John turned back to Rachel and whispered something to her then turned back around. "Seeing you all have come for a wedding we do not want to disappoint you."

Rachel pulled at his sleeve and he turned to see what she wanted. When he turned around he was laughing. "Rachel says the minister left with the other groom. So if someone will find us a minister we will this day have a wedding."

"I know where one lives," Thomas Thrasher yelled back remembering the minister he had sold his land to several years before. "And if he is not home I will find someone to ordain." The gathering laughed at his insistence.

"Can we eat while we wait for him to get here?" one of James Lee's husky young son's yelled out. Everyone started laughing and cheering at the same time.

John turned to Rachel, "Now go find yourself a place to wait. Remember, I'm not suppose to see the bride before the wedding." He reached down and swung her around once, ending with a big kiss meant to please the crowd, and not one soul showed disappointment.

Chapter 26

Early November 1766
Seneca Creek

The first snow came early this year, falling silently in the night, wrapping the cabin and fields in a blanket of white. And now, Rebeckah eagerly climbed to the top of the steep hill. It was a pilgrimage she had taken whenever possible on the day of the first big snow; ever since, as a young girl, her mother had sent her to a poor family's cabin with a basket of food. The mother of the children had died only a few days before that snow and their father had used the spirit cup, as her mother called it, to forget his dismal situation. The faces of those little lost children, not even as old as her Solomon was now, had made an imprint on Rebeckah's heart, one that she would never forget. There had been no fire in the fireplace on that cold snowy day, and although she was young, she knew how to start a fire. It was something she had watched her brothers do when they were in the barnyard on a cold day. As she left the cabin, their sad, yearning eyes had followed her down the path, and she vowed then and there to find a way to help them. It was that day that she had first fallen to her knees in the snow to say prayers for the well being of those almost orphans, just like the elders at the big church did upon hearing of a dire need.

And now, on this day of the first snow, Rebeckah pulled her cloak tightly around her against the cold and again made her way into the forest to say her prayers. The quietness surrounding her journey set the place for her song, and the crunch beneath her feet, the instrument on which it was played. She turned to look back at her footprints perfectly encased in the crisp clean layer of white. What was it about the snow that made her feel so fulfilled? Was it the rite of passage into her own petitions, her own needs? Or was it the ushering in of a time of quietness for her family as they sat by the fire, cracking roasted nuts and retelling the stories they remembered of their own young years. Whatever the reason for her feeling this way, whatever it could be called, this was her own time alone to say her prayers of petition and thanksgiving. And again today, she wondered what happened to the little children who had given her the need to pray that day so long ago.

She looked down at her own cabin with heavy puffs of smoke coming from the big rock chimney. That meant William had put on another log. The reflections from the fire flickered on her windowpane and sent signals of love through her heart. By now her children would be finishing the honey biscuits she had left on the table, and William would be sitting by the fireplace checking his papers. Because of the snow, their chores had been finished early, and after the meal she had slipped out to come in search of the perfect spot to say her prayers. It had become so much of a ritual that she had begun making lists of the prayers she wanted to remember, weeks before the snows would come.

As she turned to go on, she noticed a small pack of wolves standing at the edge of the woods. Their eyes were keenly fixed on her every move. She picked up a handful of snow and threw the ball in their direction but they did not move. Even when she hissed and stomped her foot, they stood their place. Their husky bodies were poised to attack if she threatened their domain, which she had no need to do on this day. There was something beautiful about these animals with their thick brownish gray fur and their piercing eyes.

Feeling the cold to her bones did not stop her from her appointed journey, and she continued to walk farther into the woods. With each deep breath she remembered the prayers she wanted to recite and the one that she dreaded to remember, the one that would not go away.

As she came to a clearing she spotted a fallen log. It would provide the altar for her prayers. She again, as in years past, knelt for a while, but now more than last year, on aging knees that ached too soon. When she pulled herself up onto the log, she wondered if the feeling of forgiveness was going to come this year, truly forgiven for the sin that had haunted her memories too long. But she knew until she had the courage to tell William of the sin, dealt at the hands of his dear friend, she could not be made whole.

Rebeckah's prayers were long, with petitions for health, and for wisdom, oh, most of all for wisdom. For without wisdom who could predict where a wife and mother would lead. And there were petitions for a loving and thankful heart. That alone could make a lot of things right. She remembered to give mention that God had been so gracious to send Mr. Lashley to save Rachel from a lonely life—and from Mr. Hollock. She could not help but smile at the memory of Rachel speaking the vows with John Lashley, and how he had convinced the guests to help pull the weeds and hoe the dried ground before they left for home. He had aptly called it, "A wedding present for Rachel." The thought reminded her to add another prayer, "Oh, God, please give a child to Rachel to make her marriage complete before she becomes too old."

Rebeckah started back down the hill. Somewhere beyond the path she could hear a bird. She stood still to see where such a beautiful sound was coming from. Her eyes searched the frozen branches. It was a lone red bird. The sighting of such a beautiful bird always made her feel she had received a blessing. As she moved down the hill she again stopped to listen for the bird to call for his mate.

The season wore on and William went to mark on the one remaining page of his calendar. If he was to have one for the next year, he should have already placed his order with the printer. He would have to remember to write out a copy of the next few months from the example Dowden's Ordinary always kept for that purpose. "This is the twenty first day of December," he called out to Rebeckah. "If you want to go see your family now is the time. I tried to dig the ground yesterday but it was too frozen. I want to do some repairs to the barns but that can wait. Decide where you might want to go and if the weather holds good we can go. Today looks clear, not too warm and not too gray, nothing that forewarns a blizzard," he said as he looked out the door to the sky. He called for the boys to come with him to finish the morning chores. "Just as soon as breakfast is over we can begin loading up."

When the boys returned, Absolom handed his mother a basket full of black walnuts. "I picked these for you. Father said you might have a hankering to take some walnut cakes with us."

William took the gun down from the hook over the fireplace and filled his pouch with enough shots to take care of them in case a wild animal threatened. "We will be stopping at the tavern on the way to hear the latest news. If I miss as much as a month of hearing what is being reported, it could affect what crops I choose to plant for next year. I find it makes no sense to plant the tobacco shoots if the King has a mind to tax it half over."

"And I would like to go see how Richard Willis is faring. He was so weakly last winter, I dare say he may not live to reach another spring. Your poor sister, Elizabeth, certainly has hard luck with husbands."

Rebeckah's knees went weak just thinking about going to her sister's cabin again. It was not her idea of a pleasurable family trip. Elizabeth did not take to idle talk with anyone, now or never. As the oldest daughter of her family, the memories of Elizabeth being at home when she was a child were faintly dim in her mind. "William, what will you do about the cattle?" she asked, hoping if she reminded him there was no one to see to the feeding of the cattle if they were to be gone that long, he might decide against going to see Richard.

The need for help was a painful reminder that White Horse had not returned. "I have no choice but send John down to give instructions to Job and his sons to check on the cattle and do the chores. I've been thinking on hiring them to watch the place anytime I am away—maybe help with the planting too."

Rebeckah gave the boys the job of cracking the walnuts, while she gathered up the ingredients for the rich batter. Nancy pulled the larger skillet off the hook on the wall and put a spoon full of lard in it and set it back on the fire grid to get hot. Rebeckah poured the rich batter into the sizzling hot skillet and sat it back on the grate to cook slowly. "These cakes will have to be the short ones this time. There is no time to wait for the high cakes to bake in the side oven. But my guess is you will eat them just the same." She sent Absolom to fill a basket with dried fruits from the root cellar, while she ran up the steps to gather the plunder they would need for the trip. She called down to Nancy to roll up the meat from last night's meal into what little bread was left.

She stood at the top of the steps unable to concentrate on what she needed to take with them. A trip to see family was what Rebeckah looked forward to all year. But now, with William mentioning going farther up to Richard and Elizabeth's, the excitement had turned sour. She was again faced with the situation she had not been able to deal with for so many years. It had been almost twenty years since she had been there, and the thought of going to see Elizabeth in her own home gave her a pain at the pit of her stomach. Her parents had forced her to go to the funeral of Elizabeth's second husband, William Norris. Her father insisted she needed to put the past behind her.

After William Norris's funeral, when Rebeckah had tried to question her sister, her father had intervened so swiftly and told her she was to never bother Elizabeth again. Rebeckah had wanted so much to ask the important question, but as long as her father was alive it was forbidden. Even after her own marriage she had not dared go against what James Lee had ruled on. Then Elizabeth had married Richard Willis and they always stayed to themselves, not going to *Chestnut Ridge* if they knew any other family member would be there. Rebeckah had hoped to speak privately to her sister when she came for her father's burial but Richard was so ill she never left his side. And they had not come to Rachel's wedding because of the illness. She would have to wait for him to get better or die, whichever it was to be. So much could change once she talked to Elizabeth, and she would have to deal with that. If only her father had not been so controlling. She feared she might be running out of time. Even Elizabeth was not as well as last year. Until she could be free to pry into the past, Rebeckah knew there was no use approaching her.

Going to Elizabeth's place would mean nothing to her sister. Even if she came to help. Elizabeth was like that. Rebeckah remembered what Rachel had told her. It had something to do with Robert's wife being called into court by this sister. She wondered what that could have been about. That was so like Elizabeth to go to the courts to have them settle something that a few words probably could have made right.

What reason could she give to William that would allow her to stay at Eleanor's or Sarah's? He could not be expected to understand why she chose to stay away. If he knew—if he knew the pain, would he still insist she go? She shivered just thinking about it.

Rebeckah's thoughts were interrupted. Nancy was calling up to her from the foot of the steps. She was worried about the Walnut cakes scorching. "I'm coming, just give me time to gather up the clothing," she said, as she pulled the clothes from the wall hooks and rolled the quilts.

While William waited for his family to get the belongings ready to leave, he sat at the end of the table reading something from a medical book he had purchased at an estate sale of a man who had studied to be a Doctor.

Rebeckah pulled the hot cake from the fire and decided to try approaching the conversation of not going by sounding concerned for Richard Willis and the intrusion it might cause. "William, do you think it wise to pile in with the children on poor Richard at a time he may be pondering his very life and death?"

The approach seemed to work because William thought about Rebeckah's question for a moment, then admitted, "You may be right, Rebeckah. I could leave you and the children with one of your sisters, and go to see for myself." Then he went on reading as if the conversation had never taken place. He flipped the pages, his finger going up and down the columns of the book. Finally he looked up, "I have been checking my books to see what Richard's symptoms read like, and in all probability it appears to be close to the *Bright's Disease*." William looked down at the book and began reading out loud, "It says here that it is a diffuse, progressive, degenerative disease of the kidney characterized by dropsy of the upper and lower parts of the body. And it says death often occurs." He looked up to see if Rebeckah was listening. "Or, then again, Richard could have what they call Dead Palsy. That is a loss of motion and feeling in a part of the body."

Rebeckah wanted to seem interested and reminded William how bad he was when they came to her father's burial. "Richard appeared to lose his body to the ground and would have fallen if it had not been for the help of Will Sierra."

William had not seemed to notice she had once again talked her way out of going to Elizabeth's place.

It was almost nightfall when the Littlefield's slow moving team of oxen crossed the branch of the Middle Seneca and pulled up the hill to Alexander Grant's cabin. They had tried to go to the Betterton's first, but to their surprise no one was at home. Rebeckah began to fret that maybe something had happened to one of the family, and she and William had not been at home to receive the news.

"Or maybe they have just gone to visit us," young William suggested without cracking a smile.

Rebeckah could always depend on being entertained by this son. He held a dry sense of putting his approach to life into words. She tousled his hair and told him he was probably right, then added, "Oh dear, maybe we should have left some of the Walnut cake to make them feel welcome." Everyone, even the family patriarch laughed.

Sarah had seen their wagon coming and rushed out to meet them, waving and laughing at once. Had it not been for her bad knees she probably would have jumped for joy like she used to do when they came down her road. Having family visit during these dark short days of winter was a time for rejoicing.

The evening was good, with plenty to eat and more than enough stories to exchange. By the time the younger children had been put to bed and the older cousins had used the Littlefield wagon to go for a wagon ride, the conversation in the cabin got around to Rachel's wedding.

"Have you ever seen anyone so happy as sweet Rachel standing next to that Mr. Lashley at her wedding?" Sarah confessed.

The two women talked about how fine looking John Lashley was and how utterly grateful Rachel should be. Finally, Sarah blurted out, "Well, what I am wanting to ask is do you think Rachel is too old to bring a baby to the marriage?"

Rebeckah, not wanting to put a critical tongue to her sister's baby making abilities, tried to soothe the curse of her possibly being barren. "Maybe her years have been too hard on her to produce a child so soon after the vows. I've heard of such. Or sadly, maybe not ever."

"I just wonder what would have happened if she would have married Grove Hollock. His wife gave him children so we know—"

Before Sarah could finish her sentence, Rebeckah abruptly stopped her. "Are you suggesting that Rachel should have married that man? Sarah, he would have killed Rachel with work."

"I'm not suggesting a thing, but what I wonder is, will it be more humiliating to Rachel to know she is barren or to deal with a man with a lot of children? If she had married Grove Hollock then those that did not know Rachel would have just thought they were her true born babies and she would not have to feel so barren at their glances. I've tried to inquire of James and Annie when they rode through a few days ago coming from Rachel's. Annie told me she had tried to ask but was put off by the Lashley's. Oh, there I've said it. It sounds so strange to call our Rachel by any name other than Lee."

Rebeckah's voice was tender when she changed the subject back to the wedding. "When Rachel said her vows I felt a wave of relief come over me like I've not felt in a long season. He's some younger but that is good. He will be strong enough to carry the farm work without relying on Rachel to do both jobs." Rebeckah reached down and pulled at her woolen stockings, then said, "Give them a little time Sarah, and maybe we will have smiles to report." Then she added, as if invoking the divine intervention, "If the good Lord intends it to be, so it shall be."

The men had begun talking about news from the docks. It was Alexander who opened the talk about William's change of heart. Ever since he had admitted it to Robert Lee, it had been the topic of conversation at all the gatherings of the family. And tonight was no exception. It was like they all had to make sure they had heard the words right. "Was it terribly hard for you to change sides, William?"

"Indeed it was. I was a stubborn Englishmen." William said, adding, "It is painful to see what has happened since I left the Hants."

"How do you read the reports that have come in of late?" Alexander asked. "I was down at the docks only a week ago, and I am worried about what the new minister of parliament—oh what's his name, Townsend, that's it, is proposing to keep the colonists from profiting on our exports."

"I'm afraid we are headed for an all out confrontation sometime over the next few years. Parliament is not going to let up on us. If it is not one tax it will be another. They just do not understand what we have worked so hard for over here," William lamented.

That thought brought up an entirely new line of conversation, keeping the men in their own corner of the room.

Sarah took an extra needle from the pin cushion and handed it to Rebeckah. "Here, you just as well help me finish this quilt. I thought I would take it to Rachel on our next visit. The women sat admiring the latest pattern she had cut. Their talk turned to recipes and the cost of a new wash bucket for the house. Eventually they got around to talking about how Anne and John Hughes had been acting of late.

"Have they had anymore to say about Rachel since she married?" Rebeckah asked.

"Only that she found some weeds beginning to grow along the road." The women laughed at her comment. To think Anne had nothing better to do than count the weeds along the road proved how irrational their sister could be when it came to pointing fingers. "You don't expect Anne to give Rachel credit for anything, do you?" Sarah laughed.

"Maybe we should all descend on Anne's and John's weed patch to count their shortcomings," Rebeckah suggested.

The men turned to see what the women were laughing about and then went back to talking, now feeling safe to talk about rumors of moving to South Carolina and a report on how well William Wofford was doing since moving there.

William turned to make sure Rebeckah was still preoccupied. "Have to be careful when I mention that State. At the very word Rebeckah has been known to rise up and get plain wicked over the talk," William said with a sort of chuckle and a twist of the mouth.

Alexander almost gave the talk away when he began to laugh at the idea of Rebeckah getting mean over anything.

William pulled the smoke from the pipe Alexander had handed him. "I understand William Wofford is still having good luck down there. Have you noticed? Just when you think he is on his last leg the man springs a surprise."

"He left John Wofford so saddled with debt after he pulled out to the Carolinas, I thought John was going to have to sell every bit of his land to pay his relation's debts," Alexander said, as the men continued to analyze William Wofford and the ways he seemed to make his monies.

"I've heard just about everyone can find a life and good living with the indigo plant. Have you thought of moving, Alex?" William asked his brother-in-law.

Alexander was quiet for a moment then said, "Just last week, John brought a letter over wanting to see if I read it to mean the same he was reading it. William Wofford bragged of reasons why John should break up his house here and move down. He said the creeks are full to the banks with more fish than he can ever eat. And his boys never come back to the cabin without at least three of the wild game. Their table is always full, he allows."

"I met up with two men at the blacksmith shop who were getting their wagons readied to make the trip. They allowed just about anywhere you go nowadays, there is talk about moving. That indigo plant has them all excited." William turned to look at Rebeckah before he went on, making sure to lower his voice. "Robert has been trying to talk me into considering a move. He seems to think we are going to run out of good land here before long. It upsets Rebeckah if she even hears of someone talking about moving. She acts like the desire itself will latch onto her family's backs and carry them right off."

Before Alexander could answer, the dogs outside the door began barking and he got up to see who might be coming at this close to sundown. "Sarah, it's someone riding up real hard. Looks like Will Sierra Norris's horse," he called to his wife.

They all rushed to the door to see what could possibly cause this fast of a ride.

William Norris yelled out the news, not waiting to get off his horse. "Mother wanted me to come tell you she thinks Richard is dying, and she would like for you to come sit with her."

After the door had closed, Sarah's voice was less than kind. "You'd think after losing two other husbands, she would know how to handle a death. Now that is not considerate of me, I know, but sometimes Elizabeth acts like she is the queen of this family—almost as much as Anne does."

Alexander had pulled his heavy coat from the hook by the door and thrown William his. "William, there isn't time to wait for the women and children to load up. It would be best to take my horses and go see if we can help," Alexander said. "Sary, you and Rebeckah can follow with the wagon and oxen when the day light is up. Your knees will hurt in this cold, and there won't be a place for you to get comfort there."

A light snow had fallen in the night and covered the wagon with a dusting. Rebeckah took a broom and swept it clean before she called for the others to come. The older boys had the oxen hitched to the wagon by the time Sarah brought her brood from the house, and little Alexander and Solomon were already in a fuss over who would sit where.

By the time the wagon pulled into the road leading to the Willis cabin, Rebeckah could feel the hand of her past pressing hard on her shoulders. She took a deep breath to ease the memory and shut her eyes tight to forget. Finally, Sarah's voice brought her back to the present.

"I do declare! If poor old Richard has died, you would think the hired hands would be given the day off, out of respect. But that is Elizabeth for you," Sarah said, pointing to a group of men standing next to the barn watching a man pitching hay out of the loft into a wagon below.

When the women and children got inside, who should call out a greeting but poor old Richard, frail but still breathing.

After the women had paid their respects and helped get the meal on the table, it was decided Alexander should take Sarah and her children back to the comforts of her own cabin. With Sarah's swollen knees and the constant pain, she would be no help with the chores. Alexander would bring the wagon back to pick up the Littlefields on the morrow.

Rebeckah could have insisted she be the one to take Sarah back home. Elizabeth was not an easy sister to get along with; still she was blood kin. And since she had been forced by circumstances to come, it was not right to leave a person in need. Especially if it was your mother's first born daughter.

At a time like this you would have expected Aquilla to bring Elizabeth's own daughter, Elizabeth, to help stir the food pots. But as it was, she had a sick child and could not come. Elizabeth's son Will Sierra and his wife Sarah were good to help. But Sarah had recently delivered of a dead born baby before its full time and her pain was still coming on.

So the least Rebeckah could do was help scrub the pots stacked in the corner of the kitchen, left over from the meals of several yesterdays. And when she went to the flour barrel she found it almost empty. She could not leave this overworked, although difficult sister, at a time like this.

She needed water before she could begin the work and called Absolom and young William to get the pail and go to the creek. "I will need several pails full from the looks of the stack in the corner." She looked at the iron pots and skillets. Would Elizabeth be upset that she was taking charge of her kitchen? It was obvious that something needed to be done. She wondered how long it had been since her sister had any free time aside from caring for her husband.

Rebeckah lined the children up and handed out the chores according to their age and sent them out. Nancy's job was to keep the babies quiet. As night fell and the bowls of broth had been eaten and washed, Rebeckah made up the beds for the children in the new room Richard had added to the cabin. It was never easy to bed down on a strange floor, but tonight everyone seemed more than willing to lay their heads down after a day full of work. William settled in a chair by the desk that had once belonged to Elizabeth's schoolmaster husband, William Norris. He lighted the candle and picked up the only book still on the top and began to read. It was one he remembered using so many years ago in the school's classroom.

What little the women talked while scrubbing the pots was done in slightly-above whispers. Richard would become agitated Elizabeth had said.

Elizabeth went to the root cellar and brought a basket of clothes that needed ironing. "I do not have time for talk without work. You just as well help as the next." Her voice held a tone of curtness, making Rebeckah wonder if her staying was even wanted.

When all the light conversation had been exhausted, mostly about the weather; how cold it was or how early the snow had come, they continued to iron in silence, until Rebeckah inquired about the new room.

Elizabeth took a deep breath, then admitted, "Richard is very good at spending the fortune my first husband left for me."

Elizabeth looked at her sister for a moment before she spoke again, obviously trying to decide what to tell and what should be kept to her own thoughts.

She measured out the words at first. Her speech was defensive and hard. "Richard is my third husband. I don't know if you remember William Sierra, my first." She looked up to see if Rebeckah responded.

To Rebeckah's memory, this was the first time her sister had ever mentioned her first husband or his wealth in her presence. But then William Sierra had died when she was very young.

"You had moved over here and it was just before we moved to *Chestnut Ridge*. But I do remember him." Rebeckah had a sense that Elizabeth was getting at something by the way she kept looking at her.

"My first husband, Mr. Sierra, was some years older than my age. We both lived in Charles County and moved to this place shortly afterwards. He named this place *Sierra's Love* after his name and because we loved it so much. Elizabeth and Will were born here. Then he died." Elizabeth spread out another cloth on the ironing mat and sprinkled it with water, then went to the fire and brought a hot iron from the holder to the table.

Elizabeth had always been a private person but tonight there seemed to be a need to talk as she rushed into the conversation, almost like she had waited to tell her side of the story. But why to her, when so few words had been spoken between them for years?

"Mr. Sierra left me well off and the news got around that it was so. Then the schoolmaster came. Father had known the family in Charles County." Elizabeth's face had grown weary in the light of the fire and held onto the table as she slid into the chair, leaving the hot iron to get cold. She stared into the candlelight and fingered the soft tallow remains dripping onto the table as she talked. "His family used to drive past our place on the way to their church services. They were Catholic. Father was always real friendly to them, unlike some people who did not want that religion to come into the colonies. Most people were worried it would divide and take away from the Church of England. But our salutations were still not much more than a how do you do. The Norris family seemed to be real nice people. Father knew the Jenkins family as well. That was mother Norris's family. When Mr. Norris came he said he had heard I was widowed. He said he remembered me from those wagon rides past our place. He inquired of me about the schools in my area. He was looking for land to build a new school, he said, one where no school had been. Then he asked if he might build a school on the edge of my property."

Elizabeth stopped for a moment and looked into the firelight, pondering on what had happened. "I was quite relieved to have a man around again. The children were small and he would hold them on his lap and tell them stories. Hearing them laugh once more made me decide he was a good man, and by now he was a member of the All Saints Church in Fredericktown." Elizabeth paused and began to move the candle farther away, not really mindful of what she was doing, but appearing afraid the light might portray some weakness in her soul. Her voice had taken on a tone of anger again. "He knew I had monies and that is why he came."

Rebeckah did not wish to hear about William Norris and tried to change the subject to something she had heard from her William. "My husband loved teaching the children in your school."

Elizabeth was quick to break in, "Not my school. It was William Norris's school. I just happened to have the land from Mr. Sierra's part."

Elizabeth again spoke up. "Did you know William Littlefield then?"

"No, I had not met my William when he taught here."

Rebeckah rushed on to take the conversation back to her own telling. "William has told me you would come to the school to bring hot honey rolls to the children. He said you were kindhearted."

Elizabeth bit her lower lip, trying to hide the emotional feeling that had welled up in her. She picked up another piece of clothing and set the iron to it.

Richard had begun to cough and the women did not talk, listening to see if he would call out for help. They continued to iron the clothes, taking one iron after the other from the hot fireplace, replacing a cold one to heat in its place.

William was blowing out the candle he had used to read by when Rebeckah looked around. She watched him put the book on the shelf and go into the new room to bed down. Her eyes followed him and caught sight of the same six leather chairs lining up at the edge of the room. The two spinning wheels still sat across the room with the large chest between them. Nothing had changed. Her sister had not changed a thing since her second husband had died. She remembered the stack of paper that sat on the high shelf on one wall. It was untouched, along with the jug that held the sealing wax. And the bells, she counted them, all six of them sat on the shelf where they had rested since the last time she was here almost twenty years before. What were missing were the books. Only the one William had been reading remained. Mr. Norris had been a collector of all sorts of books, or so they had been told. Maybe it was Elizabeth's way of bragging about the intelligence of her second husband in a time when his name needed upholding.

Rebeckah picked up a needle and thread and sat down by the fireplace to let the light guide her while she mended a wool stocking. "What happened to the books you used to have on the shelf?"

"Richard took them into town and sold them once when I had gone to the Woffords. He sold more than the books, but I got most of it back. This last husband did not like reminders of how educated those before him were. Besides he wanted the monies to spend the way he wanted. It was the books that paid for the new room and many more of his items. Poor William Norris would have died to know his fine selections of reading material had gone for such a needless expenditure."

The clock chime struck the bell nine times and all was quiet when it stopped. Maybe it was the disgusting mention of 'poor William' as Elizabeth had referred to her late second husband or the sight of this room again. Something pulled at her mind and took her into the private talk before she could reconsider.

She looked up at Elizabeth, and asked the question born over twenty years ago. "Where did he take my baby, Elizabeth?"

Elizabeth let out a gasp and looked straight at Rebeckah, her eyes carrying the shock.

Rebeckah did not move. Her look piercing—her needle still poised to take the next stitch. The silence of the room accentuated the seriousness of the question.

Elizabeth spoke in a cold voice, edged with strong will, as if something so long ago had finally been allowed to come out. "You know Father said you were never to be told."

"Father is dead now," Rebeckah cornered the reply.

Elizabeth did not offer an answer. Silence again filled the room.

"Tell me, Elizabeth, where did your husband take my baby?" Rebeckah said in a more pleading voice.

Elizabeth did not look up as she spoke the carefully measured out words just barely above a whisper, intended to be heard by no one but Rebeckah. "You can call his name."

"I have no pleasure in speaking of him at all. It is only the baby I wish to know about," Rebeckah said.

"William Norris was a good man for most parts of our marriage." Elizabeth said.

"William Norris deceived your marriage vows and love, Elizabeth. You surely know this," Rebeckah pointedly reprimanded.

Elizabeth stared at the floor when she spoke. "He was a good man. I am the one to whom blame should be laid."

"Oh no," Rebeckah swore, shaking her head in protest. "No, no, no. He was a most capable manager of his own deception, dear sister."

Anger rose up in Rebeckah, letting the pain come to a boil. "You did not deserve to be hurt like that by a man whose intentions were cruel."

"Rebeckah, William Norris was not a cruel man."

"You think I do not know about his cruel ways, Elizabeth?" Rebeckah drew in a hard breath before she spoke. "I was barely fifteen, and sadly, mother had yet to warn me of the unseemly cruel ways a man can take."

"I do not wish to hear this."

"Elizabeth, I have kept those horrid days away from your ears, not because I wanted to save your pain, but because I was bound by Father's codes of honor and the pain of having to relive it and what it would do to my husband and family. Now I know if I do not cleanse my soul, my pain will never heal."

"Does William know?"

Rebeckah only shook her head that he did not know.

Elizabeth stood up and went to the hook by the door. She handed Rebeckah a wrap and took one for herself. "You do not want the children to hear, I feel certain." She pulled the latch and the cold night air flushed in. The moon had found its way into the clear sky and at first neither woman said anything as they walked. Elizabeth broke the silence. "Did Mother and Father blame me for my husband's violations?"

"They never spoke of it. Besides how could you be to blame for something that happened when you were not close by to see." Rebeckah told her.

"Where did it happen?"

Rebeckah pulled her arms tightly around herself to shield against the cold, "Remember when Father sent me to take lessons from Mr. Norris? He had just opened his schoolhouse. Father wanted me to learn how to read and write. He was going to send Martha and Rachel but they both came down with the measles. It was my misfortune to be afflicted with the rash earlier."

"I remember, Robert brought you to stay with us," Elizabeth said.

"Mother had made me two new dresses. She called them my 'learning dresses.' I was so excited to be the first in our family to go to a real schoolhouse. Every morning I came from your cabin down to the schoolhouse. I had been taking lessons for some time. That night Mr. Norris told me I should wait for him to go home because it was getting dark outside and he said there had been rumors that a wildcat was prowling after dark. I was really scared of the big cats so I willingly stayed late. And that night just before we were to go home, we heard a loud screech and I began to cry. Mr. Norris came over and put his arms around me. I thought he was being kind and watching out for me. But he did not let me go. He said for me to be still or the big cat would break in."

Rebeckah shivered. She could not go on. Remembering the pain was too much and she began to run down the path letting the tears come. By the time Elizabeth got to her, she was on her knees in the snow, shaking uncontrollably.

"I did not know. He told me it was you who led him on. He said it was my fault for allowing you to come for the schooling." Elizabeth reached out, and in the first time Rebeckah ever remembered her sister showing a kindness toward her, she put her arms around her. "I should have known."

"And you thought it was my fault all these years? You thought I was the cause?" Rebeckah began to cry again.

Little by little Elizabeth began to offer up an excuse as to William Norris's character, like it was something she was expected to do. "I could not give William Norris children. Something had happened after Will Sierra was born. It left me unable to bear more children. Mr. Norris took my children to be his own. At first I thought that was good. And of course, he insisted they be given the name Norris. I had to talk hard to convince him they needed to retain their father's name so when they grew up they would know who they were. He let me write in my Bible, Elizabeth Sierra Norris and William Sierra Norris. I do not doubt he loved them as his own. But if I had been able to give him a child of his own—" she let the words fade away.

"He wanted them to have a good life. Even in his will he insisted before anything was paid we should buy the books, *Whole Duty of Man* and *Government of the Tongue* and *Drelincourt on Death* for little Elizabeth. Such big books for a little girl. He wanted so much for her to grow up smart and wholesome," Elizabeth said, putting her hand on Rebeckah's cold hand. "See, he was not all bad, Rebeckah."

"He caused me so much pain, Elizabeth. I do not know how you can defend his heart."

"He did go into the courts and make the payment. Two Thousand pounds of tobacco is a lot of money, Rebeckah. Otherwise, they would have given you the lashes, seeing that is what they do to girls that have babies without taking the vows with a husband first—that is what they do," Elizabeth said, still coming to his, maybe their defense. After all, the tobacco crop was raised on her inheritance land.

Elizabeth pulled her cloak tighter around her body. She stared long and hard into the night sky, remembering the past with Rebeckah but taking a different road into her thoughts.

Rebeckah broke the silence. "That was such a hard time for Mother and Father. Did you not notice that Father never came to your place again until the burial? Then they made me come with them. They thought it would heal my pain to know I never had to see him again." Rebeckah shook her head in anguish.

"Mother made me hide for as long as it took to have the baby. Each time they heard someone coming down our road they made me run to the barn and hide out like a common farm animal. I had to wear big aprons over my stomach when I started getting big. And I was told to always have something in my hand with which to cover my stomach, like a ·basket of hand sewing. By then Sarah had married and moved away. There were just the younger ones left at home. Eleanor might have guessed something was wrong when I kept gaining weight. I remember mother kept pretending I was eating too much when we sat down at the table, so the others would think that was the reason for the larger dresses. I was so distraught I hardly ate at all.

Father spoke with an old woman they knew who lived on the other side of where they used to live. She said she would see to me birthing a baby. She was the only one that ever knew the secret, outside of you. They told the others I was going to work for this old lady. That is why William has never learned from anyone in the family about the baby. The sheriff would never have come, nor would have known either, except a wagon full of missionaries came to the old ladies house to convert us. They had just come from one of the big meetings where that famous preacher had cried out that God was angry with all of us. One of them saw me and inquired as to my name. They said I was a sinner and needed to be punished and they were going to tell the Sheriff. It wasn't even my fault," Rebeckah said, and started crying again.

Elizabeth put her hand out and patted Rebeckah's back. "So that is when the sheriff came?"

Rebeckah nodded her head. "He came that night to tell me I was going to be brought to court. The next day I had the labor.

The trial was in Upper Marlboro. No one knew my name or my face. Father paid for a lawyer to defend me, keeping me from having to go before the jury. He did not want anyone there to see my face."

"I know when my husband had to go to court it took all the monies we could get."

"I just wanted to keep my baby. If I could have, I would have run off with her when she was born, but I had no monies."

Elizabeth let out a moan. "I had no idea you were having a baby until the sheriff came here while Mr. Norris was in the schoolhouse. I read the citation that he should appear in court to pay the fee for your body. I cried all night long. William said he could not resist your flirtatious ways."

"No, no, no. I never flirted with him," Rebeckah said with fire in her voice. "I looked up to him because he was the teacher."

Elizabeth spoke now with a heavy sadness. "Our times together had rough spells before, but after the citation it was nothing more than a man and woman staying in the same house."

The two sisters were quiet for a while, letting the words passed between them settle in their minds.

When Rebeckah spoke, her words were touched with yearning. "Did you ever see her, Elizabeth? She was so pretty, so tiny and soft in my arms." Rebeckah shivered from the cold and begged her sister. "I just want to see her again. Is she small of build? Does she have brown hair like mine? Please tell me where your husband took my baby."

"I cannot tell you, Rebeckah, not because I desire to see you tormented but because I rightly do not know. Mr. Norris brought her to me just after she was born. I did not know then she was your baby. He told me a former student had died in childbirth and her parents wanted him to find a good home for her baby because they were in poor health. I believed him. I had no reason to think otherwise. She was only here for a day or so and then he took her away. He would not tell me where he was going—said it was for my protection."

"Oh why, why, why?" Rebeckah cried out.

"I'm sure it was to a good family. After all, it was his daughter too."

"His daughter too! It was my birthing that gave her life. All he did was take away my innocence and dropped her off for someone else to love. Everywhere I go I search the faces, looking for someone that has the look of my face, someone that resembles my Nancy. I all but ask them what birth date they go by. Her twenty-second birthday has passed and she is probably married. I will never know her. My daughter is out there somewhere Elizabeth, and I will never know her," Rebeckah said, as she repeated her painful cry.

"Did you give her a name?" Elizabeth asked.

"I called her Mary—like our mother's name. But no one is going to keep her rightful name, seeing she was too young to know it and since they had been told to keep her birthing a secret."

"You named another by the same name?"

"The first after the mother that helped me get through those hard times and the second Mary as a memory of the mother we had just lost."

"What about William? How will your husband take your secret after all these years?" Elizabeth asked.

"I have thought of that, and I am ready to bargain with that heartache when it comes. Somewhere out there is a beautiful girl, possibly a wife and mother that I will never know. That is punishment far greater than worrying what William would do. Now it is too late. If only Father had allowed me to know."

"After the sheriff delivered the papers here, that is when I found out the true story. Father told Mr. Norris if he would find a good home for the baby, a place where it could grow up not knowing of the past, and how it got here, then he would not call the sheriff on him."

Elizabeth stood up and spoke like an older, maybe wiser, sister. "Father did it for the baby. Maybe that was the best chance for life he could give to her—and to you."

The two women started back to the cabin slowly. "The trial is over and we have cleansed our souls, Rebeckah. It is time to embrace what we have left." Just before they got to the door, Elizabeth turned back to her sister. "I will inquire to William Norris's relations to hear of any girl child being given out so many years ago."

When Rebeckah slipped between the quilts on the pallet next to her husband, she wondered how she could ever tell him the dark secret she had held so long, always being afraid of his disappointment in her. If she had told him before the marriage, would he have gone elsewhere for a wife? Could he forgive her now after their children were born to him?

Her thoughts of guilt ran deep. Maybe the horrible guilt was not because of the baby. It was not of her doings. Her horrible guilt that hunted her down each day since was the secret kept from her husband, not trusting him to understand—to forgive her. Sometime near morning she prayed, "Help me God to know when he is ready to hear the truth."

She put her hand gently on his back as she whispered in a voice too soft to be heard. "Please do not hate me, William."

Chapter 27

Late December 1766
Upper Seneca Creek

When Alexander Grant returned with the wagon early the next morning, William was satisfied they had done all they could for Richard Willis and Elizabeth. Anxious to return home, William turned to Elizabeth who had followed them out, "I do not believe we will be back this way for a spell, unless of course—you never know—" William left his words hanging, leaving them open for interruption.

Rebeckah reached out to her sister, and for the first time in over twenty years, a new heart felt understanding passed between them.

As the wagon slid over the half frozen ground, Rebeckah sat stolidly on the seat next to William. Even when he asked if she had a good visit with her sister, she only nodded. He looked at her with a frown, questioning if something was wrong, to which she assured him she was all right, just tired, which was not an untruth. He could not possibly understand how deep her tiredness was planted.

For so long the guilt had been on her heart. And now for the first time since the dreadful happening, she had opened her heart to Elizabeth. It would be in God's timing to find a safe place to tell her husband. A new host of conflicting thoughts began to spring up. How would she know what to do? What could she say that would ease his pain? He would naturally question why she had not told him before they stood with the preacher. Would he feel it almost inconceivable that his wife of so many years had kept such a dark secret from him? And why had her family not given a hint of the secret leaving him to marry a woman he thought to be pure? Even more distressing for him would be to find his good and true friend, the schoolmaster William Norris, had deceived him into thinking he was a godly man.

Rebeckah was so deep in thought she did not hear the wheel crack on the wagon, sending everyone sliding downward to the side. One more jolt and baby Lucy would have been flung to the ground.

Quickly she began checking everyone as they sat covered with plunder at the bottom end of the wagon. Nothing more than a few bruises had resulted from the tumble. But it had left William frustrated beyond reason. He shouted for the boys to unhitch the oxen. "Rebeckah, don't just sit there like the queen. Get the children out of the wagon. We can't turn it over to fix the wheel with a full wagon." He continued to grumble about the poor work of building this new wagon. "I just bought this thing—unscrupulous blacksmith work they have performed." He watched as Rebeckah began to roll up the quilts and pass them off to young William. Then he yelled, "Nancy, I told you to get that plunder out of the wagon!"

Nancy began to cry as she threw out the baskets of food onto the ground. Her father could be stern, but rarely did he yell at her.

With a baby under each arm, Rebeckah tried to crawl over the side. She could not safely manage to get her footing with no free hands so sat Mary down in the wagon. This caused a rush of screams from the child for fear of being left. Young William, who was always good with Mary, ran over to lift her over the side and held her tightly to console her. William and Absolom lifted the wagon to its side, holding it in place while John pulled the pegs from the wheel. The crack was more severe than first thought, and there was nothing else to do but go to a nearby farm house to find help.

William turned around to look across the countryside for a cabin. "John, you come with me. Bring the whip, I will leave the gun with your mother." He turned to Rebeckah, "If you see something threatening, do not hesitate to shoot. We will be back as soon as we can find help."

Rebeckah and her little group hunkered down next to the underside of the tilted wagon and watched as William and John started down the road. By now the cold raw wind had found a way to their bones. Rebeckah remembered the coals her sister had sent to keep their feet warm. If they were lucky they would still be hot enough to spark a fire. She sent Absolom and young William to find dry wood.

After what seemed like hours in the cold, Rebeckah heard a wagon coming over the hill. With relief she saw it was a farmer returning with William and John and hopefully with the tools to fix the broken wheel.

The old farmer, who she soon learned was named Henry Hinsbinder, yelled a greeting to the small group and said, "My wife, Prudence, insists you and the children take my wagon back to our cabin. This cold will give no favors."

It did not take a second invitation. Rebeckah piled the children into Henry's wagon and headed in the direction of the gray smoke coming from a newly stoked fireplace. "It's just over the creek there," Henry pointed.

The farmer's wife greeted them at the door with hot steaming cider and a friendly laugh. Before the cider was downed, Rebeckah knew this woman was someone with a gentle soul.

The two women sat on the bench near the fireplace, while the children sat on the floor listening to the women talk. Rebeckah had told her of her sister's wedding and all that went with it. They had all laughed, even Nancy and young William when remembering how John Lashley had rushed in to take Rachel's hand away from Grove Hollock.

Rebeckah noticed a small pair of skates hanging on a hook by the fireplace and asked, "And what of your family—I see they skated."

Prudence began to unfold the story as if it was a piece of paper with writing on all sides. "Once, yes, once we had a son. And a fine looking boy, he was too. He was much too young to find a wife, but that he did just the same. And then he felt it his duty to go help defend the land for the family. So off he marched down the road out front to help win the war against the Frenchmen. It wasn't long after he left our cabin that his Betsy gave birth to a little boy. She was so young and the baby just too big. She is buried on that hill over the ridge. Our Joseph never knew he had a son or that his wife had gone on before him. Guess he did not have the practice at shooting that some of the boys had. They said he just didn't pick up his gun fast enough. They got him the first day he was out."

Prudence wiped away the tears with the edge of her apron. "We were left to love that little baby boy, our son's wife had called Joseph. I guess we did not do a good enough job cause we let harm come to him."

As she started to tell the story she gazed into the fire, almost like she was seeing the events play out again before her eyes. "I had seen a small dog down by the road the night before and thought nothing of it. Dogs come and go, you know. Then the next morning while I set the fire for the wash, I let little Joseph, just barely two years old, play in the yard. I knew when the little boy started screaming that something bad had happened. I ran to him fast and could see the teeth marks of that old dog deep in his leg. Later that day I saw the dog again and he had long strings of white foam coming out of his mouth. It wasn't long after that that little Joseph started acting real strange. He had one fit after the other and I knew, I just knew the worst. He tried to climb the wall over there and fell back down. He even tried to bite his grandpa. We did everything to help his fits but nothing could stop them. I cleaned out all my medicine bottles trying to find something that could help him heal." Her voice became soft and she almost whispered "nothing would help. We just had to watch him go mad."

Rebeckah and the children sat stunned, listening to the tragic story. Then with determination to finish the story she spoke up. "In a few days he stopped fighting and got real still, he didn't breath anymore." She shook her head and began chanting "So sad, so sad, so sad, so sad." Rebeckah waited as Prudence gave out a long sigh and looked at her. "I don't allow dogs to come here anymore. Only my dogs."

Prudence jumped up as if to break the memory and went to the old chest under the window and began to pull out small toys for the children to play with. "I reckon these are doing no good stored away like this. She handed the boys some stone marbles. Then she dug a little deeper to find a doll. Two-year-old Mary sat spellbound when Prudence began to rock the rag doll in her arms, singing a strange sounding song with German words. When Prudence stopped singing, she handed the doll to Mary, "Here little one, you may have this doll." Mary giggled with delight as the woman placed the doll in her tiny arms.

Prudence turned to Rebeckah and explained, "Betsy made the doll before her baby was born, thinking it might be a baby girl."

When Rebeckah protested the gift, Prudence waved her off. "I have a warm place in my heart for your little ones this day, so please do not take that feeling away from me. No one comes this way anymore, and it has been so long since my heart felt full." Then she reached down into the bottom of the old chest and carefully brought out a piece of paper. Rebeckah could see what looked like a certificate with the beautiful German design painted on the face of it. "Oh, you must have come from the German lands."

The woman beamed with delight that someone recognized the art form. "Yes, yes. That was our country so many years ago. My father and mother brought me over on a ship to dock in Pennsylvania. My Henry also came from there when he was a bit older than my age. My father painted this baptismal certificate for our son." Again, the sadness crept into her voice. "My father was a painter of the old scripts." She gently laid the fragile paper on the table.

Rebeckah stood for a long while admiring the handy work on the certificate and found herself tracing the symbols of the old Germanic mythology with the prancing lions and horses standing on their back legs, looking as if they were stationed there to hold the words in place. The vibrant red, yellow and blue colored hearts and tulips intertwined making a border for the words. The brush marks could still be seen over the delicate scripting of the words.

She looked up at her host. "When I was a small child my father took our family to the fair. We stopped to watch a man standing in front of an easel painting papers like this one with a goose-quill pen. My sisters and I tried it when we returned home. It did not turn out so well." Rebeckah laughed at the memory. She looked down at the paper again, her laughter ending in a gasp. The date of birth given on the paper was two days from the day of the birth of her first born but with a different year. When the farmer's wife asked what was wrong, she simply said, "I knew someone that was born at that time of the month. She looked away and began to change the subject by going over to admire a quilt in the process of being laid out. "Do you take part in a quilting bee?"

"It has been a long season since I have been asked to join into a circle. I guess the other women thought I was not of the mind to social after the boy died." The woman started to say something else, but the sound of a wagon stopped their conversation.

Rebeckah quickly gathered up the children and started for the wagon. As the farmer's wife helped carry baby Lucy to the wagon, Rebeckah stopped. "Prudence, I just remembered that Mrs. Dawson is unable to keep her place at my quilting table. I would feel it an honor to have you pick up her needle. We meet the first Wednesday of every month." She quickly gave the instructions on how to get to her house several miles away and then did something that once would have been unlike her, she reached out and gave Prudence a hug.

Once outside of earshot, William looked at his wife in puzzlement. "Rebeckah, you don't have a quilting bee on the first Wednesday. Or on any other day of the month for that fact."

Putting her arm in his, she smiled. "Sometimes, William, we bemoan a terrible thing, like a broken wheel, and before you know it, it can be changed into a blessing all of its own. When we get home please mark your calendar that I will be busy with my new quilting bee on each Wednesday first."

William took a long look at his wife and shook his head. "I swear to the powers that be, Rebeckah, after all these years I still do not know what is in your mind."

That had been the last trip for the season. William refused to take the family out in the wagon until he had taken it back to the blacksmith, with a piece of his mind attached to it. So for the rest of the winter season there was nothing else to do but find pleasures at home.

The children entertained each other with games and story telling. Solomon never tired of hearing the old stories of *Jack and the Giant* and always got upset if the storyteller let the Giant win the battle. It was all Rebeckah could do to get the older boys not to tease him as they told the stories over and over again on a cold evening beside the fire. Sometimes if they were not allowed to let the Giant win, they tried a new story.

It was one they had made up around the true facts of Savage Mountain. For years, as a way of keeping their children in line, parents had threatened to take their unruly children to this high mountain with its peaks reaching up into the clouds and its deep crevasses far below the road. Indians were said to hold nightly war dances around scalps hanging from tree limbs. By the time Absolom's imagination took hold of the story, it did not take much more to convince the young Solomon that he heard there was a scalp with their name on it and the spirits were just waiting for them to come claim it.

It did not matter that the story made no sense, Solomon was convinced he was doomed to die if he did not behave.

William had actually broken with his serious reading and laughed as Rebeckah whispered, "Maybe if we had told that story to Solomon before we went to the fair, we could have stayed for the finish of the race."

Nancy had stitched her third sampler sitting by the fire light on the cold evenings, and the last one held the bright colors like the colorful certificate Prudence had shown them.

Now on this evening William had finished entering all the land sales of his neighbors and brothers-in-law and had even begun to make some markings on paper for an extra room to add to their house. As Rebeckah watched his hand trace the lines again that would give her room to set up the quilting frame for, as he put it, her sociable life, she wondered all over again how she could ever tell him the secret that would almost destroy his feelings for her. Only time would tell if she could bring herself to break the trust he had in her.

The sound of John putting on his moccasins, preparing to leave, as he had done on so many evenings of late, brought her mind back to the worries at hand. "Do you have to go over there again, John?"

He took her questions as mere statements of her dislike and felt no need to answer. By now his mother should have known it was obvious that he had every intention on courting the new girl visiting the Dawson's for the winter.

But to Rebeckah it was more than just his courting that worried her. She had been told by Elizabeth Dawson that the girl was staying the winter and the only explanation was that she just needed to be here. Rebeckah wondered what would happen when the girl went back home. Was John walking into a heartbreak?

When the sound of his horse was no longer heard on their path, Rebeckah turned to William, "Have you thought anymore of sending John away to school at one of your English academies where he could become a lawyer or doctor someday? He has always done well with your book teachings, William." Then she lowered her voice so only he could hear. "If he were to marry now there is no way he could go."

William did not respond to her idea as she had hoped and tried another plan. "William, did you see that wicked rut in the road up by the turn-off taking you to the Fredericktown road? I nearly lost the horse in there on my way to the mill. I would be thinking they should be calling John to join the road crew again real soon. You might tell him to go see if he is needed." What she was really asking was could they arrange to send him far away from the Dawson's visitor.

325

Still her husband did not respond to her reasoning. In frustration she marched over to her window. A spring storm was forming in the sky and she could see threads of lightening in a distance. She smiled. A good hard rain would surely wash out enough roads, and the road crew would be called.

Toward the end of March, William received a letter from Alexander Grant saying it would be a good thing to have a meeting before planting season began. The weather had stayed cold and the Maple trees were not dropping the sap fast enough to bring the buckets in daily. It was a good time to break away and attend the meeting.

The meeting had been short with only distant rumbles of British conflicts, nothing that could affect their lives that much. Alexander mentioned that James Lee's old property was looking better than it had in years, even before he had been forced to let the family manage the farm for him.

"And the roof has been fixed and the barn has a new door. Guess that is enough so soon after this new man took over."

"Does anyone of you know who this man is that we let Rachel marry?" one of the brothers-in-law asked.

No one seemed to know anymore than the rest but one of them gave his okay, "Just as long as the weeds stay down I am happy."

As the men got up to leave, Thomas Betterton gave the shock of a warning of things to come for the family.

"I've sold some of my *Thomas and James* land to John Seager, and Margaret Ward bought the *Lye By Lying* section that hugs the end of the land."

The first reaction was, "What was John Seager doing buying up all the land?"

"John just bought a part of John Wofford's land last year without giving anyone else a chance at it," John Hughes harshly complained.

The next comment from Betterton left the men stunned. "I'm unloading my land now because I plan on moving to the Carolinas when the time is right—can't see it makes sense to pass up such a good offer."

Thomas Thrasher turned to Robert Lee and with a tinge of anger said, "Is this some of your doings, Robert?"

They all had remembered several years ago shortly after his father had died, Robert had been convinced he wanted to move. But nothing had come of the talk until now. Slowly, the talk began to be about how they each could get the good land deals Betterton had been promised.

"For certain, land is scarce in these parts. I've never seen so many wagons coming into the state from Pennsylvania, even New York, looking for land sales."

The men began to analyze the profits they could get from their land sales. Still, one question bothered them. What was about to happen in the Carolinas if the British cracked down on more taxing? Would the Indigo be worthless, could they grow tobacco on that land if the parliament held back the paper monies in favor of using tobacco as payments? Would the land be good for products to export?

One by one, the men left the ordinary, and William went to pick up his mail bundle from the owner. All the while the thoughts of what was happening to their family held his attention. He dreaded having to tell Rebeckah her sister was moving. She would jump to the conclusion, and rightly so. Her close family was being pulled apart by the need for making a better life.

When William returned home he had good news before the bad. "A letter was there for you from Rachel," he said, hoping it would take some of the pain away when he told her Thomas Betterton was planning on moving Eleanor to the Carolinas.

Rebeckah's first response was, "How did you know it is from Rachel? Have you opened it?" After the mean spirited way Rachel had been treated when she got word of Grove Hollock, the women had put out a decree to the men in the family that they were not to tamper with the letter if secured by a wax seal.

"Well, I do know how to read, Rebeckah," he reminded her, then half muttered, "Besides she always draws those silly little flowers around the edges."

Rebeckah took the folded paper from her husband, noticing, "Her secret must be important because she has sealed it with two waxes instead of just one." She carefully peeled the seals away from the edge and began to read.

"Sister, I want you to be the first to know I am with child. John says the laces on my waist front are getting shorter. I guess that means I could give birth in about August. That is what Anastasia tells me also. I told her but no one else. Please come for the birth if you can. I am so happy but scared. John is very good to me. Lov Rachel."

Rebeckah began shouting, "God is good, God is good." And before the writing on the letter had worn dull, everyone in the cabin, as well as any neighbor who had dared venture close to the Littlefield cabin had memorized Rachel's words. But strangely, no more talk of Eleanor moving had been spoken. It was as if by not talking about it, it would not happen, or if it were to happen she would deal with that when the time came. For now, she had a new purpose to her day.

Rebeckah had spent a good part of a morning writing and rewriting a letter to her sister. *"My dear sister Rachel. With joy in our hearts, Nancy and I have begun picin a birthin quilt for you on your day of delivry. Mother would hav lovd to be ther to help. you can count on me to com."* With the help of William's dictionary book she had written the words in her own handwriting and put the seal on it. Then she had written words to her sisters, Sarah and Martha, to give the news. Also one to Eleanor to say how sorry she was that they would be leaving before Rachel's baby came. Those words were included in hopes it would make Thomas decide to stay long enough to see the blessed occasion. After the letters were sealed she convinced William it would be a shame to hold the letter until his next trip out. To her surprise he had given approval that John could carry the letter. "I'll send him by the new blacksmith next to the mill to leave a plow for welding, and Beall's Tavern is close by. They will pick up the mail almost as quickly as at Dowden's."

For the next few weeks Rebeckah and Nancy had searched every garden and cellar for roots that could produce the dyes needed to make the linen material a delicate pink color. And every evening they had sat late before the fire, piecing the tiny cutout rosebuds into a circle that would form a wreath among green leaves. It just would not do for Rachel to give birth without her own birthing quilt, complete in the pattern of the rosebuds. For as long as Rebeckah had remembered the talk, this quilt had been a part of the preparation of a birth.

Rebeckah raised her eyes up from the quilting to look at her daughter. She spoke softly, "Someday, Nancy, I will be sitting before this fire making you a birthing quilt."

Nancy giggled, not looking up. She continued to work the tiny stitches up and down through the quilt top while the smile stayed on her lips.

Chapter 28

Summer 1767
The Lower Seneca Creek

It was harvest time and no sooner was one meal finished before it was time to prepare the table for another. On this night, Rebeckah looked at the stairs going to the bedchambers and wondered if she had the strength to make it to her bed. As she leaned against the wall to gather what little energy she had left before taking her first step, her knees began to give way to a slide.

Sometime at the edge of morning, William heard the red rooster crow in the barnyard. "It is time to set the fire," he said as he reached over to nudge her out of bed. When he could not feel her lying beside him, he turned over in the dark room and called her name, but there was no answer. He slipped his feet into his shoes and went down stairs to find his wife. To his surprise she was still at the bottom of the steps, leaning against the wall where she had sat the night before. His first reaction was of concern. It was not all that uncommon for a woman of Rebeckah's age to fall over dead during the hard work during harvest time.

William reached over to make sure there was still warmth to her body. When he was satisfied she was still breathing, he began to scold. "Rebeckah, why are you sleeping down here? You know your bones will be too stiff to pick up the cooking pots." William reached out to try to help her up but she wanted no part in it.

"If the fire in the outside cooking place is not started before the sun comes up there will not be enough heat to cook all the food for the hired hands, and carpenters." He looked at his wife again. It was true she was working harder than ever before. Maybe they needed more help. "I'll go start it for you but you need to get up right now. I can't do everything for you." William looked down at his wife, still leaned up against the wall. He stopped halfway to the door to deliver a scornful thought, "Just remember this, Rebeckah, it was your quilting women that gave us the need to hire the carpenters." William was referring to the new room that was being added on to accommodate the quilting table.

Without opening her eyes she said, "Oh, forget the room, William. I'll just take the sleep instead."

But sleep was not to be. Her day had been addressed when the farm hands could be heard coming up the road, breaking the silence of the morning. The sound brought back the image of the King's army trampling everything in sight that day as General Braddock marched his troops to Clarksburg, and William had taken the family to watch.

When she finally opened her eyes, the sun was just beginning to give rise to the day, exposing the long timbers forming the frame of the new room. Just the look at the size made her smile. It would be nice to tell her sisters she had a fine new room. And it was a big room. None of her sisters or brothers had such a room. Even John Hughes had not afforded Anne such a space as this.

By the time William and the boys, and even Solomon, who now went daily into the fields, had finished the chores at the barn, the sun was up above the tree line. The hired hands had already been in the fields for over an hour and would be breaking for the early noon meal.

Rebeckah and Nancy worked in silence as they cut up the first bushel of potatoes; another bushel waited at her feet for the fixing. It took a lot of food to feed this many men.

Rebeckah, still half asleep, turned to her daughter with almost no expression in her voice, and said "Nancy, only a few years ago the farmers considered this potato only food for the pigs and chickens. Now we are spending all our waking hours cutting them up to feed the hungry hired hands." She took a deep breath before saying, "I'm not certain that says that the hired hands are like pigs, or they have acquired a taste for the pig food." Rebeckah began to laugh, maybe out of tiredness, but all of a sudden it all seemed so funny. Her daughter caught the infectious moment, and before the laughing was over both were holding their sides at the thought of feeding the hired hands pig food.

Between the laughs, Nancy looked at her mother with a new respect. "Mama, Father is right, you find a way to make something funny out of nothing."

Rebeckah reached out and patted her daughter's hand, "Sometimes that is the only thing we have, Nancy. Your grandmother taught me that a long time ago."

A sound from the road caused Nancy to drop her knife and turn to search for the rider.

Rebeckah wondered why the sudden change. "What is it, child?

"I thought maybe Nicholas Dawson had come to fetch the wagon."

"Oh, is he supposed to be coming?"

"Father said one of the Dawson's would be coming to borrow the wagon. Do you think it might be Nicholas?"

Rebeckah looked up at her daughter with a puzzled look. "Nancy, you have asked of Nicholas before. Is there something I have not seen?"

The thought of Nancy, at almost seventeen, having a warm heart toward Nicholas, made Rebeckah smile. She knew of no one better to trust the heart of her daughter to, than the second son of Thomas and Elizabeth Dawson. It brought back the memories of her childhood when she had also watched for a certain neighbor boy's visit, but he had not come. Almost as soon as the smile came it was replaced with a lump in her throat. She remembered there were no more suitors calling for her after—Suddenly, the thought of not telling William about the secret, after vowing to make it right, sent a pain to her stomach.

As the sun rose higher in the morning sky, Rebeckah's eyes went in search for a cloud. If only it would rain or at least cloud up.

The sound of the carpenters hammering another long board to what would be the roof caught her attention. In her mind she could picture what it would be like when finished. William would have a room to open his school for the neighboring children, and she would have a quilting frame on the other side of the wall. William had even drawn in a window on the plans to give light to the stitches as they sewed.

William had sent to a London warehouse for catalogs so that he might select the furniture as he remembered it from his grandfather's big house in England. Rebeckah's mind began to wander as she imagined what fine things he would buy.

Her thoughts came to an abrupt end when Nancy kept calling to her. "What is it Nancy?" She asked rather crossly as she let out a deep sigh, realizing she could not even entertain a daydream without being interrupted.

"When are you going to Aunt Rachel's for the birthing? What if the baby comes before it's time—like Mary and Lucy did and you are not there in time?"

"She won't go into labor that soon. This is her first baby and besides her body is older now and the birth will come slowly. In my last letter, Rachel said Dennis Madden had offered to come for me before her due date if your father has not already taken me."

The summer wore on. No sooner was one crop brought in than another was waiting. It was a good year for harvesting, making it impossible for Rebeckah to make plans to go to Rachel's. She looked at her calendar and marked the day she felt it was necessary to leave, if she was to be there in time to help with the birth.

Nancy's worries had not been wasted. And now, John Lashley stood before them announcing the new arrival.

"Rachel went to the birthing bed weeks before we planned," John said, a smile creeping over his face. She would not rest until I came to tell you about our new little lassie."

Wiping the tears that were making their way down her cheeks, Rebeckah asked, "She called her Mary, didn't she?"

"Has someone been here before me?

"No one has been here. I just know how much Rachel loved our mother. It was the name she would use." Rebeckah began to ask questions all in one breath. "Did she have a hard birthing, who was there with her? I wanted to be the one to hand her first born to her, but little Mary had her own timing, I guess."

"Rachel did a very good job of birthing, hardly a cry until the very end." John began to laugh as he explained, "I knew Rach had birthed her before Elizabeth came out to tell me. That little one of ours has the strong lungs of a pig caller."

Everyone laughed at the description of his little daughter.

"So Elizabeth was with her?" Rebeckah asked.

"Yes, she was in good hands. I made sure of it. I ran over to John's place to get Elizabeth when we first thought Rachel's travail was beginning, and then John went over to fetch Anastasia Madden to come. You know Elizabeth herself is due to birth, almost any day now John says. We wanted to have Anastasia there in case Elizabeth should have to go to her bed as well."

This news of another baby for John and Elizabeth was a complete surprise to Rebeckah. No one had bothered to come with the news. Rebeckah turned to her husband with a strong look, "Why didn't you tell me John and Elizabeth were planning on a birth?" She said shaking her finger at her husband, accusing him of forgetting part of the news he was to bring home.

William was taken by surprise as much as Rebeckah, not that it meant as much to him, but he did admit, "John Lee rarely comes to the meetings since his leg break and no one had reported it."

"See, William, I told you we were so far away from any of the family that I just as well live in the next country. I wonder what other news I have missed?"

John Lashley looked puzzled. "You did know your sister Martha had a baby boy back in early May, didn't you?"

At that news Rebeckah let out a half squeal. "I knew it was planned, but why did someone not send me word? Oh, poor Martha will think I have ceased to care."

William did speak up in defense of not knowing that news. "Rebeckah, you know I have not had time to attend any meetings since the harvest began early this summer."

John picked up his rifle and started for the door. "I best be getting back on the road. I came first to tell you. That is what Rachel instructed me to do. Rebeckah, I will let you notify the rest of them. I will tell James and Annie when I stop for the night at their place. I didn't want to leave Rach so soon after the birthing was over, but the first thing she asked was for me to come give you the words first hand."

Nancy whispered something in her mother's ear as John was preparing to go.

"Oh, my soul, I almost forgot," Rebeckah said, telling John to wait.

Nancy had quickly climbed the steps to the bedchambers and came back with a tied up bundle.

"It is the birthing quilt, Nancy and I made for Rachel. I thought I would be bringing it in time. But she will have it tomorrow. Be so kind as to give it to her." Rebeckah shoved it under John's arm.

With his hand still on the door handle, he said. "I almost forgot, Rachel said I was to tell you Mary is the prettiest baby she has ever laid her eyes on."

After John Lashley had gone, Rebeckah turned to William and in a wave of triumph said, "I guess you can properly inform the men in the family that John Lashley was the best selection for my sister. He cares for her well being, and with his good looks they will have beautiful babies. I would hate to think of her little Mary having to look like another of the Grove Hollock's brood."

William could only stand in disbelief at the mouth full of observations his wife had just spoken.

She started out the door to finish the washing, then turned back to face William. "Shocking as it may be to your thinking, there are times a woman knows best."

Chapter 29

Late October 1767
Dowden's Ordinary

The brisk October winds had begun to blow a thick pad of orange and golden leaves over the road and against the fence lines. After the long hot summer William always liked the feel of fall in the air, and this morning as he made his way to Dowden's all seemed especially good.

Only Thomas Thrasher was there before him. Even Alexander who usually presided was not there after calling the meeting.

"What's this I heard about you selling some of your land back in July?" William asked Thomas Thrasher as he sat down with his tankard. "Was it the land your father owned—the *Benjamin* piece?"

"Yes, that and a small section that was once a part of *Laybrinth.* It sits at the edge of *Benjamin.* This man, John Trundell, sought me out the other day when we were up there tending to mother's grave. And he had the monies to pay on the spot. Sixty pounds was a good price I felt. Father would have been pleased to know we got so much for it. He loved that land. I sure hated to part with it, but now that mother is gone it was just growing up with thistles," Thomas explained.

After that bit of news, they sat back listening to the men in the room relay pieces of news they had been privy to in their travels. The topic of how much winter wheat they could scatter and the prices they could expect next July harvest seemed to be their main concern.

Another man in the corner spoke of the boycott growing over the shipment of tea coming in from England.

After listening to the man expound for a while Thomas and William turned back to talk.

"Guess that will be the next big item we will have to handle. It sure is good to have you on our side, William," Thomas said.

"I'm a little slow to change my thinking. But this time, after what happened to me, I would have been a fool to not change," William admitted. "My surmise is that it will not take parliament to the end of the year to force another tax. I guess we should be thankful we are not tea drinkers."

"I do not suppose there are many that find the tax on the glass or the paint that inconvenient. Now for the lead and paper, that is another matter. But the revolt on that seems to have quieted down as well," Thomas said.

"As long as it does not press my monies bag too much, I guess I'm not willing to go to jail over it," William said.

The man in the center of the room was talking loud enough to disrupt the conversation, so they stopped to listen as he railed on about Ben Franklin acting as spokesman sitting in on parliament. "He has already given the colonists early warning to upcoming problems. But I heard from a good source that the Lord Townshend was not in good health." His friend sitting with him mused, "But not sick enough to forget how to fill the King's pockets with colonial monies." Everyone in the room laughed a hardy laugh.

Just as everyone was beginning to enjoy the idle talk, a man in a heavy leather fringed coat with moccasins came through the door. He seemed intent on making sure the establishment heard his news. "Any of you gentlemen planning on going up past Cresap's fort from here should know the Indians are on the war path up that way. I've just come from inspecting the chain carriers work on the Mason-Dixon line. We were standing on the summit overlooking the creek below and could see a very disturbing situation developing."

No sooner were the words out of his mouth than a crowd began to gather around him as he continued to talk.

"I'm headed that way as soon as I leave my meal," a man dressed in coarse traveling clothes yelled back. "What should I know about my trip?"

The man delivering the news turned to address him. "I stood with several of the axemen still working. Not more than fifteen, I'd say, still work because of the threats from the Indians. As I said, we could see down below a long party of Indians painted up for war, weaving their way along the water's edge. The spokesman that accompanies the axemen said it probably is over the hunting rights."

Another traveler broke in, "Who did you say was riding with them?"

"Seems the Governor or Lord Baltimore has given his word on the rights. An escort spokesman for the Six Nations rides with the chain carriers to keep piece. Even while I was there, he was getting his horse saddled to go down to intercept the party. Since my work was done, I decided it was a good thing to head back this way. Last night when I bedded down next to an old tree, there came another man along the way to try my same tree. He had come from the border a few hours after me and had been told that the escort in charge of the Indian complaints had come back up the mountain to meet with the axemen. The threats were too great and they sent the axemen back to their base camp in Pennsylvania. Their lives and any travelers that got in the way are in danger."

"Not for sure that chain is ever going to get all the way to the end anytime soon," Thomas told William, and both men went back to chewing on their dinner's tough meat.

"Give them time and there will be another urgent call for help," Thomas Betterton said, walking into the room in time to hear the speech. As he removed his outer coat, he went over to pick up a tankard of cider and a plate of food and sat down at the table with William and Thomas.

He wasted no time in formalities and opened his talk with shocking news. "Gentlemen, there will be one less Thomas to deal with in your monthly meetings."

"What are you talking about?" William asked.

"I've sold the rest of my land—two days ago," Betterton announced.

"You did what?" Thomas Thrasher and William lashed out the words in disbelief.

"Betterton, do you realize what you are doing?" Thomas Thrasher asked.

Thomas began to give them the reason as best they would listen. "The offers I am hearing from the Woffords in Carolina has caused me to set the figures down. My land here has become so thin I barely get a stack of tobacco to grow full size. You men know that. Both of you have complained. And don't say you have not thought of pulling up and moving."

"It was just idle talk. I never meant to go as far as moving," Thrasher said.

"William, I know you have complained about the planters getting too close on all sides as the land is divided."

"You are right. I do not abide with living in my neighbor's yard," William confessed.

I'm not sure we will have food for the table in another year. I can not find a fat rabbit to skin because they have nothing to eat as well." Thomas went on to try to convince the men he was doing the right thing.

The men just shook their heads over the news. "Once one of you men load your wagon, the next will see it as a way out," Thomas Thrasher said. "I remember when Robert Lee was going to pull up his family and move. That has been awhile back. Wonder if he is still giving it mind?"

"I talked to Robert about it just a week ago. He said his wife's parents set such a fuss about him taking Elizabeth away that he had to stop talking about it," Betterton said, then went on to explain. "Robert is not going to move. Elizabeth's parents have been good to them and moving is just not a possibility with Richard Watts."

William laughed, "That might be the reason he would want to move. Richard can be a real scrapper sometimes. Wasn't he the one that bit off the ear of one of the Wofford boys during a confrontation over a loose pig?"

"According to Elizabeth Norris, Robert's wife has a bit of her father's temper." The men still called her by her second husband's name when speaking in conversations, because that was who she was when they had married her sisters. "I guess you heard about that?" one of the men said.

"Seems Elizabeth Norris got the last word—she called both of them into court on assault charges."

"I'd say Robert has his hands full with that wife of his," Betterton said, raising his eyebrow in a knowing way. "For whatever reason, he has not talked about a move of recent." .

"And what is Eleanor saying about the move?" William asked.

"What can she say," Thomas said of his wife. "I've told her that is what it will take to keep the family fed. She had some tears when she signed the dower release."

"Who did you sell to?" Thomas Thrasher asked.

"John Riley bought two hundred and fifty eight acres, and James Taylor bought a little over one hundred and ninety one acres of *Thomas and James*. We will be ready to pack up just as soon as I get the wagons ready. I believe we can sell most of the goods to the new owners and be ready by middle of November if the weather holds out. That should get us to warm weather before the snows come to this part," Thomas Betterton said, feeling confident in his planning.

"You are not traveling alone, are you?" Thomas questioned, feeling more than a little annoyed that someone was uprooting from the family.

"Of course, not. Do you think I am a fool? There is a train forming for the first week in November, but they say it usually takes a week or so to line up the wagons. I should be ready by then. If not, I have told John Riley he may have to wait to move on land until we can meet a gathering going south."

"Well my place is better bottom land than you can find in Carolina. I'll be staying put," Thomas Thrasher said.

"If I had rich bottom land like yours, I'd be staying put too," Betterton agreed.

The men sat in silence for a time, mulling over what Thomas Betterton had just said.

"Speaking of Elizabeth Norris—I mean Elizabeth Willis. I was over there last week and she cannot leave Richard even long enough to go feed the chickens and gather the eggs," Thomas Betterton explained. The men just shook their heads as a way of sympathizing. "We need to set up a schedule to go help a couple of days a month. She has hired hands but that does not give her help with Richard."

The tavern was beginning to fill up with loud travelers, making it hard to be heard. William turned, looking at the crowded room and said, "Where have all these people come from? It used to take the evening meal time to fill this place up."

"There are just more people everywhere you go. The roads are clogged with wagons."

"It used to take a long day to get all the way to the warehouse, and when I went last week it took me almost twice as long."

"Have you men been to the court house of late? The line goes all the way around it just to set a deed in place," Thrasher said, then turned to the other Thomas. "If you don't like a crowd, maybe it is a good thing to move to the Carolinas."

William folded his note taking paper and paid his bill and was about to leave, when Mrs. Dowden threw her hands up in the air as a way to get him to wait. "I've got a bundle for you."

He took the bundle of mail and leafed through it to make sure it had his name on it. There had been times when the owner's wife had sorted the mail to the wrong bundle. He could see the catalogs he had ordered had come in. That would satisfy Rebeckah's need for news. He was not sure if he was ready to tell Rebeckah about her sister being carried off to Carolina just yet.

When William came around the bend in his path just at sunset, he could not believe how big his house looked from the road. It was a good addition and he was proud to have it completed. Now with the harvest all in, what bigger pleasure than to sit at one of his big windows and watch the sunset on a cold evening.

Each evening after the chores were finished, Rebeckah pulled the catalog down and took it to the chair with the Betty Lamp hanging onto the back. Then she lit the oil in an almost ceremonial way, and announced to her family that she was going shopping.

Each page of the catalog was like opening the door to a world she had only heard about on occasions, unlike any she had ever seen. There were fancy curtains with the extra piece of material draped at the top of the window, pictures for every wall and tall candles that sat in elegant gold pedestal candleholders. When she came to the pages with rugs on them she turned the tip of the page under as a way of holding it for safekeeping. There were more rugs than she had ever seen. Some had strange curly designs on them and others, the ones she liked best, were described as having bright flowers in the center. It would be a good thing to have a rug to keep the babies from getting croupy from the cold wind coming through the cracks.

On another page, there was a cherry wood writing desk, just like the one William had described his grandfather had owned. It had drawers in which to store his teaching papers and even a hole ready cut for the inkpot.

She turned the page and spotted the fine china like Mrs. Allnutt showed off on her shelf. Their neighbors next door were the Allnutts, and although she never considered them wealthy, it was true Mrs. Allnutt had some nice things. Rebeckah had unknowingly been privy to stories about how the first wife's relation, the Lawrence family, had given their daughter many fine surroundings before she died. Now the second wife had married into those family treasures. This had not made peaceful times, especially when the second wife Mr. Allnutt had chosen was considered of lessor class than the Lawrence's daughter. The situation had become so embittered, Mr. Allnutt finally said that was enough bickering and moved his children and his new wife to the land next to the *William and John.* For whatever reason they had moved. Mrs. Allnutt now had some very pretty plates of china to sit on her cabinet shelf.

Rebeckah turned a few more pages that showed things she had no need of, and was about to put it back on the shelf when she noticed something called Oyl Cloth. She looked up at William, "Have you ever heard of the word Oyl used with the word cloth? It says here that I need it for my tabletop and it comes in four different colors." William did not look up from his dictionary. He was busy writing a letter in response to something he had seen in the newspaper.

Rebeckah continued to look at the Oyl Cloth, especially the one that said red and white checked. "I guess it would keep the splinters out of my fingers," she said under her breath, not wanting to disturb her husband. She turned a few more pages. On page sixty-seven she noticed a bed with a curtain around it to keep the bugs out. Then she spotted something that made her laugh. Lifting the catalog from her lap, she took it over to the table and pointed it out to William, whispering in his ear, "They even have a chair with a lid to hide the pot." She laughed lightheartedly, "Sure would stop you from kicking it over in the dark of night." William looked up horrified at his wife's jesting. "I don't sit with nonsense talk, Rebeckah."

Somehow his comment had not been meant so literally, and when Rebeckah got tickled, he got up and went outside, leaving his dictionary still open on the table next to the catalog picture.

Rebeckah knew she had crossed the line of jesting and turned to another page in the catalog.

Nancy finished her row of tatting and came to look over her mother's shoulder. "It will not be long before your father will build you the wooden hope chest like this one." She pointed it out to Nancy. You will need it to store the quilts and linens you have made. Before long a special man will be knocking on our door, all nervous like, to claim you as his wife."

William had come back in the door and heard Rebeckah's reasoning. His voice was deep and deliberate. "Rebeckah, have you gone silly over that book? I will not have you filling Nancy with notions before her time. He took the catalog from the table and put it defiantly back on the shelf. "I should never have brought the catalog home."

"William, your daughter is eighteen years old and you will not be able to keep her at home for ever." Rebeckah had spoken her piece, leaving the others in the room surprised at the tone of voice she had spoken to their father.

The conversations had ended between William and Rebeckah over the catalog but not the dream. After the men had gone to work the fields, Rebeckah and Nancy would run to the shelf to take down the catalog, snatching brief moments to plan what Rebeckah would order and what might one day find its way to Nancy's own home. Nancy always turned to the page showing the little dressing table, skirted in lace. On the top it had a cushion for the tall pins they used to hold their dresses together. Nancy ran her hand over the picture as if wishing it would appear right then. "And look, there is even one of those little glass bottles for the sweet smelling oils. Oh mother, this is what I would want in my house if I married Nicholas." Nancy covered her mouth with her hand, letting out a soft laugh, trying to suppress her forwardness at assuming she would marry the Dawson boy.

After a few days of coaxing, William had finally consented to the order of a few items and had added some that he would need for his school.

He sealed the order and gave it to John. "Take this to the ordinary to post when you go with Benoni to work the roads next." It was that time of year when the men assigned to keeping the roads in traveling condition would call together the neighbors to help. For several years Benoni Dawson and John had gone in place of their fathers.

Rebeckah went to the calendar chart. "Let's see—if we place our order now, it could arrive by next spring. We could have a nice get together to share our new room, don't you think, father?" She questioned William, speaking for the children. A smile broke on her lips, at the thought of how her room would look with candles in each window like those she had seen in the catalog.

Chapter 30

March 1768
Lower Seneca Creek

One by one, Rebeckah lifted the papers William had nailed to the wall just inside the door. All twelve pages of months and days had been nailed up, one on top of the other and he gave out instructions not to remove a single page. It was a way he could look back to see what he had written the months before, almost like a diary. Only his was for the farm work he did or needed to do. Dowden's always provided an example at their ordinary. It helped make certain each colonist stopped for the Sabbath on the same day. If you could get to the printer you could buy one, but this year William had decided to make his own.

When he first put it up he had announced to the children that this year was called leap year.

"Come help me find the day that will leap onto the end of the second month page," he had called out to the children. They had gathered around their father to see the small cut out square he stuck to the end of the month of February. For several days afterwards the children had gone to the calendar to see if the new day was still attached onto the last day of the month.

This calendar was to be used by William only. Now that he had hired six new hired hands it was important that he keep the records straight as to what needed working each day.

Rebeckah looked at the first page and could see he had made markings on the January 1768 page.

Word came Lord Townshend died September. Lord North takes his place in Parliament. The news had not disturbed William, she remembered. He said there were rumors telling how the Lord Townshend had stood before parliament so tipsy with drink most to the times, and when he made his speeches before parliament, his talks were full of jostling words that made the men in the chambers laugh for lack of making sense.

She turned the page to February. William's notes for that month related to the plantings.

When she turned to the March 1768 page it read,

Sold to Jacob Waters, of Ann Arundel County, one hundred fifty seven acres for fifty pounds sterling.

Rebeckah had gone with her husband to Ninian Beall's inn to find someone that could take her dower release. Jacob Waters was in some way related to her nephew William Sierra Norris through his new wife, Sarah Waters. Possibly William knew how they were related but she did not.

When Mr. Waters had signed his name, Rebeckah noticed he had put the word millwright after it. On the way home she had asked William what exactly was the job of a millwright.

He had been bothered with her question as she remembered.

Why was it a man knew everything, and when a wife asked about it he became annoyed to have to explain? She had told him she rightly knew where she left her corn and waited all morning for someone inside to make the meal along with a lot of noise going on inside the building. That was about all she knew.

He finally stopped grumbling and told her what she wanted to know. He said millwright had to scout out the best place on the creek to set the big wheel. If the wheel is not set in the water just right then the wheel could not give enough energy to the workings within the mill.

He had turned to her and said so serious like, "Building all those cogs and notches that carry the grain to the grinding stones have to match up just right or it will make your grain either too course or too fine. I've heard the millwrights say they can tell just by the sound of how something is connecting the cogs whether it is working right or not. They have to be good at their work or they do not last long at the job."

She laughed now, remembering what William had said about her stomping her foot because the flour was so coarse. That was true. She hated it when the flour was so coarse she could not get a cake to rise in the side oven and it came out like a rock from the side of the road. And that was because the miller let the cogs move too slowly. William had even told her how flour would sometimes catch fire from the heat of the grinding stones moving too slowly. She remembered once when she got her grain back she had complained about a burnt taste.

Rebeckah agreed they could use another mill. The last few times she had taken the corn to grind she was forced to wait in long lines for half the morning.

Selling the land had been hard for William. But he had explained the options. He told her he had planned on having enough extra land so he could let the worn out tobacco land have a rest. He had intended to use the new cleared land he had sold to Jacob to grow the tobacco on for a year or so and let the old land rest.

All this worry had made him turn restless in his bed at night, just like when he thought they were headed to war over the stamp tax.

"Land is our life Becka" he had told her. "To lose it by whatever means is hard. Building the new room emptied my moneybag almost to the bottom. If I sell the land I will have enough to fill my bag and order the school supplies. I guess you could say it is like war. One side is going to lose no matter how hard you fight."

Rebeckah thought about what else he had said about the roads, which made sense. "Selling to a millwright would mean the roads would be kept up better. The farmers would insist on it. What good is a mill if your wagons break down before you get to it? And you can be pretty certain that a blacksmith shop will be built next to it. What good is a mill if it won't work? Before you know it, a town will have sprung up and we will be like the people living in Fredericktown, all crowded into each others business."

Now Rebeckah worried that if he did not get the school permit and the crops could not grow enough, they could not afford to send the boys off to schooling like William had hoped to do.

If her boys were to become the gentlemen or esquires of their day, they needed more special teachings than what William could give. It had long been a dream of hers to see that one of them became a doctor. There was no one in this part that could cut out the new disease called a cancer tumor or fix a heart. The only doctoring most families could have was just what the mother of the house had on her doctoring shelf. That would mean he should take the tutoring at some eastern school with skills in doctoring.

Rebeckah let out a sigh at the thought. Those dreams would never come true for John. As much as she protested, John still insisted on just tiling the land to gain enough monies to get married. Absolom was sixteen and should have already been sent away to school. Young William loved school probably more than any of the boys, but Absolom should not be denied an education just because another child loved it more. And for Solomon, he was just too unpredictable to know what he would choose to be. Would they have money enough to send them all?

Suddenly, a chilling thought came over Rebeckah and she pulled her shawl tighter. Did William sell the land to Mr. Waters because he was planning on moving? The news of Thomas and Eleanor moving had come with so much grief for Eleanor, but there was nothing she could do about it. When the men in the family got it in their minds that they were moving you simply started packing what little you could take. She knew once the close knit group of men started unraveling the gathering, all of them would decide to go.

She took in a deep breath and looked again at William's calendar, chiding herself that it made no sense to worry what tomorrow would bring. She had heard that somewhere, probably—yes, most likely from the minister's sermon on a time when they went into All Saints Church.

343

Her eyes went back to searching the months ahead. After news of Rachel's little Mary, and then a few weeks later, the news that her brother John's wife had birthed Emelia, it seemed pretty certain there would be little need for spaces to enter a birth. The Lee girls were near upon the "old woman's hex" if not already taken in by it. But then, maybe her sisters Martha and Rachel, they being the youngest, might have one more baby.

She spoke to the calendar as if it was her collaborator with ears to hear. "That was until this morning," she said rubbing her tummy where she had felt the first kick..

As she lifted each sheet she called out the month. "April, May, June, July." Then she put a mark at the first of August and again spoke to the calendar. "Right in the middle of harvest." She let out a soft chuckle.

As Rebeckah turned back the pages to the present month of March she realized it was the seventeenth day. It had been on this day in 1756 that her nephew, Mary Wofford's John Junior, had ridden from the home place where he had been helping with the farming. She still remembered his words "Grandpa looks to be dying. Grandma Mary sent me to get Mr. Butler to write the will, and then I found the Madden boys at home to set the witness names." That was a few months before young William had been born. So much had happened in her life since then, including having three more babies. She looked over at Lucy, her dark eyed baby daughter who had just had her third birthday a few weeks before, and painfully remembered the travail of this last birth.

That evening, Rebeckah swept the last crumbs from the floor, and when she went to hang the broom outside the door she noticed William's candlelight in the barn window. Pulling her shawl from the hook, she called to Nancy to watch the little ones and started to the barn.

William had his back to her when she opened the barn door. She was struck with what a handsome man he was. His white shirt, with the dropped shoulders and full sleeves, revealed even at fifty years old, he maintained a strong back. He stood next to his workbench, sharpening his tools as he did every night since White Horse had gone away. "I thought it be kind of me to forewarn you I will not be fixing the hired hands meal this harvest."

Annoyed at the insolent comment, William began to lecture on why her attitude could not be abided. "This is sheer nonsense, and you know I do not like playing the fool."

His words made Rebeckah laugh. Still William still did not turn to look at her.

"Then you should be hiring a woman to come in," Rebeckah said, with more seriousness.

"Exactly what are you getting at, Rebeckah?" His impatience was growing even greater by now. "Rachel must be with another child. You think your sister cannot breathe a good breath without your help?"

Again she laughed at his reasoning, and went over, putting her arms around his neck like she used to do when they were young. This time it was to whisper in his ear.

"Oh," He said, letting the word fall flat. When he did turn to face her, the tinge of anger had left his voice. "What is this, some kind of jest between yourself and the unborn to make my life through harvest more difficult than it is already?" There was another pause, then, "Tis true, it would be a good thing to have another field hand."

"And if it is a boy will you name him George?" she teased, knowing his feeling toward the King of late.

"If I have to name him George, I would prefer it be a girl."

William blew out the candle and in a rare move, took his wife's hand as they walked back to the cabin.

For that night all was well on the *William and John.*

By late March the farm was coming alive. The maple trees had to be tapped for the precious sap that would sweeten their Journey cakes next winter, and if the British placed another tax on sugar, the maple syrup would be the sweetness for Rebeckah's recipes. So it was with stern instructions that William sent the boys to do the tapping and placing the spout in place. "Find the right spot to make your hole. We cannot afford to lose any of the drippings."

This year for the first time, Solomon had the job of placing the bucket in the proper place to catch every drop of syrup. Tomorrow they would return with the sled to collect the buckets.

By month's end Rebeckah and Nancy rushed their regular chores in anticipation of the gathering that evening when the neighbors would come to help stir the big cauldrons of boiling syrup to a beautiful brown color. There was much honor in the stirring, and if you let the pot scorch, you were looked upon as a careless person, unworthy of the honor again next year.

As the night came around the farm, Nancy watched the road, hoping the Dawsons would come. Her father had said the youngsters, as he called them, could have a dance on the barn floor and had even sent John and Absolom to sweep the hay away and position the torches to light the space. It would be Nancy's first dance since she and Absolom were allowed to pick up the steps from Verlinder Dawson. Verlinder knew all the steps. She had taken lessons from one of the traveling teachers that had come house to house. Nancy had caught Absolom grinning each time Verlinder took his hand and stepped off the dance at her teaching, but he would never admit to liking her. Even though Nancy and Absolom did not always get along in a friendly manner they had been forced to practice together at home as Rebeckah hummed out the tune.

As the first wagon lumbered into their pathway, Nancy could feel her heart begin to race. It was the Dawson's wagon. Nickolas jumped from the wagon, and his eyes caught sight of Nancy. Try as she might, she could not keep the smile from her lips. In an awkward sort of way, he gave a greeting and walked past her to talk to Absolom. As the evening wore on the Allnutts and several more wagons had pulled in. The dance started when John and Benoni took up their juice harp and violin. Nancy all but forgot her steps when it was time to change partners, and Nicholas grabbed her hand in his and put the other hand on her waist. She felt she could live a lifetime remembering the joy of this moment.

After they had gone away Nancy sat in the dark looking at the stars, remembering how it felt to dance with the boy she hoped to someday marry.

Chapter 31

May 1768
Lower Seneca Creek

His back aching from bending over too long, William reached up for the corner of his workbench and slowly pulled himself up, a task that seemed more difficult the last year or so. But getting the farm work done meant there was no getting around a few aches and pains. Today it had been the job of repairing his old stone sled. This morning he had sawed hardwood runners and fastened them with pegs. If the runners were cracked it was a sure wager they would split under the heavy load. He remembered the first time he had seen one of these sleds named for hauling the heavy stones from the fields. He was courting Rebeckah, and James Lee showed him how to build one. Without the sled, William could never have carried the stones from the fields to build this barn.

It had been over a week since the threat of frostbite on the new growth, and this morning the boys had gone out to the field to remove the hay from the new plants of tobacco.

William loaded his shovels onto the sled and headed for the field. There was a certain pleasure a farmer took each spring as he stood on his land and surveyed what could be the promise of a good crop. The sight of his land, cleared almost to the top of the hill and all the way to the bottom where the white oak stood on one side, and where the twisted tree trunk stood on the other boundary, made him proud. At the last count he figured there were close to seventeen hundred acres left after his sale to Jacob Waters.

He and the family had cleared every acre that he intended to clear, leaving the forest line untouched for now. It was needed to break the winds and keep the hillside from coming down on them. His apple tree orchard had survived the years and was free of worms, as rightly as he could tell. Before coming to the colonies he never knew the importance of growing apples. Now if someone leased a piece of land, it was put in the contract that the man leasing was required to plant a hundred apple trees and fence it in. Without the apple cider a family could die of thirst.

There were six new field hands hired for this season and he hoped to put more to work. This left him free to do what he had intended to do when he first came to the colonies.

William no longer felt the tinge of pain at the thought of selling the portion of land to Jacob Waters. There was hope in sight. Building the new room to begin his school had made the sale necessary, but when his classroom was full, the exchange would be worth it. He turned around to look again at his newly finished room. That reminded him—he needed to order a school bell so it would be ready when he acquired the permission to hold classes.

He had hoped the province would sponsor a school, as had been voted on by the assembly, but that was taking too long to set up. There were so many children on all sides of his road that needed book learning if they were ever to have a chance at being more than a dirt digger. He did not speak that to the other farmers, but there were times he felt it after a crop failed or when the King's men unfairly fixed the prices. He knew to have a chance in life the children had to learn to read and write and do the numbers. And the only way that could happen was if he became a schoolmaster to these parts. This meant finding the time to go to Fredericktown to meet first with the Reverend Bacon, and then with the trustees of All Saints Church.

The Reverend Thomas Bacon was the authority on colonial education. William felt it would help if he could explain to Reverend Bacon that he had been hired to teach with their late church teacher, William Norris. Although, the fact that it had been twenty years since William had picked up a pointer to teach a lesson gave concern. The reason was the same each year, too many weeds to hoe or a barn to build or sows to wean but never time to serve as teacher.

The rumor of the reverend's poor health, William remembered, had been on everyone's mind when he and Thomas Dawson had ridden together to the warehouse to pick up seeds for planting. The illness had come over him while spending the years in the damp port of Annapolis. He had been there for several years setting to paper the important and now famous rules between church and state. And this illness appeared to have all but taken away his breath.

A new thought surfaced. Who would take up the Bible in the pulpit for Thomas Bacon? Would the new minister be favorable to educating the children as Reverend Bacon had been? If not, where did that leave the schooling?

He turned to look back to his cabin. What a big room they had to accommodate the school. He picked up his shovel and began digging a row of holes for planting. For now, he had to work the farm or there would be no monies to open a school, even with approval.

The warm sunshine filled the new room as Rebeckah put the last of the quilting tools in the trunk. As she closed the lid, the sound echoed in the big room that had only the quilting frame sitting in front of the fireplace at one end and the big windows letting in all the light of the outdoors. William had said the new furniture would be here by the end of May, and when she checked the calendar this morning it had said it was the twenty first of May. Every sound on the road made them all run to the door to see if a rider was coming to tell them their order was waiting at the docks. She knew when William got permission to open a school this room would be his room. But until then she could enjoy her new furniture placed as a sitting room. And there would be times when school was in recess when she could say it was her room. But for now, it made a good quilting room.

Prudence was the only one that had been able to attend the quilting this week. A true bond had developed between the two quilters. Who would have ventured to guess that the broken wheel could bring so much pleasure? It was almost like they had been friends for life. There was never a mean word coming from Prudence's lips, even when life was hard. And now, she had a lot to worry about. Poor Henry could barely lift a bucket of water, much less hang the crop of heavy tobacco leaves on the barn hooks. Rebeckah wondered what would happen to them.

From somewhere within her brain an idea began to form, and it seemed like the solution to all their problems. If William built a cabin near their house, like he had done for the Sittlers, then Henry could help with some of the lighter chores like the kitchen garden. It was easier work, with no heavy lifting to hurt the bulge in his side. And this would give William more time to oversee the farm hands. Rebeckah sat down on the trunk lid letting the idea spin around in her head. Prudence could even cook at harvest time when the baby was born. She knew William well enough to know he would do whatever it took to keep the older couple from doing without. If they were helping with the chores it would not hurt their pride to receive favors once in awhile. Besides, William liked Henry's talk of an evening.

It was all Rebeckah could do to keep from running to the field to tell William of her idea. But knowing her husband as she did, she knew the idea had better wait for him at the cabin.

But before William came, Thomas Dawson had ridden into their road and on into the fields.

"I just came across a wagon coming from Fredericktown and they had news of Reverend Bacon taking a turn for the worse. I remembered you had the need to talk with him about the school. If you are still thinking it necessary, you should go today."

"I was afraid I was waiting too long to see him," William said as he stopped to wipe the sweat from his brow with his sleeve. "Without the Reverend's voice on the matter I am afraid I cannot secure an audience with the trustees of the church, and I cannot afford to school without their support."

The men knew the Reverend was held with such high respect from Lord Baltimore that a lot he had accomplished was most likely from that relationship. But still, he had done more than most ministers and teachers. Somehow he had even been allowed to do the unthinkable task of approaching the slave owners about schooling their slave children. Now, many of them could read and write their numbers. Reverend Bacon always went beyond the call of duty.

"Who do you suppose Lord Baltimore will assign to the pulpit?" William asked.

"I can only speculate to that, but if rumors hold any bearing, I've heard talk that a gentleman schooled at Oxford by the name of Bennett Allen is in line for a big church. All Saints is the wealthiest Church in the Province, so I feel these rumors have merit. Besides, this man is said to be a relation, or maybe it was friend, to Lord Baltimore. These may be old rumors from about two years ago," Thomas explained.

"I remember it was indeed about two years ago, like you said, that I heard Lord Baltimore had instructed Walter Dulaney and his brother to introduce a man with exceptional schooling from Oxford to the people in hopes of finding a church for him," William said.

"According to the man that I was talking to, this Mr. Allen had hoped for a large church but had to settle for the very small one on the coast someplace. It did not take long for him to start complaining about how underpaid he was and how degrading to him it was, considering his advanced education. Then I found out he had bragged about coming to the colonies to seek his wealth," Thomas said.

"Has anyone heard this fellow deliver his educated sermon?" William asked.

"According to the man, he is more famous for his over drinking than his sermons."

"Oh, let us hope he does not come to All Saints. He could ruin that fine church in no time." William shook his head as he said it.

Thomas brought up a point of worry. "You know how much the people of Fredericktown loved the elder Dulaney before he died. If his sons bring a recommendation to them they probably will seriously consider the proposal."

"Yes, and the Dulaneys are not about to ruffle the feathers of the Lord Baltimore—you know that."

"It sounds like this would be an unfortunate turn if All Saints Church were to be the next step up for this Mr. Allen."

350

After Thomas left, William went inside to give the news to Rebeckah and discuss his need to try once again to speak to Reverend Bacon. "Assuming the news is current on Reverend Bacon's health, and the rumors are true, I had better go now before this new upstart takes over. If I could get Reverend Bacon's approval, then the trustees would listen to my application as well. And the use of William Norris's name as the teacher in whose school I taught surely would offer a good recommendation."

Rebeckah had been silent as he talked, until the mention of William Norris. She stood up and pointed her finger at him, something that was so uncharacteristic of her. "You can stand on your own merits, William. There is no need to give his name along with yours. "

William looked puzzled as to what might have caused his wife to become so caustic. "William Norris was one of the best, I guess you know."

Rebeckah caught her breath. She quickly changed the subject away from the schoolmaster to their new room. "You have the room to teach the children, and your order of hornbooks should be arriving within the month."

William's mind was still trying to figure out why she had taken such a strong position against his mention of William Norris. He returned to his thoughts of how he could convince Reverend Bacon's wife to allow him to have a few words with him. He reached over and forked a piece of meat from the skillet hanging over the fire. "I will take the horse. John will stay here this time to help you. If you would like to make some of your special gift foods I could take them to the reverend's wife."

William went outside to finish the chores and stopped at the gate to gather his thoughts. Tonight the blaze of the orange sunset was more brilliant than he ever remembered. It spoke of strength.

He felt Rebeckah's hand on his arm.

After a time she broke the silence. "Some day you will be the better schoolmaster, William," she said softly.

He reached out and pulled her hand to his, his eyes never leaving the slowly fading light.

"You are a good woman, Becka."

Chapter 32

May 24, 1768
Fredericktown

The big clock on the Courthouse struck the seventh bell as William reined his horse through the streets. He could see the crowds already gathering around the church and home of the Reverend Thomas Bacon. In the small cemetery behind the church, the gravediggers had begun throwing the fresh dirt from a hole that would be the Reverend's grave.

As William neared the church his thoughts went back to the events of the day before. He reflected on the almost missed opportunity of yesterday and his mind recited the old adage, *Wait not till the morrow what tasks thy hand finds today.*

Upon hearing how gravely ill the minister was, he had gone to the Reverend's home in the middle of the afternoon and was instructed by those in line that he was to sign the doorkeeper's guest book to register his respects. When he stepped to the front door, she asked him to give his name and title. William had told her he was a teacher as well as a landowner and handed her the food offering Rebeckah had made for him to bring.

Now he was convinced it had been the hand of God's intervention that he was allowed in. No sooner had he taken his place at the back of the line, than the doorkeeper had come out and called his name. He was told the ailing minister wished to speak with him.

Reverend Bacon had been very weak, and his breathing shallow. But from somewhere within, a fire had still burned deep in his soul for the education of children. He gave William his notes, made some weeks before, and asked him to read them back to him. The old gentlemen closed his eyes and listened as William read the notes, nodding his head each time a new point was read. When William finished the reading, the reverend opened his eyes and asked what he thought of the notes and if anything needed to be added. William respectfully gave confirmation that he had long ascribed to the reverend's ideas and even spoke of some new thoughts. The conversation was limited due to the difficulty in the elderly man's breathing, and soon a doctor appeared at the door to insist the Reverend should rest. There had been no time to ask for a recommendation before the trustees, but it no longer mattered. He had been in the presence of a great mind and that sufficed the trip.

William had slept leaned up against a tree near Carroll Creek, as did many of those waiting at the parsonage yesterday. And before daylight someone across the creek had awakened them by calling out that the Reverend Thomas Bacon had died.

He had decided to wait until after the funeral to return home. By this afternoon word should have reached the brothers-in-law about the reverend's death and they would be making their way to Fredericktown. He would attend to business as long as the shops stayed open. After that, he would wait for the family with their own family news.

William dismounted his horse and looped the reins over a branch on the tree. He made his way through the gathering, hoping to hear news of the funeral time. Halfway through the crowd he began to realize what was on everyone's mind. It had to do with the Governor's choice as to who would fill the now vacant pulpit. Everyone knew it was just a formality to say the Governor would announce the person. The Lord Baltimore was the one who chose whom he wanted, and then he gave the name to the Governor to announce. This morning the speculation was that it was the person Lord Baltimore had assigned to St. Anne's Church. It was the same one Thomas had told him about just two days ago.

One man in the crowd even confessed to a secret lottery, set up to wager on the selection. The fact that the Lordship had told the Dulaney brothers to introduce the Mr. Allen fittingly added some credence to the probability as to his selection. To feed the rumors, someone came running into the crowd telling of seeing just this morning two men with the looks and age of the Dulaneys. They said they were carrying papers in hand going into the church vestry. It was all very secretive.

This news enraged the crowd. How could they put someone like Mr. Allen at the heart of the wealthiest and largest church in the province? A man standing on the left of William was discussing the known fact that the man had a heavy drinking problem.

"He even goes as far as to throw violent temper fits because they were not paying him enough to keep a good drink in his place," one man said.

As William walked farther into the group, yet another rumor had been started. This one accused Mr. Allen of lying about attending classes at Oxford. William stood for a moment to hear the reply from a man that evidently lived in the eastern part of the province. "This I know, education or not, this imposter knows the power of the newspapers. He called himself by the pen name of *A Bystander* and used the newspapers to attack those that disagreed with him. His tyrants were long and became a tit for tat for those that read the outbursts."

William shook his head at the ranting. But when he heard an even more scandalous account of how this Mr. Allen was acting, he turned to speak directly to the accuser, "Surely this is not true."

"Oh, it is for a fact. I live near the house where he sleeps. This scoundrel has taken his own sister to be his mistress. My neighbor saw him through the window curtains carrying on like a man in love. He said it was a most shocking thing to witness." The man telling the story turned again to speak to another.

William sickened at the vicious talk spoken just outside the door where such a fine man of God lay in his coffin. How could this moment become something like the loose talk around the tavern bar?

Late that day when the Town Crier stood on the Courthouse Square to cry the news, William was there. Strangely, what usually held the news from around the province, on this day held only the grievous words no one had wanted to hear.

> *Hear ye, hear ye, this day 24 of May God save King George the third. Today a most solemn day in our heart with news of our beloved Reverend Thomas Bacon has been taken from among us by death.. His funeral set at the strike of High Noon at the Church of All Saints on the morrow.*

William had again been forced to sleep under a tree near the tavern, and counted his blessings to even finding a tree to lean against, considering the swarming crowd. When the sun hit his eyes, he folded his saddle blanket and went to the creek to wash his face. Not that the muddy creek water would do anything for cleanliness, but it was cooling. He could feel his wig beginning to slide to one side and decided to find a window reflection to try to make the adjustment. There was nothing so embarrassing as to lose your wig in the time of a public moment. He needed Rebeckah here to help him.

After securing the wig as best he could, he went in search for one of the vendors that had set up yesterday shortly after the death announcement. The spirit of enterprise was alive and well in this crowded town and no one was convinced it was to aid the grieving parish. They knew a good moneymaker and the time to advance it.

One by one, William met up with John Wofford, then Thomas Thrasher and James and Robert Lee. Alexander Grant was almost too late to hear the eulogy as he had been in the fields and had not heard of the death until late last evening when Will Sierra had come by to tell him Richard Willis was getting even weaker.

"I am surprised John Hughes has not come. He must be ailing as well, or he would have not missed the rumor mill surrounding the selection of the new minister," William speculated. The men, sitting on the ground at the courthouse yard, all laughed. Knowing John as they did, they knew by now he would have been in a fight over something. By the time they made their way to the church grounds most of the men had finished telling what their wives had told them to share about the family. If enough news of family came back with them, it made for a happy homecoming. Other than that, no one mentioned the problems with the parliament or even the expected prices of the crops that year. Nothing outside the local story seemed to interest them on this day.

The crowd overflowed into the street during the funeral. No sooner had the service ended, and the body put in the ground, did the rumors begin all over again. A new one circulating seemed to be an answer to the problem though. If all went as planned by the vestry, they might have found an answer to saving All Saints Church from this prestige hungry Mr. Allen.

It was reported a man identified as vestryman, George Murdock, had sent a letter with signed petitions to the Governor, laying out the plan to divide the large parish. This would take away the wealth from the larger church and divide into two smaller churches, thus taking away the interest of Mr. Allen as a way to fill his pockets.

No sooner was that rumor cheered than a more disturbing rumor began burning. Someone had seen a man in a fine suit of satin being unloaded from a new two-seated buggy in front of a house on the next street over from the church. A man coming to this part of the country in a fine buggy had to be important, or in this case, someone thinking he was that important.

After awhile William had heard enough and decided to ride along with Robert Lee on the way home. The roads had not held up to all the added travel the last few days, and now deep ruts made the travel slow and dangerous. A horse could stumble and break a leg before you could correct its path. For a time they talked about the funeral but shortly got around to talking about the planting season.

When William mentioned to Robert that his sister was again with child, Robert looked at William. Then in an almost blunt tone asked, "William are you good to Rebeckah?"

William was incensed. "Robert, you have the gall to ask such a question. You have seen how I treat her. She is a good wife. I have no reason to be quarrelsome. It is insulting you would question me."

Robert just shrugged his shoulders, "Father once asked."

Later, after turning from the road near Robert's place, he thought about the question and wondered why father Lee had posed that question to his son. James Lee was long dead leaving the answer unattended.

Once William reached home his need to make up for lost time in the fields put Roberts comments in the back of his mind. In fact, it was not until he saw Thomas Dawson with his wife Elizabeth riding into his path one afternoon late that he even thought again about the trip to Fredericktown the week before.

At first, William surmised they had come to hear details of the funeral, but it turned out in fact, Thomas and his son Benoni had been in Fredericktown in time to hear the eulogy but left before the burial.

"I just got back home this afternoon from going to the warehouse at Georgetown. I told Elizabeth she could visit with Rebeckah while I filled you in on what happened a few days later after the funeral," Thomas said with a sort of chuckle to his words.

The men waited for Elizabeth to climb over the side of the wagon and go in to see Rebeckah before they began to talk.

"I can only surmise what it concerns. I've never heard so many vicious rumors as were burning through the crowd," William admitted.

"I heard them too. Rather rank in their nature, I would say. Had I not heard them for myself I would not have believed what happened afterwards. And I'm sorry to say most of the rumors were spoken with truth. It is a disgrace to All Saints integrity. According of all the men today, what happened afterwards was so outrageous it could only have been at the hands of a half-mad man."

The story was as black as the rumors that had fed it. The news of the vestryman trying to see to it that the parish could be divided was true and had fallen on Bennett Allen's ears. He was about to be dismissed before he was confirmed and wasted no time in seeing to the confirmation.

"Mr. Allen had gone to the church and found the doors locked. He had gotten hold of the keys, some said from sweet-talking the serving maid. Then he let himself in and bolted the inside lock so no one could come to pull him out. The he preformed everything in the book of confirmation to make him the minister."

"Thomas, are you telling me this Mr. Allen read all the lessons and scriptures to himself? If I remember correctly there are thirty-nine items at least," William said in amazement.

"He was most wise to the rules of the church that says that once he was confirmed as minister, the Governor or the people had no power to rid the pulpit of his person."

"And no one was in the pews?" William asked.

"Not one soul."

"How did they know he said the vows? How do they know he did not lie?" William asked.

"The vestrymen had been called when it was discovered the keys were missing, and they went to the church. As they banged on the door they could hear Mr. Allen reciting the vows loudly so as to be heard by those at the door," Thomas explained.

"It sounds like this man has misused his fine education, if he indeed had one, to think up ways to get what he wants," William admitted.

"Oh, that is not the end of the melee," Thomas said, as he went on to tell the story. "After his confirmation was complete, this insidious man went to the tavern and bragged about it to the locals. They said after the members heard this, they had gathered at the church and padlocked the door and kept the key on their person to make sure this thief could not again gain access. When he came again and found it locked they said you could hear Mr. Allen yelling profanities all down the street."

William shook his head in disbelief. "And to think, Reverend Bacon so wisely issued a paper against that kind of talk sometime back. What a slap in the face to the memory of such a fine minister."

"He would not be outdone. Mr. Allen was at the church on Sunday by four in the morning. He found the ladder used by the workmen when doing roof repairs and climbed into the high church window. You know the little one over by the organ? When the parishioners arrived, they discovered he was already standing at the pulpit. Several of the vestrymen tried in vain to pull him out." Thomas laughed, "Don't suppose his wig looked real good by that time."

The men laughed at the thought of this pompous fellow with his wig half pulled off.

William started to say something but Thomas held his hand up. "Let me finish. Mr. Allen put a gun to the head of the lead parishioner."

"He what? Are you serious?"

"Yes, I'm telling it like they told me at the warehouse. And one man there had seen it all happen in person."

"Was anyone injured?"

"Only Bennett Allen's reputation, I guess. The rest of the congregation backed off and he released the man. It seems some of the congregation managed to climb up to the windows and began throwing rocks at Allen. I think he must have been in fear of his own life by then, minister or no minister. They said he ran from the building, yelling threats to all involved, including the Dulaney brothers."

"You mean he is gone for good?" William asked.

"Oh, he is gone, but not for the good. Under the bylaws of the church they will still have to give him pay until he dies, I suppose. He was confirmed after all. There are no provisions in the bylaws that say how many or if any have to hear the confirmation. The Governor has no more power over it."

It was getting dark and Thomas called for Elizabeth to come. He turned back to tell William, in hushed voice, so not to disturb the women. "We better be getting back home, there has been another sighting of a wildcat roaming the barns and fields the last week."

After they left, William went to the barn to finish the chores. Rebeckah found him there.

"William, I have been thinking since it is only two months when the baby arrives and you will be so bothered by the harvest, maybe we could bring Prudence and Henry up to help out."

He agreed that would be a good idea.

"It is too bad we don't have a small cabin close by that they could bed down in when you need them. It sure would be comforting to me when you are away." Rebeckah had planted the first of her plan, hoping William would pick up on it and decide to build a permanent cabin for them. She purposely went over and picked up her barn broom and began to sweep around the left over lumber William had instructed the carpenters to stack in the barn to keep it dry. She let a short piece fall from the stack. "Oh, no, if I have to sweep around this left over lumber for the rest of my life, I'm going to get hurt. You'll probably come home some night and find me flattened out under it all."

William said nothing but just shook his head and gave what sounded like the beginning of a laugh. Then he bought into the effort. "You would like for me to build a cabin for Prudence and Henry?" Still he did not commit, again shaking his head at her attempts.

"I was just thinking how that big bulge on Henry's side is so much worse and he can't load the heavy tobacco crop from his field now. They will starve to death without monies. Poor Prudence is beside herself with worry," Rebeckah lamented.

"True, that bulge is big," William said, baiting her along to see what further ideas she had devised.

"He would be good working the kitchen garden and some small chores. And it would be no problem for Prudence to see to the harvest meals."

"And what do Prudence and Henry think of this idea, Becka?"

Rebeckah grinned. She knew he was onto her plan. "They like it, William, they really like it—well Prudence does, I can't say we have told Henry yet. But you know if Prudence likes it then Henry will think it is good."

"Hum," was all William said, and went back to his work.

For now, William had to once again put away the dreams of being a schoolmaster, even though the meeting with the Reverend Bacon had made his resolve even greater. Someday he would find a way to teach.

The furniture finally came from London, and Prudence came to help put up new curtains. They spent long hours braiding a bright colored rug, like the one described in the catalog, to go in front of the fireplace. The new high back chair would be William's and she would keep the Betty Lamp hung to the back so he could read whenever he desired. Next to the tall windows she placed the rocking chair that her father had made. Now when the baby came she could sit there to nurse and be able to look into her beautiful hills.

Rebeckah marveled at what a good life she had. She had picked up the pen to write letters to all of the family, telling them about the new room and the good things happening to her. There was even a suggestion she now had the room to put the sleeping pallets out to have them all come for a Christmas celebration. It was something she had missed since coming from her parent's place. She remembered the time when everyone from neighboring farms would go from house to house to see the big bonfires burning in celebration of the Christ Child's birth.

And true to Rebeckah's request, William and his sons had spent the extra hours at the end of each day putting the logs in place for the little cabin just down the path from their own home. At the end of one long day as he looked at the nearly completed cabin, he remembered the question Robert had asked. He quietly muttered under his breath, yes, Father Lee, I am good to your daughter.

Everyone cheered as Henry's old wagon lumbered up the path with the first load of plunder. By nightfall, Henry and Prudence would be moved into their new cabin. Rebeckah couldn't say it was better than the old cabin, not to Prudence and Henry, but in her thinking it was. It had been heavily chinked to make sure there were no cold drafts and the roof would not leak. That was better than the old cabin. But it was not home to them—yet. Maybe after a few years they would think of it as being home. But today, they were moving, although willingly, from the birthplace of their son and grandson. Maybe the hardest of all to leave behind were the stone marked graves of their son and grandson lying next to the mother.

Rebeckah's children had already begun to think of them as the grandparents they no longer had. Even John, in his near grown up ways, would lean against the fence and talk to Henry over some thought he had.

Life could not have been better now, Rebeckah thought. Well, maybe if she could see Rachel more often. Who knows, she had thought, another plan beginning to surface, maybe Henry and Prudence would go with her to see Rachel this autumn after the baby was born.

In August Rebeckah gave birth to a baby girl. It had gone well. Maybe it was her state of mind that gave her such an easy birth. "All is well," she had written in the announcement letter to Rachel. "All is well."

Chapter 33

Spring 1769
Dowden's Ordinary

The horse lot at Dowden's ordinary was unusually crowded this morning when William rode in. That could mean one of two things had happened. There had been a very important bit of news brought by a traveler or the newspapers from the upper part of the colonies had been delivered.

Everyone was up in arms again after parliament had found another way to press the colonists for more monies. And the newspaper from Boston spared no ink in complaining about it.

William gave his horse a swat and handed the stable boy a coin to throw a handful of food into the trough. The ordinary was filled with smoke, even at this early hour. He spotted the stack of newspapers sitting on the table. Dropping a coin into the jug, he picked up a paper. He looked around the room to see if any of the family had arrived for their meeting. When he did not see anyone he looked for a chair in which to sit and read until they arrived.

The room was shoulder to shoulder, back to back of men with newspapers pulled to their faces. Finally a man got up and William quickly claimed the chair.

The headlines read *British Customs Officials Fear Reprisals*. It had all started last year when the British Custom Officials had swarmed the docks in Boston, claiming they had proof that John Hancock was bringing in a ship with unregistered merchandise on the invoice. The officials had climbed onto the ship and pulled the captain off and then seized the fine looking sloop called *Liberty*. John Hancock was the richest shipper in the colonies, and if the custom officials could show he was smuggling it was their belief they would make an example of how powerful they were by taking it over.

This did not sit well with the people of Boston, and soon a young bullish crowd began to go down the streets yelling that they were there to stop this from happening. It did not take long for the custom officials to hear the warning. Fearing the outcome of this anger, they immediately wrote to parliament and told them if they were to do the job, parliament needed to send over a large force of soldiers for their protection. But before the soldiers could arrive, the officials had run for their lives, taking a boat to a safe island off the New England coastline.

Now, as William read the paper, it was not uncommon to hear someone around him yell out in support of a story. The man at William's side turned to him and pointed to a paragraph. "It says here one of George Washington's friends had come into the newspaper office and showed them a letter he had received from Washington stating he believes if the British do not back down on the trade limitations we will be forced to take up arms against the King." The man pulled off the spectacles sitting on the bridge of his nose and turned to look William in the face. "That is strong talk. Washington is a man of his words, and if he goes so far as to write his friend of the concern, then he believes it."

Before William could comment, Alexander Grant tapped him on the shoulder. "We are all here, as many as could come, and I'd like to make quick work of this meeting. Richard Willis is not any better, and I need to go there as soon as our meeting is over."

William folded the paper, putting it under his arm and started to the table that Alexander had claimed for their meeting.

"I talked to Will Sierra yesterday and he said it is about all he can do now to keep his mother's work done since Richard has gotten so bad. He's been called to sit on the grand jury, you know. And I'm thinking he is still a sheriff. He was, the last I heard," Alexander explained.

"You are right, it is only the family thing to do—offering help to Elizabeth, I mean. She has had her share nursing sick husbands."

The men set a schedule as to who would go to the Willis farm. Once that was attended to, they then moved on to other items they found urgent.

"Gentlemen, remember, do not drink any of that tea stuff coming from England," a man yelled out from another table. "We have to stop 'em taxing us somehow." With that reminder the men in the room cheered for the rebellion.

Everyone laughed and went back to exchanging the family news.

"Guess some of you have heard the news relating to James Jr." This kind of talk would be considered gossip by some, but the men refused to label it as such. To them it was staying informed. Alexander went on to relate something James Jr. probably would just as soon not be talked about, and maybe this is why he had chosen to stay away this day. "Seems James's boy, Richard, has bound himself to trouble again," Alexander told the group. "James had to go pay up bail to get him out for assaulting the person John Michel Wydemir."

"How many times now has he been carried to the judge?" Thrasher asked. The men agreed he did seem to take on a portion of the devil from somewhere.

Before the end of the meeting it was reported that Ninian Beall had again snatched up more of the good farming land next to his tavern. "He is as greedy as John Seager, grabbing up the land," William commented.

"Now wait a minute," John said, "I've got as much right as the rest of you. I just have my pocket book ready sooner than you." The men all laughed at his defense, which was true.

"Speaking of land sales, guess you know my sister Anne's husband has given a small part of their *Indian Fields* land to John Jr. It's just like John Hughes not to share much though—even with their own boy." Robert's comment made the men laugh again, knowing full well how true it was also.

A loud commotion caused the men to look around to see what was happening as the room began to fill up with travelers. "Must have been something funny," Alexander said after the men in the other corner had settled down and were patting each other on their backs.

William knocked the tobacco out of his pipe and stood up. "Well, gentlemen, if that is all the meeting we need to do for now, I think I will depart this little bit of heaven for my road home. These crowds are not for me."

The rest of the men, not waiting to be swarmed by the midday meal rush, took one last swig of their cider, then left as well.

As William was about to mount his horse he noticed a man coming into the horse pen with a wagon full of barrels. He tipped his hat to him, feeling he had seen him someplace before.

"Didn't I see you at the tavern in Fredericktown a few years back?"

"Ja, I stop there often on my way to the warehouses."

"The night I refer to, there was talk of the last war and the young boy fell from his chair at the memory," William said, as he put out his hand and introduced himself. "As best I can remember, you lived close to the Pennsylvania line."

"Ja, I'm Jacob Brumbaugh, and I remember sharing words with you. Seems a long time past."

William pointed to Brumbaugh's wagon, "Are you coming from the port."

"Ja, I am there to fetch supplies."

"You didn't happen to hear words of the King's business with the colonies, did you?"

"I saw at least ten crates sitting on the ship. No one was unloading them," Brumbaugh said. "I heard someone say the dock hands had been given word that a ban was being enforced."

"There must have been tea in the crates. I'm surprised the King's men have not started making a stink over our lack of love for the stuff now with the high taxes," William said.

363

"Ja, and that is not the only ban we have been forced into. My wife informed me the women up where we live have gathered together to refuse the use of any materials but their own rough homespun for the clothing. It is their way of voicing against the linen and lace tax," Jacob said.

"The new Lord North may have met his match when the women decide to march onto the ship to protest," William said, both men laughing at the possibility.

As William turned his horse toward the gate, he remembered, "I almost forgot. You live up by the Mason-Dixon Line. Did they get the line finished?"

"Ja, it is finished. Come visit. The wife keeps telling me we should set up the beds for the people to stay when they come to see our fine looking border stones they brought from England."

Once outside the gate, William let the horse choose a soft trot, giving his mind time to think. There were so many places in the new land he had yet to see. It had been twenty some odd years and he had not traveled over sixty miles away from the *William and John.* The work consumed his last breath. Even now with Henry helping out full time there was no time for pleasure making. The thought of Brumbaugh's invitation had made him think how good it would feel to turn his horse toward the Pennsylvania border, set with the new stones sent from England.

By the end of May, William had more upsetting concerns than just the lack of tea for his Sunday meal. This morning he had come in to complain about seeing two more wagons with milk cows tied to the back on their way to Birdwhistle's land.

Rebeckah listened to him rant on while she sat quietly in the rocker nursing little Becka, with an eye on five year old Lucy who was still at the table messing with her porridge.

"If one more family moves in around me, I think I will pack our wagons and move. I do not like being crowded. Thomas Birdwhistle surely has little land left to raise a crop." William's tirade came to an end when his baby daughter turned her head from nursing to grin at her father, showing off the beginnings of two new teeth. She always smiled when William came near, and he had to admit this last baby was the happiest child they had brought into the world.

William went to the window to see if he could see the wagons any longer. "I'll miss the Birdwhistles," he said. "Do you remember if they were living here when we moved to this cabin? Must have been, but strangely I cannot recall." The family in question lived just down the road a few miles. Over the last few years Thomas Birdwhistle had sold off acre by acre. When the William Hawker family had bought land during that first selling, it was shortly after Rebeckah's father had died and they were just too busy to pay a sociable visit. It was when William's horse had gotten loose and William Hawker had come to inquire if the one he had found belonged to the Littlefields that they became friends. Now the last year or so they had enjoyed riding over to see them on cold winter days when no work could be done. For the most part they had children that matched the ages of their own offspring and it made for a most enjoyable outing.

John had even taken a liking to William and Susannah's oldest daughter. That was after his heartbreak over the girl visiting the Dawsons. She had mysteriously left one day without as much as a wave good-bye. But the new romance with the Hawker daughter was also destined to doom when he found out she was more interested in a boy that had come to help with the Hawker's crops by the name of Zephaniah Swann. William and Rebeckah and the children had just last year attended the wedding gathering, inspite of John's hurt feelings. And now she was almost due to give the new husband a baby. Rebeckah had even gone over to help Susannah make the birthing quilt.

Whenever William complained about more new families moving in, Rebeckah often reminded him it was not always bad news.

Now again, William repeated, "We will miss the Birdwhistles." He stood at the window for a time, then turned around to address his wife with a serious thought. "I risked my life coming over the ocean to see the new world and have not left this side of the colony. Maybe it is time to move on and see what lies out there."

"William, don't jest that way," Rebeckah said, in no mood for that kind of talk. As she spoke, the pain of watching Thomas Betterton's wagon roll onto the ferry was still very real. Eleanor had waved her white shoulder scarf as a way to be seen until the ferry had crossed the Potomac onto the Virginia land and southward. And then they were gone for good.

The summer wore on. With each load of hay William harvested, he thanked the good Lord for sending Henry to them. The poor old man struggled to keep up with the younger workers in the field, but it did not matter to William if he had slowed down. To have Henry there at the end of the day, as they leaned against the fence to talk about how the crops looked, was enough.

Henry and Prudence had spared William the task of taking Rebeckah and the children to see Rachel and her family. That alone made William doubly thankful. The only regret was that it was Rebeckah's idea to move them close by, and she did not let an opportunity go by without reminding him.

A storm looked to be brewing over the mountains, and William had come in earlier than usual. Today he had been working in the tobacco field, checking each plant for any bug that might cut at the roots before he could send the men into the field with their blades. As he gathered his tools he noticed a cloud of dust coming his way. Sunset in late August began to sink faster now, and with the approaching storm it was hard to see who was coming. By the voice of the man yelling, he knew it was Robert Lee. "I've been to the ordinary today and they gave me this letter for you. Looks to be important, coming from your old Salisbury home."

William took the letter from Robert and examined the water spots on the paper. Unlike most letters in the colonies, this one was enclosed in the fine linen envelope like those he remembered seeing on his grandfather's desk. The postmark said *Salisbury the County of Southton Miller.*

He pulled the seal from the edge and read the words written in big bold letters.

This is to inform you an Attorney of Law has been hired to settle the estate of your late father. Expect his arrival when suitable passage can be arranged.

The letter carried no name or who to expect. William could only surmise that it was some lawyer being sent from his birthplace.

Rebeckah had come from the house when she heard her brother's voice, and William handed her the letter and said, "Seems strange they would come all the way over to the colonies to settle something like this when a letter would have sufficed."

Robert talked awhile about the letter and the crops, all the while eyeing the building storm. As he was leaving, he said something that caught William and Rebeckah as much by surprise as receiving the letter he had brought. "I've given the word to Samuel Hocker that he can buy *Rich Valley.* I'll be moving back to land Richard Watts deeded to Elizabeth and me as our marriage consideration."

"Why? What cause would make you sell, Robert?" Rebeckah said, almost in desperation.

William listened as Robert tried to explain that since he had been appointed as a constable by the county, he just could not keep up so much land. But William had the feeling that what was driving him to sell was the same thing that took the Bettertons away.

After Robert left, William took the letter from his wife and went into the cabin. "I am afraid I have lost another family member," he said as he set it on the self with his books.

"Something tells me I am about to lose a brother, too. Do you think Robert is getting ready to move over to the Carolinas just like Eleanor and Thomas?" She asked.

"Your family has the right to sell their land when they please, Rebeckah. Just like I sold our land to Jacob Waters. You do not see us moving do you?" William scoffed.

"Do you think we women do not hear your talk along the fence line? We hear. And that is what worries me, William. All of you men seem to be inclinable to load the wagon and head out."

William knew what she said carried truth, but he did not want to admit how often they had discussed it. Right now his interest was on the lawyer that would be coming. "Rebeckah, you and Nancy would be advised to set your table with more than the journey cakes until this lawyer comes. I would find it sorely embarrassing to show him my wife could not cook a decent meal."

With her hands firmly set on her hips, Rebeckah reminded her husband, "William, I have been married to you for twenty years, and you have yet to go away from my table with an empty stomach."

He chose to ignore her comment. "Maybe he is coming with papers for selling it."

Rebeckah remembered William had told her when he was a mere child, after his father's death, his grandfather had taken over the controls of his father's estate. He had leased the Littlefield land to his mother's sister and her husband for the duration of the uncle's life.

"No, more than likely he is coming to give me news of my uncle's death, thereby releasing the land to us again. Maybe there is news of an inheritance."

For years, William had made a practice of writing a letter to his sister and brother whenever he went to the docks in Georgetown to hand to the ship's captain, hoping it would find its way to Salisbury and some of his family. But no reply ever came. Despair once again came to his voice, "Maybe it is to tell me my sister Anne and my brother John are now dead. But why would a lawyer come all this distance for that?"

William walked into the new room. He stood for a time looking at the trappings they had ordered from the catalog, then he went to stand at the window. The moon furnished enough light to see the road and beyond. After awhile Rebeckah came to stand beside him. "It is a good thing we have this new room to entertain this English Esquire," William confided.

Rebeckah knew he would never admit to being proud hearted, but she knew it pleased him that the lawyer could go back home and spread the news that William Littlefield had been successful in the new land.

That night William had tossed and turned in his bed. And when Rebeckah dished out his breakfast mush the next morning, she told him so. "You slept with the visit of your friend all night long, did you not? Hardly let me sleep last night for the pulling on the covers."

"Don't call him friend until I see the whites of his eyes."

William was worried. What if this lawyer would not hand over the land until William had signed some sort of allegiance papers vowing to comply with the King's taxes? There had been rumors of such when dealing with land in England. He had never let someone tell him what to do and he did not intend to do so now. He would be polite to a point. Then he would dismiss the man to the road.

William's calendar said it was October and almost two months since he had made notation of receiving the letter. But still, no Esquire. Rebeckah had given up dressing the children in their Sunday best and had gone back to fixing only one meat for the meals.

This morning Nancy had taken little Mary and Lucy to gather the eggs, with a promise she would let them chase the mice in the barn. For Mary at six years of age and Lucy at five, this was a real adventure.

There was a nip in the air, and Rebeckah decided this would be a good morning to try to find the remaining herbs for her medicine bottles. One more frost and the leaves would be browned beyond use. She went to her doctoring shelf, as she called it, and pulled the bottles down that needed replenishing. It was always a scary thing to enter winter without the medicines to cure the family.

With baby Becka on her hip, Rebeckah closed the door to the cabin and grabbed her basket from the tree stump. She could hear the honking of a flock of geese on their way south, breaking the stillness of the morning. She stopped to search the clear blue sky for the sleek long-necked bird that meant the change of seasons, as much as the beautiful orange and yellow leaves that fell in front of her path. What a beautiful day to enjoy life. It would not be long now until winter was on their doorstep, and with it the cold that froze to the bone. Getting older seemed to make the cold hurt more, and William had complained of aching bones the last year.

She waved at Prudence who was down on her knees pulling the last two pumpkins from their vines. Even though the Littlefields shared more than enough with Henry and Prudence, it was Prudence's idea that it did a person good to feel the earth in your hands and to know you had provided for one's own keeping.

Lifting her gathering basket in the air, she called out, "I'm on my way to find a few more peppermint leaves for the stomach pain bottle."

Prudence pushed her thin tall body up with her hands first on the ground and came to walk with Rebeckah. She reached out to take little Becka. The baby squealed with delight at seeing the woman they now lovingly called grandma Prud.

The two women searched under each tree and rock, pulling the strong smelling peppermint leaves into the basket. "With winter coming on, William will be calling for the oil of eucalyptus for his aching bones. When I checked my bottle this morning it was nearly empty. Do you remember seeing any leaves down by the creek?"

"That is the first supply I set in each spring. If you need more I have enough to share with William," Prudence assured her. "Let a man begin to hurt and you would think they were dying." The women laughed at the spoken truth.

It was the bigger part of an hour when the two women returned to the cabin. Both stopped abruptly as they came around the side of the barn.

A man, some years older than William, was sitting on the tree stump next to Rebeckah's kitchen door. He was dressed in what once appeared to have been an elegant suit of traveling clothes. Politely, he stood up and bowed, "I'm Sir Robert Holmes, Esquire. I have come to do business with one William Littlefield. A jolly fine fellow at the Beall's Tavern informed me this was indeed his abode."

William was called for, and now this afternoon the two men sat in the new room talking mainly of times in Salisbury. Sadly, no word had been found of the sister and brother. The lawyer had to assume they were deceased because they had not tried to reach his office for many years.

"But ye had written many times and left your traveling address," Mr. Holmes said. "If it was not for ye being so determined to find family still living, we would not have known your whereabouts."

"And why did you come, Mr. Holmes?"

Mr. Holmes, his shirtwaist too tight for comfort, sipped again on his cider as an attempt to put off the task of divulging unwelcome news.

"I assumed you were bringing news of Uncle John's demise and needed permission to again lease my father's land," William said rather bluntly.

"I am regretful to bring this kind of news when you had hopes of the other. The truth is thy uncle has not paid the taxes for the last ten years and the place has been sent to foreclosure. We just need your signature on the papers saying thou hast been informed."

William's face showed anger as color began creeping up his throat into his face. "You what? You just admitted you knew where to find me. Why did you not send a letter notifying me of the unpaid tax?"

What once had been a near smug look on Mr. Holmes' face, now bordered on real fear. "Well, I—I—we did not consider you able to render the taxes due." The man looked around the room surveying the holdings. "I must say we were mistaken."

"I am not an unforgiving man, but this draws close to the line. I will feed you and bed you down until we negotiate the terms of reclaiming my land, or you can find the road tonight."

Mr. Holmes put his papers back in the satchel he was carrying, and as an attempt to secure his room and board, for the night at least, he began to talk about what a nice place William had made for himself in these back woods.

The next morning after chores, William sat down with the lawyer and wrote the terms of his drawing up the papers to make the foreclosure null and void in the court.

Afterwards, they walked through the countryside, and settled into a friendly enough visit. Talking was not something William liked to participate in. But listening to John Holmes describe the old village was like he had walked the streets himself this morning. Slowly William began to ask more and more about the town and who owned what. "Whatever happened to the old castle at the edge of town. Has it blown down? I remember the winds could come blowing down from the hills, almost putting us to the ground. And what happened to the old street vendor we all loved to visit, particularly when we knew his daughter would be there. The men laughed at the memory of a young man seeing a girl.

"Oh, he died, and the girl went on to grow up sassy and still sells on the corner from her father's cart," Mr. Holmes told him. "The horses still race on a Saturday and the parishioners go to ask forgiveness for their loses on Sunday."

On this morning, unaware of how far they had walked, they came across the Sittler's old burned out cabin. William told him of the family that had lived and of their murder. "After that they burned the house down." Then William began telling the story of the old warrior, White Horse, and how it was thought the same killers had attempted to kill him. "But before I could get home and bury him, something had dragged him from sight."

This story fascinated the Englishman. "You mean you kept an Indian on your place? Was that not dangerous after what I have been told of the massacres?"

"Oh, White Horse would never hurt anyone," William said as he went on to explain about why his Indian friend had been on the place when they bought it. "Some have said there were those that wanted to make it look like the Indians had done the dirty deeds on other ravaging events so they could steal from the cabin and not be blamed. It is said they dressed as Indians to disguise their color. Maybe White Horse came across them and they shot him and disposed of his body. Don't know we will ever find out."

As evening came upon them the two walked across the field. The sun had all but disappeared behind the ridge when William pointed to the shadows along the creek. "On some nights we see White Horse walking along the bank."

The old lawyer looked confused. "Either thou art delusional or have sipped too long on the cider jug." But even as he talked something moved in the shadow and the Englishman could not disprove the story.

The next morning as they were on their way to the mill to meet Jacob Waters, William pointed to the tall cone shaped mountain in the distance. "We call that Sugar Loaf Mountain. It takes its name from the Sugar Loaf sitting on every woman's table. Many a traveler, lost in the forest, has found his way out by looking for the peak on the Sugar Loaf."

Each day after the chores were finished, William had taken the lawyer to meet the neighbors. What started off to be no more than a nip in the air had turned cold. Mr. Holmes began to notice the fur caps the farmers had pulled from their wall hooks and asked William, "I would like to know where I might purchase one of those fine looking caps." William had laughed when he told John and Absolom about how the lawyer had discovered the necessity each colonist male had come to rely on a squirrel cap.

William had refrained from letting the conversation with the lawyer bring up the distrust he felt over the parliament, much to Rebeckah's relief. And one night when she had asked, he whispered, "This man is a guest. He has no way of understanding the sometimes cruel and underhanded ways of the officials. Nor would Mr. Holmes understand my turning traitor to his thinking, seeing I was schooled in the English ways."

Late one afternoon, Mr. Holmes had gone to the calendar and turned to announce "Sir William, my departure is drawing nigh upon us. Two days hence and the fair ship will be returning to my homeland. If I am not on it, your papers will not be filed in time."

The family all gathered around the big fireplace for one last night of stories. Tonight the Englishman spun the tale of the pirate he had encountered in his youth while sailing to the West Indies. And with each log that turned over on the grate, sending sparks flying, the eyes of the children grew wider. Never had they heard such a death defying story. Finally, at the end he turned to William. "Did you ever meet the swashbuckling Calico Kidd's son?".

"I've heard stories," William told him.

"Happened before thy time." Mr. Holmes then abruptly changed to the serious side, maybe like the lawyer he was, trying to finalize a case with one last heart gripping story. "I remember the last time I saw thy grandfather was on the road into London with a load of woolen rolls to sell at market. We talked for a spell and he told me of your father's death and the short life of your mother. He was still grieving over the loss and told me of two older children and a wee little one. That must have been ye, Sir William."

"So you knew my grandfather?" William asked.

"Ah, yes. And your grandmother as well. Oh, what a fine tune she carried. I heard her in the church once. Did you ever hear her sing, William?"

"She sang songs to me at bedtime. The others were too old for that ritual. That was before I was sent away to the guardians and never saw her again—" The last memory fell silently before them.

The lawyer, in the quietness of the room began to sing ever so softly the haunting melody William had sung that night at the fair, the year Solomon had caused them to come home so soon. It was the song every Englishmen knew as a farewell song. *For when I go I will not come, forbid me not to stay. My heart, my love, is in the land where my spirit has not trod, where my spirit has not trod."* William did not sing with the others. He began to half clear his throat as if something was caught inside him. Rebeckah knew it was his way of dismissing the thought of saying good-bye to the last person that could speak of knowing his family face to face.

The next morning, Solomon, trying to be a grownup, lugged the lawyer's satchel to the wagon. They were all going with William to take him to the main road to catch the stagecoach.

"You can thank John and some others for your convenience of a stagecoach. Until this year the path was too rough to carry the large covered body."

The tavern steps were crowded with people waiting for the Stagecoach pickup. Mr. Holmes climbed over the side of the wagon with his satchel as Rebeckah handed him a parcel containing food she had fixed for his trip. John had climbed down as well and took something from his pocket. Absolom and young William grinned from ear to ear.

"Mr. Holmes, seeing you liked the fur caps so well, Absolom and young William and I went to the fields in search of the thickest furred squirrels and have made you one to keep your ears warm for the trip home."

It was obvious the old gentleman was pleased as he placed it on his head in a ceremonial way. Everyone cheered.

As they waved goodbye, their visitor was switching his head from side to side to keep the furry tail wagging back and forth for as long as they could see him.

The calendar by the door said December this morning. William and the boys had finished their chores early. The first snow had fallen quietly before daybreak. Now it was middle afternoon and William had expected Rebeckah to set the honey biscuits on the table as she had done almost every year since their life together. She would put on her heavy cloak and wrap her scarf around her head, but say nothing. He would watch her make her way up the hill to say her prayers. But today she made no motion to leave. When he asked, she simply said, she thought the Lord knew what was on her heart while in her warm cabin just as well as on the cold hillside.

Rebeckah let the words fall flat and picked up the yarn from her basket and began rolling it tightly into a ball. What she did not say was that she could not again ask God to take her guilt away if she could not do what she had promised.

Sometime in the night Rebeckah awoke to the distant sound of a horse breaking the crusty snow on the road. The dogs began barking, then the sound of snow crunching under foot made her sit up. It was bad news. No one would come this time of night, with snow on the ground, if it did not call out bad news.

Richard Willis had died late afternoon and news was just getting down that far.

Once again the family stood around a grave. Poor Elizabeth stood next to her husband's coffin, wearing for the third time her black widow's cap. She stood next to her children, Will Sierra, with his wife Sarah beside him. Elizabeth and her husband Aquilla Compton were there, the four children, Mary, Thomas, Elizabeth and William next to them. Richard Willis was the only grandfather they had known. Rebeckah watched the children shivering in the cold. Their little daughter Mary, at eight years old seemed to know her grandmother's pain and had gone over to hold her hand throughout the readings. So much pain had passed over this woman's life, Rebeckah wondered how she had held up.

Elizabeth had stood with her eyes closed through most of the readings, and Rebeckah wondered if she was asleep on her feet, or just not able to look beyond the grave.

Only a small group had attended. Outside of Elizabeth's own family and her brothers and sisters living close enough to get the message, no one had come. Well, maybe a neighbor or two and a hired hand, and that was all. She could not help but think how many more friends her father had drawn for his burial. But maybe it was the cold that kept them away.

Alexander Grant leaned over to William and confided he and John Wofford had secretly dug the hole about a month ago, ahead of the freeze, knowing that Richard could not live much longer. They had covered it with brush, so Elizabeth never knew.

"You seem to be good at that," William said, nudging his side without changing the somber expression on his face. Both men remembered how their wives had accused them of hastening the death of their father because they dug his grave before the last breath.

Rebeckah shivered. Her cloak did little to keep the cold from her bones. Because of the heavy snow, Prudence and Henry had called on them to leave the children in their care. This was the first time since John was born that she had gone anywhere without a child on her lap. A strange, disjointed feeling came over her as she watched the Compton children.

Before mid afternoon the burial meal had ended, and the house had been cleared and swept. Everyone but William and Rebeckah had gone back to their own cabins.

Elizabeth had asked William to help her look for a will that Richard might have left, thus delaying their leaving time.

"If he had one, it would be stuffed in Mr. Norris's desk somewhere. I've not looked in that desk since William died," she admitted.

A suffocating fear came over Rebeckah. If everything was in place as William Norris had left it, then what else might her husband find? She watched William methodically take each piece of paper from the little compartments and briefly examine them before going to the next. Rebeckah knew that if the Bastardy papers were given to William Norris when he paid off the court, he would have stored them in this desk. She remembered when she had come for her schooling, William Norris would sit at this desk to work each evening. Elizabeth had told her never to disturb him when he was at his desk, because that was where he kept his important papers. Her heart began to beat fast and she felt like a caged bird, frantically trying to think of a way to get out.

William tugged at a large roll of papers stuck together in the back. of the compartment. As he pulled them loose a folded brown paper, sealed on all sides with sealing glue, fell from it. He remembered seeing the paper once before when he had been asked by the schoolmaster to find a piece of paper on which to write his will. It had not been his business to inquire to the nature then. Now he wondered what information it contained that made him seal it so securely.

He did not say anything after reading the outside cover words but set it to one side.

Rebeckah watched as he went back to searching for a will. Was he going to ask Elizabeth about the contents? Was that why he had set the brown paper aside from the other papers? Rebeckah tried to get her husband's attention.

"William, shouldn't we start home before night falls? The children will be anxious as to our whereabouts."

"Rebeckah, I'm trying to find something for Elizabeth," He said crossly and waved his hand to dismiss her. "The children are fine with Prudence and Henry."

Will Sierra and his wife, Sarah, had returned to check on his mother. Seeing William was occupied, they began to ask Rebeckah about the progress of the mill Jacob Waters was building. Before she could answer, William spoke to Elizabeth over the conversation. "Elizabeth, what is in this brown envelope that William has all sealed with sealing glue?"

Elizabeth went over to see. "What does it say, William? You know I can't see the words any more."

"It says, *Paid to the courts two thousand pounds tobacco*. It must have been a severe violation to be charged that much. I do not see a date on it. Maybe it was before you met William."

Elizabeth took a deep breath, so tired she could not think straight. When she looked at Rebeckah she questioned without thinking of the consequences. "You didn't tell him, did you?"

"Tell me what?" William asked, looking to both women.

Elizabeth, almost as a way of covering her mistake for asking, went over to the desk and took the paper from William's hand. "I'm just too weary to worry with this just now, William. I'm sure Richard would have told me if he had written a will." She pushed the papers back into the desk and closed the lid.

As the darkness came in around the room, it matched the fear creeping into Rebeckah's life. She knew she could not get out of telling William now. He was a smart man. He would know something was wrong by the way Elizabeth looked at her, then closed the desk so abruptly.

William went out to the check on his horses and realized it was too late to chance making it home tonight. He threw out some feed and started back toward the cabin.

He could not get his mind off the faded brown paper and what it meant. Why had they kept it secretly sealed for so long? What had happened in this family that would make Elizabeth react the way she did tonight?

Chapter 34

December1769
Leaving Elizabeth's Place

William brought the wagon around and waited while Rebeckah came with the quilts and bundle of clothing. She turned to give Elizabeth the assurances that they would return in time to plant the crops.

By this time, Elizabeth looked so broken it probably did not matter that they were leaving so soon after the burial. What she needed more than anything was rest.

The December sun was just beginning to find its way into the early morning sky as William cracked the whip to get the horses going. The worries of the evening before seemed buried under the need to get back home before nightfall.

Rebeckah turned to William as he reined the horses onto the main road. "William you are a good man to offer to help plant Elizabeth's crops this year." She patted his arm with her hand and then folded her arm through his.

He removed her arm from his and cracked the whip harder. The horses began to run and the rattle of the wagon left talking impossible.

Rebeckah wondered why he was in such a hurry. There was no sign of a storm coming. Sometime about midmorning, they had reached a clearing looking out over the valley below, and he pulled the horses over to rest.

William seemed to be preoccupied in his own thinking but that did not stop Rebeckah from talking about what a pretty sight it was to look down into the valley. And she even wondered if some cabin was close by to take in the view every day. It was an attempt to break the silence William had enforced all morning.

When he pulled the wagon over to the side to let the horses rest, Rebeckah took it as the time to look for the sweet bread Elizabeth had insisted they bring with them. She was caught by surprise when his voice became angry.

Anger had festered since yesterday in William's mind. Without saying anything he had tried to discern what Elizabeth had been hiding when she posed the question to Rebeckah. The very words were, "You have not told him?" That could only mean one thing. A long held family secret was sealed in the brown envelope. There was one thing he could not abide with, and that was deceit. "Sit down Rebeckah. What is going on? And do not think of lying. I have had all the sidestepping I will tolerate."

Surprised at his hostile talk, she turned back to face him. "William, I have never lied to you."

He turned around to face her, and the veins in his neck pulled against his skin as he spoke. "You and Elizabeth are privy to something you do not want me to hear. I found those same sealed papers when I wrote the schoolmaster's will. They are untampered to this day. What horrible deed causes you to guard the contents so zealously?"

Rebeckah's lips began to quiver. She suddenly felt trapped and afraid to answer. Never had she seen his anger so strong.

He reached out and caught her wrist, squeezing it hard. "Tell me what you know. I've never let anyone take me for the fool and I will not do it with you, either."

"You are hurting me, William."

He dropped her hand and could see the red marks where he had squeezed her wrist. "You and the family are keeping something. What is it? I will find out and it will be better if you told me now."

Rebeckah began to cry. Her eyes unknowingly began to look for an escape from telling him the truth he expected her to tell.

William's voice demanded an answer. There was no getting away. This was the secret she had promised God she would tell. But now, why was her soul splitting apart with the truth.

The tears were coming so fast she could not talk. What had been built up in her for years was finding a release. William did not offer a way of stopping her. His glare was cold.

Finally, the hysteria slowed and she was able to speak. "I wanted to tell you, but I was afraid."

She began to reveal the horrid events that led up to this moment, the painful secret she had kept all these years. She told of the Sheriff, John Cook, coming to her door with the summons, even before the baby had been born, and how her father had paid Thomas Clark to attorney for her case, and Thomas Gantt had been the foreman of the jury. And most sadly, how William Norris had taken her baby.

"Your family kept this from me all these years? What did they take me for, a fool?" William went on to condemn the family.

"No one knew, at least that is what my parents said." She now wondered if her father had threatened everyone that knew. And after so many years it had passed from their thoughts.

William's anger looked frozen in place. He did not speak.

"William, please do not blame me for what someone else did." She waited for him to say something. He still said nothing, so she spoke again.

Her voice, just above a whisper, begging, "Hate me if you like—if it makes you feel better, hate me, but do not set the blame on me."

William just stared into the distance—one hand griped the whip while the other held the reins.

She tried to speak again but the words came out wrong. "It was not your fault. You had nothing to do with the cruel way your friend violated my innocence. It was before you even knew him. I have tormented over how you would feel when someone you respected so much was found to be a man of deceit."

Before Rebeckah could say more, William lifted the whip to the horses. In his haste, the whip lashed back toward Rebeckah and without warning, stuck the side of her face as the horses lunged. In a sudden moment of anger he had done an unthinkable act. He abruptly stopped the horses and turned to look at her face.

She began to cry again and jumped from the wagon.

Stunned at what had just happened, but not enough to make him forget what it was that she had said. "How do I know it was not your leading him on that caused him to do such a thing?"

"William, how could you say that about me?" she said between the sobs. Her words fell on a stone heart.

"Why else would you keep this secret? I do not know who I married, Rebeckah. William Norris was just a man I thought was my friend. It is the fact that you deceived me all these years that causes my humiliation."

William jumped from the wagon seat, grabbing his rifle from the back of the wagon and headed into the woods.

Rebeckah caught her breath in fear. Was he going to end his life? She heard a shot. Then silence. She started to run into the woods when she heard a volley of shots, one after the other, going into different directions in the woods. She was afraid one of the shots would hit her if she went after him.

Finally he walked out. He put the rifle in the back and climbed up on the wagon seat. He picked up the whip and yelled, "Get in."

She carefully approached the wagon and got up on the seat, afraid he might lash out at her again. He turned to look at her and could see the imprint of the whip still on her face. This time it was anger at his lack of control that went to his heart. He had never hit his wife. Furthermore, he hated those that did. It was a violence he had never understood, and now he was no better.

They rode on in silence. Just before they turned onto their own path, he stopped the wagon.

From the road you could see a large portion of the *William and John* and the fields stretched out forever in a pure white covering. The barn standing high above the many out buildings reflected the bright sun off the snow and gave the place a crisp clean look.

Among all that whiteness, the orange-red barn door stood as a testament of what had happened when he let Rebeckah have her way.

What he said now was a way of taking back his control over everything. "I am going to paint that door brown—dark brown." He did not look at Rebeckah as he cracked the whip making the horses jump.

Rebeckah knew it was his way of giving warning that she could no longer expect to be given wishes.

The children and Prudence were waiting at the door when William pulled the horses to a stop. He let Rebeckah climb over the side and then took the wagon on to the barn. It was all Rebeckah could do to keep from showing her desperate feeling just now. But to bring the innocent into this heartbreak was of no use. She gave each one a hug and turned to Prudence. "It was a good thing you insisted in keeping the children at home. It was very cold on the road." She hoped the redness of her face would be construed as coming from the cold wind. But oh, what she really wanted to do was break down in her old friend's arms and cry forever.

William had not come to the cabin until very late that evening. Nor did he say anything to Rebeckah when he did. He spoke the children in a friendly sort of way, giving the boys a long list of instructions on how they needed to do the work. Rebeckah wondered if he was going to punish her sons for her failures.

That night William had worked at the table in the new room. Once when she went in to say something to him, he rebuffed her conversation. His eyes still burned with anger and she wondered how long he would fester the anger.

She turned and went up to the bedchambers.

After she had climbed the stairs he began to think about all the times James Lee had not volunteered the words. It would have been less damaging then. He would have simply walked away. And if he had come back it would be because he loved Rebeckah more than his good name. As he thought about it now, the deceit of secrecy angered him beyond his comprehension. The feeling of restlessness came over him like a cloud leading the storm. There was no reasoning to his anger. Why had he come to the colonies? More importantly, why had he stayed? His refusal to comply with the overseer in his homeland over unfair treatment then, seemed to speak to him now, without reason.

In the middle of the night Rebeckah reached out and he was still not there. She knew this new revelation was hard to take and he might decide to permanently sleep downstairs. Or at least until the school classes could start.

It was not until she heard the crunch of horses feet prancing in the snow did she get up to check. When she came down the steps she could see the fire in the fireplace was fresh with extra logs. William must have been working by the fire until late. Then she saw the piece of paper propped against the candlestick.

Her very soul stopped breathing as she read the message. William had written it in simple words.

Rebeckah, I am leaving. I cannot stay knowing you and your family have played me for a fool all these years. I have hired Jeb to oversee the farm for you. Henry thinks I just have gone in search of more land. You can tell that same story if you like. I wish the children a good life. I have left you the monies to run the farm. Make it last until you can learn how to make the crops grow. William

Her hand found the bag of monies under the note. She sat down on the bench and began to cry. It was no easier than if William had died and been put in the grave. How could she live without him?

For what seemed like hours she sat looking at the letter. Finally, she folded it over and over until it was a small little wad of misery and put it on the high shelf under the unused papers. Could she tell another lie to cover what had caused all these problems? Could she tell her children and family and even Prudence and Henry that he had just gone in search of new land? As she sat starring into the slowly dying fire, she guessed it was not a lie after all. William had implied it was new land for the family when in real it was new land for himself. She wondered if he would go back to England.

She went to the door to look at the horse tracks, evidence that his note was real. She found herself, foolishly wanting go follow them, to find William and beg him to come home. But she knew that was hopeless. Once a man's pride had fallen there was not much else to live for.

When the children came down to eat the first meal, she sent the boys to do the chores as always. She had explained the half-truth to them that morning, as she had begun to call it. Nancy was the first to give her displeasure at the thought of moving. How could she leave just as Nicholas Dawson was beginning to talk to her?

Snapping back, Rebeckah gave a piece of her mind in response to her daughter's statement, and Nancy did not know why her mother reacted in such a harsh way.

By the noon meal she felt sick. Every fuss the children put up caused her head to throb. She dropped the stirring spoon into the fireplace and reached in to grab it, burning her hand badly. She again sat down and cried. The children thought she was in pain from the burn, which was in part truth, but it was more the thought that she was all alone now without William to lean on.

It was not until Nancy watched for Nickolas to come and he had not, that Rebeckah let on to her daughter that sometimes things happen to break your heart. "It takes more tears than you know you have to put it aside."

Nancy looked at her mother as if knowing. Her whisper seemed to say she knew what her mother was really saying. "Father, is not coming back, is he?"

Rebeckah began to cry. And for the first time Nancy seemed more like the consoling mother than the child, as she put her arms around her mother. "Sometimes, the hurt in your eyes when you looked down the road told me he was not coming back."

Days went by and then weeks. It would be time to set the buckets under the maple trees again. Still she could not help herself. She still judged her days by how many times she looked toward the road hoping to see a sign of a horse racing for the house. But William did not come.

It was bound to happen sooner or later. One day she let the truth slip from her lips as she talked to Prudence. The older woman said nothing at first, then reached over and patted Rebeckah's hand and simply said, "You will be fine dear."

Nothing more was said about it. She guessed Prudence had told Henry, because he seemed to stop and talk to her more often. When something needed to be fixed he proceeded to take care of the chore. Just the fact that some one else shared her pain helped get her through the next few months.

Chapter 35

Late February 1770
Lower Seneca Creek

Guilt worked on Rebeckah's thoughts as she turned her horse into the path that led to Susanna and William Hawker's cabin. So much so, she hardly gave notice at the turn in the road where two men were felling trees to set the walls for another log cabin. That would mean William was right, the Birdwhistles had indeed sold more land.

Her mind was on the fact that she should have come just as soon as the news of the death had come, but that was shortly after William had left and nothing was handled as it should have been back then.

Now that she was here, what would she say that could make them feel any better? The Hawkers' daughter had been such a pretty girl and so full of anticipation over the birth of her first born.

Susanna came to the door holding the baby and looking older than her age. Rebeckah handed her the fried fruit pies she had made this morning as a condolence gift, then reached out to take the baby. As they talked, the baby's grandmother began to explain how hard the father, Zephaniah Swann, had taken the death of his wife. "He absolutely refused to hold this precious little son after he was told his wife had died." Susanna reached over and patted the baby's tiny hand as she continued to tell the story. "He said every time he looked at little Hezekiah he would think of his wife's death. I can't see how that would make him not want the baby, but he said that. So we are raising him. It just makes us love him more to think his sweet mother gave her last breath for him."

The two women sat next to the fire for half the morning speaking of the feeling of grief over the loss of a loved one. While Susanna spoke of the loss of their daughter, Rebeckah silently remembered the loss of her own baby, not from death, but at the hands of another.

Again, as in so many times of late, she told of William being away looking for new lands to buy. She wondered if anyone had thought to question the reason further.

She got up to go and handed the baby back to Susanna and suggested that she bring the children over to visit sometime. "Our son John is just a little older than your son William, so they probably both have other interests, but your Margaret and Diana and our young William could spend enjoyable moments doing the dances."

Rebeckah thought to herself after giving the invitation that young William would die of embarrassment at the suggestion he dance with a girl. At fourteen he would rather be practicing to bring home the dinner with his bow and arrow. She realized her thoughts had strayed and left Susanna waiting. "And your Elizabeth looks to be about the age of our Solomon. Please come. It would be good for our children to have a visit to provide excitement." Rebeckah took a closer look at the child. Something told her she was not well and she wondered if Susanna had been too busy with the new grandbaby to notice. She had seen children like this, children whose look said they did not have enough blood to color the face. Sadly, these young ones usually died young. She thought of her own children with their bright healthy faces and again gave a silent thankfulness to her maker.

Once Rebeckah was on the road leading back to her cabin she let the horse slow walk, and even stop to graze along the way. It gave her much needed time to think, for once she stepped foot in her cabin it would be back to work as usual. She corrected her thinking. Nothing was as usual since William had been gone. It had been over two months and she had done more work than she thought herself capable of doing.

William had left Jeb in charge, and she had found him less than competent at running the farm. In desperation to save the crops she had taken over the task of directing the planting. Henry tried to keep her informed as best he could. Again, she thanked the Lord for sending this couple her way.

She stopped the horse on the road just before turning onto her path. It was the same spot William had stopped the wagon the day before he left. William had been true to his word, and the night before he left he had painted it a dismal dark brown to show his displeasure at her request so many years ago. Suddenly a resolve swelled up in her and she determined to paint it a brighter orange red than before. She would show William that he could not defeat her for long. The thought gave her courage.

No sooner had her courage been born, it was dashed. William was not coming back to see her new door.

She sat looking out over her field, remembering how the land had looked when William moved her onto the first one hundred acres. He had worked so hard. She had done her share, that was sure. Up to the birthing day of the babies she had worked and then returned to the fields with the babies in a sling against her chest.

She turned to look farther into the hills. William had saved all their extra monies and bought over fifteen hundred acres ten years later. And now he had given it up just to save his honor. Wasn't that the way he had put it?

Slowly, but defiantly, a new thought began to find a place in her thoughts. It did not matter if William witnessed the repainted door or not. She would do it for her own feelings. To look out her window at something bright and cheerful made her feel good, and that was enough reason to paint it red again.

Her reliance on William to provide a life had been pulled from her, as the old saying went. She could do nothing to bring her husband back if he chose to stay away. It was his misfortune to miss the good times with his children or the bounty from his land. But she could enjoy what he had left. Now the lives of her children were in her hands and she would not waste it away because of a foolish man's pride.

Somewhere, from the back of her thinking, a verse came to give her confirmation of her thoughts. She had memorized it once when William had read it at the nightly scripture readings. It had made her heart feel good when he said the words. She tried to remember how they went. Give her of the fruit—of her hands—oh what was the ending? She started again. Give her of the fruit of her hands, and let her own works praise her gates. She tried to reason where the thought had come from after all the years. Finally, knowing it had been remembered was enough.

She gave her horse a swat and headed on home.

The weeks wore on, and one by one, the family and friends began to come around to inquire when William was coming back.

First it had been Thomas Dawson riding to her door to bring the news to William, not realizing he was gone. John and Absolom had come to stand with her and listened intently as Thomas told what he knew.

"The British shot a man in Boston in early March. I do not know much about it only that it sounds bad." It had happened, so the news came, that on a night with snow covering the town a group of men were heckling the British army. They said it had been going on for some time and over a hundred colonists were throwing rocks at the soldiers. One of the officers hit a young boy with the butt of his rifle after he made an insulting remark. The colonists were shouting something about killing the soldiers. It had all happened so fast, and in the end there were several Bostonians lying dead in the snow—murdered they called it.

Thomas ended his story and said, "Well, I just thought William would want to know this news. When he comes back tell him I delivered it."

Rebeckah thanked Thomas for coming and assured him she would pass the words on when William returned. She closed the door and took a deep breath. She had not had to give a more detailed answer. To lie to Thomas Dawson was unthinkable. He had always been considered their best friend and ally. She wondered how William could have gone away without telling him. But he had, and now she was having to lie to make it alright.

The thought of explaining William's absence had passed, but the thought of the shooting stayed with her all evening. It was John who started the conversation. "Mother, Absolom and I have been talking. We want you to know we have been training with our rifles and if an uprising comes we will go help if we are needed."

She looked closely at her boys. How old would they have to be to fight a war? It sent a shiver up her spine. John was twenty-one and she was sure any day he would want to leave home with the other boys to find a job at the docks or some warehouse. And Absolom was almost eighteen and was restless to the point of leaving before his time. They would go sooner or later, she knew. But please, not to take up a gun against someone!

Rebeckah knew what it took to run a farm. But what she did not know was how to direct someone to make it happen. Her lists seemed to grow longer and longer of things that needed to be tended to or paid for. Their taxes surely needed to be paid before long. And she remembered William talking about how the Governor always called for so much tobacco to be given for the church improvements. Would she have enough left over to pay the new hired hands she had been forced to employ?

William's old calendar of last year held the information. She had stored it on the shelf in case she needed to refer to something. He had put up a new calendar the night he left. It still hung on the wall, empty of ink marks as a testament of his departure. She went to the shelf and found the one he had taken down.

Rebeckah sat down at the table and began to pick through the pages of last year. To see William's handwriting in his large scrawling penmanship gave a tug at her heart. When Nancy asked what was causing her mother to wipe her eyes so often, Rebeckah realized how deeply she missed this man.

Before she could read through the pages of last year, she heard the dogs bark and Benoni Dawson calling out, "I've brought a letter from Alexander Grant."

The letter held no real news, just questions. He was writing to inquire why William had not come to the last three meetings at Dowden's Ordinary without sending a note to explain.

Alexander's letter had been the first to question William's absence. A couple of weeks after Alexander's letter, came a letter from Thomas Thrasher. It seemed on the last visit to the ordinary William and Thomas had discussed racing their horses at the May Fair. Now Thomas was waiting for his decision. Rebeckah had politely answered the letters as best she could without letting on William had given no intentions of returning.

James Lee paid his sister a visit around the middle of April and her world began to crumble.

"Well, sister," James always addressed his sisters by the same calling, as if he could not remember their names. "I thought William would like to know I have sold all my land. But I see he is not home yet." He began to tell her the story of his land sales. "Actually, I sold the first part to the Jones family. Annie was so distraught that a few days later I bought a small piece to live on from the Birdwhistles. But if I do live and breathe, I was offered almost twice as much for it that same day. So I sold it. Annie was not one bit nice about it. But I figure a man has got to do what he knows is best. We will be moving to the Carolinas to join the Bettertons just as soon as I can find a wagon train with enough space for at least two of our wagons."

Rebeckah suddenly burst into a tearful frenzy. "Oh, James, how could you?"

James had a puzzled look on his face.

"I need you and Robert to be here to lean on since—" she did not finish her sentence.

"Since what? What's wrong with William? He treats you good, doesn't he?"

Maybe it was that she was tired of pretending that William was just away or the feeling of desertion, now by her brothers as well. She could not stop herself if she wanted to. The story spilled out.

"William is not coming back. What I told the others was not the whole story. He has left us for good."

For the first time in her life, James put his arm around her as she let the past few months dissolve into tears of honesty.

"I had hoped William would be lining up with our wagon but I guess you won't be moving now," James said.

After James's visit everyone in the family knew William had left for good. The fact that the truth had finally come out had a healing effect on Rebeckah. She was able to follow some of her resolves without being questioned. One morning in May she went to the barn and began mixing from all the jugs of paint makings that William often used. At first it turned out too pink. Finally, after adding all the sesquioxide of iron ground in oil and resin and more raw linseed oil, it turned the color she so wanted. A bright orange red paint to prove her point. After the job was finished she stood back to enjoy the first real feeling of revenge she had experienced since William left. The next day she called Prudence and Elizabeth Dawson, who had come for the quilting that morning, to come see her handiwork. They both patted her on the back and laughingly agreed, "William cannot take your bright door away from you."

That evening, John came in with news that a group of young men were going to the port of either Annapolis or Baltimore to help build the big ships. A call had gone out that the colonies were in need of more ships. "I feel strongly, mother, that it is my place to help. I will send monies back to pay for a new hired hand."

The news sent shock through Rebeckah. How could she make the farm go without workers. She proceeded to give a harsh talking to her sons, all of them, that if she did not have support on the farm she could not make it produce enough to keep it.

Rebeckah stood straight and without emotion before them. "Your father is not coming back. He has chosen to find another path in his life after all these years." She reckoned the truth was all she had left to give them resolve, now that the rest of her family knew. Their faces did not show a sense of shock. They were wise children and probably had already suspected it.

It was Nancy that seemed to be happy with the news. Not that she did not love her father, it was just that she had been afraid they would move like the rest of the families. Now she could stay here and still have dreams of marrying Nicholas Dawson someday, even though she had begun to wonder why he did not come around as much. Several days passed, and for Absolom the news of his father not coming back seemed to give him a new more restless feeling. He complained about the work, or about what they were not having on the table or about the others in the family getting off easier on chores than he was. So it was only a slight surprise to Rebeckah when she got up one morning and found he was gone. At eighteen he felt he was free to do as he pleased. William would not come back to punish him. And he knew Rebeckah had little strength to wield a whip. The only other man around was Henry, and his bulge hurt too much to give a whipping, even if Rebeckah had insisted.

In the fall of the year Rebeckah's work was lessened with the crops in. Today she had worked through the day with all the children in the apple orchard. That was the one crop that had flourished but she could not take the credit. Mother nature had done her part.

By the end of the day she was able to sit down at her table and revise her list of things she absolutely needed from the warehouse. Even with more lines drawn through the list she wondered where the monies would come from. A new loneliness settled in as she watched a ray of sun finding a path through the small peephole, intended for seeing those coming to the door. It was only a sliver of light, but it highlighted the blue bowl holding the newly picked apples, then forced its way to the wall. She sat for what seemed like ages, watching the light get smaller and less bright. It was like a forewarning. Her life was getting smaller with each family member that left. She could hear Mary and Lucy, laughing in the next room as they played with the new doll dresses Grandma Prud had made for them. Two-year-old Becka had fallen asleep on the rug next to the fireplace. What a contrast she thought. Her life getting smaller while these little ones were growing into new persons of their own making.

Rebeckah heard Solomon and young William outside racing to the door. "Mother, mother, you should see this long hair. I got it from the old gray horses tail. It is so strong there won't be a fish that can break it," Solomon yelled, trying to tell his mother before young William could blurt it out. "And we found, like you told us, the young hawthorn tree growing next to the creek. Those thorns are so sharp not a one of those slippery fellows can get away from us tomorrow."

Listening to her son's plans, she smiled and said, "Tomorrow maybe you will bring me a mess of fish for dinner." She slowly pulled herself up to stoke the fire and stir the stew that had been cooking all afternoon. Even her meals had shown no interest of late. The thought of a fish dinner would be a welcome change.

It was a shot of new life given by the Almighty when word came from Rachel, saying she and John were bringing another child into the family. This time Rebeckah knew there was no hope of attending the birthing and quickly wrote a letter. She mentioned that due to being needed at home she would not be able to come. She realized Rachel had probably been told about William leaving her. But even if not, a letter detailing it was not the place to make it known.

By late October, Prudence and Henry had helped her make enough Apple Butter to line the root cellar shelves, and her barrels were full of sweet cider just waiting to age with time. Rebeckah had allowed the children, all but the three little girls, to go with Prudence and Henry to a Apple Butter stirring at the Dawsons. She had chosen to stay at home, not wanting to face the stares of those less known neighbors wondering why William had chosen to leave her. Nancy had come home with high hopes that Nicholas really did like her. Young William had surprised them by dancing a jig with all the girls. Solomon had pretended he thought it all so silly, but Grandma Prud suspected he was just itching to take part real soon. She had told Rebeckah when they got home, "That young William is becoming a ladies man and Solomon is just a step away."

When Rebeckah closed the barn door after finishing her last chores for the evening, she could feel a definite chill to the night air. A pack of coyotes howled at the edge of the woods. She remembered William always said when that happened it was time to check the tobacco barn to assess the crop drying on sticks hanging from the roof. She went inside and put a note on the calendar to remember to go check on it.

She cautiously opened the door, prepared for a bat to fly in her face. It had happened before. One look and she was appalled at how few stakes were being used. William always had a full barn. It would not be until next year that they would be dry enough to take to the warehouse, but she already knew she had been a failure at raising tobacco. William would be so embarrassed at how poorly she had managed his farm. But then, he would never know unless an acquaintance met him in some far-off port.

Rebeckah had been unable to hire enough people to see to the plows and the gathering in of the field, and in the end she had very little to show for all the work she put out. It would have to be enough this year. Maybe by next year she could understand the ways of farming.

She closed the tobacco barn door and went to check on Jeb. Henry had taken young William with him to help Jeb. This was the day they had chosen to slaughter two pigs. It was not a job that Rebeckah had a stomach for. The sound of the squealing pigs was far too painful. She had taken the younger children with her to the mill and asked Prudence to go along. Of all the years she had lived here only once did she remember having to stay around for the gruesome task. William had been good to her like that. She could clean them and salt the meat and stuff the sausages, but she just could not bare to listen to them in their final minutes.

By the end of the week, after all the grease parts were readied, she had started her lye soap making in the leach barrel. And with the leftover grease she would make her candles for the long winter evenings, just as soon as it was cold enough to set the hot tallow. Prudence had promised to help her make the Bayberry candles she loved to smell at Christmas time. Together the two women, with Nancy and the girls following along, had searched the woods looking for the berries to boil down and add to the tallow.

The sound of a wagon coming up their path sent Rebeckah rushing to the door. To her surprise it was Sarah and Alexander's wagon. One look at her sister's face and she knew it was not just for conversation they came. She had seen that look on both Eleanor and Annie when they were loaded up to move. It was like a plague. Once one man got the itch to move it spread to the next family.

After their short visit, Rebeckah waved to them as long as she could see the wagon. And even after they were out of sight she followed the dust along the road. It was the same as with the others—and now they had gone, one by one.

The middle of December the first snow came, and Rebeckah wondered if she had the strength to take her feet to the top of the hill. Last year she had not made the journey, and look what happened. William had found out about the secret and now he was gone from her. Maybe if she would have gone—no, she knew better than to blame God for his leaving. She looked again at the snow-covered trees and something inside of her needed to go find the peace of the countryside. Rebeckah told Nancy to watch the children, and if Grandma Prud or Henry came, tell them she was just taking a walk. She did not want to have them worry about her absence nor come upon her prayers.

Her needs were different this year. The guilt was gone. Not telling William her secret had been wrong and he had a right to feel angry. She thought about it all the way up the hill. Never before had she felt so empty of spirit. Why had God made the secret known and now chastised her for telling the truth? She could only offer up thankfulness at being able to care her children and ask that the little ones be kept safe from disease and that Nancy find contentment. And she prayed for John and Absolom—especially for Absolom. He needed a turn of heart. The boiling inside him would do him no good.

It took all the strength she had to get up from her knees and start back down the hill. This year she did not take the time to stand before the beautiful snow covered trees or see the ornaments of nature spread out before her. As she started back down the hill something tugged at her heart. What was it that caused her prayers to seem so empty; so unfulfilled? Defiantly she had refused to mention William's name. These were her prayers and it was his decision to not be a part of their life. The pain of that thought pried at her soul. Was God not giving her peace as a way to prepare a benevolent heart? How could she refuse him her prayers when he had been the center of her thoughts since the day she agreed to be his wife? She wondered where he was by now. Was his health good? He would have turned fifty-two this year and by now would need more eucalyptus to soothe the pain of his knees and back. And ever since he had fallen in the creek right after the return from her father's burial, he had taken more colds.

As Rebeckah came to a clearing she caught sight of a stone path just under the snow and remembered how he had set it along the edge for her that first year before John was born. He had been afraid she would lose her footing on the rough hillside when bringing him his dinner. She stopped and looked around the farm and everything that held his presence. How could she be so calloused to enjoy the work of his hands while refusing to request his good health before the Father?

A prayer, at first just a whisper behind the words, then a prayer, earnest from the heart, for the man she had hoped to spend the rest of her life. She turned and began to pick her steps down the hill. For an instant she could almost hear her mother's gentle voice as her long ago words settled on her heart. *"When you do something for someone else, you heal your own wounds."*

Before nightfall a new round of snow covered the steps of those outside and when they heard Nicholas Dawson ride up to her door they were surprised. Rebeckah ushered him into the cabin. "What brings you here so late this evening. Is anything wrong at your place?" She knew Elizabeth had missed the quilting table for several weeks.

"No, mam, I just brought you a letter Benoni picked up two days ago when he went to Dowden's. Father and Benoni have been helping a cow with her birthing and mother thought it might be something important."

"Nancy, pour this half frozen boy a mug of hot cider," Rebeckah told her daughter and watched as Nicholas followed her daughter with his eyes. Finally, he remembered the letter and he took it out of his coat pocket and handed it to Rebeckah.

Rebeckah looked at it and stuffed it in her apron pocket, not wanting to read it just now in the presence of others.

She quietly motioned for the others to come with her into the new room, leaving the two young people alone. Rebeckah could hear them talking and laughing but very shortly she heard the door close behind him and his horse race off. She pulled the letter out of her pocket and saw that someone had written *Elizabeth Willis* in small letters at the top next to the seal. She tucked it back in her pocket to be read in privacy. It was bad news most likely. That is all she had gotten of late, with the exception of Rachel's letter, and she wanted to be sitting alone when she had to face it.

After the children had sat for the scripture readings and all except Nancy had gone to the bedchambers upstairs, Rebeckah sat looking into the slowly dying embers for sometime before she pulled the letter from her pocket. It was as she had suspected. Elizabeth, along with her son Will Sierra, and her daughter Elizabeth and husband Aquilla had sold their land to William Waters. Rebeckah could only guess that he was the father of Will Sierra's wife, Sarah, and maybe the brother of the Jacob Waters that bought William's land several years ago. There was one good piece of news. It would be a few months until Aquilla would be moving. They were going to the upper part of the first Carolina and not following the Bettertons, because Aqilla liked that land better.

Rebeckah could tell someone had written this for her sister because Elizabeth did not know how to write. Her thoughts went to the person of William Norris and wondered why he had never taught Elizabeth how to write. Rebeckah's William had been proud of her when she knew the letters and tried to write them out. That was one more difference in the two teachers.

She looked back at the letter and wondered from the sound of the letter who it was. Probably, her daughter had written it. William Norris had left money for someone to buy her books in his will provisions, and she was to get some education.

Letting the letter drop to her lap, Rebeckah sat again looking into the fire. Life was growing smaller. Once her sisters moved away, they would be too busy with their new life to remember this place. When they passed over the water to the Virginias she might get a letter or two the first year, then after that they were gone from her. There was no use trying to hold on to them.

When she heard John Hughes had also sold his land it was no surprise to Rebeckah. For one thing, John Hughes was not going to let the others get better land than he had, even if he had to travel three months to get to it. Strangely, Robert Lee was the first one to speak of moving and here he was the last one to sell his land. She wondered if his getting the job of constable had caused him to put away the thought of moving. Who could say what he would do when his time was up. It was probably just a matter of time and he would follow the others. Thomas Thrasher had vowed he would not leave. He loved his land and there was no reason to go. But they lived so far away they just as well be gone. With Martha expecting another baby next spring, she knew she would not venture out often.

Young William had become the man of the house almost overnight. Not that he was old enough but because his brothers had left. When a man came to ask for a reading of a word from his father's Dictionary, Rebeckah had taken it down from the shelf and handed it to her son. And without hesitation he opened the book and fingered the words until he found the right one, then read it as well as his father would have done.

Rebeckah decided if he could do that well with the book it was time she let him teach Solomon, and to her surprise Solomon did not object. He seemed to like the way young William explained the lessons. And Mary had shown an interest in making the letters when young William had drawn little pictures for her to write under. Rebeckah was amazed at his love of teaching.

"You will make a good schoolmaster, Will." She surprised herself at leaving off the word that had always described her son from his father. No longer did the word young fit his person.

William looked up at his mother and smiled.

When the letter came from Rachel it brought both joy and sadness to Rebeckah. Rachel had given birth to a baby boy. He was named Arnold, and she wondered where that name had come from. No one in her family was named Arnold. She smiled as she reread the words Rachel had put on the paper. Her smile left her lips as she wondered if she would ever see this little Arnold.

Rebeckah went to the calendar and lifted the December page. She marked the date of little Arnold's birth, then looked at the square for today. It was twenty-fourth day of December and that meant the year was fast coming to an end. She flipped the pages she had filled this year on her own and felt a sense of pride. Now she would have to find someone that could copy a new one for next year. She might send Henry to the ordinary to make one. But Henry's eyes were failing and he might miss a day or put two days where one should be. She could send Will with him to do the job. It would make him feel proud to be respected enough to make the calendar for the year, like his father had done.

What was once a very special day that the children all looked forward to, was now not much different than any other day. When their father was there they always celebrated with a big meal. As a special surprise he would write a fine story and set something for everyone's interest. Once he had used all the children's names as characters in the story and in the end handed each one a trinket. That had been as close to giving an actual surprise as they had come.

Sadly, she knew her stories would not be good enough to be a special gift. Upon telling Prudence of this fact, Grandma Prud did not fail her. She suggested she and Henry help Rebeckah make a small surprise for each one. For days this had kept them busy after the others had gone to bed.

After all the children were asleep, even Nancy, Rebeckah went to the chest and pulled them out and set them on the table. There was a comb for Nancy, set with the feathers of the red bird. Henry had gone into the woods and found the feathers. For Will and Solomon he had made a whistle like the one he had brought as a child from Germany. It did not match the sound of the whistles Rebeckah's father had made, but she did not tell that to Henry. The boys would like it because he had carved W L into one and S L into the other one. For the three little girls Grandma Prud had made a tiny rag doll and Henry had quickly sawed and nailed a miniature cradle for each doll.

Rebeckah picked up a doll from its cradle. She smiled when she noticed Prudence had been careful to paint each doll with a different face so there would be no arguments over who owned which doll. She put the doll back in its cradle and sat down on the bench. Her thoughts went to the doll her mother had made for her when she was about Lucy's age. The memories came uninvited—even the good ones sometimes carried pain. She was thankful she had them, but so wished the sad ones would be forgotten.

The clock began to chime and ended with the eleventh bell. She pulled herself up from the table and started for the steps, pausing to look at the reflections left by the moonlight. This was the night her family was to have come. William had given her permission to plan it after the new furniture had arrived. She and Nancy had planned all the recipes they would cook and where to set the food out. There would be so much to eat and everyone would be talking and laughing at once. Then someone would announce it was time to go sit under the stars and William would bring the torch and light the big fire to celebrate the Christ Child's birth. The carols and visiting would start and go on for hours until the logs burned down. Then they would take their bedrolls and curl up next to her fireplace in the new room. All of them! It would be just like when all the family had returned home each Christmas at Chestnut Ridge.

Then Richard Willis was so near death they cancelled it until this year— that was before—

She went into the empty room and looked out at the sky. The moon seemed to be so much brighter tonight. But that was how the December sky always looked, clear and crisp, inviting you to bring your sled and a friend for a ride under its covering. Fingering the cold windowpane, one by one she repeated the names of her brothers and sisters and her nieces and nephews and Prudence and Henry and the neighbors' names, the ones she knew. Then ever so lovingly, she recited the names of her own children.

But still, for sometime she did not move from the window. Finally, she wiped her eyes and quietly whispered her thoughts.

"Joyful Christmas, William, wherever you are."

Chapter 36

April 1771
Lower Seneca Creek

Holding the pen away from the paper so not to drip the ink, Rebeckah read what she had just finished writing.

Dear sister Martha I am sory yu hav ben so sick having
this nu baby. Lov Rebeckah oh yes, John and Absolom
hav gone from hom so I can not come visit.

She set the pen down and began blowing on the paper, reading again the words she had written. There was no time to wait for Will to check her spelling or for her to look them up in the dictionary this morning. Henry was coming to take the letter to Beall's tavern on his way to visit his friend who was gravely ill. It was a trip he took just about every week now. And since Beall's tavern was on the road, he always stopped to check the basket for any mail waiting with their name written on it.

Only Martha and Rachel answered her letters. Henry had gone to Dowden's Ordinary and asked for any mail with the Littlefield name on it to be sent on down the road to Ninian Beall's tavern. Ninian was someone they had known for years, and he set out a friendlier place for Henry to visit.

Rebeckah folded the letter's edge and secured it with the hot wax symbol, then she put the paper and the inkpot back onto the shelf. Afterwards, she went to the wall calendar and wrote a notation saying she had written to Martha. As was often her practice, she flipped back over the last months since the year started to see what she had accomplished. To witness it written on paper seemed to give her the confidence to stand up to the task.

Today she would go to the field to begin picking up the rocks dug up by yesterday's plowing. It was something the children loved to help with, and she had asked Prudence if she could bring them a midday meal so they could have one of the "eat on the ground" fun days.

Mary and Lucy skipped on ahead, trying to keep up with Will and Solomon, while Rebeckah carried Becka in one arm and a big stick with the other. The stick was for forcing any stubborn rocks from the ground.

Following behind the others, Nancy carried the quilt. From time to time she would turn and look toward the road. Rebeckah noticed this and suspected she was hoping Nickolas Dawson would happen by. It had been a long while since any of the Dawsons had come. Maybe it was because Henry had picked up all the messages or that the British soldiers had all gone back to England and there was no need to relay any disturbing news.

The children kept up a lively chatter, punctuated with giggles as they piled the sled high with rocks of all sizes. Will and Solomon would then pull it to the side to reinforce the fence line higher than last year. The children would race the sled to the side and unload it by throwing the rocks against the fence line.

Working with the stick, on a particularly stubborn rock buried under the hard ground, Rebeckah heard a scream and turned around to see Nancy and Will running over to little Becka. She dropped the stick and ran to the lifeless baby. There was a large lump on her head and blood was pouring down her face. Mary and Lucy began to cry knowing something terrible had happened to their baby sister. Solomon stood next to the sled still not sure what had happened.

Rebeckah quickly picked up the tiny figure and ran toward the cabin.

If only White Horse was there, she thought. It was an old habit when anyone needed medicines he had been the one to call on. Instead, she yelled for Solomon to get Grandma Prud to come quick.

Solomon took off running.

"Tell her to bring the medicines for a bad bruise." If anyone outside of White Horses had an herb collection, it was Prudence's well-stocked doctoring shelf.

Frantically running ahead of her mother, Nancy quickly folded the quilt to make a padding for the table. At not yet three years old, their brown-eyed Becka, with her cute little ways, was the darling of the family.

Rebeckah put the baby down and began talking to her to try to break the stupor. They all came to stand by the table and try to wake her up. But nothing helped.

Prudence came with Solomon and quickly went to work wringing out the cold water rags and bathing the child's face and hands. When that did not help she tried warm water. She put a small amount of lavender water on her handkerchief and placed it over Becka's nose. Next, she took the strong Confrey leaves from her bottle and rubbed the bruise. Nothing helped. Becka still lay lifeless when Henry returned home at the end of the day. Her breathing was shallow and her white face spoke of a shock somewhere within her tiny body.

The children left to do their chores without being told, then returned to stand silently beside their mother, watching Becka's little chest barely extending itself to take in a breath.

Everyday, Rebeckah and Prudence spent hours trying to force little spoonfuls of brown broth down her throat. This, more often than not, caused a choking sound, and they would quickly turn her over and hope it found its way into her stomach. She could not live much longer if she did not have liquid. Everyone took turns at sitting with the child. Everyone but Rebeckah. She never left her baby's side, not even to sleep.

On the second day, Henry went to get the Dawsons to come sit with Rebeckah in her watch. One by one, other neighbors heard the news. Everyone came with the same whispered mournful words.

On the way back to their own cabin, after a hopeless day of waiting, Henry had told his wife in confidence, "Maybe I should be finding the wood pieces to make a small coffin."

The thought of losing her little Becka sent Prudence into a hysterical moaning cry.

Nancy heard Grandma Prud's pitiful moans as she was returning from milking the cows. Dropping the bucket, thinking Prudence had bad news, she ran half screaming and half crying, to the cabin. "Becka, don't die, don't die"

But nothing had changed when she got to the cabin. Becka still slept. She turned to her mother and asked what was wrong with Grandma Prud. Rebeckah only shook her head in despair. By now Nancy felt her mother was slipping away in the same way Becka was leaving them.

Robert and Elizabeth Lee received the word and came to sit, as well as Will Sierra and his wife Sarah. Aquilla Compton came with wife, Elizabeth, and brought Elizabeth's mother, Elizabeth Willis. Benoni Dawson had offered to carry the news to the Thrashers, and Will Sierra was going to get Rachel and her family when daylight came. They all knew if the baby died, only Rachel would be able to console Rebeckah. That was just the way they were with each other. It had always been that way.

Rebeckah looked around at the faces of her family and thought about how she had dreamed of the Christmas celebration with all of them present. But after William left that dream had been dashed. Now they had come, but it was to watch for the death angel. How cruel life had turned.

Everyone bedded down in the new room for the night. They could hear Rebeckah still whispering to Becka in words that seemed to make no sense. Prudence was sitting in the rocker next to the door, saying nothing, just waiting. Suddenly, in pure exhaustion, Rebeckah collapsed to the floor. Prudence screamed for some one to come help. She called Rebeckah's name in panic. Somehow the commotion, the noise or sensing that her mother's voice had stopped talking, or whatever it was, brought Becka from the coma, and she began to whimper.

Rebeckah's face was washed in cold water and she was given the lavender cloth to breathe through. She opened her eyes to the sight of her baby's little arms reaching for her and crying the most precious words any mother hoped to hear. "Mummy, mummy."

A life had been saved and everyone departed for their houses, satisfied that all was well.

It was Rebeckah that was the first to notice the frail little body did not seem to hear the sounds around her or see someone across the room. Rebeckah kept this to herself until one day Prudence was watching the same thing, having never admitted it. They looked at each other; both knowing something was not right with the child.

"We will work with her, Rebeckah. She will get better," Prudence said, in a most defiant way. That was all that was said. It was the unspoken bond between the two women that said they were so glad to have the child back that whatever the injury had caused, with time it could be overcome.

Only once did Rebeckah let herself remember Susanna Hawker's little Elizabeth who still lingered with less color than before. Is this how others would think of Becka? Would they be afraid to talk to her about it? Even worse, would they see things she did not see?

Life was back to a near normal routine. Rebeckah went to the fields to check on the crops as before, but she did not stay as long. And she gave Nancy the job of watching Becka, leaving any other work to someone else's hands.

When they heard Thomas Thrasher's wagon come into their path it was a real surprise.

"Marthy, heard about your baby's near death, from your brother, Robert. She just about went crazy with worry when she heard it and wanted me to bring her this far on my trip to the warehouse. I told her if she had the baby on the road it would do neither one of you any good. But I did promise to stop and check on you. William being gone and all, Marthy has been worried sick about you."

"Oh, Thomas, it is not our well being that needs to be discussed here. It is Martha I need to hear about. She wrote that carrying this baby is harder on her than the others and that her feet have swelled out of her shoes. I thought Elias was going to be her last baby, but then these things happen."

"Well, I don't have anything to say about that. But I am supposed to tell you about the wedding we had at our place last month."

"A wedding! For mercy sake, with Martha in such a condition? Why didn't she write me about it?"

Thomas, not a man of much description, felt uneasy giving so much detail. "I guess you remember Westall Ridgely that lived close to my parents place. He married Sarah and lives close to us now. Their son, William, took a liking to our Mary sometime ago, but we felt she was too young to be marrying a man his age. But he set his mind to it and waited for her. Mary claims it was one of those fanciful happenings that she fell in love with his charm. That was the way Mary put it to her mother. He is somewhere close to thirty-five now, and Mary is twenty-two so I guess they know their minds. I gave my assurances to them. Marthy says our Mary has a mind pretty much of her own." Thomas laughed when he remembered, "Marthy said she felt a bit awkward dancing the dance with the wedding party, seeing she is getting pretty round with this baby coming."

Thomas spent the night in the new room and they talked about William being gone and other matters. He gave her much credit for dealing with his leaving and managing so well. When Rebeckah waved good-bye to him the next morning, it was with a feeling of well being. Thomas had made her feel good about herself.

Nancy had not said much during the visit and Rebeckah wondered if she was finding it painful that her cousin had gotten married and Nancy did not have her man yet. But as Thomas rode off Nancy told her mother, "I'm not going to marry a man that old. I want someone that can still do the jig and not have his back throw out."

The others laughed at her reasoning but it seemed all too real. Will poked her in the side and said, "You want to marry Nickolas Dawson, don't you?"

Nancy protested and began to pretend to pound Will on the head with her hand.

Rebeckah watched the children jest with each other and was glad there was still joy between the family members after all that had happened.

Sadly, Nancy's hope in the future faded. Elizabeth Dawson announced at the next quilting table, quite innocently, and not knowing of Nancy's feelings, "Nicholas has begun to court his brother Benoni's wife's sister. We are so pleased. It will be nice to have two of the Machall girls in our family, and Mary is such a sweet little thing."

That was all that was said, but for Nancy it was enough to crush her heart. She had run from the cabin without saying anything or letting on to the women sitting hunched over the quilt frame. But Rebeckah knew. She knew it possibly was the worst thing that had ever happened to her daughter, and there was nothing she could do about it.

By the middle of summer Rebeckah had no time for anything but going to the field to oversee the hired hands. Their lives all depended on her making a better crop than last year. She had given Will the job of overseeing the book keeping and he had announced last night that they were doing better, maybe even better than the last year William was at home. Rebeckah tousled his hair. She knew it was her son's way of making her feel better. But the news had been good to hear and she announced to those still at home that just as soon as the last crop was in the barns, they were going to go see all the relatives still living here.

"I feel if we do not go, after a while there will be no one that knows us." The pain of not being able to stand and wave goodbye, as one by one of her family had left for South Carolina, still caused tears to well up.

More and more neighbors came to talk farming. She was now considered one of the women that was making a living with her land and many wanted to know how she did it.

The news of the outside came slowly, more slowly then when William would go to the brother-in-law meetings at Dowden's, but it came. Rebeckah had heard something had happened to their Governor Sharpe and a new man had taken over by the name of Governor Eden. And someone passed on the news that the British were still agitating the colonists if they tried to set the rules. She did not waste her time on such things like William had once done. Instead, she left it to Thomas Dawson to tell her when something was distressing his own household. And by chance news came that Absolom had been seen down in Kentucky. A couple of men, traveling that way, had talked to a boy who told them he had lived just off the Seneca Creek. And he had gone on to brag about leaving home just after his father had walked away. The traveler had returned through Frederick County on his trip back to Pennsylvania and had spent the night at Beall's Tavern. When he saw that the Seneca Creek passed nearby he had relayed the words. Henry had brought the news back after one of his trips.

Rebeckah shook her head in bewilderment. "It is amazing how the news gets to where it wants, but when we want to know something of William's whereabouts it stays silent." That was all she said. She did not question Absolom's safety or why he had gone. That was for Absolom to worry over. She figured both William and Absolom had chosen their own destiny and had to deal with it in their own time.

She had more things to do now, like keep the children within her own walls safe. By now, whenever William's name came up, she simply said she did not waste her energies as to his whereabouts any longer. That was all she would say, and people stopped questioning her about him. Her answer sounded final and maybe she fooled most of the people, but she knew at the bottom of her heart she cared for both of them. John was a different matter.

He wrote when he could, but not as often as Rebeckah wished. And he had promised to send monies just as soon as he could. She was satisfied he cared and had written back that there were no immediate needs she could not handle, and he should keep his money in case he found a wife to marry.

Today's calendar said it was the second day of November and Rebeckah decided it was a good day to make a last trip to the pumpkin patch. By now, most of the hired hands had been sent home and Henry and Prudence were all she needed. The only job she found hard to handle was keeping the woodpile filled without letting on it was a problem. Henry insisted he could still pick up the axe, but they all knew one swish of the instrument could cause his bulge to come open and he would be gone from them no matter how many herbs Prudence kept on her doctoring shelf.

Rebeckah loaded the first good pumpkin onto the wagon. When she turned around to pick up another, she noticed a cloud of dust coming from the road. Once it passed her standing she gave it no more thought until a voice behind her said, "Mother, I've come home." She turned around in surprise.

Absolom gave no explanation for his leaving or his home coming. He looked and acted older, but was thin.

He picked up the rest of the pumpkins and put them in the wagon. Rebeckah could only thank the Lord for sending more help so Henry could work less. At least, that is what she had intended to think. Suddenly she found herself crying with joy. Her wayward son had come home.

That evening, as they sat around the fireplace, Absolom kept the family spellbound with one story after another of his trip down the Potomac in a small boat, just like George Washington had done last year. "George Washington is a fearless man. Did you know, he started out at the top of that big river and went all the way to the ocean in a small boat. Did you know he has made speeches in both Virginia and Maryland to get them to clear out the river so big boats can go from the top all the way down to meet the Chesapeake Bay waters? I can see why he did that. A ride down that river is more exciting than any war he fought in. It sure is a pretty river. Makes me want to try it again." He turned to his younger brother and said, "Young William, next time I will take you."

"I'm called Will now, Absolom."

Absolom seemed not to notice his brother had grown years older in maturity since he left.

"He is almost as tall as you are," Rebeckah said, seeming to say it in praise of the son that stayed by her side during these hard times.

Absolom listened to his mother talk, but when she finished he did not seem to care about Will's growing taller. He did not seem to notice anyone in the family, not even his baby sister's not hearing his words. He just went back to telling his own story.

"All the twists and turns. You really have to watch the river ahead to make sure you don't wreck the boat on the rocky shoreline. I watched real close as we got close to the mouth of Seneca to see if maybe I could see any of you in the wagon crossing on the ferry. Guess you were not coming that way going to Aunt Martha's place. I did see someone looking like Benoni and Nicholas Dawson in a wagon, but they didn't hear me call to them. I'll figure on them wanting to go with me the next time when I tell them all about how dangerous it was when we got to the rocks. Then, when we reached the Great Falls, we just came down one of them before we realized it was on us. After that, I have to admit we rowed it to the side and carried it past the next fall. Too dangerous, they had told us. Sure did beat plowing the fields."

Will spoke up, being the logical one, "Are you planning on staying home now to help us?"

"I've been thinking, maybe I could go work with John to learn how to build my own boat if he is still there. Then I could carry people with me down the river and they would pay to see all the sights."

While his brothers and sisters sat wide-eyed over his stories, Rebeckah wondered if he had gone up fool's hill too long. What was to become of someone with such take off dreams?

"I met up with a boy about my age that was traveling with a wagon train that stopped for the winter. You would have liked him, Nancy. He talked like Mr. Holmes, father's friend that came to visit from England. But he got sick, and we had to leave him back at the place of the rocks."

Absolom was so caught up in telling about his boat almost sinking when it hit a big rock and how his heart went into his throat when going over the first big falls, that he did not notice his mother quietly sitting in her rocker, not saying a word.

"Just staying alive took all our energies every day when we put that boat on the river. And I did a good job with the paddles. It made me know I was not intended to be a simple farmer."

"Mother needed you." At fifteen, Will sounded so grown up and responsible as he talked to his older brother. "We had to pay people to come help."

"I'm nineteen now and can do as I please," Absolom said, giving an annoyed look at his brother's insistence. "Why should I stay home to work when Father left to do his own looking?" He shot back at William.

Rebeckah sadly shook her head, but said nothing.

"At first, I just wanted to see the river at the top after hearing what George Washington had said about it. Then when I met up with Albert and he was going to ride the waters all the way down, I decided to go along. At the end of the Potomac, someone said they had heard Daniel Boone had gone all the way into Kentucky and they were going to see for themselves what it looked like. They asked me to go with them."

"You and Nicholas Dawson were always talking about how brave you thought Daniel Boone was—and a good fur trader," Nancy said, and in her saying so, admitting she had listened in on their conversations.

"How did you know all that?" Absolom said with a frown on his face, but he did not wait for her answer. Instead he began giving more detail of all he knew about Daniel Boone. "He led the exploring from North Carolina down into Kentucky. Did you know he and his brother were captured twice by the Shawnee Indians and lived to tell about it?"

"And did you find satisfaction being away from your family?" Rebeckah asked, not looking up from her sewing.

Absolom looked at her face, and saw the new lines of worry and sensed a disappointment. He was silent for a moment, trying to decide what to say. When he spoke the excitement had gone out of his voice. "I guess I was just mad at Father for leaving home without telling us."

Rebeckah did not say anything to make her son feel better. She just nodded her head and as she got up to put the girls to bed, she put her hand gently on his shoulder as she passed by.

Absolom, as planned, had caught a ride with Thomas Dawson on his way to the docks. John would teach him how to build his boats. But much to Rebeckah's surprise, her son had returned home with Thomas at the end of four days.

Thomas dropped off the returning son to his own cabin, and as they watched Absolom pick up a hoe and go into the fields, he offered not much more than Absolom had as to a reason why he returned so soon. "I guess your Absolom decided the docks was not the place he wanted to be."

As Thomas turned his wagon to go he called out a bit of news. "The non-importation on shipping from England has ended and the merchants are again rushing to bring in goods from the warehouses. If you want to order anything I will see to it someone picks it up for you when it comes in."

After Thomas left she went back into the cabin. The older children had gone with Prudence and Henry to the mill to help load the order of grain into the wagon. The youngsters just went along for the joy of the outing. Rebeckah took a minute to go sit in the new room to celebrate the quietness of the day. She sat down in one of the chairs William had let her order from England before parliament enforced the non-importation act, and she remembered the excitement with which they had unloaded it from the big wooden shipping box. Life would never be that carefree again, she supposed. As the sun passed the mid-afternoon mark in the quiet room, she fell asleep in her chair.

The sound of the wagon returning awakened her. She could see the sun had slid farther to the west, and she jumped up in shock at allowing sleep to come upon her, uninvited. How could she have fallen into such a melancholy mood that it would take her working hours away? It was not like her, and it served no purpose to be so foolish. Life was not for looking back. And if on the occasion you did, it could be a dangerous threat to how well you survived.

She turned to go to the kitchen to make the mush for the children's meal, but not before stopping to look around the room again. At least, once she had the things of which dreams were made.

Chapter 37

January 1772
Lower Seneca Creek

The sound of ice hitting the window awoke Rebeckah before daylight. She slipped out of bed to look out at the dark sky. The windows were mostly covered with snow. It was not the first snow of the season but appeared to be the heaviest.

All morning it snowed. She doubted poor Henry and Prudence could even get out of their cabin door. She went to the window to make sure the red flag was not hanging out. It was their prearranged signal calling for help. What she saw was the comforting sight of smoke circling from the chimney.

Absolom and Will made it to the barn to put hay out for the cattle, but that was as far as they could go. If it did not stop soon it would cover the livestock still in the field. She could lose them all and remembered the occasion of her father's dying time when she had insisted they leave before gathering up the cattle. She remembered at the time the hurt she felt at William's scorn that she might have caused him to lose all he had worked for if they froze to death. Now she knew why he had been so upset.

Pulling another log onto the fire, she went to the salt barrel that sat next to the door outside. She took a slab of fat back out and came back inside. She would send the boys to catch a squirrel before the evening mealtime.

Again, she went to the window to look down toward Prudence and Henry's cabin. It was times like this she wished William had built the couple's cabin closer to her own place. But at the time, they wanted them to feel in charge of their own surroundings. A motion along the road caught her attention. As she turned her head slightly to the side she saw what looked like someone riding toward their house. Her first thought was of concern. In weather like this only those needing help or bringing bad news would be out on the road. She watched the road for sometime but the object did not seem to come closer. Had it been her imagination? But when she looked again what had looked like a rider was no longer there. She moved back to sit by the warm fire.

By evening the boys had indeed found several squirrels and on the way back to the cabin delivered one first to Prudence to cook for her dinner.

Once back home, Absolom told his mother about finding strange looking tracks leading across the field. Someone had been dragging something. It seemed to be headed for the creek.

The news disturbed Rebeckah, and she remembered what she had seen earlier, thinking someone was traveling on the road.

"Where did the tracks come from?" she asked. "Could it be White Horse? I have not seen him in the shadows since your father left. I supposed he moved on—or died."

"I could not tell. The snow covered most of the tracks. We just happened on them on the side of the hill where the wind had not blown so hard."

After Rebeckah put the squirrels in the frying pan, she went to check her pouch of shots and set it by the door with the rifle. Most people by now knew the Littlefield cabin was without a man to protect them. Henry could help but was too far away to hear her cries if any harm was to come.

The younger children were put to bed early that evening, and Rebeckah began her usual speech to the older ones about protection. It was not her first time to drill them, and by now they just looked at her, listening with half an ear. The dogs had been put in the barn during the snow, leaving the cabin without a first warning. Shadow was the only one left capable of doing much harm to an intruder. Gabby was too lame and hard of hearing to move upon someone fast.

She dismissed her fears when she heard nothing for several hours. Maybe it had been a wolf dragging his prey to the den, she thought. Finally, she told Solomon and Nancy they could go on up to bed. Will and Absolom had made a practice of sleeping downstairs since their father left and she went in to give them one more piece of instruction. "If you hear anything, come get me."

Sometime in the night Rebeckah thought she heard the dogs barking. About the same time, Will, whispered an urgent summons from the bottom of the steps. "Shadow was barking real loud from inside the barn. It was like he heard someone coming around. But then he stopped."

Rebeckah grabbed for her shawl and hurriedly took the steps downstairs. Absolom was standing by the window and motioned to his mother to come watch the figure of a man walking around the cabin.

She whispered, "It must be Henry checking on us. Maybe he heard Shadow barking."

Before they had time to check the other windows, a knock on the door caused them to jump. Rebeckah braced herself as she picked up the rifle, "Henry?" she called out. "Is that you?"

The voice on the other side sent shock through her body.

"Open the door, Rebeckah." The voice was not harsh, neither was it kind.

She pulled the brace from the latch. The man standing in front of her had a long beard and she let out a gasp at what she saw. His clothes were caked with heavy snow, stained with blood. Rebeckah stood as frozen as the man, but not from the elements. He did not make a motion to come in until she opened the door wide for him to move through.

Without waiting, she began to talk. "You are hurt. How did it happen?"

"It is White Horse's blood."

"You've seen White Horse?" The boys began to question William at the same time.

William, weary from the travel, lifted his heavy bear hat from his head, revealing a thinner, balding man hidden beneath the fur. He shook his head sadly. "I've brought him back to die at his own cave. It was what he wanted and I promised him I would." William spoke without looking at Rebeckah.

Rebeckah rushed over to the pot hanging at the back of the fireplace and began to ladle up some broth she had started last night from the left over squirrel meat.

She put the broth cup on the table and motioned for William to sit down. "You said you brought White Horse back to die. How did you find him?"

William's voice was barely understandable as he began to tell the almost unthinkable story. "White Horse came all the way to the South Carolina border to find me. He said Becka was near death after a stone hit her in the head. We started back that very hour and had just crossed over the Potomac on the Maryland side when a party of renegade Indians made a run at me. White Horse stepped in front of me and took the hatchet intended for me.

Rebeckah shook her head at the long held mystery of how this old Indian seemed to always have secret lines of communication. Little could she have guessed he was watching them so closely as to know Becka was injured.

William shook his head slowly, obviously reliving the attack. His voice was pained as he prophesied "White Horse has fought his last fight." He dropped into a quiet solitary grief as the firelight cast deep shadows on his face. At first those standing around could see the watering of the eyes as he spoke. "He wanted to be left alone to die on his own pallet as is their custom." Suddenly William began a strange moan as he tried to keep from breaking down, unsure of how to cry after so many years removed from his youth.

Rebeckah's hand trembled as she started to touch his hand but drew back. Suddenly, he reached out for her and pulled her to him in a trembling embrace as he choked down a moaning sound. Then he abruptly released her and made long swift strides for the door.

They could only let him go without a word. When he did not return she sent the boy's back to their beds in the new room and sat in her rocker by the fire.

Her heart and mind at first cried out, and begged for reconciliation. Oh, how she had missed the sound of his voice; more than she had known was possible. Slowly, she thought of what had brought him back and recounted that he had not even so much inquired if Becka had lived or died, even if that was his reason for turning back. Suddenly, the hurt caused by this man flooded her mind. She was forced to remember all the times she had been faced with hardships after he went away. And yet she had still opened the door to him and offered him broth.

The clock chimed the hour two more times and she continued to probe her feelings until the sun came up bright on the sparkling pure white snow. As she went to the window to look out at the covered fields, she wondered what had happened to him. It was so unlike him to weaken before his children.

Rebeckah sent the boys out to do their chores as usual and then pulled on her heavy coat as soon as the breakfast had been cleared away.

When she knocked on Prudence's door she wondered what took them so long to come. Just as she was about to go away, the door opened. Prudence looked tired.

"Is everything alright? I thought I should check on you and to let you know William—" She stopped short. William appeared behind Prudence.

Rebeckah turned and ran toward her cabin without looking back. William had gone to Prudence and Henry, rather than sit with his own family in his grief. All the time he was gone she had hoped he would discover his need for her companionship, but now it was obvious that was not to be. She ran until she could not get a breath in the cold wind.

Unwilling to let the children see her tears she went into the barn. Her body went limp and she reached out for the center post for support. The heartaches of the past two years erupted into loud outbursts, her lungs gasping for air.

She did not hear the barn door open. She cried until there were no more tears, finally sliding to the ground, and wiped her eyes with her sleeve. She jumped when she saw William standing by the window looking out at the snow-covered hills past their cabin. If only she could have run from this place, away from the sight of William's disapproving eyes. But she felt frozen in place.

William broke the cold silence. "White Horse refused to die until he could come home. I paid a farmer to bring us a ways in his wagon, but when the blizzard closed the roads I could only half drag him, half carry him the rest of the way." He still did not look at Rebeckah. "I guess I never realized how important one's own dying place can be."

"I am sorry about White Horse, William."

"He risked his life for me—for the family. He stayed away for our safety."

"What are you saying?"

"When the Sittler's cabin was burned to the ground and they were found murdered, he saw the people that did it. It was not the Indians that dealt the murderous blows, as some accused. It was a band of white men, just boys really, living near here. They were bent on stealing the Sittler's wagon and horses. White Horse heard the screams of the Sittler children as they were being hatched to death. They set to make it appear it was Indians that killed them. They shot White Horse when he tried to help the children but he was able to slip away. He heard the attackers issue a warning that if he was ever seen around us again they would kill all of us."

Rebeckah let out a gasp. "Oh, William, the children!"

William was quiet for a time, then said, "He was keeping watch over us just the same."

The story left Rebeckah in shock. All she could think of was how horrible the Sittler's death had been. No conversation now could make that better.

Silence again bore into the cold. Finally she asked, "What happened to your horse?"

"I had to put him down." William still did not look at her as he talked. "I've walked from the New England part of the colonies almost to South Carolina. I had a lot of thinking to do, and I guess God was making sure I had the time to do it. I could have bought one, but I didn't have anyplace to go in a hurry."

A long pause marked the time. They could not seem to move from where they stood.

"Along the way I taught school in nice plantation homes."

"Will teaches Solomon and Mary their books now."

"Will? Is that what you call him?"

"He became a man when you left. He adds and subtracts my crop earnings for me."

William's eyes stayed on what was outside the window.

"Henry said John has gone to build ships, and Absolom ran away last year to Kentucky in search of Daniel Boone's trail." This time he turned around to look at his wife, "Prudence said Becka came back from death's door not the same as she was before. How could you let that happen to her, Rebeckah?"

The accusation was hurtful and made Rebeckah want to cry. But she looked hard, straight at her husband. "You were not here to pick up the rocks so I could see to the children." Then she muttered, "You were not hear when we needed you."

There was silence again before he took a deep breath and walked over to the door to leave. He turned back and said, "I want to see the children."

"You know you can come any time you wish, William. They are still your children, even if you do not desire to be my husband."

He did not comment on her words.

Rebeckah's feeling darted between wanting to lash out mean words to him for leaving but at the same time wanting to run to him and beg him to stay the rest of his life. Pride stopped her. If he chose to stay it had to be because he loved them and wanted to be there.

"I will sit with them at the evening meal," he said as he went out the door.

She stood at the open door and watched him go through the field to the creek where White Horse had dug a cave many years ago. She had never understood the ways of the Indian. William would have built a cabin close to the barn but he refused the offer. For the old warrior, being at one with nature was the intended plan.

Rebeckah sent Absolom and Will to gather big logs that would burn brightly for the evening, then began to gather the ingredients for a skillet of cornbread. She went to the root cellar to cut a large slice from the ham she kept for special meals, all the while thinking about the favorite recipes she could make. When she returned up the steps she went to the shelf where she kept her best dish and took it down for William to eat from. A sad realization hovered over her that William had given her no reason to believe he was staying longer than the meal and she should not let herself give in to hope.

"I'll just make cornbread tonight," she announced to Nancy as she put the plate back on the shelf and did not bother to explain her thinking.

Late afternoon, William opened the cabin door and came into the warm room. The children came to greet their father, but Rebeckah noticed, for the older ones, the awareness that it had been his choice to leave them two years ago with out saying good-bye, played on their words. Becka was just a baby when he left. Her lips puckered, and she began to bawl. William seemed helpless to know what to say to make her stop. She ran to her mother and buried her face in Rebeckah's apron.

"She does not know me, I guess," he said as he took off his heavy coat and hung it on the hook by the door.

410

Rebeckah wanted to scold at William and say, why would she remember him, but she did not give voice to her thoughts. Instead she looked at his very nice but well-worn set of clothes and surmised his teaching salary must have been good.

He stood at the door looking around the room. Rebeckah wondered if he was simply trying to remember it or was he being critical of how she cleaned the house. Then he walked into the new room. Mary and Lucy stood shyly watching his every move. Will and Solomon held back but finally followed him into the room. No one seemed to know how to act around this long absent father.

By mealtime the children had begun to say a few words to him, and when Rebeckah called them to the table William lifted Lucy up on the bench and patted Mary on the head as she sat quietly beside her sister. Becka still refused to look at him and buried her face in her mother's apron.

William said the blessing and Rebeckah handed him the Bible for the scriptures. She felt his hand in the exchange.

The meal was served as usual with the first meat selection being offered to William. The talk was slow to come. Once it was the best part of their day together. Now when he talked they listened with respect but still not returning the conversation.

William noticed the silence and seemed to try to bring them out. When he talked he spoke with a soft and kinder tone. "With each new sight I looked upon, I wished to share with you when I saw you again," he told the children. Was it his way of telling them he had intended to return?

Absolom on the side of being rude, asked his father the unspoken question. "Are you going to leave us again?"

William looked up in shock at his son's directness. He looked at Rebeckah as if to say how dare letting your son be so insulting to me. But he said nothing. All the same she knew his way of thinking.

All was quiet for too long, and finally William began to tell of an interesting man he had met coming from Pennsylvania.

"I engaged in conversation with a man at the Mason Dixon boundary line. We had both gone there to see the marker stones brought from England for the purpose of dividing the states. He introduced himself as Robert Whitacre." William looked at Absolom in an attempt to bring him into the conversation. "This Mr. Whitacre makes a practice of herding his cattle to the docks in Baltimore. You remember, Absolom, the ships waiting on the dock to transport down the coast?"

Absolom did not respond to his father's question, and Rebeckah suspected he was deliberately holding back as a way of rebelling against his father.

"I traveled with Mr. Whitacre and his fellow workers for the most part of two weeks. I began to enjoy the conversations amongst them as to their way of life and to understand their philosophy to which they subscribe."

It was obvious the children did not know what William was talking about. He looked around the table at the blank faces and began to make an attempt at explaining what he had seen.

"They profess the Quaker life and have a fine soul within them," William said.

Rebeckah had said few words as her husband talked, but she did comment on the Quaker experience. She spoke in a soft voice, not wanting to appear pushy, but wanting to help the older children's understanding of what their father was talking about. "Father used to tell us about the early Quakers that settled here before we moved to Chestnut Ridge. They moved to Maryland after they were treated in terribly cruel ways across the border."

She noticed everyone had turned to listen to her now. "The authorities put hot irons on their tongues if they were found to be a member of the Quaker faith. As we were riding by their land, Father would point out the land where Mr. Snowden and his son-in-law James Brooke had come to find refuge. Their land was as far as your eye could see, and I remember wondering how someone get the monies to buy that much land." By now Rebeckah was rushing ahead in a furry of words. "Mother used to say Father felt blessed to own his one hundred acres. The Snowden's and the Brooke's owned thousands of acres." She nervously dropped her eyes and let her words fade away, suddenly aware this was William's story, not hers.

William had waited for her to finish, then picked up his story again, "They subscribe to a quiet life of letting the spirit of God move them from within. One man told of living a simple life and letting the fear of God shake within him until nothing but love came out. But I suppose it was more than their words that struck me to notice. It was the way they treated each person they came in contact with. When they took up this faith they set the slaves free. To them all men are equal. They bring a different way to look at life."

Rebeckah watched William and it was true he seemed to have taken on a new kinder manner with the children.

They finished the meal in silence. William got up from the table and almost as soon as he had come, he left. But not before he noticed Rebeckah's hand-made calendar on the wall where he once had nailed his own copy. He lifted the pages to see her writing but said nothing.

Turning around at the door he called for his son, "Absolom, by now it is most certain that White Horse is waiting for his burial rites. I will need your help tomorrow morning." He turned and eyed Will standing next to his brother. "You are almost as tall as your brother, young William." He corrected himself. "I mean, Will. I will need you, as well."

After he was gone Rebeckah could only surmise he was sleeping at Henry's again tonight.

True to his word, the next morning at daybreak William whistled for his sons.

Confusion had ruled her dreams the better part of her sleep that night, and she felt doubly weary. She got up to put the water pot on the hook over the fire to begin boiling the grain for their breakfast. Then she went to her window. She could see William and her sons almost down to the creek road, each carrying the tools to build the burial frame for White Horse's body, as was the custom of his long lost tribe.

Absolom and Will returned at mid afternoon without their father.

Rebeckah remembered Absolom's question of last night and wondered what William's answer would be. "Did your father say if he was leaving?"

"No." It was all the explanation Absolom gave. Will said nothing.

Late that afternoon Rebeckah went again to the window. She gave the reason to her thinking that it was Prudence's candle for which she looked. When in truth she knew it was William she was looking to see. Sure enough, he was standing at the gate leading to the fields. How many times had William stood in that very place, checking his fields, talking with Henry or hoping to catch a glimpse of the shadowy figure of the old Indian after he had disappeared?

The sun was sinking over the cold snow covered fields. Rebeckah knew without a word being said that William had come to stand respectfully in this place on the sunset of the old warrior's final day.

When morning came, Prudence and Henry knocked on Rebeckah's cabin door. It was the first time they had left their cabin since William had come two nights ago. She was beginning to feel deserted by them in favor of William. This time they came to beg her to go to William.

"He is gathering his belongings to go to the road again. It is his stubborn pride that keeps him away. It will do you no good or him either. He loves his children and needs to be a part of their lives."

At first Rebeckah resented the plan—resented Prudence for presenting it. At first she shook her head. This is William's decision; By his choice I am not a part of it.

"At least tell him good-bye," Prudence begged. Never had she heard her friend try so hard to convince her of something. Finally, she wiped her hands on her apron, then untied it to find a clean one to tie on before putting on her cloak.

The cold morning air took away the tiredness as she found her way to her friend's cabin.

She tapped lightly on the door and it was opened almost before her hand rested at her side. Had he been watching her footsteps coming through the snow?

William stood before her a cleaned up man. His long beard had been trimmed to the precise exactness before he had left home. And his clothes seemed neat again. Prudence must have tended to them for his trip. It was like seeing the husband she had known all these years. He was courteous as he stepped aside to let her in. She went to stand in front of the fireplace, warming her cold hands. He chose to stand by the table. His height seemed taller than before.

When he spoke his voice was firm. "I did not expect to see you before I took my leave. I presume Prudence and Henry must have come to you."

Rebeckah nodded her head but said nothing.

"I am glad you have them to turn to." He appeared to be ready to say something else but instead just looked at her. Then he pulled his cloak from the hook and took the door handle in his hand before turning back. "I missed my children, Rebeckah. It is too bad it had to be this way."

Before William could go out the door Rebeckah broke into uncontrollable sobs. He turned around. She looked almost frail holding onto the fireplace mantel. Her pale blue dress with her white dust cap and clean crisp white apron reminded him of the first time he had come to her father's place. Elizabeth Norris had sent him over to deliver a plow her husband had borrowed the month before he died. Rebeckah had come to the door that day and he had been smitten love blind by her dark spitting brown eyes. After that he had asked for a job of the Beall's farm close by the Lee's farm so he could come courting.

William hesitated with his hand on the door latch. "If only you had not kept the truth from me." His words fell at her feet as he turned and pulled the door closed behind him.

As he started down the path the words of the men traveling with Quaker Whitacre bore into his thinking. But they were not his words. Those words belonged to another kind of man, one that could turn the other cheek.

William's mean spirited thinking of his youth still held him on the path almost to the main road. He had been taught to not let grief overtake his mind. As he continued to walk in the cold morning air, he wondered why he had come back? Sure it was because White Horse's had requested it. He knew that much. After the brutal attack, White Horse had made the request that he be taken back to die in his own cave and buried as was his tribe's custom. In return he had entrusted to William the story of the Sittler's death and his vow to keep William's family safe by not coming near them again. But after the Indian's revelation, he had fallen into a deep trance and spoke no more. The old Indian would have never known he died somewhere besides his own grounds. And now William thought about it. He had given his word. And his promise had meant so much he had risked his own life to bring him back during the blizzard.

So why was it now that his promise to Rebeckah, given at their marriage vows so many years ago, to care for her, to provide for her, now did not count with his soul?

William continued to walk until he could see the top of the new gristmill. The one the Jacob Waters had gone to work in after William had sold him some land. Just passed the mill he would take a little path to the main road. And from there he could catch a ride with some wagon. Oh how he wished for his wagon and horse. But that had to stay at the *William and John*. It would have been cruel to take that away from Rebeckah and the children. He thought about it. He may be mean spirited at times, but he was not cruel.

He would go warm by the fire at the mill for a time and then move on for good.

But as he approached he could see a chain wrapped around the door handle. He slid down onto the porch to shield away from the wind and fumbled in his pocket for the meal Prudence had made.

An eerie unfriendly quietness surrounded him. There was only an occasional snap of a frozen limb falling to the ground or the sound of some creature jumping into the tiny stream that still trickled from the falls. Not even the big grist wheel could turn in the frozen creek bed. Large icicles hung from the roof edges like a collection of daggers just waiting to pierce the ground below.

In the cold desolate surroundings he thought about what his life had become. All of his educated ways did him no good when it came to heart matters. From an early age he had learned to rely on his temper to fuel the decisions of conflict. At least they were his decisions, he consoled, and not something put over on him.

From somewhere up above he could hear a bird screech out for its mate. He held his hand to his eyes to shield the sun and watched as the bird swooped and circled at the top of a tall tree. He envied the foul for finding a nest to go home to.

Suddenly, within the deep confines of his angry heart came the longing to settle himself back to his own place and give up the pride that had sent him on his aimless journey. Rebeckah's frail look standing by the mantel came again to his eyes. The thought of putting her through the pain for his own justification burned his soul. He sat for a time thinking about their life together. Not once had Rebeckah given him grief until now. He remembered her words. She had said please don't hate me for what someone else did. How was it he was willing to make excuses for the wicked so called friend-schoolmaster but hold Rebeckah guilty for not wanting to divulge such a abominable affliction to her body? More than anyone he should have cursed James Lee for swearing the secrecy.

Eventually his thoughts came around to admitting he would have done the same to protect his daughter from cruel gossip.

Were his thoughts becoming dull in the cold? Not even conscious of his change of heart he was beginning to feel the grace of forgiveness of which those following the Quaker spoke. No more was the senseless pride decaying his thoughts.

Slowly the words came again, surrounding, hovering—prodding. From somewhere within his soul the grace of God was replacing the rancorous pride.

As he sat questioning the decisions he had made and why, a wagon lumbered up in hopes of finding the mill open. William did not recognize the fellow and he surmised it was one of the men Henry spoke of last night that had moved in while he was gone. Finding the mill closed, the man turned his wagon around to leave. As he did he offered William a ride.

William shook his head. "Thank you just the same. I'm headed in the other direction."

He pulled his stiff body up and started down the path, finding his frozen footprints facing him on his way as he formed the words in his mind. Forgiveness for what he had put his family through might not come, but he had to try.

It was almost dark when he came up the path to his cabin, and he could faintly see through the frosted windows the image of Rebeckah sitting with the children at the table. Suddenly his heart was overwhelmed with gratitude. He had found this woman he had brought to be his partner for life, once before. Now he was finding her again. And the contrition he felt was almost more than he could bare; and very unfamiliar.

The dogs gave no warning of his coming. Their master had returned home again—for good.

Chapter 38

Summer 1772
Lower Seneca Creek

William returned. And Prudence and Henry still grinned each time they saw Rebeckah standing with him.

Indeed, something had changed this man, although there were times he found his old ways more comfortable. He was still the head of the house and reminded Rebeckah of that fact on occasions but never with anger. "I am who I am—better now but still stubborn," he would say. She would simply tilt her head a little to the side and purse her lips and he knew he had said too much. All she had done in his absence was never far from his mind.

Rebeckah had found an old log out front by the road that she called their *talking seat*. It was a place for reconciling, a place where they could look out at all their land. Sometimes it took the sight of their land to serve as a leveling stick in their thinking.

Rebeckah could have been bitter for what perils William had left them in, but the future was much too important than setting blame. What was a husband without his honor, she would say to Prudence on times he had been hard contrary. One by one their grievances were brought to the old log to be solved in private. William was not to throw up to her something she had done wrong, and she was not to point out his foolish anger in front of the children.

It was when he offered to make inquiries as to where William Norris might have taken her baby girl so many years ago, that made her know a new William Littlefield had come home. No longer did his pride get in the way of a loving soul.

Life went back to how it had been two years ago. William went into the fields, his sons following behind him, and Rebeckah tended to the children in the cabin and kitchen garden. Now on occasion, William would come in from the field and ask Rebeckah for her opinion as to the plantings to produce better crops. Her answers were always subtle solutions. Nothing that would make him feel he was bowing down to a woman planter. That suited her just fine. No, by no means did she miss going to the fields to scold some hired hand for letting the young tobacco plants wilt. Now it was her quilting table that gave her honor.

Rebeckah smiled as she pulled the needle up through the cloth to make another row of stitches on a quilt that had been set aside for two years. She ran her hand over the design and decided it should be a late gift for Martha's daughter Mary for her marriage to the Ridgley boy.

Martha had sent a letter a few months back. She reached into her quilting basket where she kept it for safe keeping and again she laughed out loud. The picture her sister had drawn on the front was a drawing of an old woman sitting in a rocker, her hair wildly flying all over her head. At least that was what it looked like. Martha was not a good artist. But it was the humor in her sister's drawing that made her laugh. The picture showed the woman holding a baby in both arms. It said,

Me tryin to hold my new grand child and my own baby Eli at same time

Rebeckah put the picture down and began to make her stitches again. When would her children give her a grandchild? When would any of them find a wife or husband? Poor Nancy was convinced she would be a spinster now that she was twenty-one, and her Aunt Martha's daughter, Mary was already a mother. If only someone new would move in close with sons and daughters her children's age, Rebeckah thought.

Something William had talked about when he came home came to mind. He had said there was so much better land in the Carolinas, and fine robust younger men were filing in to clear the forestry to grow healthy crops and build their cabins. He had laughed when he added, "They say the only thing missing is enough young women to marry."

Rebeckah put the letter back into the basket and got up to look out her window. It was something she did often of late. Decisions were made clearer when looking out into their fields. Slowly, ever so slowly, the ideas William had set out had taken hold. Better land, better chances for the children to meet their mates on lands full of promise.

The thought of leaving Martha and Rachel, especially Rachel, who had just started her family, was heart breaking. But could she make peace with her heart if she deprived her children of a better life. Even Robert had brought up his desire to move when William met him at the ordinary. They were both ready to follow the others to one of the Carolinas. Rebeckah thought about her sister Elizabeth now and wondered how she was faring. She had moved with her daughter Elizabeth and Aquilla to the upper borders of North Carolina last October after he sold his last cow. Now Elizabeth's son, Will Sierra, said he was thinking about moving to one of the Carolinas.

And this summer when the crops all but dried up on the overused tobacco land she was sure they would be moving. After managing the farm while William was away, she understood about fresh land.

The first part of August, William went to Ninian Beall's tavern to post a notice that the *William and John* was for sale. Upon this news, people came by often to look over the land and inquire of the price. On one of the days a fine looking carriage pulled onto the Littlefield path. Two well-dressed men got out, and before they came to the door they had walked all around the cabin. Rebeckah could hear them giving favorable remarks about the looks of the place. William was sent for, and before the man left he had put in his bid for the home place and four hundred and thirty seven acres surrounding it.

Within a week all the land had a buyer. William marked his calendar and pointed out the day to Rebeckah. "On this Friday, August twenty-first, I will take you with me to Fredericktown to find witnesses for the deeds and have you release your dower. By then all the buyers will have their monies in hand."

On the appointed day, Rebeckah sat up straight, listening to the clerk as he methodically read off the land being sold and asked if she released her dower to each claim.

The first one read made her feel better about selling. She knew it was in good hands.

Benoni Dawson, one hundred and ten acres bordering the land of Thomas Dawson, his father for One Hundred and ten pounds

Rebeckah thought, with another baby coming anytime now, as best she remembered it was their fourth, he probably needed more cropland than what his father's land afforded.

Again, the clerk read the name.

Samuel Hooker, bought two hundred and nine acres for two hundred and fifty pounds

William had told Rebeckah this Samuel Hocker was of the same family as William Hawker that now lived on the Birdwhistle land, but his name was written differently. Rebeckah's thoughts went to the time when she had gone to pay her sympathies over the death of William and Susanna Hawker's daughter and wondered how Susanna was holding up raising her daughter's baby.

The clerk read another name.

Richard Wootton buys the cabin and four hundred and thirty seven acres around it for two hundred pounds.

Rebeckah could see it was the man who had come in the fine carriage. William had explained Richard Wootton was from a socially fine family. And his wife had a reputation for loving a fine party with dancing. The story was she had danced all night at the new Hungerford Tavern. Rebeckah could not help but wonder if they would find her cabin and all her new furnishings acceptable.

The clerks again read the remaining sales, all to the Beall family.

Andrew Beall Jr. buys Six Hundred and eighty-seven acres. for six hundred pounds

William had explained that by buying so much land he was in line to be considered a large landowner before long. Rebeckah listened to the rest with half an ear. Charles Beall had carved out a strip of one hundred and forty acres and Ninian bought only ninety-nine acres. William had already told Rebeckah that Ninian owned much of the land around their area, so he probably had not wanted to invest in more.

At the end of the day William climbed up on his wagon seat and turned to Rebeckah. "Do you know how rich we are Rebecky? We are rich! One thousand three hundred and sixty pounds rich."

Rebeckah's thoughts went back to when her father's estimation was filed. Rachel had told her it was valued at sixty pounds and that was more than most men had when they died. She wondered what her father would have said knowing his little girl was now worth so much. She sat stolidly on the seat as the pain of leaving was all too real now.

When she did not reply he turned to her and asked, "What? No want list?"

"Seems to me, it does a man no good to have money but no bed to lay his head on when night comes."

William reached out to take her hand. It was something he did since he came back. "I'll get you a bed, a fine bed."

They had started with a small room and a dirt floor, and he had added the bedchambers in the attic and finally the new room with all the settings. How could she give that up so easily? How could William not seem bothered by that thought? She decided his indifference must be what they liked to call a man thing.

"You have the catalog, Rebeckah. You can order more furniture than before.

Besides, since John has given his word that he will be coming home to make the trip with us, John and Absolom can handle the reins on another wagon in which to load more of your plunder."

When the first geese flew south William knew the wagon master he had signed on with would feel it was now safe to travel. Ever since the first day of September, when the warm air along the coast line had sent a terrible hurricane on shore in Virginia and North Carolina, killing fifty people, he had decided to delay the trip until cooler weather prevailed. John had come home as promised, and together they packed the trunks with what they could take. Rebeckah never stopped trying to find more spaces to pack some small keepsake. But in the end, most of her things were either packed for someone else, sold with the place, or thrown away.

At the end of the week she stood in the almost empty cabin and began to cry as she wrapped the last big jug and put it into the trunk she was taking to Rachel. It was so hard to break up her house. Her babies had been born here. That was enough to make it a special place. Prudence and Henry had come to live next to this place.

Prudence was the dearest friend she had ever had and it was breaking her heart to give her up. Henry and Prudence had refused the offer to move with them and were moving back to their old cabin. Their reasoning was that they had their son and his wife and little boy buried there and they just could not bear to leave them.

The wagon John and Absolom would be driving was loaded and rolled into the barn for safe keeping. They loaded the remaining wagon with the things Rebeckah would be taking to Rachel, and a few things for her brother John. Then next week she had a few keepsakes to leave with Martha as they passed by their place on the way to meet up with the wagon master on the Winchester road.

Just after rolling the wagon into the barn William heard Henry calling to him. "William, I need a moment of your time if you can spare it." Henry was a man of few words, and he wondered what was so important that he would come over to talk with him so late in the evening.

When William returned to the cabin he had a smile on his face.

"What?—What is it making you smile like that?" Rebeckah asked her husband.

"Henry and Prudence are coming with us."

The children let out a big whoop of a yell and Rebeckah smiled for the first time in days.

"He said they had decided it is far better to be a part of the living, than to grieve for both the living and the dead. Prudence just could not live without seeing her little Becca everyday—well, the other children, as well. They will have their wagon ready when we return from Rachel's."

The chilly early November wind hit their faces as the wagon rolled along the road leading up to Chestnut Ridge. Rebeckah braced herself for the bump in the road that had been there since the day her father first moved them to this land. She had been thirteen and a long way from being lady like.

Her heart ached as she let her eyes search the ridges with their heavy growth of trees—her favorite tree. How many times had she climbed up into those thick leafed branches with her sisters and younger brother, John? It was a place where she could go to set her dreams. One tree in particular had been her favorite, a sanctuary for her young soul. It was her own secret hiding place where she could sit without anyone disturbing her thoughts. Once when her mother had called her several times, and more crossly the last time, she had pulled at the quilt too fast and a piece had torn off. She imagined if she climbed that tree today, she would still find the tattered piece caught on the limb.

Rebeckah let out a deep sigh and William turned to look at her. "I was just thinking, William, when I am old will I remember the feeling of this place?" Tears welled in her eyes but she did not cry.

How could she bear to tell Rachel the sad news they were leaving next week ahead of the winter snows?

William was the first to see Rachel standing by the gate. "She must have heard our wagon."

Rebeckah braced against the wagon seat and took in a deep breath. It was important that she be strong for Rachel's sake. So many of the family had moved, and now she was losing her as well.

William stopped the horses, and Rebeckah jumped off to embrace her sister and for the first time realized Rachel was again with child.

"Oh, Rachel, look at you. Why did not tell me you were expecting another baby?" Rebeckah said, as she hugged her sister gently.

Wearily, Rachel looked at her sister and asked the obvious question. "Rebeckah, why have you come? You are moving away too, aren't you? It is the same way the others have come—suddenly without warning, to walk among our parents graves one last time."

The question, asked with such pain in her voice, made Rebeckah quickly turn away, and with a sense of urgency she began to point out the changes that John Lashley had made to their father's old place. "I see you have a new barn. That is good. Father talked of building a new one." She nervously created talk away from why they had come.

Rachel looked around the farm only nodding in reply.

"We came by our brother John's place on the way, but no one was home," Rebeckah said as a way to prolong answering Rachel's question.

"They sit with Betsy's ailing mother," Rachel said flatly.

"I saw a new barn at his place, as well," Rebeckah offered. All the resolve she had built as a fortress to the pain was about to fall in around them. She so wanted this trip to be a fine memory of smiles and not one of tears. She turned back again and saw tears in Rachel's eyes as well.

Rachel did not wait for the answer. She turned and went to her cabin.

Was this the way they would spend the last visit together, skirting the pain? Rebeckah wanted to talk until they were hoarse and fill her mind with funny stories they both remembered.

When William, with his son's help, carried in the old trunk that had been their mother's, Rachel leaned against the mantel and began to sob helplessly.

"I knew it, I knew you were leaving." Little Mary and Arnold had never seen their mother cry like that and pulled at her skirt for safety against what was wrong. Rachel wiped her eyes and picked up two year old Arnold and pulled Mary to her.

The others in the room just looked on without knowing what to say. No matter how many promises they could have given for a return visit, they all knew it would not happen. No one ever came back.

John Lashley had seen the Littlefield wagon coming up his path and had put down his axe and started for the cabin. When he saw the tears in his wife's eyes, he asked, "What is it? Has someone died?"

"Rachel and Rebeckah are finding our moving to the Carolinas hard," William explained.

John went over to his wife and pulled her to a bench to sit down. And the show of emotion he felt for his wife was a lesson in compassion. Rebeckah had never seen anything so tender. Her eyes cut to William as if to say, why are you not that kind to me. But she said nothing. It was just the thought she wished she could say.

The conversation at the evening meal was quiet, like a veil had fallen over the table and those that sat around it. The younger children were dismissed to go with Rachel's little girl Mary to see the new puppies born just yesterday. John and Absolom sat with the family for awhile before tiring of the boring talk and went outside to talk. Nancy went to sit by the fire and find some handwork from her aunt's mending basket.

The grownups struggled to make interesting talk. William finally resorted to telling the story of seeing the new mansion Philip Key had built on the large plantation near the Pennsylvania border. "It has big white pillars holding up the two story front porch, and the walls are covered in brick ordered from England. And each night it is said the honorable Mr. Keys calls his slaves to the quarters, and he reads them the scriptures and they sing their songs for him in return. I was there one night passing by on the road and I heard the most beautiful singing coming from those slaves."

William being taken up in the moment did a rare thing and began to sing the old song he had heard. "Well, children, go where I send thee, well, they're gonna send thee, one by one." Realizing he was making a show of himself, he stopped abruptly. "Well, it goes something like that. Very pretty indeed sung in the evening time by those fine workers. I dare say with that kind of treatment, none of his slaves have been listed as runaways on any street corner posts in years." When he was finished with his story telling, the conversation began to dull as the men picked up the talk of more problems with the British. "They won't stop until we have another war," John said and William agreed.

Rachel got up from the table and motioned for Nancy to follow her up the steps. She pulled a small trunk from under her bed and gently took out a scarf. "It was your grandmother's scarf that she kept for special church visits. I want you to have it."

When Nancy protested, knowing that Rachel must have been saving it for her little daughter, named after her grandmother, Rachel still insisted.

"You are the spitting image of your grandmother. I did not see that until tonight. She would have been so proud to have you wear it."

Before Rachel had finished, she had given out little pieces of memories of the place. John and Absolom each had an old tool from their grandfather's old toolbox. She gave Solomon the pick of her father's knives he used to make the whistles, and the little girls had small pieces of lace made by their grandmother. "There, you can have your mother make you doll dresses," she said. Will stood quietly waiting his turn. He knew what he wanted but did not want to ask for it. Rachel went to the back of the room and pulled something off the shelf. "Father always said he wanted you to have this when you grew up. Since I won't be seeing you then I best give it to you now." Will wiped his eyes with emotion but the smile was there. It was the thing he had promised his grandfather at the burial that he would do for him. It was his grandfather's cane he used to fetch for him when they visited. He hugged his aunt. "This is what I always wanted."

And so started the good-byes. Long after the others had bedded down for the night, and after all the tears had been wiped away, they did as Rebeckah had hoped. They talked. Rachel even laughed about how William had been so determined to marry her off. "I am certain it was the act of divine intervention. I would never have said the vows with my John Lashley if it had not been for William."

Rachel asked if she had heard from any of the others since they had gone and the answer was no. "I knew they would forget us back here, just like you will."

"We are different than the rest, Rachel. We will always speak from the letters."

"And I'll pass your words around to Betsy and John and the children," Rachel said, as she thought about how sad they would be that they had missed Rebeckah and her children. "Maybe it was a good thing John is gone. He promised to punch William in the nose the first time he saw him after his return. He took his leaving you like that real mad like."

Rebeckah laughed at the thought. "Please let them know we are alright now. William is a good man."

"I'll remember everything you said and give it to them." Then Rachel went over to pick up their father's Bible. "I need to make sure we have all the names right." The two sat reciting the names of all the births happening for the last few years. Rebeckah remembered one. "I do not see the birth of Robert and Elizabeth's last child. I can not rightly remember the date but it was between the time you married and now." Rachel got out the pen and wrote in, *Birth of John Watts Lee*, and fixed a question mark after it. "I will ask Elizabeth the next time she comes. Robert will not remember." They both knew how true that was of a man. "He will only say, well he is walking now, how old can that be?" Both laughed at the thought.

The two read the words so long Rachel had to get up and light another candle to read by. When they got to John's family, Rachel sounded like a doting grandmother to her brother's children. "I've helped get everyone of them birthed in that house. John Jr. and Sarah are such fine young people. Do you remember what a hard time they had getting them started? I went with Mother many evenings to help hold them. Their little tummies would be seized with colic. Twins are like that. Sarah is seeing a fellow on a regular time and our brother is vowing to send her off to South Carolina with the next person."

"We will take her with us. But she has to promise not to find a husband before our Nancy does." They laughed at that idea.

Rachel went back to reading the names. "Daniel is fourteen now, then they had James and Elizabeth and Dorcus and finally little Emelie. She is short of just a month of our Mary's age."

The talk turned to when they were young and their voices softened and a gentle feeling passed between them. It was a tie that could not be changed. They had been the best of sisters. The miles apart would not change that. "I'll write. You will see," Rebeckah said again. "I had to write letters to everyone when William was gone. With him not being there to carry the news to the others, no one knew I was still alive."

That was the first time Rachel had heard her sister talk about that hard time. "Your letters never sounded hurtful when you wrote. How could you not be full of hate for what he did to you?"

For a moment Rebeckah was silent. Then the admission came of what she had refused to tell anyone before. "I cried every day, Rachel. Sometimes because I was so mad at what he had done, but then other days I cried because I missed the sound of his voice so much. That is why I am willing to move. I never want to be without him for as long as we live. He has changed." Rebeckah went on to tell the story of the Quaker that William had traveled with and it had changed him. "We are not Quaker, but we can still find peace in their ways."

After all the talk was over they still sat quietly next to the fire, unable to let a minute go by unused. Finally, Rachel said, "This baby within me is going to fill my days with joy. I just know it. Not that the others have not, but it is most likely the last I will bear. I am almost forty-three. I had better make this one my joy." She leaned back in James Lee's old rocker. John Lashley had repaired it so Rachel could rock her babies in it. Rebeckah watched her as she closed her eyes, trying to memorize all the looks of her face one last time. It was as bad as sitting near a deathbed, knowing the person beside you would not be around much longer.

The next morning they would leave. The wagon train was lining up at the end of the week.

It was early when the two women put on their shawls and walked slowly down the hill to the graveyard. William and the boys were busy loading the sleeping pallets into the wagon.

"Don't tarry long, Rebeckah we need to be on the road." He watched as the two sisters started toward their parent's graves and knew it could be a hard time if they stayed too long.

Rachel and Rebeckah carefully made their way down the hill. They stopped to look at each grave in the small cemetery. Dennis Madden's parents had lived on the other of the Lees long before Dennis bought their brother's land. One of their relations was buried there. There was one unknown grave with only a rock to show where it was. A man traveling through had asked to bury his small daughter. And before he gave his name he had quietly departed. They had kept the grave cleaned as if it was one of their own. The grave at the edge of the path was of an old farm worker who had died while plowing the field.

Then there were the graves of their parents.

Rebeckah bent down and began to sweep the leaves from the graves. When she stood up she looked back at Rachel.

Both, unable to keep the tears from their eyes, reached out for each other. Finally, it was Rachel that spoke.

"Go Rebeckah—go now so I will always remember us as a family here with our parents. It is better than seeing your wagon disappear at the end of the road."

Rachel reached down and picked up a fresh Chestnut leaf that had just fallen from the tree. She gently folded it into Rebeckah's hand. "Take this with you, Becka. It will help you remember the feel of Chestnut Ridge"

And so they had gone that day. And through the years, when the lonely hours came upon her on a cold night in Union, South Carolina, Rebeckah would take down her Bible. Pressed between the pages was the leaf Rachel had folded in her hand that day so long ago. And for a moment, family did not seem so far away.

Ann Littlefield Coleman

Printed in the United States
1183300001B/368-372